全国高校数字媒体专业规划教材

数字媒体专业英语

Professional English for Digital Media

吴军其 李 莎 熊桂枝 主 编

图书在版编目(CIP)数据

数字媒体专业英语/吴军其,李莎,熊桂枝主编. —北京:北京大学出版社,2014.9
(全国高校数字媒体专业规划教材)
ISBN 978-7-301-24390-9

Ⅰ. ①数… Ⅱ. ①吴… ②李… ③熊… Ⅲ. ①数字技术-多媒体技术-英语-高等学校-教材 Ⅳ. ①H31

中国版本图书馆 CIP 数据核字(2014)第 129931 号

书　　　名：**数字媒体专业英语**

著作责任者：吴军其　李　莎　熊桂枝　主编

丛 书 策 划：唐知涵

责 任 编 辑：泮颖雯

标 准 书 号：ISBN 978-7-301-24390-9/G·3836

出 版 发 行：北京大学出版社

地　　　址：北京市海淀区成府路 205 号　100871

网　　　址：http://www.jycb.org　http://www.pup.cn

电 子 信 箱：zyl@pup.pku.edu.cn

电　　　话：邮购部 62752015　发行部 62750672　编辑部 62767346　出版部 62754962

印 刷 者：北京宏伟双华印刷有限公司

经 销 者：新华书店

　　　　　　787 毫米×1092 毫米　16 开本　24 印张　410 千字
　　　　　　2014 年 9 月第 1 版　2014 年 9 月第 1 次印刷

定　　　价：48.00 元

未经许可,不得以任何方式复制或抄袭本书之部分或全部内容。
版权所有,侵权必究
举报电话:010-62752024　电子信箱:fd@pup.pku.edu.cn

目 录

Chapter 1　The History of Digital Media …………………………………… (1)
　Part 1　The History of Communications Media ………………………………… (1)
　Part 2　Computer Graphics …………………………………………………… (7)
　Part 3　Workstations …………………………………………………………… (8)
　Part 4　Personal Computers …………………………………………………… (9)
　Part 5　CD-ROM ……………………………………………………………… (11)
　Part 6　The Internet …………………………………………………………… (13)
　Part 7　Games ………………………………………………………………… (14)
　　　New Words ……………………………………………………………… (15)
　　　Notes ……………………………………………………………………… (15)
　　　Selected Translation …………………………………………………… (17)
　　　Exercises ………………………………………………………………… (18)
　　　专业英语简介 …………………………………………………………… (18)

Chapter 2　The Basics of Digital Media …………………………………… (21)
　Part 1　Hardware ……………………………………………………………… (21)
　Part 2　Software ……………………………………………………………… (29)
　Part 3　DSP and Digital Media Art …………………………………………… (30)
　Part 4　Others ………………………………………………………………… (34)
　　　New Words ……………………………………………………………… (36)
　　　Notes ……………………………………………………………………… (36)
　　　Selected Translation …………………………………………………… (37)
　　　Exercises ………………………………………………………………… (38)
　　　专业英语的词汇特征 …………………………………………………… (39)

Chapter 3　Digital Images …………………………………………………… (42)
　Part 1　Outline of Digital Image ……………………………………………… (43)
　Part 2　Formats of Digital Image ……………………………………………… (44)
　Part 3　Capture of Digital Image ……………………………………………… (46)
　Part 4　Digital Image Processing ……………………………………………… (49)

Part 5	Output of Digital Image	(69)
	New Words	(74)
	Notes	(75)
	Selected Translation	(76)
	Exercises	(79)
	专业英语常见的语法现象	(79)

Chapter 4 Digital Audio ...... (82)

Part 1	Outline of Digital Audio	(83)
Part 2	Formats of Digital Audio	(84)
Part 3	Capture of Digital Audio	(86)
Part 4	Digital Audio Processing	(90)
Part 5	Output of Digital Audio	(99)
	New Words	(103)
	Notes	(103)
	Selected Translation	(105)
	Exercises	(107)
	数的表示与读法	(107)
	常用的数学名词	(109)
	数学公式的表示与读法	(110)

Chapter 5 Digital Video ...... (112)

Part 1	Outline of Digital Video	(112)
Part 2	Formats of Digital Video	(116)
Part 3	Capture of Digital Video	(118)
Part 4	Processing of Digital Video	(120)
Part 5	Output of Digital Video	(131)
	New Words	(134)
	Notes	(135)
	Selected Translation	(136)
	Exercises	(139)
	专业英语翻译的标准	(139)

Chapter 6 Electronic Word ...... (142)

Part 1	Outline of Electronic Word	(142)
Part 2	Formats of Electronic Word	(144)
Part 3	Capture of Electronic Word	(149)
Part 4	Processing of Electronic Word	(153)

Part 5　Output of Electronic Word ……………………………………… (155)
　　New Words …………………………………………………………… (157)
　　Notes …………………………………………………………………… (158)
　　Selected Translation ………………………………………………… (158)
　　Exercises ……………………………………………………………… (160)
　　从句的翻译 …………………………………………………………… (160)

Chapter 7　Digital Layout and Design …………………………………… (164)
Part 1　Introduction, Birth …………………………………………… (164)
Part 2　A Brief History of Publishing ……………………………… (166)
Part 3　Digital Layout and Design: The Equipment ……………… (173)
Part 4　Support Programs …………………………………………… (176)
　　New Words …………………………………………………………… (177)
　　Notes …………………………………………………………………… (177)
　　Selected Translation ………………………………………………… (178)
　　Exercises ……………………………………………………………… (181)
　　被动句与长句的翻译 ………………………………………………… (181)

Chapter 8　2D Animation ……………………………………………………… (188)
Part 1　Outline of Traditional Animation …………………………… (188)
Part 2　Formats of 2D Animation …………………………………… (193)
Part 3　Capture of 2D Animation …………………………………… (203)
Part 4　Processing …………………………………………………… (207)
　　New Words …………………………………………………………… (210)
　　Notes …………………………………………………………………… (211)
　　Selected Translation ………………………………………………… (212)
　　Exercises ……………………………………………………………… (214)
　　文献检索简介 ………………………………………………………… (214)
　　文献检索方法简介 …………………………………………………… (216)

Chapter 9　3D Animation ……………………………………………………… (218)
Part 1　Outline of 3D Animation …………………………………… (218)
Part 2　Formats of 3D Animation …………………………………… (222)
Part 3　Capture 3D Animation ……………………………………… (226)
Part 4　Process 3D Animation ……………………………………… (233)
　　New Words …………………………………………………………… (247)
　　Notes …………………………………………………………………… (248)
　　Selected Translation ………………………………………………… (249)

  Exercises ·· (252)
  互联网上常用的数字媒体技术专业资源 ··· (252)
  数字媒体技术专业论文投稿期刊 ··· (253)

Chapter 10 Virtual Reality ·· (254)
 Part 1 Terminology, Concepts and Timeline ······················· (254)
 Part 2 Application Areas ·· (257)
 Part 3 Social Implication（1） ··· (258)
 Part 4 Social Implication（2） ··· (260)
  New Words ·· (261)
  Notes ·· (263)
  Selected Translation ·· (264)
  Exercises ·· (265)
  科技论文的结构与写作初步 ··· (265)

Chapter 11 Multimedia ··· (277)
 Part 1 Introduction to Multimedia ··· (277)
 Part 2 Types of Multimedia ·· (279)
 Part 3 Application of Multimedia ··· (292)
 Part 4 Multimedia System ·· (295)
  New Words ·· (298)
  Notes ·· (298)
  Selected Translation ·· (299)
  Exercises ·· (300)
  投稿指南 ··· (300)

Chapter 12 Web Design ··· (309)
 Part 1 Overview of Web Design ··· (309)
 Part 2 Technologies Involved in Web Design ······················· (314)
 Part 3 Tools for Web Design ·· (328)
 Part 4 Type and Application of Web ····································· (335)
  New Words ·· (337)
  Notes ·· (337)
  Selected Translation ·· (339)
  Exercises ·· (342)
  应用文写作 ··· (342)

Answers to Exercises of Each Chapter ································ (371)

Chapter 1　The History of Digital Media[①]

▲ **Knowledge Objectives**

When you have completed this unit, you will be able to:
- State the history of communications media.
- Take a brief look at some of the major inventions throughout history then preceded it and influenced its development.
- Recognize the recent development of the Internet and computers.

▲ **Professional Terms**

abacus and mathematics	算数
cave drawings and paintings	壁画
communications media	传播媒体
computer graphics	计算机图形
internet	互联网
motion pictures	电影
personal computers	个人电脑
the printing press	印刷机
workstations	工作站
written language	书面语

Part 1　The History of Communications Media

Oral History

Then: For countless millennia, before the advent of written and drawn history, most of our social information, customs, and history were passed down in the oral tradition. Storytelling was the primordial form of communication and handing down information and tradition. There were no permanent records of events, and early societies consisted of roaming bands of hunters and gatherers. Agricultural societies developed as people began to live in permanent

---

[①] M. D. Roblyer, *Integrating Educational Technology into Teaching*, Third Edition, Chapter One, The History of Digital Media.

locations. Trade began to develop between different regions. Along with the development of trade came cross-cultural exchange and the economic and social benefits of dealing with others from faraway places. In contrast, societies like the Chinese protected themselves from conquering societies with the Great Wall. In both cases, written language, letters, and books developed as means for people to trade and communicate over long distances.

Now: Storytelling remains one of the most important and effective ways to communicate, even with modern technology. The motion picture is one of the most popular forms of entertainment. The quality of the storytelling is often a major factor in a film's success.

Abacus and Mathematics

Then: A simple calculation device invented by the Chinese to make counting easier and faster (see Figure 1-1). The concept is to have different rows stand for different levels of units. This approach to mathematics was the foundation of digital mathematics. In the early 1800s Charles Babbage designed an analytical calculation engine that was intended to perform calculations mechanically. Because of this and his other work related to the mechanization of mathematical calculations he is known as the Father of Computing.

Figure 1-1 This is an abacus. Counting is done by moving the beads along the rows.

Now: Digital numerical systems form the basis of how computers work. Everything is reduced to ones and zeros, allowing for extremely fast calculations and data handling.

Cave Drawings and Paintings

Then: The cave drawings discovered in France are some of the earliest evidence of the power of the image. Many art history courses start with these drawings, and for good reason. They point to the power of the image and the desire of people to communicate with each other and to make a record of their cultural and personal history.

Now: Images are still a major part of how we communicate. Although photography allows us to reproduce an image exactly as we see it, drawings and paintings can give us a glimpse of things we cannot see, the creations of our imagination. An artist's rendition allows us to look back through history. We can enter fantasy worlds we never dreamed of through the imagination and skill of the artist. The need to escape from our daily reality was, and still is, served by those who can create visions other than those we see every day.

Chapter 1 The History of Digital Media

Written Language

Then: The Chinese language is thousands of years old and developed out of a pictorial. It has been refined over the centuries and now contains about 7,000 characters. Words and concepts are made through the association of the characters used in the language. This also makes it difficult for the Chinese language to be adapted to a keyboard with a limited amount of characters. Egyptian hieroglyphics formed an early bridge between images and written language. The Greeks and Romans were very influential in the development of writing. The Roman alphabet is the basis of the English written language.

Now: The development of a standard character set allowed for greater numbers of people to communicate with each other. English is the main language used on the Internet, although there are many other language options. More and more, digital communication via e-mail is becoming the standard. Handwritten and even typewritten letters are becoming less common. E-mail is now becoming a major form of communication among those digitally equipped.

Books

Then: Books were one of the first permanent records of events, traditions, and societies. The Egyptians used papyrus to record their writings. The Chinese are credited with the invention of paper, which was used to preserve sacred Buddhist texts. Early books were drawn and written by hand, and were thus very valuable. Most early books were created by monks. Texts that are thousands of years old have been discovered in Europe, the Near East, and Asia.

Now: Interestingly, Amazon.com was the first well-known e-commerce Web site. It sells books. It now has built-in artificial intelligence that tracks your book buying habits and recommends books that fall within your area of interest. It has become, in a sense, an enormous digital library that only needs your credit card number for you to purchase the books. New trends are evolving in publishing that will eventually put all books on-line, and you will be able to order the books on a print-to-order basis.

The Printing Press

Then: The invention of the printing press made books and other written material available to a much wider audience and began the era of mass communication. No longer were handmade books available only to a select few. The printing press allowed for hundreds and eventually millions of copies of Bibles, historical records, and so on to be distributed and read.

Now: Printing has made a significant move from high-cost commercial presses to local desktop printers in people's homes, which have the ability to print photographic-quality images. What cost hundreds of dollars to print just a few years ago can be printed inexpensively and selectively by end users?

Photographs

Then: Photography started in the 1800s with tintypes and glass negatives (see Figure 1-2). Black-and-white photography became a popular medium for newspapers and eventually for creative and personal photography. Color photography followed in the 1900s and became the standard for all kinds of image making, both commercial and personal. The four-color process used in printing is photographically based.

Figure 1-2 This old Wands family photograph was printed on a glass negative.

Now: New technology is moving printing and photography to a digital standard. The invention of megapixel cameras and the resulting higher resolution are fast making digital photography a standard professional medium. It is already in wide use on the Internet and in newspapers.

Telephone

Then: Invented by Alexander Graham Bell in 1876, the telephone allowed the transmission of voice and music over wires. Long distance vocal communication became a reality.

Now: Telephones have become wireless and still hold a major place in communication technology. Digital phones can carry both digital and voice data. Personal digital assistants allow users to send e-mail and access the Internet.

Electricity

Then: Although it is difficult to believe, people used to go to Times Square in New York in the early evening to watch the electric lights be turned on. Thomas Edison invented the electric light in the late 1800s. Electricity allowed inventions like the stock ticker, telegraph, and radio to become widespread.

Now: Electricity forms the basis for much of modern society's daily routine. It pervades almost all of our normal daily lives. We ride to work on electric trains, work inside buildings lit with fluorescent lights, and spend much of the workday using computers. We go home and watch television, surf the net, or go to restaurants and music clubs to hear electric music. Restaurants with wood stoves and nonelectric music are a rarity. We go to sleep and wake up to an electric alarm clock and start the cycle all over again.

Typewriter

Then: The typewriter ushered in the era of individual printing. Personal and business communications could be typewritten much greater speed faster than they could be written longhand. The original QWERTY keyboard was invented to minimize collisions between keys that were frequently struck.

Now: Typewriters are slowly becoming obsolete, thanks to word processors, but the original QWERTY keyboard is still with us.

Motion Pictures

Then: Thomas Edison invented the motion picture camera in 1891, launching the era of movies as entertainment and documentaries. Early films were black-and-white until the color process was invented (see Figure 1-3). Early cameras were cranked by hand. The frame rates of old films were low, just fast enough to exploit the persistence of vision of the human eye, but slow enough to keep the cost down. The addition of sound moved the frame rate to 24 frames per second, where it stands today.

Figure 1-3   Motion picture film was widely used until video became common. It is now mainly used for feature films, commercials, and short independent films. This is a photo of 16 mm film.

Now: Movies are a $7-billion-dollar business worldwide. It is a major form of entertainment. Over the past decade, large theaters began turning into multiplex theaters with smaller screens but more choices for the audience. Experiments with digital cinema are underway but remain extremely expensive. The cost of making multiple prints of the original film is still less than making theaters digital and distributing the films over the Internet. Considerable effort is being made to perfect video compression to allow full-screen movies to play in real time over networks.

Radio

Then: Radio was invented by Gugliemo Marconi in 1874, and he received an American patent in 1900. It was called the "wireless telegraph", and it could transmit signals across distances without wires. One of the major milestones was when he sent a signal across the Atlantic Ocean in 1901. Lee DeForest continued the development of radio with the invention of the audio vacuum tube, which allowed for better signal transmission/reception and amplification. This was followed by Edwin Armstrong's invention of FM radio, which eliminated the static associated with AM radio. AM radio was based on the concept of amplitude modulation, where the radio signal is linked to the strength or amplitude of the signal. FM radio is based on frequency modulation, where the signal is linked to the frequency with which it is transmitted.

Now: Radio continues to be a popular mass medium. Both AM and FM radio stations thrive. Programming is extremely diverse, ranging from talk shows and National Public Radio to popular music, to niche stations playing only jazz or specific genres of music. New developments include using the Internet to transmit radio programming. Listening is no longer restricted by geography.

Television

Then: The invention of television relied on the development of a cathode ray tube, or kinescope, as it was called by its inventor, Vladimir Zworykin. He applied for the patent in 1923 and first demonstrated it in 1929. Another individual who had a major role in the development of television was Philo Farnsworth. In 1927, he was the first person to transmit a television image. The image transmitted was a dollar sign. Television was showcased at the 1939 World's Fair in New York, and the TV era began. The first public television station was WQED-TV, which began broadcasting in Pittsburgh in 1954. Several years later, color television was developed. The early years of television were dominated by the three major networks, ABC, CBS and NBC. This was followed by the development of CATV, or cable television, which provided better reception to certain local areas and offered a wider range of programming.

Now: In the United States 98% of homes have at least one television. The number of hours a typical viewer watches television is staggering. Cable networks are now fully developed. Television stations are now broadcasting content over the Internet. Although it is neither full screen nor of high quality, many people see this as the trend for the future. Just as Amazon.com provides suggestions for books to read, future television systems will provide lists of programming suited to one's taste. The concept of prime time and watching television programs at a specific hour is changing. Video on demand will be the new paradigm of the digital broadcasting era.

Part 2 Computer Graphics

Computer graphics existed long before they were used to create digital media. The ability of the computer to handle increasing amounts of data and more sophisticated calculations made it a natural for creating graphic representations of mathematical formulae. Early computer graphics systems relied on programming to create images. Early plotters drew thin black lines on a piece of paper. Some of the other early images were made with ASCII character sets, with periods and commas representing light areas and number signs and asterisks representing the darker areas. These primitive methods of creating imagery relied on mainframe computers. Terminals were nothing more than a keyboard and a dot matrix printer. The idea of a video monitor was still new and kept in the control room out of access of remote users. This was during the mid-1970s, and the Internet had existed for quite a while as a text only research network of government administration, the military, and universities. Access to the Internet was slow and cumbersome, but the seeds of the future were there. It was obvious that this new technology was going to evolve and grow into something more useful and more accessible to people other than scientists and programmers.

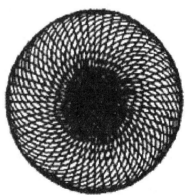

The early machines were known as mainframes. IBM held a near monopoly on computers in the early days. The IBM 360 was the most sophisticated machine at the time, and at Syracuse University, where I was a graduate student in the mid-1970s, it formed the basis around which the campus network was built. I was taking an Experimental Studios course and was using a language called Art Speak (see Figure 1-4). It was written in FORTRAN and gave a series of commands to the plotter to create complex mathematical drawings, reminiscent of the toy Spirograph. The time it took from handing in your stack of punch cards to seeing the printout was about 1/2 to 3 hours.

Figure 1-4 I created this line drawing in 1976 using Art Speak.

Another sign that technology was about to make a leap was the arrival of video games. Previously, games like ping pong and football were the main pastime for young people. Then a game called Space Invaders arrived. A silent group of characters slowly marched down the screen as players tried to eliminate all of them before they got to the bottom. This was an example of an early use of raster, or pixel-based, graphics. Close on the heels of Space Invaders came Asteroids. This game had a different look, and the player was now in the center of the screen with 360 degrees of rotation and the images were sharp and clear. It was the first vector-based game.

Part 3 Workstations

Large mainframe computers were very expensive and beyond the reach of most businesses. While development was continuing with these machines, General Electric was working on another graphics system, called Genigraphics. This system was used to make slides for business presentations. Until then, all of the artwork had been done by hand and then photographically double-exposed to add the type. Traditional methods of producing slides were expensive and time consuming. Genigraphics was a very high resolution system that became the standard for still computer graphics.

During the same period, a group of artist/programmers were working on a new computer graphics system called Synthavision. This software was based on government research concerning the behavior of radiation. The research was looking at how surfaces reflected or absorbed radiation from atomic bombs. The people developing Synthavision figured out a way to add color to these surfaces. Objects were built with primitives (i.e. rectangles, spheres, planes, etc.), and a new computer animation system was born. The early Disney movie Tron used this system.

Dolphin Productions, a well-known studio in the early 1980s, used digital and analog methods to create graphics. Digital Effects and several other companies that produced computer graphics were appearing. On the West Coast, John Whitney was experimenting with digitally controlled machines that created computer graphics.

Most of these early computer systems were large and cumbersome, and they required a lot of maintenance. Shortly after these systems were developed, a new generation of systems was born. They were called workstations. Companies like Via Video, the IMAGES system from the Computer Graphics Laboratory at NYIT, and Silicon Graphics began to produce very expensive workstations in the $75,000 to $100,000 range. Computers were just beginning to fall within the reach of the business and creative production communities. The Quantel Paint Box, one of the first video graphics systems capable of producing broadcast quality graphics, became available.

Systems like Via Video and IMAGES were still affordable only by large corporations and these systems were used mainly to create slides for business presentations and graphics for corporate videos.

Part 4 Personal Computers

In the early 1980s, intense research into developing smaller and more affordable computers was underway. In 1982, IBM introduced the IBM PC, a basic computer, capable of 16 colors and very poor audio. Early software was mostly business software like spreadsheets, word processing, and a business graphics package called Lotus Symphony, which included the spreadsheet Lotus 123 and a simple graphics package.

In parallel with this was the development of the Apple computer. The Apple II had graphics capability and the ability to display 256 colors as compared to IBM's 16. The early Macintosh computers were black and white (see Figure 1-5). The most significant feature of the Macintosh system was referred to them as "desktop publishing". Early

Figure 1-5 This is my first Macintosh 512e, bought in 1985. it has 512k of RAM, an 800k internal disk, and an 800k external disk for a total of 1.6 MB of storage. This was state of the art at the time. I used MacPaint, MacDraw, MS Word, and Pagemaker software to produce design work for print and film.

graphic programs included MacPaint, a pixel-based program, and MacDraw, a vector-based program. Shortly thereafter, several page composition software packages emerged, including PageMaker and Ready Set Go, which later developed into QuarkXPress. The first desktop publishing systems with a Macintosh, a scanner, and a LaserWriter cost about $10,000 and were extremely primitive by today's standards. However, this system caught the eye of forward-looking graphic design professionals. The profession was quickly divided into two camps. The more vocal of the two proclaimed the computer as a new revolutionary tool for design professional. The almost as vocal other camp decried that the computer was not capable of creating professional quality work, that the typography was poor and the images were low resolution. We all know the outcome, and as 16-, then 24-, then 32 bit color became available and typographic controls increased, more advertising agencies, design studios, corporate graphics departments, and individual designers jumped on the bandwagon.

The desktop revolution has come of age and won over the entire design community. At the present time, the great majority of magazines and books are produced using desktop publishing, or digital design as it is now called, software.

Imagery was not the only area that was undergoing a fundamental revolution. MIDI, the musical instrument digital interface, was invented in the mid-1980s, and it has revolutionized the recording and music industry, along with the development of digital audio and CD technology.

The original intention for the development of MIDI was to sell more synthesizers. If there were a way that keyboards could talk to each other, it would be in the interest of a musician to own several of them, so that they could create a wide range of sounds. Early music synthesizers like the MOOG and the ARP were analog. Sounds were created by turning knobs. The first digital synthesizer was the Casio CZ1000 (see Figure 1-6). The innovation of MIDI was that this was converted into a digital process. MIDI was run by a digital clock, which became the time keeper. Notes, or keys, were numbered 0 through 126, and given parameters like pitch, duration, note on, note off, velocity, and after touch. Because the clock ran at 384 cycles per second, MIDI was so sensitive that a digitally recorded performance played back with MIDI was indistinguishable by the human ear from the original performance. Not only was this revolutionary, but the data needed for MIDI files was small and within the capabilities of low-cost computers. Very soon, MIDI sequencers and scoring software emerged, which allowed musicians to control a whole range of synthesizers and compose with digital control over tempo and harmony and gave them the ability to go in and fix mistakes by changing the MIDI data.

Figure 1-6 This is the Casio CZ1000, the first digital synthesizer. It has a total of 16 preset sounds, 8 waveforms, and MIDI in the out. It was the first affordable MIDI synthesizers.

MIDI also became the scourge of recording studios. In the past, musicians had to play a song over and over again until they got it right. There were limitations on the number of tracks you could record on, and tape generated hiss. MIDI changed all that. Musicians now bought inexpensive sequencer systems for their home studios and perfected the performances with MIDI before going into a studio. Professional recording studios had to jump on the digital bandwagon to keep from going out of business. Slowly, digital was beginning to replace analog in the audio business. There is a saying in the industry, "audio precedes video". What is meant by that is that technological developments that happen in the audio business eventually work their way into the video business. The data-handling needs of audio are much smaller than those of video, so that as technology advances, the ability to handle video is increasing.

Standards started to emerge. The first IBM machines were VGA and used a video card called the Video Graphics Adapter, which had a resolution of 320 by 240. The next step up was SVGA, which had a higher resolution of 640 by 480 and the ability to have 256 colors.

During the mid to late 1980s, good quality video for computers was still very expensive, and the state-of-the-art video system at that time was the AT&T Targa Graphics board. These first came out in 16-bit color, and then evolved to 24-bit and 32-bit color. They also had the capability of storing a single video frame in the frame buffer. Compared to the Quantel Paint Box, which at that time was well over $100,000, $3,000 for a TARGA board seemed a bargain and was what we would now call "prosumer." Along with the TARGA boards came a video board for the Macintosh, and other vendors began to create full-color systems for the Macintosh and the IBM. The race was on to see which computer would win the popularity contest. The Macintosh was popular with designers, artists, and academics. This was partly due to an aggressive campaign by Apple to get the computer on college campuses. The IBM was popular with corporations and businesses. For the time being, the Macintosh was the computer of choice for design professionals.

After the computer came of age as a graphic design tool and word processor, the computer industry needed something to sell more computers. Technology was also catching up with people's imaginations and the color, audio, and video capabilities of the machines were increasing by leaps and bounds.

Alongside this was the further development of the more expensive workstations. Silicon Graphics incorporated developed machines with built-in rapid graphics calculation capabilities. Companies like Wavefront, Alias, and Softimage were developing 3D animation software. Star Wars ushered in a new era of special effects. Even before computer graphics had made its presence known, animators were attaching digitally controlled stepping motors to the Ox berry camera and creating digital photographic effects that had not been possible before. The star gate sequence in 2001 was an early example of this.

Along with these developments came the focus on multimedia. There was a call to develop a multimedia standard for computers so that there could be more compatibility. Not all software that was on the Macintosh worked on the IBM PC and vice versa. There were endless debates as to which platform was the more desirable and which machine should one buy. During the late 1980s the Macintosh had the edge on design and audio, and the IBM had the edge in the corporate community.

Part 5   CD-ROM

Another significant development during this period was the development of CD-ROM technology as a storage medium (see Figure 1-7). Before this, the only removable media available were floppy disks and SyQuest drives that had storage capacity of about 1MB and 44MB or 88 MB, respectively. As image quality increased so did file size. The CD-ROM was capable of storing 650 MB. Since computers of that time were able to create and store text, images, audio,

Figure 1-7 CD-ROM disks were the first storage medium to hold a significant amount of data. 650 MB of storage enabled the development of multimedia. These disks could store text, images, audio, and digital video.

and video on their hard drives and CD-ROMS, a field emerged from this technology called Multimedia.

In the early 1990s the CD-ROM medium started to become widespread, spawning the development of interactivity. At the time the Internet was text only, but CD-ROMs could hold text, graphics, audio, and video. CD-ROMs were hailed as a new era in computers. There was also a major sales effort to promote these new uses of computers. The "multimedia standard" was born. The promise was huge. Computers could hold 250,000 pages of text on a CD-ROM disc, high-quality audio was now an option as evidenced by the success of the audio CD, and the early stages of digital video were becoming evident, with the rapid public acceptance of the QuickTime standard. Finally, CD-ROMs could be made interactive. Macromedia was one of the major players in the early days of CD-ROM authoring. Their professional-level software, Authorware, was cross-platform and very versatile. It was used for a lot of early interactive applications. Multimedia was now used for business presentations, making interactive books and converting films to the interactive format. There was a lot of research and development in the multimedia area.

However, a large problem began to develop: compatibility. Since most Macintosh systems were sold as complete units, with standard graphics and audio capabilities, CD-ROMs tended to work on most Macintosh machines, although they ran much slower on older machines. Also, Apple was the only manufacturer of Macintosh computers, and there were no clones. PCs had some serious problems with CD-ROMs. IBM manufactured their machines, and a host of clone manufacturers built competing machines using a wide variety of graphics boards and sound cards. There was very little standardization. As a result, commercial CD-ROMs did not work on all PC computers. Sales of CD-ROMs were disappointing, and many companies scaled down their operations or closed altogether.

This was in the early 1990s, right when the Internet was getting ready to explode. The rapid growth of the Internet signaled the end of the CD-ROM era, and sales of CD-ROMs became smaller and smaller. People wondered why they should spend $40 for 650 MB of data on a CD-ROM when they could access gigabytes of data on the Internet for free. CD-ROMs are still widely used, mainly for software and content delivery. Many of the early compatibility problems have been solved.

Part 6　The Internet

The Internet has caused a cultural and technical revolution both in the United States and abroad. We are still in the early stages of this revolution, and although almost every television commercial lists a Web site and many of us spend countless hours on the Internet, we have yet to see the full impact of this revolution. Before we talk about what is happening now, let's take a look at the history of the Internet. We have traced the recent history of new media to the present, but Internet history goes back to the 1960s.

The Early Internet

The Internet was started in the 1960s as a way to link research institutions supported by the Advanced Projects Agency (ARPA). Arpanet, as it was known, allowed various types of computers to talk with each other through the development of Internet Protocol (IP). It was a text-only system.

My first professional exposure to the Internet was as a Senior Information Scientist for Sandoz Pharmaceuticals in 1972. We used an Internet service provider that connected us to various on-line storage and retrieval systems. We could access the National Library of Medicine through a service called MEDLINE. The National Library of Education had a service called the Educational Resource Information Center (ERIC). Several other on-line resources were also available. The method used for on-line research was very similar to ones we use now. You would type in keywords and see how many matches you had. By carefully selecting the keyboards, I would narrow down the choices to about 30 to 50 articles. I would then enter the print command and wait. The typical wait for response on the Internet in 1972 was 5 to 15 minutes. I would enter the command, return to my desk, and then wait until I heard the printer typing out my results. We joke now about how WWW stands for "World Wide Wait", but we have come a long way in 30 years and still have a long way to go.

In the mid-1980s we started to see further development of the Internet through the establishment of NSFnet. This was a high-speed network created by the National Science Foundation with a speed of 1.5 Mbps.

One of the most significant developments that have allowed the Internet to develop into what it is today appeared in the early 1990s. The World Wide Web (WWW) was developed at the European Laboratory for Particle Physics (CERN).

In 1993, the National Center for Supercomputing Applications (NCSA) developed Mosaic, a graphical user interface for the Web. A few years later, Netscape and Internet Explorer were invented.

Although new developments continue to happen on the Internet on an almost daily basis, the rest is really history. The number of users on the Internet is still growing exponentially, and we are continuing to see new areas develop. Some rapidly developing areas are the increasing of access speed through cable modems and DSL. Streaming media now allows audio and video to be streamed over the Internet. Shortly, we will have full-screen video and high-quality audio available to people with broadband connections. One of the major organizations involved in this development is the World Wide Web Consortium (W3C), which collaborates with industry and is located at the Massachusetts Institute of Technology (MIT).

Part 7　Games

The history of digital media would not be complete without an in-depth discussion of the development of video games. In some ways, this industry has been one of the driving factors of the digital revolution. One major manufacturer of early video games was Atari (see Figure 1-8). Recently, video games became a $7-billion-dollar industry worldwide, surpassing the film industry. The future of video games also looks promising from both a creative and technical perspective. To get the big picture, we'll take a closer look at the history of video games. Video games evolved along the same pathway as personal computers.

Figure 1-8　This is an early Atari video computer system. Games were played by inserting a cartridge into the slot and attaching the system to a television.

One of the earliest video games was Pong. Played much like ping-pong, the "ball" moved back and forth across the screen, and the object was to keep it in play. As the game progressed, the ball started going faster and faster. It could be played either as a single player or dual player game. Another early game was Tank. This vector-based game moved through a 3D world made up of line drawings. The object was to destroy the other player.

As video games evolved, they began to work more with 3D, and a significant development was the addition of textures to worlds and characters. This relied on the increasing speed of computers and additional memory to store the textures.

The next development in the video game revolution was the addition of sound. With more memory, sound could be stored and played back, adding realism and more impact to the game play.

CD-ROMs greatly affected what video games could be. With 650MB of data available, the quality of the imagery and methods of game play could be greatly expanded. This is currently a limiting factor for games. We will see the development of using DVD technology for video games in the future due to their advanced storage capabilities.

Recent developments for video game development include networked games like Doom and

Quake. As bandwidth increase on the Internet, global multi-user video games will develop. The creation of new game machines, like Sony Play station 2, is pushing the envelope for game play.

New Words

    primordial   *adj.* 原始的;根本的;[生]原生的
    permanent   *adj.* 永久的,永恒的;不变的
    megapixel   *n.* 兆像素
    representations   *n.* 代表;表现;表示法;陈述
    persistence   *n.* 持续;固执;存留
    synthesizer   *n.* 合成器;合成者
    fundamental   *adj.* 基本的,根本的 *n.* 基本原理;基本原则
    cumbersome   *adj.* 笨重的;累赘的;难处理的
    association   *n.* 协会,联盟,社团;联合;联想
    roam   *vi.* 漫游,漫步;流浪 *vt.* 在……漫步,漫游;在……流浪 *n.* 漫步,漫游;流浪
    conquer   *vt.* 战胜,征服;攻克,攻取 *vi.* 胜利;得胜
    calculation   *n.* 计算;估计;计算的结果;深思熟虑
    analytical   *adj.* 分析的;解析的;善于分析的
    reproduce   *vt.* 复制;再生;生殖;使……在脑海中重现 *vi.* 复制;繁殖
    imagination   *n.* 想象力;空想;幻想物
    pictorial   *adj.* 绘画的;形象化的 *n.* 画报;画刊
    negative   *adj.* 负的;消极的;否定的;阴性的 *n.* 否定;负数;底片 *vt.* 否定;拒绝
    transmission   *n.* 传动装置,变速器;传递;传送;播送
    usher   *n.* 引座员,带位员;接待员;门房 *vt.* 引导,招待;迎接;开辟 *vi.* 作招待员;当引座员
    distribute   *vt.* 分配;散布;分开;把……分类
    reminiscent   *adj.* 怀旧的,回忆往事的;耽于回想的 *n.* 回忆录作者;回忆者
    cumbersome   *adj.* 笨重的;累赘的;难处理的
    maintenance   *n.* 维护,维修;保持;生活费用
    spreadsheet   *n.* 电子制表软件;电子数据表;试算表
    indistinguishable   *adj.* 不能区别的,不能辨别的;不易察觉的
    original   *n.* 原件;原作;原物;原型 *adj.* 原始的;最初的;独创的;新颖的
    scourge   *vt.* 鞭打;蹂躏;严斥;痛斥 *n.* 鞭;灾祸;鞭子;苦难的根源
    compatibility   *n.* 兼容性

Notes

[1] Images are still a major part of how we communicate. Although photography allows us to reproduce an image exactly as we see it, drawing and painting can give us a glimpse of

things we cannot see, the creations of our imagination.

译文:图片依然是人们交流方式的重要部分。摄影能够让我们像复制图像一样看到我们想看到的东西,而绘图软件能让我们发现我们看不到的东西,那是我们想象力的创作。

- glimpse of 瞥见;一瞥
- 在"Images are still a major part of how we communicate."中,"of how we communicate"做 part 的定语,how 引导方式状语,指代人们交流的方式。
- 在第二句中,although 引导的是让步状语从句,在"...drawing and painting can give us a glimpse of things we cannot see..."中,"drawing and painting"是动名词短语做主语,"we cannot see"做 things 的定语,that 可省略。

[2] The ability of the computer to handle increasing amounts of data and more sophisticated calculations made it a natural for creating graphic representations of mathematical formulae.

译文:计算机处理大量数据和复杂运算的能力使其适合于绘制数学公式的图形。

- amounts of 大量的
- 在"...made it a natural for creating graphic representations of mathematical formulae"中,"a natural for creating graphic representations of mathematical formulae"作 make 的宾语补足语,即短语 make it sth. 中,sth. 做宾语补足语。

[3] It was obvious that this new technology was going to evolve and grow into something more useful and more accessible to people other than scientists and programmers.

译文:很明显,除了科学家和程序员,对于更多的人来说这种新技术正在演变成为更有用的和更易接近的技术。

- grow into 成长为;长大到能穿着;变得成熟有经验
- accessible to 可归属的;可归因的;可亲近的,有权使用的
- It was obvious that... 强调句型,即,很明显……
- other than 除了,除……之外

[4] ... almost every television commercial lists a Web site and many of us spend countless hours on the Internet, we have yet to see the full impact of this revolution.

译文:尽管几乎所有的电视商业广告都列有网站,我们中的许多人也花费大量的时间在互联网上,但是我们仍未看到这场革命的全部影响。

- spend...on 在……方面花费
- although... 引导让步状语从句,译为:尽管

Selected Translation

Part 2

计算机图形

　　计算机图形在被用于制作数字媒体之前就已经存在了很长时间。计算机处理大量数据和复杂运算的能力使其适合于绘制数学公式的图形。早期的计算机绘图系统依靠编程来创建图形。早期的绘图仪通过在纸上画细黑线来创建图像。其他的一些早期图像是用 ASCII 字符集来表示的,句号和逗号代表亮一些的区域,数字符号和星号代表暗一些的区域。这些原始的绘制图像的方法主要依靠电脑主机,而终端只不过是一个键盘和一个点阵打印机。视频监控的观念对于访问控制室的远程用户来说还是新鲜的。20 世纪 70 年代中期,互联网已经以文本的形式存在了很长一段时间,但它仅仅研究政府管理、军队和大学的网络。访问互联网不仅慢而且不方便,但是它的未来却是光明的。很明显,除了科学家和程序员,对于更多的人来说这种新技术正在演变成为更有用的和更易获得的技术。

　　早期的计算机是大型计算机。早期 IBM 公司在计算机发展中一直接近垄断地位。在那时,IBM 360 是最复杂的机器,在 20 世纪 70 年代中期我就读研究生的锡拉丘兹大学,IBM 360 奠定了校园网建设的基础。我选修了一门实验室课程,这一课程中使用了 Art Speak 语言(见图 1-4)。它使用 FORTRAN 语言书写,并输出一系列的指令给绘图机用于绘制复杂的数学图纸,使人想起斯皮罗图。打印输出的时间大约是 1/2 到 3 个小时。

　　技术飞跃的另外一个标志是电子游戏的出现。以前,乒乓球和足球等是年轻人的主要娱乐方式;而后是"太空入侵者"游戏产生。一组沉默的角色慢慢从屏幕上方向底部行进,而同时游戏玩家试图消灭这些游戏中的角色。这是一个早期的使用光栅或基于像素、图形的实例。紧随"太空入侵者"之后出现了行星游戏,这个游戏有不同的外观,玩家位于屏幕的中心可以 360 度的旋转且图像轮廓分明。这是第一款基于矢量图形的游戏。

Part 6

互　联　网

　　互联网已经在美国及美国以外引起了文化和科技革命,但我们仍处于革命的早期阶段。尽管几乎所有的电视商业广告都列有网站,我们中的许多人也花费大量的时间在互联网上,但是我们仍未看到这场革命的全部影响。在我们谈论目前互联网的发展之前,我们先来看一下互联网的历史,我们可以将新媒体追溯到现在,但是互联网的历史可追溯到 20 世纪 60 年代。

早期的互联网

　　互联网起源于 20 世纪 60 年代,主要是用来连接 ARPA 所支持的研究机构。众所周知,随着 IP 协议的发展,Arpa 网能够实现不同类型计算机之间的通信,但这是一个纯文本系统。

我第一次比较专业地使用互联网是在 1972 年作为高级情报学家对 Sandoz 药品进行研究时。我们使用互联网访问在线存储检索系统；还可以通过联机医学文献分析和检索系统（MEDLINE）服务访问国家医学图书馆。国家图书馆的教育服务叫做教育资源信息中心（ERIC）。一些其他的在线资源也可以访问。在线检索的方法与我们现在的使用方法非常类似：输入关键字就会看到许多的匹配项，通过仔细筛选，可将匹配的文章减少到 30 到 50 篇，然后输入打印命令，等待打印输出即可。1972 年互联网的反应时间是 5 到 15 分钟。我输入命令，回到我的书桌旁，然后一直等到听见打印机打印出结果。我们现在取笑 WWW 是代表"全球等待"，但我们已经等了 30 年并且仍有很长的路要走。

20 世纪 80 年代中期，互联网的进一步发展是 NSF 网的建立，这是一个由美国国家科学基金会建立的速度为 1.5Mbps 的高速网络。

20 世纪 90 年代初，产生了其中一个最重要的发展，即欧洲粒子物理学（CERN）实验室开发了万维网（WWW），这使得互联网发展成现在这个样子。

1993 年，国际超级计算机应用中心（NCSA）开发出了一种适用于网络的图形浏览器：Mosaic；几年后，Netscape 和 Internet Explorer 问世。

尽管互联网几乎每天都有新的发展，但它终究会成为历史。互联网用户依然呈指数形式增长，新领域的发展也不断出现。一些飞速发展的领域如通过调制解调器和 DSL 提高访问速度。使用流媒体技术可以将视频和音频上传到网络。不久，我们还可以通过宽带连接为人们提供全屏视频和优质的音频，位于麻省理工学院（MIT）的与工业有紧密联系的万维网联盟（W3C）是最主要的组织者。

Exercises

1. Explore the connection between written language and pictorial history. Trace your culture roots or those of a culture you are interested in, and collect a series of early images and writings. Use this research either to write a short paper on this period in history or to produce a series of images based on this time.

2. Do an in-depth study of one of the important inventions of predigital or digital technology. Try to discover what led this person to making that invention. What was his or her educational and professional background? What social and culture conditions prompted the inventions? Write a short biography of your subject and the effects of his or her invention. Speculate on what would have happened if the invention had not been made.

专业英语简介

信息技术的飞速发展，给社会带来了重大的变革，各国之间的交流也愈益广泛，各种国际学术会议也不断举行。但是，教育学、心理学以及数字媒体等相关学科的文献和会议，大部分都是用英文写的。所以，掌握好专业英语的阅读、翻译和书写的方法对我们了解最新的技术动态、吸收先进的科技成果是至关重要的。数字媒体专业英语是数字媒体专业学生学好数字媒体课程的一门重要工具,也是一门必修课,同时它也与公共英语密切相关。作为数字媒体专业的大学生,尽管他们既有数字媒体基础知识,也有不错的公共英语基础,但一看到那些英文文献、英文资料、英文会议还是有些不知所措。如何在较短的时间里将专业英语掌握好呢?首先要了解数字媒体专业英语的三大特点。

一、专业性

专业英语的专业性体现在它的特殊专业内容和特殊专业词汇。词汇是构成句子的基本元素,对词汇含义不能确定,就很难理解句子内容,甚至得出可笑的、相反的结果。很多公共英语在专业领域内被赋予了专业含义,这就要求我们熟悉所学专业。如:communication(传播)、elaboration(细化)、development(开发)。

新词汇层出不穷,有的是随着本专业发展应运而生的,有的是借用公共英语中的词汇,有的是借用外来语词汇,有的则是人为构造的词汇。有些专业词汇是需要对专业知识有相当的了解之后才会明白意思的。如:Communications media(传播媒体)、Abacus and Mathematics(算数)、Computer Graphics(计算机图形学)、Cave Drawings and Paintings(壁画)、Written Language(书面语)、The Printing Press(印刷机)、Motion Pictures(电影)。

二、灵活性

专业英语一般讲述的是基本理论、数字媒体的开发与应用等,这就决定了专业英语的客观性和灵活性。在学习过程中,尤其是在阅读专业文章时,必须尊重客观内容,不能主观想象。为了表示一种公允性和客观性,往往在句子结构和词性的使用上比较灵活。如:

① Regardless of the quality and sophistication of computer hardware and software, the success of technology often depends on the support and encouragement that students and teachers receive in using it.

不管计算机硬件和软件的质量和复杂性存在怎么样的差别,技术在学校的成功更多地取决于我们如何支持和鼓励学生和教师使用各类技术。

② What's more, by means of information technology, education can thus be made available outside of working hours, at the weekend, during working hours in cooperation between companies and educational institutions, as well as in a completely different part of the country from that in which the teaching is taking place.

另外,在工作时间之外、在周末,在公司和教育机构合作的工作时间,或者是和上课地方完全不同的场所的情况下,学习者也可以通过信息技术受到教育。

三、简明性

为求精炼,专业英语中常希望能够用尽可能少的单词来清晰地表达原意。这就导致了非限定动词、名词化单词或词组以及其他简化形式的广泛使用。

1. 动名词短语可用来取代时间从句或简化时间陈述句,如:

Before being executed, the program should be loaded into main memory.

2. 过去分词短语可以取代被动语态关系从句,现在分词可以取代主动语态关系从句,如:

① In Britain electricity energy generated in power station is fed to the national Grid.

② The number of people working in the field of educational technology can be larger in the future.

3. 不定式短语用以替换表示目的、功能的从句,如:

The best way to introduce this theory is through Gagne's model.

总的说来,与普通英语相比,专业英语很注重客观事实和真理,并且要求逻辑性强,条理规范,表达准确、精练、正式。专业英语有如下显著特点:

- 长句多
- 被动语态使用频繁
- 用虚拟语气表达假设或建议
- 在说明书、手册中广泛使用祈使语句
- 名词性词组多
- 非限定动词(尤其是分词)使用频率高
- 介词短语多
- 常用 It... 句型结构
- 单个动词比动词词组用得频繁
- 常使用动词或名词演化成的形容词
- 希腊词根和拉丁词根比例大
- 专业术语多
- 缩略词经常出现
- 半技术词汇多
- 缩写使用频繁
- 插图、插画、表格、公式、数字所占比例大
- 合成新词多

Chapter 2　The Basics of Digital Media[①]

▲ Knowledge Objectives

When you have completed this unit, you will be able to:

* Know how your computer works.

* Being able to troubleshoot, configure, and optimize a system will save hours of lost time due to crashes, lose files, and other problems.

* Review and explain the basics of how computers work, how they are put together, and how they can best be adapted for digital media production.

▲ Professional Terms

analog-to-digital converters	模数转换器
Central Processing Unit (CPU)	中央处理器
digital media art	数字媒体艺术
digital media	数字媒体
disk drives	磁盘驱动器
DSP	数字信号处理
GUI	图形用户界面
motherboard	主板
operating systems	操作系统
processing	处理器
software applications	应用软件
system configuration	系统配置
video editing and compositing	视频编辑和影像合成软件

Part 1　Hardware

Processing

This is what happens to the data once it has been entered into the computer. The main

---

[①] M. D. Roblyer, *Integrating Educational Technology into Teaching*, Third Edition, Chapter Two, The Basics of Digital Media.

components of a computer include the central processing unit (CPU), the motherboard, and storage devices. The motherboard contains all the printed circuits that enable the CPU to talk to all the other components of the computer. The motherboard is connected to a monitor, mouse, and keyboard by direct connections or circuit boards (i.e., a video card).

Central Processing Unit (CPU)

The central processing unit is the "brain" of the computer. However, it is incapable of working unless it is turned on and loaded with the system and application software. We'll talk more about this later. The CPU is where the calculation and manipulation of data happen. CPUs are generally referred to by clock speed, brand, and generation. Current clock speeds are in the 500 to 800 MHz area. Ten years ago, clock speeds were in the 33 to 66 MHz range. We can expect to see clock speeds continue to increase in the future. Another way to get more speed out of a computer is to have multiple processors. Dual processor machines are becoming more common, and high-end computers can have 4, 8, 16, or more processors working together.

The two main manufacturers of computer CPUs are Intel and Motorola. Intel CPUs evolved through the 286, 386, and 486, the Pentium I, II, and III machines. Motorola CPUs are 80260, 403, Power PC, G3, and G4.

Motherboard

The motherboard is the main circuit board on the computer where everything resides and/or gets plugged in. The CPU is on the motherboard, as is the memory, system bus, and connections for disk drive, expansion cards, video card, audio card, hard disk, peripherals, and so on.

Bus

The bus is the pathway through which the data travels around the computer. The bus connects the CPU with the hard drive, video cards, audio cards, ports, input devices, and so on. Buses have speeds, just as motherboard do. Several buses have been developed over the years, starting with ISA, EISA, and Video Local Bus. Currently we are using the PCI bus technology. Bus speeds evolve with processors speeds and are intimately linked to the speed of a computer. If a really fast CPU is installed in a machine with a slow bus, the speed of the computer is limited by the bus speed.

Memory

RAM is the random access memory that exists on the motherboard. Most computers come with 64 or 128 MB of RAM. For better performance, especially with digital media computers, it is recommended that at least 256 MB is installed. For high-end 3D computers, very large images, or video, 512 or more RAM will be helpful. The general rule for RAM is to buy as much as you can afford.

Disk Drives

There are many different kinds of disk drives. Most computers have a single hard disk. This is where the operating system and application software resides and where the data files are stored. The cost per megabyte has been dropping with time and hard disks are getting larger and larger. Now 18 and 36 GB drives are common.

There is also removable media, such as floppy disk (see Figure 2-1), CD-ROM, removable hard drives, DVD, and so on. Floppy disks are inexpensive and hold about 1 MB of data. They are starting to be used less frequently because of increasing file size. Zip drives are very widely used. The original zip disks had a capacity of 100 MB, and now a 250-MB format is available (see Figure 2-2). They are relatively inexpensive, stable, and many people have them. CD-ROM has become a standard format for the delivery of software, video games, and other types of data. The cost of CD recorders has dropped and many machines now come with them built in. The cost of CD media has also fallen dramatically. CDs are stable and easy to store and carry. The popularity of audio CDs has made them also a very popular form of data storage. In the future, DVD will become a major form of data storage. DVD writers are currently very expensive but prices will fall just as prices for CD-ROM writers have fallen. DVD has the advantage of storing very large amounts of data. As DVD players become more popular, we will see an increase in the use of DVD writers and disks for data storage.

Figure 2-1   A high-density floppy disk. It can store 1.4 MB of data.

Figure 2-2   A 100 MB Zip disk. With increasing file sizes, Zip disks are becoming very common.

Input

Input is the manner how the data entered into the computer (see Figure 2-3). The most frequently used input device is the keyboard. There are many different types of keyboards, and if you are going to spend significant time in front of a computer, it is a good idea to examine the various keyboard options. Two common ones are the standard QUERTY layout (see Figure

2-4) and the ergonomic layout, which is designed to create a minimum amount of stress on your hands. There are many sizes and shapes of keyboards, and they can work on different machines. Some keyboards have special keys. For example, the AVID keyboard, this has functions assigned to keys to speed the video editing process (see Figure 2-5). Keyboards are not expensive, so it is a good idea to choose one that matches your hand size and work style.

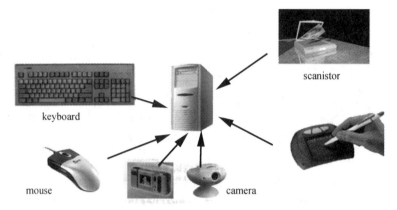

Figure 2-3　How different types of data can be brought into the computer.

Figure 2-4　A standard keyboard for an Apple computer. Notice the QWERTY layout of the keys. It also has function keys at the top and a numeric keyboard at the right.

Figure 2-5　A keyboard for an AVID digital video editing system. Look at the keys and notice how they have been assigned to different functions of the software.

The second most frequently used input device is the mouse. There are many kinds of mice, as well, but they generally break down into the one-, two-, and three-button models. The basic metaphor for their use is the click and drag method. There are mechanical mice, which use a track ball that glides over a surface (see Figure 2-6). There are also optical and laser mice, which use a beam of light as a reference. This is again a matter of personal choice. There are also several alternative input devices, such as track balls, joy sticks, game controllers, and so on.

For drawing with the computers, the graphics tablet is an excellent idea. It allows you to draw and sketch in a way that is similar to drawing. The Wacom tablet is the most popular, and the tips have a pressure control stylus (see Figure 2-7). They come in a variety of sizes and shapes. They even have different types of styli, which emulate a pen or airbrush (see Figure 2-8). All of this is a matter of personal choice, but it is well worth the money to set you up with an input system that matches your hand size, work style, and personal preference.

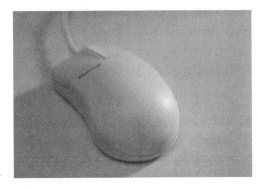

Figure 2-6 A mechanical mouse for an Apple computer sitting on a rare ILM mouse pad.

Figure 2-7 A WACOM graphics tablet. This is a 12 by 18-inch model. It came with a mouse and a pen.

Figure 2-8 A close-up view of the WACOM mouse and pen. Notice the five buttons on the mouse. It can be programmed for a variety of functions.

Scanners are used to bring flat art and photographs into the computer. Scanners work by converting the image into digital form through a row of charge-coupled devices on the arm of the scanner as it moves over the art. The resolution of scanners varies with their quality, but 1440 dpi scanners are fairly inexpensive. Once an image has been scanned, it can be modified with an image processing program like Photoshop.

Audio Input

Audio input can happen in three ways. The first is through a built-in microphone or external microphone. Generally, microphones that come with computers are of low quality, and this type of input is recommended for memos, recording ideas, and other nonprofessional purposes.

If you want to record high-quality voice into the computer, it is generally better to use a professional quality microphone, which is run through a mixer before it is plugged into the computer's audio input jack. The same applies to music.

Although removable media and CD-ROMs generally do not fall under input devices, many people use software to pull prerecorded audio from audio CDs and images from clip art CDs into the computer. This type of input should be mentioned here because of its widespread use.

Video Input

Input can either be through a camera or video cable. The same standards for audio apply to inexpensive video cameras. They are good as webcams and for recording low-quality video, but for professional uses, video should be shot in the highest quality possible and digitized into the best machine available. However, a simple setup, such as a digital video (DV) camcorder and Firewire can create very high-quality digital video. We should mention here that, currently, the DV standards for the Internet are still not full screen. However, DV, VHS, and other consumer and prosumer standards can be used for video for the Internet. Professional systems like the AVID are designed for professional quality video and are therefore much more expensive than the typical desktop video solution using Firewire (see Figure 2-9).

Figure 2-9 An AVID editing system. It is a specialized system with three monitors: two RGB and a NTSC video monitor. There are also several hard drives to allow for sufficient storage. There is also an audio mixer and external speakers.

Firewire was developed to allow for the high-speed transfer of data between peripheral devices. It is most commonly used on DV camcorders for inputting and outputting video, but it is also used for many other devices, such as digital cameras, hard drives, and printers. Firewire allows for very high-speed data transfer rates and is 30 times faster than Universal Serial Bus (USB). Currently, Firewire can support up to 63 devices and cable lengths of up to 14 feet. It also allows you to plug it in without turning the computer off. It is also called IEEE 1394 or iLink.

Output

It is easy to see that the type of output we can get from a computer can be very broad, including images, video, CD-ROMs, DVDs, Web sites, and software applications (see Figure 2-10).

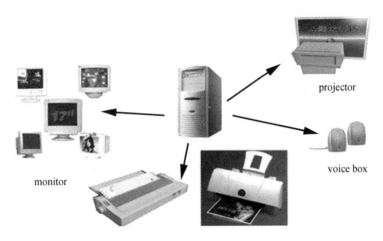

Figure 2-10 This diagram shows how data and other media are output from the computer.

The Computer Image

When an image is displayed on a computer screen, what really happens? What are its components, and why does it look the way it does? Working from the monitor inwards, the size and type of monitor is the first consideration.

Monitors come in a standard range of sizes. Large monitors are more expensive. One of the most common monitor configurations is 17 inches, measured diagonally. The older standard was 15 inches, and there are still millions of computers with 15-inch monitors. Large monitors range in size from 19 to 21 inches. Other specialized monitors have unique layouts for print or digital video work. The new generation of monitors is the flat screen LCD variety.

Video cards drive monitors. The video card determines the resolution of the image and how fast the information is fed to the monitor. Video RAM speeds up the display of the image and allows for higher-resolution images to be displayed. Resolution is determined by the number of pixels that make up the image. Standard resolutions are 1680 by 1050, 1024 by 768, etc. (see Figure 2-11). The more pixels or resolution an image has the sharper and more realistic it will appear.

1024*768   1440*900   1280*1024   1680*1050

Figure 2-11 These are standard computer monitor resolutions. As the speed and memory of a computer increases, you can take advantage of higher resolutions.

In addition to the resolution, color depth is an important component of the image. Three different types of color depth are black and white, 256 colors, and 16.7 million colors. Another way to describe the color depth is by using bits. The number of bits that are assigned to a pixel will give it the color possibilities. Two-bit color is black or white. Eight-bit color gives a range of 256 colors, and 24-bit color gives a possible range of colors of 16.7 million and is photographic in quality. This is based on different levels of red, green, and blue. For example, $8*8*8=256$.

While color depth is used to determine the number of colors created, the color systems used in computers are important to understand. The additive color system is defined as colors that are combined using light; for example, monitors and video. When this happens, red and green make yellow, green and blue make cyan, red and blue make magenta, and all three together make white, as shown in Color Plate 2. Print uses the subtractive color model, which means that colors are created by adding dyes and pigments together. Color Plate 3 shows how this model works. In print, there is a slightly different terminology. The inks are called cyan, magenta, yellow, and black-or CMYK. In this model, all colors add together to make black.

For videotape, color bars are used as a standard, as shown in Color Plate 4. Whenever professional video is shot, 60 seconds of color bars are recorded at the beginning of the tape as a color reference. In the editing process, different reels of tape are adjusted in the studio by referencing them to the studio's color bars, or "house bars." Color bars are also used as a reference to adjust how a video monitor looks. Another way of defining the color of light is to use the color temperature, as shown in Color Plate 5. Measured in degrees Kelvin, 3200 degrees is photographic white. Sunlight is slightly blue and is 5500 degrees Kelvin. A standard light bulb emits a warmer yellow color and is measured at 2800 degrees Kelvin.

Printers

One of the oldest forms of computer output is paper prints. Recent developments in technology have brought color printers down to as low as $100. There are several types of printers. The early dot matrix, or impact, printers are becoming more difficult to find. These printers worked much like a typewriter with a ribbon and print head that had a mechanical matrix that matched the pixels on the screen. They have been replaced by laser printers and ink jet printers. Laser printers use lasers and a heat transfer process to create images. Black-and-white laser printers are very good an affordable, but color laser printers are more expensive and require more complex technology. Ink jet printers are the most common kind of printer. They work with ink cartridges that are digitally controlled and are relatively inexpensive. Some of the most popular brands of ink jet printers are Epson and Hewlett-Packard. By using archival inks and paper, artists can create high-quality images. Recent developments allow ink jet printers to use pigments instead of dyes. This allows for prints to be much more archival. Ink jet printers are also extensively used in design and publishing.

Part 2　Software

Software is the means by which things get done on a computer. Two basic elements are needed: the operating system and the software application. The operating system is the basic set of instructions that tells the computer what hardware components it is made of and, in essence, what it can do. Software applications allow specific tasks to be done.

Operating Systems

The operating system is the set of software that is loaded into the computer when it is turned on. There are also instructions that reside in the computer when it is turned off. The instructions that the operating system gives to the computer are to bring it up to speed so that software programs can be used. Several operating systems are currently in use. They have varying degrees of compatibility and are moving toward being more compatible in the future. In the early days of personal computing, it was to the manufacturer's advantage to be exclusive. For example, the Macintosh computer was the first to have a graphical user interface (GUI), and this was its major sales feature. Early IBM and clone computers used the text-based Disk Operating System (DOS). To compete with the Macintosh, the Windows operating system was developed by Microsoft. Now, with the development of the internet and cross-platform software, the differences between operating systems are more of a hindrance than a marketing advantage. The two main operating systems are the Macintosh OS and Microsoft Windows, but there are many other operating systems, such as Linux, Irix, and UNIX. Linux is becoming very widespread due to its open architecture, low price, and stability. For many Web services, it is the operating system of choice. It is important to have a good knowledge of the operating system of the computer you are using. Operations such as file transfers, copying, renaming, deleting, color palettes, and changing the resolution of your monitor are functions of the operating system. Once the operating system has been loaded, other software programs can be installed on the machine.

Software Applications

We will talk about various software applications in detail in the later chapters. This section will give a brief overview of applications that are used for digital media design and production.

Internet

A tremendous amount of software has been written to deal with the creation of Web sites. HTML is still the standard for creating sites, but many packages have evolved that eliminate having to write code from scratch. There are simple HTML editors like BB Edit, and a whole range of more sophisticated Web site creation software like Adobe Golive and Macromedia Dreamweaver. Macromedia Flash is a vector-based software that is used to create Web sites and animation for the Web. Additionally, programs like Adobe Image Ready, Macromedia Fireworks, and several others support creating images for the Web. We can expect to see this category of software evolve over the next several years as Internet standards change and different software companies complete for dominance in this area.

Programming

Programming languages are used to create software packages. Most software packages come with a tool set, and you have to work within the limitations of the software. Considering the sophistication of the software available, it is rare that one needs to be a programmer. However, programmers are among the most desired and highest paid individuals in the field today. This is because programmers are essential in many situations. One of the fields that they are in most demand is the Internet. Given the rapid changes in the Internet, programmers can create applications for the Internet that give their companies a competitive edge. Feature film and special effects studios also use programmers extensively to create effects that no one has seen before. The Hollywood film industry is highly competitive, and while off-the-shelf software packages are common, big-budget feature films always strive to create something new that will give the audience a reason to go see the film. Some of the languages that Web programmers use are HTML, XML, Java, and JavaScript. The C and C + + programming languages are in wide use by video game, computer graphics, and special effects programmers.

Part 3　DSP and Digital Media Art

Analog-to-Digital Converters

Mice, keyboards, pens, and digital data from networks and files create input data that is in digital form. Images, audio, and video need to be converted into digital data before they can be used and processed by the computer. This process is done with analog-to-digital converters (ADCs). Converters generally sample the signal coming in and convert it into digital data. For example, we can look at the sky during a sunset and see a smooth range of colors, from the fading yellow of the sun, to the gradated colors of the sky and clouds, to the overhead dark sky. When an image like this is sampled, it is divided into a number of discrete elements, both in terms of resolution (pixels) and colors. The image might then conform to a digital image standard by being 640 by 480 pixels in height and width and 256 colors. True photographic color is 24-or 32-bit samples using 16.7 million colors. At this level of quality, our eye cannot tell the difference between the original photograph and the digital image. The same thing happens with audio. The analog-to-digital converter for CD-quality audio uses 16-bit samples at a frequency of 44.1 kHz. This level of sampling is beyond our ability to tell the difference between the analog recording and the digital recording.

Painting and Drawing

This group of software packages is used to create, edit, and manipulate images. There are two types of painting and drawing programs. The first group works with bit-mapped images, or images composed of pixels. The second group is vector-based. These programs create images by using curves, lines, and shapes, which are drawn by using mathematical operations. There are advantages and disadvantages to each type of program. Bit-mapped programs, like Adobe Photoshop, are good for dealing with photographic images, scanned images, and illustrations (see Figure 2-12). Images are composed of pixels of a particular resolution and bit depth.

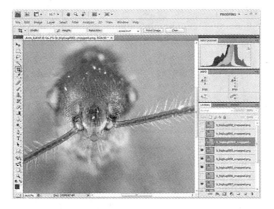

Figure 2-12 A screen grab from Adobe Photoshop. Photoshop is a bit-mapped software that is used for working with photographic and other pixel-based images.

A pixel refers to a picture element, or the smallest component of an image. It can be thought of as a square dot on the screen. Images on the computer are composed of thousands of pixels; each one assigned a particular location on the screen and color. Typical screen resolution for a computer image on your monitor would be 640 by 480. As mentioned earlier, the bit depth, or the number of bits assigned to each pixel, determines the color of the pixel. Screen location is generally done with x and y values. For example, 0, 0 might be the top left of the image, 320, 240 in the middle, and 640, 480 at the lower right corner.

The second type of painting and drawing software is vector based. The two most popular software packages using this type of system are Adobe Illustrator and Macromedia Freehand (see Figure 2-13). These software packages define shapes through mathematical equations, rather than by using pixels. In doing so, they can be changed in a variety of ways without losing the precision of the mathematical curves. This is often referred to as resolution-independent to software. For example, a very small vector graphic can be scaled to many times its original size and train its smooth edges. A low-resolution bit-mapped image, on the other hand, will start to show its pixels if it is enlarged too much. Resolution independence is one of the strengths of this category of software. Also, the file sizes of vector-based images tend to be smaller than bit-mapped images. We will see continued development of this type of software in relationship to the Internet based on this fact, as well as combining bit-mapped and vector-based functions into a single software package.

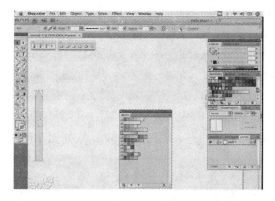

Figure 2-13 A screen grab from Adobe Illustrator. This is vector-based software. Although the tool palette may look the same, the software operates very differently from Photoshop. It relies of mathematical formulas, rather than pixels to form images.

2D Animation

This type of software allows one to create animation on the computer. It is similar to painting and drawing software in that there are bit-mapped and vector-based animation programs. Bit-mapped programs use a series of still images to form the basis of the animation. They also have built-in controls to allow for "inbetweening," or allowing the compute to create the motion by calculating the images that fall in between the start and end position of the animation. Macromedia Director, Adobe Premiere, and Metacreations Painter are three popular 2D animation software programs. There are also high-end packages like US Animation and Animo that are used for television and feature films.

3D Animation

Three-dimensional animation has made considerable progress in the last few years. Packages that once were extremely expensive and only affordable by the major film studios are now available for personal computers. Three-dimensional animation allows users to create a mathematical world within which animation can be created. Feature films, video games, and TV commercials are the places you see 3D animation most often. The learning curve for this type of software is fairly complex. In order to create an image, you must first create a 3D mathematical model of the object, and then assign surface properties like color, and texture to it. After this has been done, a scene is created by placing the model in an environment with a camera and lights. Animation is then done by key framing the object in various positions. After an extended period of refining and testing, the images are then rendered into 2D images by the computer and output to digital video files, videotape, or film. Two examples of high-end software packages that have been adapted to personal computers are Alias/Wavefront Maya and Softimage XSI. Other popular packages include Discreet 3D Studio MAX and Lightwave.

Video Editing and Compositing

Because of the large amount of data needed for video, early video editing programs for personal computers worked mainly with smaller digital video formats like Quicktime. The most popular of these is Adobe Premiere. With the rapid increase in computer speed, low cost of RAM and hard drives, and the development of Firewire and USB, it is now possible and affordable to edit video on a personal computer. One of the first systems invented was called the AVID, and it is still standard for the broadcast industry. A complete AVID system is expensive and beyond the reach of most small studios. However, new software, like Apple's Final Cut Pro includes many of the editing features of an AVID system but costs much less. It is slower and does not include all of AVID's features, but the capabilities of software like this are impressive.

Another category of this software is compositing and special effects software. One of the most popular packages is Adobe After Effects. This software has can work with a wide range of files and is popular with large professional studios as well as smaller ones. High-end compositing systems like Discreet Inferno and Flame are very expensive and the realm of Hollywood and broadcast environments. Software like Shake, Combustion, and After Effects can produce many of the same effects of the high-end software. Again, they are slower but are much less expensive. Many studios use these packages in addition to or in place of the high-end systems. Compositing and special effects software allow you to combine live action, 2D animation, and 3D animation to create all kinds of special effects on these images.

Part 4　Others

System Configuration

To configure a system means to assemble a computer system designed for a specific purpose. It may be s simple home computer, a Web design computer, digital audio system, or digital video system. System configuration includes specifying both the computer components needed and the software needed. When designing a system, you need to look at costs and functionality required. Many computer companies allow customers on Web sites to configure a range of machines tailored for specific purposes and costs.

When you configure a system, the first thing you consider is what the system is going to be used for and what the budget is. Home computers are generally bought preconfigured and cost the least. High-end professional systems are generally designed by the buyer and are relatively expensive.

There are two schools of thought when it comes to putting a system together. One is that you buy the latest, most expensive computer. The reasoning is that your system will be state of the art and that you will get the longest life out of the computer. The down side to this approach is that the currently available software may not have been rewritten to take advantage of the new hardware. New systems also tend to have "growing pains," or compatibility problems with hardware and software. These problems are generally worked out within 6 to 12 months after the new machines are released.

The second approach is to buy a system that is one level down. The reasoning here is that it is considerably less expensive, and it will also be compatible with all current software and hardware. The difference in speed between the slightly older machines is usually 10%, which is not a major compromise. There are exceptions, though. For instance, the Macintosh G4 platform is considerably faster than the G3 platform.

When putting together a Macintosh system, these are several factors to consider. Macintosh machines are generally reasonably priced, so I would recommend getting the fastest, most expensive system you can afford. When looking at RAM, I would try to get 512 MB if you can afford it, but 256 MB is adequate for most uses. It is handy to have 512 MB when you are working with several programs at once, very large images, or video editing. For input, I recommend finding a keyboard that fits your hands and suits personal preferences. Keyboards are inexpensive and come in a wide range of configurations, as do mice. You will be spending a lot of time in front of your machine, so the keyboard and mouse setup should be one that agrees with your working style. You may want to consider a Wacom tablet, especially if you are going to do photo retouching. They come in several sizes and price ranges. Most artists feel that the mouse is not a good tool for drawing.

Regarding monitors, buy the largest monitor you can afford, preferably 17 inches or large. Currently, 17-inch monitors are relative inexpensive, and there is a big price jump when you look at 19-or 21-inch monitors. However, if you use software that has a lot of windows (e.g., ProTools, Macromedia Director, Photoshop, etc.) screen real estate becomes very valuable. I use a Sony 19-inch monitor and am very happy with it. If you have to spend a lot of time moving windows around on the screen so that you can see what you are working on, you are wasting time. Macintosh machines can accommodate multiple monitors easily. This is another option.

You will also need a scanner. Scanners come in a range of prices, and you get what you pay for. If you are going to use it a lot, buy a really good scanner. You will get better quality images, and they tend to work faster.

You will also need a printer. Ink jet printers have come down in price considerably over the past few years. For a few hundred dollars, you can get a really good printer. Epson and Hewlett Packard are two of the most popular brands. I have both and am happy with them. You may want to consider the all-in-one approach as well. Hewlett Packard's Office jet series has a scanner, copier, printer, and fax machine in one box. It is also a good idea to have a CD writer. They are inexpensive and provide for a good method of backup and a way to transport your data. Most computers have CD drives, and this is an advantage when sending work to clients.

The recommendations for PC systems are generally the same. I have a Sony VAIO system and am very happy with it. It came configured with a 500 MHz processor, 128 MB of RAM, a 20-GB hard drive, and capabilities for digital video, audio, and a built-in CD writer. For high-end PC systems, dual-processor Windows NT systems are most common.

The mouse, keyboard, computer, monitor, scanner, and printer are the basic elements of a computer system. You'll also need a modem to connect to the Internet. You may also need a digital camera, digital video camera, external disk drives for additional flexibility, USB or Ethernet hubs if you have more than one computer, and so on.

As a consultant, I advise professionals to buy systems then can pay off in one year. One year is the usual lifespan for machines, and two years is considered a good life for a production machine. After two years, new machines are significantly faster, and software releases are tailored for the newer machines.

The most common software packages used by the professionals I work with are Adobe Photoshop, Illustrator, Image Ready, After Effects, Premiere, Macromedia Director, Dreamweaver, Flash, Terran Media Cleaner Pro, Apple Final Cut, Alias Wavefront Maya, Softimage XSI, Discreet 3D Studio MAX, Lightwave, Microsoft Word, Netscape, Internet Explorer, and BB Edit. Commonly used utilities include Norton Utilities, Adobe Acrobat, and Stuffit Deluxe. Software choice is a combination of professional standards and personal preferences. Many software packages perform similar functions but are produced by different companies. The preceding is the result of my professional, personal, and teaching experience. I suggest you try out a number of competing packages and make your own decision.

New Words

  ergonomic *adj.* 人类环境改造学的；人类工程学的
  manufacturer *n.* 制造商；厂商
  manipulate *vt.* 操纵；操作；巧妙地处理；篡改
  dimensional *adj.* 空间的；尺寸的
  sophistication *n.* 复杂；诡辩；老于世故；有教养
  configuration *n.* 配置；结构；外形
  compositing *vt.* 使合成；使混合 *n.* 影像合成
  tremendous *adj.* 极大的，巨大的；惊人的
  component *adj.* 组成的，构成的 *n.* 成分；组件；元件
  multiple *adj.* 多重的；多样的；许多的 *n.* 倍数；并联
  recommend *vt.* 推荐，介绍；劝告；使受欢迎；托付 *vi.* 推荐；建议
  metaphor *n.* 暗喻，隐喻；比喻说法
  reference *n.* 参考，参照；涉及；提及；参考书目；介绍信；证明书 *vi.* 引用
  alternative *adj.* 供选择的；选择性的；交替的 *n.* 二中择一；供替代的选择
  emulate *vt.* 仿真；模仿；尽力赶上；同……竞争 *n.* 仿真；仿效
  peripheral *adj.* 外围的；次要的
  subtractive *adj.* 减去的；负的；有负号的
  pigment *n.* 色素；颜料 *vt.* 给……着色 *vi.* 呈现颜色
  terminology *n.* 术语，术语学；用辞
  hindrance *n.* 障碍；妨碍；妨害；阻碍物

Notes

  [1] These programs create images by using curves, lines, and shapes, which are drawn by using mathematical operations.

  译文：这些程序通过利用数学运算绘制曲线、直线和形状来创建图片。

  • 在"… by using curves, lines, and shapes…"中，by 引导的是方式状语。by doing sth. 译为：通过使用……

  • 在"which are drawn by using mathematical operations."中，which 引导的是非限定性定语从句，修饰 images。

  [2] They also have built-in controls to allow for "inbetweening," or allowing the computer to create the motion by calculating the images that fall in between the start and end position of the animation.

  译文：它们也具有内部程序来控制插图，允许计算机通过估计介于动画开始位置和

结束位置之间的图片来创建补间动作。

- fall in between 介于两者之间
- allow...to do sth. 允许……
- 在"...the images that fall in between the start and end position of the animation."中，that 引导的是限定性定语从句，修饰 images。

Selected Translation

Part 3

数字信号处理和数字媒体艺术

模数转换器

通过鼠标、键盘、笔输入到网络的数字数据以数字信号的形式存在。图像、音频、视频需要转换为数字化的数据后才能在计算机上使用和处理。这个过程需要借助模数转换器（ADCs）完成。转换器通常将输入的信号取样并将其转化成数字信号。例如，我们在日落时观察天空，就可以看到一系列的渐变颜色：太阳的金黄色逐渐退却，天空和白云的颜色逐渐变化，还有头顶上暗淡的天空。如果有像这样的一张图像被采样，它会从分辨率（像素）和色彩两个方面被分为多个独立的元素。随后图像可能会遵循数字图像的标准——480(H)×640(W)的像素和256种颜色。真实的摄影颜色是使用1670万色的24位或32位的样本。从这个方面考虑，我们肉眼不能分辨原始照片和数字图像的区别。音频也是如此，CD品质音频的模数转换器使用的是频率为44.1千赫的16位的样本。这样的样本也超出了我们分辨模拟录音和数字录音的区别。

绘图软件

这组软件包是用来创建、编辑和处理图像的。有两种类型绘图程序。一种是处理位图或者基于像素的图像，另一种是处理矢量图像的。这些程序通过利用数学运算绘制曲线、直线和形状来创建图片。每种程序都存在利弊。位图程序（如 Adobe Photoshop）能更好地处理照片、扫描图像和插图。图像由具有特定分辨率和位深的像素组成。

一个像素是指一个图形的元素，或者说是一个图形的最小单元。它可以被看作是屏幕上显示的单个的染色点。计算机上的图像是由成千上万的像素组成的，它们在屏幕上被分配特定的位置和颜色。在你的显示器上典型的计算机图像的分辨率为640×480。如前所述，每个像素分配到的位深和位数能决定其颜色。通常其在屏幕上的定位是由 x 和 y 的值决定的。例如，(0,0) 代表图像的左上角，(320,240) 为中间，(640,480) 指图像的右下角。

另一种绘图软件是基于矢量的。这类软件的典型代表是 Adobe Illustrator 和 Macromedia Freehand。这些软件包利用数学方程式定义图形，而不是利用像素。这样，图像可以在不丢失数学曲线精度的前提下做任意的改变。这通常被称为分辨率独立软件。例如，一个非常小的矢量图形无论被改变多少次都可以一直显示它原来的样子和精准边缘。相反，一个低分辨率的位图图像如果被放大得太大就会看到一个个的像素格。分辨率独立是这类软件的优势。当然，矢量图像的大小要小于位图图像。我们可以预测不久的将来随着互联网的发展会出现一款将基于位图的软件和基于矢量的软件结合起来的软件。

二维动画

这类软件允许你在计算机上创建动画。它与绘图软件类似,包括基于位图和基于矢量两种类型。位图程序使用一系列静止图像形成动画的基础。它们也具有内部程序来控制插图,允许计算机通过估计介于动画开始位置和结束位置之间的图片来创建补间动作。Macromedia Director、Adobe Premiere 和 Metacreations Painter 是目前最流行的三款二维动画制作软件。当然也有用于电视和高清电影的高端二维软件,如 US Animation 和 Animo。

三维动画

在过去几年里,三维动画取得了长足进步。之前的程序包极其昂贵,只有各大电影公司能够负担得起,而现在个人用户也可以购买使用了。三维动画允许用户创建一个可以制作动画的数学世界。电影、视频游戏、电视广告是三维动画应用最多的地方。学习这类软件是相当复杂的,为了创造一个图像,你首先必须建立一个三维数学模型,然后再在物体表面渲染材质,如颜色和纹理。此后,再利用照相机和灯光为场景布置环境。动画的关键框架完成了。经过一段时间的改善和测试,三维图像被计算机转化为二维图像然后输出到数字视频文件、录像带或者电影中。可以应用到个人电脑的两个高端软件是 Alias/Wavefront Maya 和 Softimage XSI,另外流行的软件主要是 Discreet 3D Studio MAX 和 Lightwave。

视频编辑和影像合成软件

由于视频需要大量的数据,早期个人电脑的视频编辑程序主要是较小的数字视频格式如 Quicktime。现在最流行的是 Adobe Premiere。随着计算机速度的快速增长,RAM 和硬盘的成本降低,以及火线接口和 USB 接口的发展,在个人电脑上编辑视频成为可能,并且也负担得起。最早发明的系统称为 AVID,它现在仍然是广播行业的标准。一个完整的 AVID 系统十分昂贵,普通的小型工作室是负担不起的。然而,一些新软件(如苹果公司的 Final Cut Pro)包含了 AVID 系统的许多特性和功能,价格却要少很多。它运行缓慢,并且没有包含 AVID 的所有功能,但是这种软件的性能还是很不错的。

另一个类别的软件是影像合成和特效软件。其中最流行的软件包是 Adobe After Effects。这款软件可以处理各种不同的文件,并且在大、小型公司中都很受欢迎。高端软件如 Discreet Inferno 和 Flame 非常昂贵,它进军的是好莱坞的领域和广播公司。其实像 Shake、Combustion 和 After Effects 这些软件也可以制作出很多和高端软件一样的效果。它们虽然慢但却要便宜很多。许多工作室使用这些软件来代替高端软件,影像合成和特效软件允许你将实景、二维动画和三维动画结合起来创建各种特效。

Exercises

1. On a sheet of paper, design and configure two computer systems for a particular purpose, one being an economical system and the other having no price limit. Examples of the uses of the system might be Web production, digital audio or 3D animation. List the

components needed and then check different manufactures on-line to get prices for these systems. Compare the two systems in terms of price and performance. Make a plan to build the larger system by expanding the smaller system by adding components in $500 to $1,000 increments.

2. Research different software packages and see how many you can locate that perform similar functions. For example, research how many 2D drawing software, 3D animation software, or video editing software packages there are. Compare the packages for price, number of features, and ease of use. Read reviews in different on-line magazines, talk to users, and try them yourself, if possible. Order the list in term of what you feel are the best software packages for your own needs.

专业英语的词汇特征

一、词汇构成

专业英语词汇有其自身的特点,一般来说,可以分为以下几类:

1. 专业词汇

这类词的意义狭窄,一般只使用在各自的专业范围内,因而专业性很强。如:compositing(影像合成)、analog-to-digital converters(模数转换)。

2. 次专业词汇

次专业词汇是指不受上下文限制的各专业出现频率都很高的词。这类词往往在不同的专业中具有不同的含义。如 communication 和 elaboration。

其中,communication 常用含义是交流、沟通,但是在专业英语中指传播、通信;elaboration 常指苦心经营、苦心经营的结果、详尽的细节,但在专业英语里指细化,如 elaboration theory。

3. 特用词

在日常英语中,为使语言生动活泼,常使用一些短小的词或词组。而在专业英语中,表达同样的意义时,为了准确、正式、严谨,不引起歧义却往往选用一些较长的特用词。这些词在非专业英语中极少使用但却属于非专业英语。

日常生活中常用下列句子:This kind of measure is not accurate.

在专业英语中,却表示为:This kind of measure is qualitative.

这是由于 qualitative 词义单一准确,可以避免歧义。而 accurate 不仅可以表示精确的,而且还可以表示其他意义,如:

He gave an accurate(正确的) answer to the question.

类似对应的特用词还有:

go down—depress　　upside down—invert
keep—maintain　　　enough—sufficient
take away—remove　　an once—immediately

push in—insert　　　a lot of—appreciable
used up—consume　　find out—determine

4. 功能词

它包括介词、连词、冠词和代词等。功能词为词在句子中的结构关系中提供了十分重要的结构信号,对于理解专业内容十分重要,而且出现频率极高。研究表明,在专业英语中,出现频率很高的十个词都是功能词,其顺序为:the、of、in、and、to、is、that、for、are、be。

二、构词法

英语的构词法主要有四种:前缀法、后缀法、合成、转化。前缀和后缀法也叫派生法(derivation),专业英语词汇大部分都是用派生法构成的,即通过各种前缀和后缀来构成新词。有专家学者曾经作过统计,以 semi-构成的词有 230 个以上,以 auto-构成的词有 260 个以上,以 micro 构成的词有 300 个以上,以 thermo 构成的词有 130 个以上。仅这四个前缀构成的词就达近千个,而常用的前缀和后缀却多达上百个,可见派生法的构词能力非常强。

1. 常用的前缀

inter(相互、之间):intersection interface
counter(相对的):counterpart
sub(低、下):subway submarine
hyper(超过):hyperons hyper plane
tele(远):telescope
photo(光;像片;照相):photosphere
super(超过):superheated
in(表示否定):inadequate insufficient
im(表示否定)(加在字母 m,b,p 之前):impossible
re(回、再次、向后):reuse recharge
over(在……上方;在……外):overwork overload
under(在……之下;次于……;不足;隶属于):underpay
dis(表示不,表示否定):discharge dissatisfy
ab(表示偏离、脱离或离开):abstract
con(共同,和,完全):confound
ex(表示"前"):exit
trans(通过,横过):transformer

2. 常用的后缀

-ist(表示……专业人员):scientist artist
-logy(论,言论):anthropology
-ism(主义;特征;状态):mechanism
-able(能……的;具有……特性的):noticeable stable

-ive(与……有关的;具有……性质的;有……倾向的):reactive effective
-ic(与……有关的;产生……的;……似的):electronic metallic
-ous(像……的,具有……特征的):synchronous porous
-proof(不透……的;防……的):waterproof acid-proof
-en(使,使成为):weaken harden shorten

3. 常用的合成(composition)方法

名词+名词形式,如 cable modem(有线通)、motherboard(主板)。
动词+名词,如 feedback(反馈)、operating systems(操作系统)。
名词+动词,如 input(输入)、output(输出)。
介词+名词,如 outside(在外边)、outgrowth(长出,派出,结果,副产物)。

Chapter 3   Digital Images

▲ **Knowledge Objectives**

When you have completed this chapter, you will be able to:
- Know what digital images are.
- Compare and contrast different formats of digital images.
- Choosing suited method to get digital pictures from various ways.
- Master the basic procedures of processing of digital images.
- Tell how to output digital images.

▲ **Professional Terms**

analog image	模拟图像
binary	二进制
bitmap image	位图
brush strokes	画笔描边
calligraphic	书法的
digital camera	数码相机
digital image processing	数字图像处理
digital image	数字图像
format	格式化
grayscale	灰度
opacity	不透明度
perpendicular	垂直的
photo CD	相片光盘
plotter	绘图仪
pressure-sensitive	压力传感的
printer	打印机
raster image	光栅图像(位图)
rasterize	栅格化
synchronous	同步的
vector image	矢量图像
videography	电视录像制作

Chapter 3 Digital Images

Part 1 Outline of Digital Image[①]

The first computer-generated digital images were produced in the early 1960s, alongside development of the space program and in medical research. Projects at the Jet Propulsion Laboratory, MIT, Bell Labs and the University of Maryland, among others, used digital images to advance satellite imagery, wirephoto standards conversion, medical imaging, videophone technology, character recognition, and photo enhancement.

Rapid advances in digital imaging began with the introduction of microprocessors in the early 1970s, alongside progress in related storage and display technologies. The invention of computerized axial tomography (CAT scanning), using x-rays to produce a digital image of a "slice" through a three-dimensional object, was of great importance to medical diagnostics. As well as origination of digital images, digitization of analog images allowed the enhancement and restoration of archaeological artifacts and began to be used in fields as diverse as nuclear medicine, astronomy, law enforcement, defense and industry.

Advances in microprocessor technology paved the way for the development and marketing of charge-coupled devices (CCDs) for use in a wide range of image capture devices and gradually displaced the use of analog film and tape in photography and videography towards the end of the 20th century[1]. The computing power necessary to process digital image capture also allowed computer-generated digital images to achieve a level of refinement close to photorealism.

A digital image is a representation of a two-dimensional image using ones and zeros (binary). Depending on whether or not the image resolution is fixed, it may be of vector or raster type (see Figure 3-1). Without qualifications, the term "digital image" usually refers to raster images also called bitmap images.

Raster images have a finite set of digital values, called picture elements or pixels. The digital image contains a fixed number of rows and col-

Figure 3-1 Example shows effect of vector graphics versus raster graphics. The original vector-based illustration is at the left. The upper-right image illustrates magnification of 90x as a vector image. The lower-right image illustrates the same magnification as a bitmap image. Raster images are based on pixels and thus scale with loss of clarity, while vector-based images can be scaled indefinitely without degrading quality.

---

① http://en.wikipedia.org/wiki/Digital_image

umns of pixels. Pixels are the smallest individual element in an image, holding quantized values that represent the brightness of a given color at any specific point. Typically, the pixels are stored in computer memory as a raster image or raster map, a two-dimensional array of small integers. These values are often transmitted or stored in a compressed form.

Raster images can be created by a variety of input devices and techniques, such as digital cameras, scanners, coordinate-measuring machines, seismographic profiling, airborne radar, and more. They can also be synthesized from arbitrary non-image data, such as mathematical functions or three-dimensional geometric models; the latter being a major sub-area of computer graphics. The field of digital image processing is the study of algorithms for their transformation.

Part 2 Formats of Digital Image[①]

JPG, GIF, TIFF, PNG, BMP. What are they, and how do you choose? These and many other file types are used to encode digital images. The choices are simpler than you might think.

Compression is a term used to describe ways of cutting the size of the file. Compression schemes can by lossy or lossless. A lossless algorithm might, for example, look for a recurring pattern in the file, and replace each occurrence with a short abbreviation, thereby cutting the file size. In contrast, a lossy algorithm might store color information at a lower resolution than the image itself, since the eye is not so sensitive to changes in color of a small distance[2].

Images start with differing numbers of colors in them. The simplest images may contain only two colors, such as black and white, and will need only 1 bit to represent each pixel. Many early PC video cards would support only 16 fixed colors. Later cards would display 256 simultaneously, any of which could be chosen from a pool of 2^{24}, or 16 million colors. New cards devote 24 bits to each pixel, and are therefore capable of displaying 2^{24}, or 16 million colors without restriction. A few display even more. Since the eye has trouble distinguishing between similar colors, 24 bit or 16 million colors is often called TrueColor.

TIFF

Tiff is, in principle, a very flexible format that can be lossless or lossy. The details of the image storage algorithm are included as part of the file. In practice, TIFF is used almost exclusively as a lossless image storage format that uses no compression at all. Most graphics programs that use TIFF do not compression. Consequently, file sizes are quite big. (Sometimes a lossless compression algorithm called LZW is used, but it is not universally supported.)

PNG

Png is also a lossless storage format. However, in contrast with common TIFF usage, it looks for patterns in the image that it can use to compress file size. The compression is exactly

---

① http://www.wfu.edu/~matthews/misc/graphics/formats/formats.html

reversible, so the image is recovered exactly.

GIF

Gif creates a table of up to 256 colors from a pool of 16 million. If the image has fewer than 256 colors, GIF can render the image exactly. When the image contains many colors, software that creates the GIF uses any of several algorithms to approximate the colors in the image with the limited palette of 256 colors available. Better algorithms search the image to find an optimum set of 256 colors. Sometimes GIF uses the nearest color to represent each pixel, and sometimes it uses "error diffusion" to adjust the color of nearby pixels to correct for the error in each pixel.

GIF achieves compression in two ways. First, it reduces the number of colors of color-rich images, thereby reducing the number of bits needed per pixel, as just described. Second, it replaces commonly occurring patterns (especially large areas of uniform color) with a short abbreviation: instead of storing "white, white, white, white, white," it stores "5 white."

Thus, GIF is "lossless" only for images with 256 colors or less. For a rich, true color image, GIF may "lose" 99.998% of the colors.

JPG

Jpg is optimized for photographs and similar continuous tone images that contain many, many colors. It can achieve astounding compression ratios even while maintaining very high image quality. GIF compression is unkind to such images. JPG works by analyzing images and discarding kinds of information that the eye is least likely to notice. It stores information as 24 bit color.

Important: the degree of compression of JPG is adjustable. At moderate compression levels of photographic images, it is very difficult for the eye to discern any difference from the original, even at extreme magnification. Compression factors of more than 20 are often quite acceptable. Better graphics programs, such as Paint Shop Pro and Photoshop, allow you to view the image quality and file size as a function of compression level, so that you can conveniently choose the balance between quality and file size [4].

RAW

RAW is an image output option available on some digital cameras. Though lossless, it is a factor of three of four smaller than TIFF files of the same image. The disadvantage is that there is a different RAW format for each manufacturer, and so you may have to use the manufacturer's software to view the images. (Some graphics applications can read some manufacturer's RAW formats.)

BMP

BMP is an uncompressed proprietary format invented by Microsoft. There is really no reason to ever use this format.

PSD, PSP, etc.

PSD, PSP, etc are proprietary formats used by graphics programs. Photoshop's files have the PSD extension, while Paint Shop Pro files use PSP. These are the preferred working formats as you edit images in the software, because only the proprietary formats retain all the editing power of the programs. These packages use layers, for example, to build complex images, and layer information may be lost in the nonproprietary formats such as TIFF and JPG. However, be sure to save your end result as a standard TIFF or JPG, or you may not be able to view it in a few years when your software has changed.

Currently, GIF and JPG are the formats used for nearly all web images. PNG is supported by most of the latest generation browsers. TIFF is not widely supported by web browsers, and should be avoided for web use. PNG does everything GIF does, and better, so expect to see PNG replace GIF in the future. PNG will not replace JPG, since JPG is capable of much greater compression of photographic images, even when set for quite minimal loss of quality.

Part 3 Capture of Digital Image

You can get digital images by the following methods:

Shoot by Digital Camera[①]

1. Preparations:

- Digital camera (Figure 3-2)
- USB cable
- Computer
- Software

2. Steps of Operation

Figure 3-2 Digital Camera

① Power your camera and look at the back of your digital camera. There are several buttons. Locate the menu button, a delete button and a mode button.

② Locate and push the arrow buttons on your digital camera to explore how they function. Some scroll through pictures and play them back for you, while others will make more menus appear on your screen.

③ Find a photo you wish to delete on your digital camera. When you are absolutely sure you have the correct photo, push your "Delete" button. A confirmation message will appear to reduce the possibility you will accidentally delete a photo. Ensure you do not select "Delete all" on this menu.

---

① http://www.ehow.com/how_2217908_operate-digital-camera.html

④ Explore the playback mode. This mode offers choices such as a slideshow or thumbnail view while the top button can offer frames. If you have a zoom, you can also click this button to zoom in on a digital photo. This will not affect the printout of the picture.

⑤ Pushing the menu button will give you a variety of choices such as recording, setup and other functions. Push the right button to advance and down button to select. Scroll to exit to leave the menu or just click "Menu" again. Be sure the proper boxes are checked, especially for features like anti-shake or red-eye reduction.

⑥ Push and hold a round button located on top of your digital camera for up to eight seconds to take a digital photo. Repeat a few times until you adjust for lighting, distance and activity level.

⑦ Ensure your batteries are charged or that you have fresh batteries if you are using disposable AA batteries, as these will be quickly used up. The battery meter is found on your view screen to the left or on the top of the readout. You may wish to use rechargeable AA or AAA batteries.

⑧ Push gently, grasp with thumb and forefinger to remove your memory card. Insert into a reader or printer for download onto your computer. It is acceptable to use more than one memory card, in fact, it is a good idea. If you are going on vacation, bring along at least two memory cards, a charger or an ample supply of batteries.

⑨ Charge your battery in its cradle or using the plugs provided, especially if you know you have an event coming.

⑩ To use your camera as a video camera, make this selection first on the menu. Depending on the manufacturer, you may have to turn the dial to a video camera or select the choice from an on-screen menu.

⑪ Add a special touch such as "night" or "scenery" photography by setting the dial to that setting or set it up in the screen menu ahead of time in your digital camera.

⑫ Understand that the number of pictures you can take varies with your memory card. This information is often displayed in the screen when you are about to take a photo. Keep in mind video takes much more space photos alone.

Input by Image Scanner①

In computing, a scanner (see Figure 3-3) is a device that optically scans images, printed text, handwriting, or an object, and converts it to a digital image.

Modern scanners may be considered the successors of early telephotography and fax input devices, consisting of a rotating drum with a single photo detector at a standard speed of 60 or 120 rpm (later models up to 240 rpm). They send a linear analog AM signal through standard telephone voice lines to receptors, which synchronously print the proportional intensity on special paper. This system was in use in press from the 1920s to the mid-1990s. Color photos

---

① http://en.wikipedia.org/wiki/Image_scanner

Figure 3-3 Image Scanner

were sent as three separated RGB filtered images consecutively, but only for special events due to transmission costs.

It mainly contains Drum Scanners, Flatbed Scanners, Film scanners, Hand scanners.

A flatbed scanner is usually composed of a glass pane (or platen), under which there is a bright light (often xenon or cold cathode fluorescent) which illuminates the pane, and a moving optical array in CCD scanning [4]. CCD-type scanners typically contain three rows (arrays) of sensors with red, green, and blue filters. CIS scanning consists of a moving set of red, green and blue LEDs strobed for illumination and a connected monochromatic photodiode array for light collection. Images to be scanned are placed face down on the glass, an opaque cover is lowered over it to exclude ambient light, and the sensor array and light source move across the pane, reading the entire area. An image is therefore visible to the detector only because of the light it reflects. Transparent images do not work in this way, and require special accessories that illuminate them from the upper side. Many scanners offer this as an option.

The scanned result is a non-compressed RGB image, which can be transferred to a computer's memory. Some scanners compress and clean up the image using embedded firmware. Once on the computer, the image can be processed with a raster graphics program (such as Photoshop or the GIMP) and saved on a storage device (such as a hard disk).

Take Screen Captures by Hypersnap[①]

HyperSnap(see Figure 3-4) is perfect for capturing images and texts that you want to include in your Help system, online tutorials, manuals, training handouts, presentations, marketing materials, Web pages, emails and more. Use HyperSnap to quickly share a picture-perfect representation of anything on your screen. It is compatible with 32 bit and 64 bit releases of Windows 7, Vista, XP, 2000, NT4, ME and Windows 98.

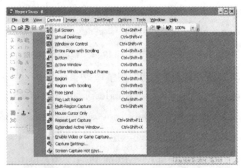

Figure 3-4 The Interface of HyperSnap 6

① http://www.hyperionics.com/

Get by Searching the Web

Searching from special websites of images, you can get the pictures you need. For example, Google: http://images.google.cn/ (see Figure 3-5); Baidu: http://image.baidu.com/ (see Figure 3-6).

Figure 3-5　Google Images

Figure 3-6　Baidu Pictures

Photo Library

Photo library is a library which collects thousands of different types of pictures and it is easy to be searched. Photo libraries are wide varieties. Some are spot by digital camera, and others are made by computer cartographic software.

The common photo galleries are great many, such as Google Gallery (see Figure 3-7), Baidu library (see Figure 3-8).

Figure 3-7　Google Library

Figure 3-8　Baidu Library

Part 4　Digital Image Processing

Digital image processing is the use of computer algorithms to perform image processing on digital images. As a subcategory or field of digital signal processing, digital image processing has many advantages over analog image processing. It allows a much wider range of algorithms to be applied to the input data and can avoid problems such as the build-up of noise and signal distortion during processing.

Photoshop

1. Workspace

The Adobe Photoshop CS4 workspace is arranged to help you focus on creating and editing images. The workspace (see Figure 3-9) includes menus and a variety of tools and panels for viewing, editing, and adding elements to your images.

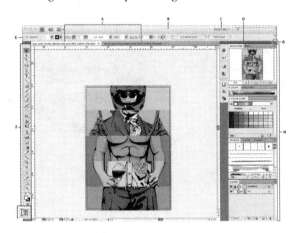

Figure 3-9   Default Photoshop workspace A. Tabbed Document windows B. Application bar C. Workspace switcher D. Panel title bar E. Control panel F. Tools panel G. Collapse To Icons button H. Four panel groups in vertical dock.

① The Application bar across the top contains a workspace switcher, menus (Windows only), and other application controls.

② The Tools panel contains tools for creating and editing images, artwork, page elements, and so on. Related tools are grouped.

③ The Control panel displays options for the currently selected tool. The Control panel is also known as the options bar in Photoshop. (Adobe Flash, Adobe Dreamweaver, and Adobe Fireworks have no Control panel.)

④ The Document window displays the file you're working on. Document windows can be tabbed and, in certain cases, grouped and docked.

⑤ Panels help you monitor and modify your work.

2. Layer

Photoshop layers are like sheets of stacked acetate. You can see through transparent areas of a layer to the layers below. You can also change the opacity of a layer to make content partially transparent. (see Figure 3-10)

The Layers panel (see Figure 3-11) lists all layers, layer groups, and layer effects in an image. You can use the Layers panel to show and hide layers, create new layers, and work with groups of layers. You can access additional commands and options in the Layers panel menu.

Chapter 3 Digital Images

Figure 3-10 Transparent areas on a layer let you see layers below.

Figure 3-11 Photoshop Layers panel
A. Layers panel menu
B. Layer Group
C. D. Expand/Collapse Layer effects
E. effect F. thumbnail

3. Selecting and masking

(i) Select

If you want to apply changes to parts of an image, you first need to select the pixels that make up those parts.

Photoshop provides separate sets of tools (see Figure 3-12) to make selections of raster and vector data. For example, to select pixels, you can use the marquee tools or the lasso tools. You can use commands in the Select menu to select all pixels, to deselect, or to reselect.

Figure 3-12 Selection Tools Gallery

To select vector data, you can use the pen or shape tools, which produce precise outlines called paths. You can convert paths to selections or convert selections to paths.

(ii) Channels

Channels are grayscale images that store different types of information

The image's color mode determines the number of color channels created. For example, an RGB image has a channel for each color (red, green, and blue) plus a composite channel used for editing the image.

Alpha channels store selections as grayscale images. You can add alpha channels to create and store masks, which let you manipulate or protect parts of an image.

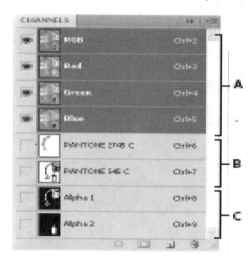

Figure 3-13　Channel Types
A. Color channels
B. Spot channels
C. Alpha channels

Spot color channels specify additional plates for printing with spot color inks.

The Channels panel (Figure 3-13) lists all channels in the image—composite channel first (for RGB, CMYK, and Lab images). A thumbnail of the channel's contents appears to the left of the channel name; the thumbnail is automatically updated as you edit the channel.

(ⅲ) Mask

When you select part of an image, the area that is not selected is "masked", or protected from editing. So, when you create a mask, you isolate and protect areas of an image as you apply color changes, filters, or other effects to the rest of the image. You can also use masks for complex image editing such as gradually applying color or filter effects to an image. (see Figure 3-14)

Figure 3-14　Examples of Masks
A. Opaque mask used to protect the background and edit the butterfly
B. Mask used to protect the butterfly and color the background
C. Semitransparent mask used to color the background and part of the butterfly

Masks are stored in alpha channels. (see Figure 3-15) Masks and channels are grayscale images, so you can edit them like any other image with painting tools, editing tools and filters. Areas painted black on a mask are protected, and areas painted white are editable.

Chapter 3　Digital Images　53

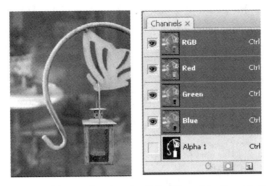

Figure 3-15　Selection Saved as An Alpha Channel in Channels Panel

4. Painting

Painting changes the color of image pixels. You use painting tools and techniques to retouch images, create or edit masks on alpha channels, rotoscope or paint on video frames, and to paint original art. Brush tips, brush presets, and the many brush options give you creative control to produce stunning painting effects or to simulate working with traditional media. You can work with several painting tools on 32-bit per channel, high dynamic range (HDR) images including Paintbrush, Pencil, Smudge, Sharpen, Blur, Stamp, History Brush, Pattern Stamp, and Eraser.

Adobe Photoshop CS4 provides several tools (see Figure 3-16) for painting and editing image color.

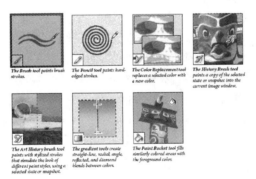

Figure 3-16　Painting Tools Gallery

You can save a set of brush options as a preset so you can quickly access brush characteristics you use frequently. Photoshop includes several sample brush presets. You can start with these presets and modify them to produce new effects. Many original brush presets are available for download on the web.

5. Drawing

The drawing tools (the Pen and shape tools) let you create and edit vector shapes. You can work with shapes in shape layers and as paths; you can also create rasterized shapes, which can be edited with the painting tools (see Figure 3-17). The drawing tools provide an easy way to create buttons, navigation bars, and other items used on web pages.

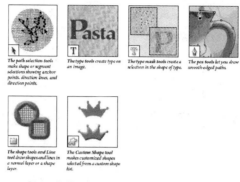

Figure 3-17　Drawing and Type Tools Gallery

Drawing in Adobe Photoshop CS4 involves creating vector shapes and paths. In Photoshop, you can draw with any of the shape tools, the Pen tool, or the Freeform Pen tool. Options for each tool are available in the options bar.

Before you begin drawing in Photoshop, you must choose a drawing mode from the options bar. The mode you choose to draw in determines whether you create a vector shape on its own layer, a work path on an existing layer, or a rasterized shape on an existing layer.

6. Filters

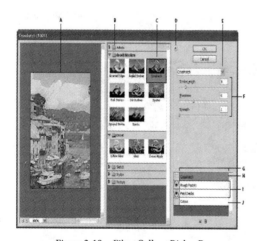

Figure 3-18　Filter Gallery Dialog Box
A. Preview
B. Filter category
C. Thumbnail of selected filter
D. Show/Hide filter thumbnails
E. Filters pop-up menu
F. Options for selected filter
G. List of filter effects to apply or arrange
H. Effect selected but not applied
I. Effects applied cumulatively but not selected
J. Hidden filter effect

You can use filters to apply special effects to images or to perform common image editing tasks, such as sharpening photos.

You can use filters to clean up or retouch your photos, apply special art effects that give your image the appearance of a sketch or impressionistic painting, or create unique transformations using distortions and lighting effects. The filters provided by Adobe appear in the Filter menu. Some filters provided by third-party developers are available as plug-ins. Once installed, these plug-in filters appear at the bottom of the Filter menu.

The Filter Gallery (see Figure 3-18) provides a preview of many of the special effects filters. You can apply multiple filters, turn on or off the effect of a filter, reset options for a filter, and change the order in which filters are applied. When you are satisfied with the preview, you can then apply it to your image. Not all filters in the Filter menu are available in the Filter Gallery.

7. Type

Type in Adobe Photoshop CS4 consists of vector-based type outlines—mathematically defined shapes that describe the letters, numbers, and symbols of a typeface. Many typefaces are available in more than one format, the most common formats being Type 1 (also called PostScript fonts), TrueType, OpenType, New CID, and CID nonprotected (Japanese only). Photoshop preserves vector-based type outlines and uses them when you scale or resize type, save a PDF or EPS file, or print the image to a PostScript printer. As a result, it's possible to produce type with crisp, resolution-independent edges.

Entering text (see Figure 3-19) this way is useful when you want to create one or more paragraphs, such as for a brochure.

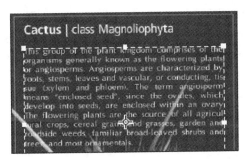

Figure 3-19   Type Entered as Point Type (top) and in a Bounding Box (bottom)

Type on a path that flows along the edge of an open or a closed path, When you enter text horizontally, characters appear along the path perpendicular to the baseline. When you enter text vertically, characters appear along the path parallel to the baseline. In either case, the text flows in the direction in which points were added to the path.

CorelDraw

CorelDraw is an intuitive graphics design application that gives designers an enjoyable work experience. The program is built to meet the demands of today's graphics professionals. Whether you work in advertising, printing, publishing, sign making, engraving, or manufacturing, CorelDraw offers the tools you need to create accurate and creative vector illustrations and professional-looking page layouts.

Before you get started with CorelDraw, you should be familiar with the following terms. (Table 3-1)

Table 3-1   Terms of CorelDraw

Term	Description
object	An element in a drawing such as an image, shape, line, text, curve, symbol, or layer
drawing	The work you create in CorelDraw: for example, custom artwork, logos, posters, and newsletters
vector graphic	An image generated from mathematical descriptions that determine the position, length, and direction in which lines are drawn
bitmap	An image composed of grids of pixels or dots
docker	A window containing available commands and settings relevant to a specific tool or task
flyout	A button that opens a group of related tools or menu items
artistic text	A type of text to which you can apply special effects, such as shadows
paragraph text	A type of text to which you can apply formatting options, and which can be edited in large blocks

1. CorelDraw application window

When you launch CorelDraw, the application window opens containing a drawing window. The rectangle in the center of the drawing window is the drawing page where you create your drawing. Although more than one drawing window can be opened, you can apply commands to the active drawing window only. The CorelDraw application window appears below (see Figure 3-20). A description of its parts follows. (Table 3-2)

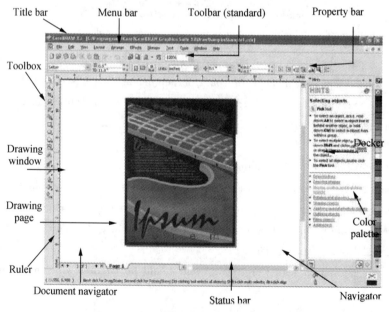

Figure 3-20   The CorelDraw Application Windows

Table 3-2 A Description of the CorelDraw Application Windows

Part	Description
Menu bar	The area containing pull-down menu options
Property bar	A detachable bar with commands that relate to the active tool or object. For example, when the text tool is active, the text property bar displays commands that create and edit text.
Toolbar	A detachable bar that contains shortcuts to menu and other commands
Title bar	The area displaying the title of the currently open drawing
Rulers	Horizontal and vertical borders that are used to determine the size and position of objects in a drawing
Toolbox	A floating bar with tools for creating, filling, and modifying objects in the drawing
Drawing window	The area outside the drawing page bordered by the scroll bars and application controls
Drawing page	The rectangular area inside the drawing window. It is the printable area of your work area.
Color palette	A dockable bar that contains color swatches
Docker	A window containing available commands and settings relevant to a specific tool or task
Status bar	An area at the bottom of the application window that contains information about object properties such as type, size, color, fill, and resolution. The status bar also shows the current mouse position.
Document navigator	The area at the bottom left of the application window that contains controls for moving between pages and adding pages
Navigator	A button at the lower-right corner that opens a smaller display to help you move around a drawing

2. Working with lines, outlines, and brush strokes

CorelDraw lets you add lines and brush strokes by using a variety of techniques and tools. After you draw lines or apply brush strokes to lines, you can format them. You can also format the outlines that surround objects.

(i) Drawing Lines:

A line is a path between two points. Lines can consist of multiple segments, and the line segments can be curved or straight. The line segments are connected by nodes, which are depicted as small squares.

① CorelDraw provides various drawing tools (see Figure 3-21) that let you draw curved and straight lines, and lines containing both curved and straight segments.

② CorelDraw lets you simulate the effect of a calligraphic pen when you draw lines. Calligraphic lines vary in thickness according to the direction of the line and the angle of the pen nib. By default, calligraphic lines appear as closed shapes drawn with a pencil.

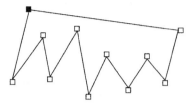 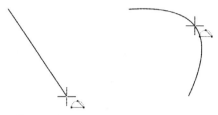

You can draw lines with multiple segments by using the Bézier tool and clicking each time you want the line to change direction

You can draw a curved line by specifying its width (left), and then specifying its height and clicking the page (right).

Figure 3-21　Drawing Lines

　　You can control the thickness of a calligraphic line(see Figure 3-22) by changing the angle of the line you draw in relation to the calligraphic angle you choose. For example, when the line you draw is perpendicular to the calligraphic angle, the line is at the maximum thickness specified by the pen width. Lines drawn at the calligraphic angle, however, have little or no thickness.

　　③ CorelDraw lets you create pressure-sensitive lines (see Figure 3-23) which vary in thickness. You can create this effect using the mouse or a pressure-sensitive pen and graphics tablet. Both methods result in lines with curved edges and varying widths along a path.

Figure 3-22　A calligraphic pen allows you to draw lines of various thicknesses.

Figure 3-23　A flower drawn by using three different artistic media lines: calligraphic lines (Left), pressure-sensitive lines of variable thickness (center), and flat preset lines (Right).

　　④ You can also draw dimension lines (see Figure 3-24) to indicate the distance between two points in a drawing or the size of objects. By default, dimension lines and the measurements shown on the lines change when you change an object's size.

Chapter 3　Digital Images　59

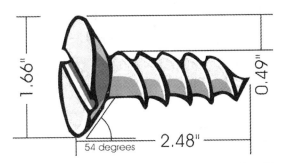

Figure 3-24　Dimension lines can show the sizes of parts of an object.

(ii) **Formatting lines and outlines**

Lines are treated the same way as outlines of closed shapes, such as ellipses and polygons. You can change the appearance of both lines and outlines by using the controls of the Outline pen dialog box, the Outline page of the Object properties docker, and the property bar. For example, you can specify the color, width, and style of lines and outlines.

(iii) **Applying brush strokes**

CorelDraw lets you apply a variety of preset brush strokes, ranging from strokes with arrowheads to ones that are filled with rainbow patterns. When you draw a preset brush stroke, you can specify some of its attributes.

- **Drawing shapes**

CorelDraw lets you draw basic shapes, which you can modify by using special effects and reshaping tools.

① **Drawing rectangles and squares**(see Figure 3-25)

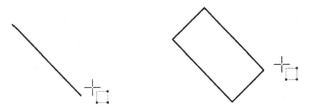

Figure 3-25　You can create a rectangle by first drawing its baseline and then drawing its height. The resulting rectangle is angled.

CorelDraw lets you draw rectangles and squares. You can draw a rectangle or square by dragging diagonally with the Rectangle tool or by specifying the width and height with the 3 point rectangle tool. The 3 point rectangle tool lets you quickly draw rectangles at an angle.

② **Drawing ellipses, circles, arcs, and pie shapes**(see Figure 3-26)

Figure 3-26 Using the 3 point ellipse tool; you can draw an ellipse by first drawing its centerline and then drawing its height. This method lets you draw ellipses at an angle.

You can draw an ellipse or circle by dragging diagonally with the Ellipse tool, or you can draw an ellipse by using the 3 point ellipse tool to specify its width and height. The 3 point ellipse tool lets you quickly create an ellipse at an angle, eliminating the need to rotate the ellipse. Using the Ellipse tool, you can draw a new arc or pie shape, or you can draw an ellipse or circle and then change it to an arc or a pie shape.

③ **Drawing polygons and stars**(see Figure 3-27)

Figure 3-27 Left to right: a polygon, a perfect star, and a complex star, each with a fountain fill applied.

CorelDraw lets you draw polygons and two types of stars: perfect and complex.

Perfect stars are traditional-looking stars and can have a fill applied to the entire star shape. Complex stars have intersecting sides and produce original results with a fill applied.

You can modify polygons and stars. (see Figure 3-28) For example, you can change the number of sides on a polygon or the number of points on a star, and you can sharpen the points of a star. You can also use the Shape tool to reshape polygons and complex stars, just as you would with any other curve object.

Figure 3-28 Left to right: The Shape tool was used to change a polygon into a star that can be shaped as a curve object. The line segments of the star were then converted to curves and adjusted to produce the starfish shape.

④ **Drawing spirals**(see Figure 3-29)

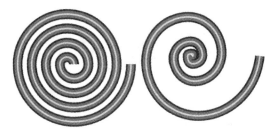

Figure 3-29　A Symmetrical Spiral (left) and a Logarithmic Spiral (right)

You can draw two types of spirals: symmetrical and logarithmic. Symmetrical spirals expand evenly so that the distance between each revolution is equal. Logarithmic spirals expand with increasingly larger distances between revolutions. You can set the rate by which a logarithmic spiral expands outward.

⑤ **Drawing grids**

You can draw a grid and set the number of rows and columns. A grid is a grouped set of rectangles that you can break apart.

⑥ **Drawing predefined shapes**(see Figure 3-30)

Figure 3-30　Using the Shape tool; you can drag a glyph to alter a shape.

Using the Perfect Shapes collection, you can draw predefined shapes. Certain shapes specifically basic shapes, arrow shapes, banner shapes, and callout shapes—contain glyphs. You can drag a glyph to modify the appearance of a shape.

⑦ **Drawing by using shape recognition**(see Figure 3-31)

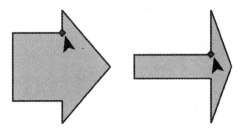

Figure 3-31　Shapes created with the Smart drawing tool are recognized and smoothed.

You can use the Smart drawing tool to draw freehand strokes that can be recognized and converted to basic shapes.

- **Working with objects**

Working with objects is an essential part of creating drawings.

① **Selecting objects**(see Figure 3-32)

Figure 3-32　A bounding box appears around a selected object, and an "X" appears at its center.

Before you can change an object, you must select it. You can select visible objects, objects that are hidden from view by other objects, and a single object in a group or a nested group. In addition, you can select objects in the order in which they were created, select all objects at once, and deselect objects.

② **Duplicating**(see Figure 3-33)

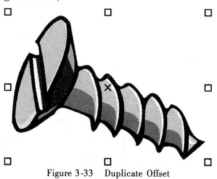

Figure 3-33　Duplicate Offset

Duplicating an object places a copy directly in the drawing window and does not use the Clipboard. Duplicating is faster than copying and pasting. Also, when duplicating an object, you can specify the distance between the duplicate and the original object along the x and y axes. This distance is known as the offset.

③ **Copying objects at a specified position**(see Figure 3-34)

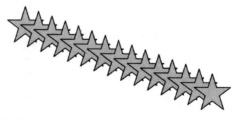

Figure 3-34　Offsetting Multiple Copies of an Object by a Specified Distance

You can create multiple object copies simultaneously while specifying their position, without using the Clipboard. For example, you can distribute object copies horizontally, to the left or right of the original object; or you can distribute object copies vertically, below or above the original object.

Chapter 3 Digital Images

④ **Creating objects from enclosed areas**(see Figure 3-35)

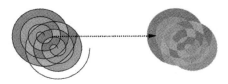

Figure 3-35 The enclosed areas created by the two spirals objects (left) are filled by using the Smart fill tool. The Smart fill tool creates objects from each area. In the example above, the original spiral objects are deleted (right), and the newly created objects remain.

You can create objects from areas enclosed by other objects. For example, if you draw a freehand line that crosses over itself to create loops, you can create an object from the loop shape. It doesn't matter how many shapes and lines surround the area; as long as it is totally enclosed, you can create an object in the shape of that area.

⑤ **Creating a boundary around selected objects**(see Figure 3-36)

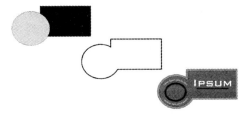

Figure 3-36 You can create a boundary around selected objects (left). The boundary is created as a new object (middle) that can be used as a cut line or Keyline for a finished logo (right).

You can automatically create a path around selected objects on a layer to create a boundary. This boundary can be used for various purposes, such as to produce key lines or cut lines.

The boundary is created by a closed path that follows the shape of the selected objects. The default fills and outline properties apply to the object created by the boundary.

⑥ **Aligning and distributing objects**(see Figure 3-37)

Figure 3-37 Scattered objects (left) with vertical alignment applied to them (right).

CorelDraw lets you precisely align and distribute objects in a drawing. You can align objects with each other and with parts of the drawing page, such as the center, edges, and grid.

Distributing objects automatically adds spacing between them based on their width, height, and center points.

⑦ **Snapping objects**(see Figure 3-38)

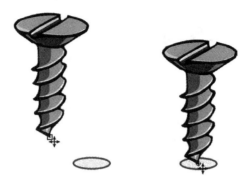

Figure 3-38 The pointer was snapped to an end node of the screw (left) and then the screw was dragged to snap to the center of an ellipse (right).

To snap an object to another object with greater precision, you first snap the pointer to a snap point in the object, and then snap the object to a snap point in the target object. For example, you can snap the pointer to a rectangle's center, and then drag the rectangle by its center and snap it to the center of another rectangle

⑧ **Sizing and scaling objects**

CorelDraw lets you size and scale objects. In both cases, you change the dimensions of an object proportionally by preserving its aspect ratio. You can size an object's dimensions by specifying values or by changing the object directly. Scaling changes an object's dimensions by a specified percentage.

You can change an object's anchor point from its center to any of its eight selection handles.

⑨ **Rotating and mirroring objects**

CorelDraw lets you rotate and create mirror images of objects. You can rotate an object by specifying horizontal and vertical coordinates. You can move the center of rotation to a specific ruler coordinate or to a point that is relative to the current position of the object. (Figure 3-39)

Figure 3-39 Rotating Objects around a Single Point

Mirroring an object flips it from left to right or top to bottom. By default, the mirror anchor point is in the center of the object. (see Figure 3-40)

Figure 3-40   Mirroring an Object from Top to Bottom

⑩ **Grouping objects**(see Figure 3-41)

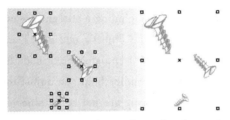

Figure 3-41   Objects retain their attributes when they are grouped.

When you group two or more objects, they are treated as a single unit. Grouping lets you apply the same formatting, properties, and other changes to all the objects within the group at the same time. CorelDraw also lets you group other groups to create nested groups.

You can also ungroup all nested groups within a group by clicking the Ungroup all buttons.

⑪ **Combining objects**(see Figure 3-42)

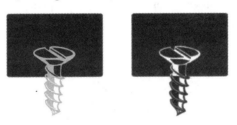

Figure 3-42   The two objects (left) are combined to create a single object (right). The new object has the properties of the last object selected before combining.

Combining two or more objects creates a single object with common fill and outline attributes. You can combine rectangles, ellipses, polygons, stars, spirals, graphs, or text.

- **Shaping objects**

CorelDraw lets you shape objects in various ways.

① **Using curve objects** (see Figure 3-43)

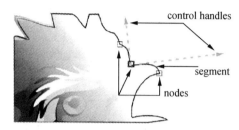

Figure 3-43　The Components of a Curve: Nodes, Segments, and Control Handles

A curve object has nodes and control handles, which you can use to change the object's shape. A curve object can be any shape, including a straight or curved line. An object's nodes are the small squares that appear along the object's outline. The line between two nodes is called a segment. Segments can be curved or straight. Each node has a control handle for each curved segment connected to it. Control handles help you adjust the curve of a segment.

Most objects that are added to a drawing are not curve objects, with the exception of spirals, freehand lines, and Bézier lines. Therefore, if you want to customize the shape of an object or text object, it is recommended that you convert it to a curve object.

② **Using envelopes**

CorelDraw lets you shape objects, including lines, artistic text, and paragraph text frames by applying envelopes to them. Envelopes are made of multiple nodes that you can move to shape the envelope and, as a result, change the shape of the object. You can apply a basic envelope that conforms to the shape of an object, or you can also apply a preset envelope. After you apply an envelope, you can edit it or add a new envelope to continue changing the object's shape. CorelDraw also lets you copy and remove envelopes.

③ **Cropping objects** (see Figure 3-44)

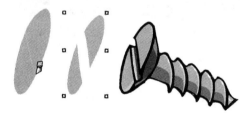

Figure 3-44　Cropping Objects

Cropping lets you quickly remove unwanted areas in objects and imported graphics, eliminating the need to ungroup objects, break linked groups apart, or convert objects to curves. You can crop vector objects and bitmaps.

④ **Splitting objects** (see Figure 3-45)

Figure 3-45 The Knife tool creates two separate objects by cutting the ellipse in half (left). The two objects are separated and used to form the top of the screw (right).

You can split a bitmap or vector object in two and reshape it by redrawing its path. You can split a closed object along a straight or jagged line. CorelDraw lets you choose between splitting an object into two objects, or leaving it as one object composed of two or more subpaths. You can specify whether you want to close paths automatically or keep them open.

⑤ **Filleting, scalloping, and chamfering corners** (see Figure 3-46)

Figure 3-46 From left to right, you can see standard corners with no changes, filleted corners, scalloped corners, and chamfered corners.

You can shape an object by filleting, scalloping, or chamfering corners. Filleting produces a rounded corner, scalloping rounds and inverts the corner to create a notch, and chamfering bevels a corner so that it appears flat.

⑥ **Welding and intersecting objects** (see Figure 3-47)

Figure 3-47 Welding the leaves to the apple creates a single object outline.

You can create irregular shapes by welding and intersecting objects. You can weld or intersect almost any object, including clones, objects on different layers, and single objects with intersecting lines. However, you cannot weld or intersect paragraph text, dimension lines, or masters of clones.

⑦ **Creating PowerClip objects** (see Figure 3-48)

Figure 3-48　Objects before Becoming a PowerClip Object: Artistic Text and a Bitmap

CorelDraw lets you place vector objects and bitmaps, such as photos, inside other objects, or containers. A container can be any object, for example artistic text or a rectangle. When you place an object into a container that is larger than the container, the object, called the content, is cropped to fit the form of the container. This creates a PowerClip object.

You can create more complex PowerClip objects by placing one PowerClip object inside another PowerClip object to produce a nested PowerClip object. You can also copy the contents of one PowerClip object to another PowerClip object. (see Figure 3-49)

Figure 3-49　In the PowerClip object, the artistic text is the container, and the bitmap forms the contents. The bitmap is shaped to the letters of the artistic text.

- **Filling objects**

You can add colored, patterned, textured, and other fills to the inside of objects or other enclosed areas. You can customize a fill and set it as a default, so that each object you draw has the same fill.

① **Applying uniform fills**

You can apply a uniform fill to objects. Uniform fills are solid colors that you can choose or create by using color models and color palettes.

② **Applying fountain fills**

A fountain fill is a smooth progression of two or more colors that adds depth to an object. There are four types of fountain fills: linear, radial, conical, and square. (see Figure 3-50) A linear fountain fill flows in a straight line across the object, a conical fountain fill creates the illusion of light hitting a cone, a radial fountain fill radiates from the center of the object, and a square fountain fill is dispersed in concentric squares from the center of the object.

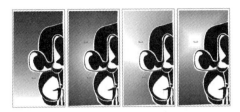

Figure 3-50　There are four types of fountain fills. Left to right: linear, radial, conical, and square.

③ **Applying pattern fills**

You can fill objects with two-color, full-color, or bitmap pattern fills. A two-color pattern fill is composed of only the two colors that you choose. A full-color pattern fill is a more complex vector graphic that can be composed of lines and fills. A bitmap pattern fill is a bitmap image whose complexity is determined by its size, image resolution, and bit depth.

3. Working with color

Your application lets you choose and create colors by using a wide variety of industry-standard palettes, color mixers, and color models. You can create and edit custom color palettes to store frequently used colors for future use. You can also customize how color palettes appear on your screen by changing the size of swatches, the number of rows in palettes, and other properties.

4. Working with pages and layout tools

The CorelDraw application allows you to specify the size, orientation, unit of scale, and background of the drawing page. You can customize and display page grids and guidelines to help you organize objects and place them exactly where you want. For example, if you are designing a newsletter, you can set the dimensions of the pages and create guidelines for positioning columns and heading text. When you are laying out an advertisement, you can align graphics and text along guidelines and arrange graphic elements within a grid. Rulers can help you position grids, guidelines, and objects along a scale, which uses units of your choosing. Also, you can add and delete pages.

5. Working with bitmaps

You can convert a vector graphic to a bitmap. Also, you can import and crop bitmaps in the CorelDraw application. You can also add color masks, watermarks, special effects, and change the color and tone of the images.

Part 5　Output of Digital Image

Printer[1]

In computing, a printer is a peripheral which produces a hard copy (permanent readable

---

[1]　http://en.wikipedia.org/wiki/Computer_printer

text and/or graphics) of documents stored in electronic form, usually on physical print media such as paper or transparencies. Many printers are primarily used as local peripherals, and are attached by a printer cable or, in most new printers, a USB cable to a computer which serves as a document source.

Printers are routinely classified by the technology they employ; numerous such technologies have been developed over the years. The choice of engine has a substantial effect on what jobs a printer is suitable for, as different technologies are capable of different levels of image/text quality, print speed, low cost, noise; in addition, some technologies are inappropriate for certain types of physical media, such as carbon paper or transparencies.

Figure 3-51 Toner-based Printers

The following printing technologies are routinely found in modern printers:

Toner-based Printers(see Figure 3-51)

A laser printer rapidly produces high quality text and graphics. As with digital photocopiers and multifunction printers (MFPs), laser printers employ a xerographic printing process but differ from analog photocopiers in that the image is produced by the direct scanning of a laser beam across the printer's photoreceptor.

Another toner-based printer is the LED printer which uses an array of LEDs instead of a laser to cause toner adhesion to the print drum.

Liquid Inkjet Printers(see Figure 3-52)

Figure 3-52 Liquid Inkjet Printers

Inkjet printers operate by propelling variably-sized droplets of liquid or molten material (ink) onto almost any sized page. They are the most common type of computer printer used by consumers.

Solid Ink Printers(see Figure 3-53)

Solid ink printers, also known as phase-change printers, are a type of thermal transfer printer. They use solid sticks of CMYK-colored ink, similar in consistency to candle wax, which are melted and fed into a piezo crystal operated print-head. The pinhead sprays the ink on a rotating, oil coated drum. The paper then passes over the print drum, at which time the image is transferred, or transfixed, to the page.

Figure 3-53   Solid Ink Printers

Solid ink printers are most commonly used as color office printers, and are excellent at printing on transparencies and other non-porous media. Solid ink printers can produce excellent results. Acquisition and operating costs are similar to laser printers.

Drawbacks of the technology include high energy consumption and long warm-up times from a cold state. Also, some users complain that the resulting prints are difficult to write on, as the wax tends to repel inks from pens, and are difficult to feed through automatic document feeders, but these traits have been significantly reduced in later models.

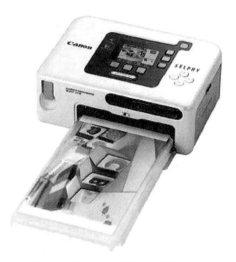

Figure 3-54   Dye-sublimation Printers

Dye-sublimation Printers(see Figure 3-54)

A dye-sublimation printer (or dye-sub printer) is a printer which employs a printing process that uses heat to transfer dye to a medium such as a plastic card, paper or canvas. The process is usually to lay one color at a time using a ribbon that has color panels. Dye-sub printers are intended primarily for high-quality color applications, including color photography; and are less well-suited for text. While once the province of high-end print shops, dye-sublimation printers are now increasingly used as dedicated consumer photo printers.

Inkless Printers(see Figure 3-55)

Figure 3-55 Inkless Printers

Thermal Printers(see Figure 3-56)

Figure 3-56 Thermal Printers

Thermal printers work by selectively heating regions of special heat-sensitive paper. Monochrome thermal printers are used in cash registers, ATMs, gasoline dispensers and some older inexpensive fax machines. Colors can be achieved with special papers and different temperatures and heating rates for different colors. One example is the ZINK technology.

UV Printers(see Figure 3-57)

Figure 3-57 UV Printers

Xerox is working on an inkless printer which will use a special reusable paper coated with a few micrometers of UV light sensitive chemicals. The printer will use a special UV light bar which will be able to write and erase the paper. As of early 2007 this technology is still in development and the text on the printed pages can only last 16 to 24 hours before fading.

Today it is common to print everything (even plain text) by sending ready bitmapped images to the printer, because it allows better control over formatting. Many printer drivers do not use the text mode at all, even if the printer is capable of it.

Plotter①

A plotter is a computer printing device for printing vector graphics. In the past, plotters were widely used in applications such as computer-aided design, though they have generally been replaced with wide-format conventional printers, and it is now commonplace to refer to such wide-format printers as "plotters," even though they technically aren't.

Pen plotters (see Figure 3-58) print by moving a pen or other instrument across the surface of a piece of paper. This means that plotters are restricted to line art, rather than raster graphics as with other printers. Pen plotters can draw complex line art, including text, but do so very slowly because of the mechanical movement of the pens. Pen plotters are often incapable of creating a solid region of color, but can hatch an area by drawing a number of close, regular lines. This

Figure 3-58　Pen Plotters

was often the fastest way to efficiently produce very large drawings or color high-resolution vector-based artwork when computer memory was very expensive and processor power was very limited

Unlike other printer types, pen plotter speed is measured by pen speed and acceleration rate, instead of by page printing speed. A pen plotter's speed is primarily limited by the type of pen used, so the choice of pen is a key factor in pen plotter output speed. Indeed, most modern pen plotters have commands to control slewing speed, depending on the type of pen currently in use.

There are many types of plotter pen, some of which are no longer mass produced. Technical pen tips are often used, many of which can be renewed using parts and supplies for manual drafting pens. Early HP flatbed and grit wheel plotters used small, proprietary fiber-tipped or plastic nib disposable pens.

Photo CD②

Photo CD is a system designed by Kodak for digitizing and storing photos in a CD.

---

① http://en.wikipedia.org/wiki/Plotter
② http://en.wikipedia.org/wiki/Photo_CD

Launched in 1992, the discs were designed to hold nearly 100 high quality images, scanned prints and slides using special proprietary encoding. Photo CD discs are defined in the Beige Book and conform to the CD-ROM XA and CD-i Bridge specifications as well. They were intended to play on CD-i players, Photo CD players (Apple's PowerCD for example), and any computer with a suitable software (LaserSoft Imaging's SilverFast DC or HDR for example). The system failed to gain mass usage among consumers partly due to its proprietary nature, the rapid decline in the costs of scanners, and the lack of CD-ROM drives in most home personal computers of the day. The Photo CD system gained a fair level of acceptance among professional photographers due to the low cost of the high quality film scans. Prior to Photo CD, professionals who wished to digitize their film images were forced to pay much higher fees to obtain drum scans of their film negatives and transparencies. Photo CD was replaced by Picture CD, also from Kodak.

The Kodak Pro Photo CD Master Disc contains 25 images with maximum resolution of 6144×4096 pixels (six resolutions per file, Base/16 to 64 Base). This type is appropriate for 120 film, 4×5, but also for small picture film, if highest resolution is required. (Table 3-3)

Table 3-3 the Variants of Kodak Pro Photo CD Master Disc

Designation	Resolution (px × px)	Size (Mpx)	Size (MB)	Intended typical use
Base/16	128 × 192	0.025	0.07	Preview (index print, thumbnail)
Base/4	256 × 384	0.098	0.28	Web
Base	512 × 768	0.393	1.13	Computer screen, TV, Web
4 Base	1024 × 1536	1.573	4.50	HDTV screen
16 Base	2048 × 3072	6.291	18.00	Print-out up to ca. 20 × 30 cm
64 Base	4096 × 6144	25.166	72.00	Professional print, pre-press, archiving (optional)

For practical use, any Photo CD images will have to convert to a modern format such as JPEG, TIFF or PNG. While there are a large number of image conversion programs available, both commercial and freeware or open source, most are capable of only basic, low resolution (often only to Base resolution, 512×768) conversions.

New Words

computerized axial tomography   计算机轴断层摄影术
astronomy   *n.* 天文学
charge-coupled devices   光耦合装置
computer-generated   *adj.* 电脑操控的
coordinate-measuring machine   坐标测量机
seismographic profiling   *n.* 地震剖面测量
airborne radar   *n.* 机载雷达
algorithms   *n.* 算法式

exclusively　　*adv.* 专门地；专有地，独占地；排外地
reversible　　*adj.* 可逆的
palette　　*n.* 调色板，(画家使用的)主要色彩，主色调
error diffusion　　误差扩散法
AA batteries　　五号电池
cradle　　*n.* 发源地，发祥地
telephotography　　*n.* 远距离照相术，传真电报术
monochromatic　　*adj.* 单色的，单频的
photodiode　　*n.* 光敏二极管，光电二极管
firmware　　*n.* 韧体，(泛指直接控制硬件的软件，也指固化在硬件中用来控制硬件的软件，比如 BIOS。)固件
acetate　　*n.* 醋酸盐；醋酸酯、醋酸纤维；醋酸人造丝
thumbnail　　*n.* 缩略图
symmetrical and logarithmic　　对称和对数
freehand　　*n.* 手画线，手绘曲线
Filleting, scalloping, and chamfering　　*n.* 圆角，扇形，斜切
peripheral　　*adj.* 非本质的；非主要的，次要的，外围的周围的，边缘的 *n.* (计算机的) 外围设备，周边设备
phase-change　　相位变化
piezo　　*n.* 压力

Notes

[1] Advances in microprocessor technology paved the way for the development and marketing of charge-coupled devices (CCDs) for use in a wide range of image capture devices and gradually displaced the use of analog film and tape in photography and videography towards the end of the 20th century.

译文：微处理器技术的进步为光耦合装置应用于广泛的图像捕获设备的发展和市场铺平了道路，并于 20 世纪末逐步替代了模拟电影、摄影中的磁带以及摄像的应用。

- pave the way for... 为……铺平道路
- towards the end of the 20th century 接近 20 世纪末

[2] A lossless algorithm might, for example, look for a recurring pattern in the file, and replace each occurrence with a short abbreviation, thereby cutting the file size. In contrast, a lossy algorithm might store color information at a lower resolution than the image itself, since the eye is not so sensitive to changes in color of a small distance.

译文：例如无损算法可能通过查找文件中反复出现的模式，然后用一个所写的形式取代，从而减少文件大小；相反，有损算法可能通过存储在比无损图像本身分辨率低的颜色信息以减小文件大小，因为眼睛对小距离的颜色变化不太敏感。

- for example：例如，作为插入语

- 无损算法与有损算法是相对的两种压缩算法,in contrast:相反。
- since 引导原因状语从句,引出存储低分辨率图像而不影响预览的原因。

[3] Better graphics programs, such as Paint Shop Pro and Photoshop, allow you to view the image quality and file size as a function of compression level, so that you can conveniently choose the balance between quality and file size

译文:比较好的图形处理程序,如 Paint Shop Pro 和 Photoshop,允许查看该图像的质量和文件的大小作为压缩程度的函数,这样就可以方便地选择以保证质量和文件大小之间的平衡。

- such as,比如,such as Paint Shop Pro and Photoshop,在此作为插入语使用。
- so that 以至于,引导结果状语从句。

[4] A flatbed scanner is usually composed of a glass pane (or platen), under which there is a bright light (often xenon or cold cathode fluorescent) which illuminates the pane, and a moving optical array in CCD scanning.

译文:平板扫描仪通常是由一个玻璃面板(或滚筒)和下面的一个明亮的灯(通常是氙或阴极荧光灯)照亮面板以及在 CCD 扫描中移动的光学阵列。

- be composed of... 由……组成
- ...a glass pane (or platen), under which there is a bright light...under which 引导状语从句 which 指代 a class pane。
- ...which illuminates the pane, which 引导定语从句限定 a bright light

[5] The choice of engine has a substantial effect on what jobs a printer is suitable for, as different technologies are capable of different levels of image/text quality, print speed, low cost, noise; in addition, some technologies are inappropriate for certain types of physical media, such as carbon paper or transparencies.

译文:发动机的选择对于什么样的工作适合打印机有很大的影响,因为不同的技术适用于不同层次的图像、文本质量、打印速度、成本或噪音,此外,一些技术不适用于某种类型的物理媒体,如:碳纸和胶片。

- ...on what jobs a printer is suitable for ... what 做介词 for 的宾语。
- as 引导原因状语从句,引出进行大量尝试的原因。
- in addition 另外,此外

Selected Translation

Part 5

数字图像的输出

打印机

打印机是一种计算机输出设备,可以将电脑内储存的数据按照文字或图形的方式永久地输出到纸张或者透明胶片上。许多打印机主要作为外围设备使用,并使用打印机电缆或者 USB 线与计算机相连,而计算机此时作为打印机的文档源。

打印机通常以它们使用的技术进行分类,许多这样的技术已经经历了多年的发展。发动机的选择对于什么样的工作适合打印机有很大的影响,因为不同的技术适用于不同层次的图像、文本质量、打印速度、成本或噪音,此外,一些技术不适用于某种类型的物理媒体,如:碳纸和胶片。

以下是现代常见的打印机:

墨粉打印机

激光打印机能够迅速打印出高质量的文本和图形,与数字复印机和多功能打印机相同,激光打印机使用静电的打印过程,但不同于模拟复印机的是通过激光束在打印机的感光器直接扫描生成图像。

另一种墨粉打印机是发光二极管打印机,它使用的是发光二极管激光阵列而不是激光将碳粉黏附到打印鼓上。

液体喷墨打印机

喷墨打印机通过推进可变大小的液滴,或熔材料(油墨)到几乎任何大小的页面上进行打印,是消费者最常用的计算机打印机类型。

固体油墨打印机

固体油墨打印机,也称为相变打印机,是热传递打印机的一种,它利用一种与蜡烛相似的固态 CMYK 型墨水,融化成一个压电晶体打印头并旋转喷洒墨水到涂油鼓上,在纸张经过此打印鼓的时候,图像被传输或固定到纸上。

固体油墨打印机是最常用的彩色办公打印机,在胶片和其他非多孔介质上的打印效果较好,购买和经营成本类似于激光打印机。

此项技术也有它自身的缺陷,包括高能耗、预热时间长。另外,一些用户抱怨所得到的打印品都难以书写,因为蜡往往排斥钢笔的墨水,并且很难自动扫描,但这些特征在以后的油墨打印机中得到了显著改善。

染料升华打印机

染料升华打印机(或染料分打印机)在印刷过程中使用热将染料转移到一种媒体如塑料卡、纸或画布,这一过程通常使用色带一次打印一种颜色。染料分打印机的目的主要是高品质的彩色应用,包括彩色照片,但是不太适合文本的打印。染料升华打印机曾应用于高端印刷,现在正越来越多地用作消费者专用的照片打印机。

无墨打印机

热敏打印机

热敏打印机的工作原理是选择性地加热纸的特殊热感应区域。黑白热敏打印机用于收银机、自动柜员机、汽油机和一些较旧的廉价传真机。不同颜色的打印需要特殊的纸张、不同的温度和升温速率来实现,其中一个例子是无墨技术(不用墨盒和色带,而只靠一种特殊的纸张,就能够随时输出一张精美的数码图片或者文件)。

紫外线打印机

施乐公司正在开发无墨打印机,它能够使用特殊的涂有几微米的紫外光敏感化学物质的可重复使用的纸,并使用一种特殊的紫外线灯条书写和擦除文件。截至 2007 年初,这项技术还处于发展中,打印的文本只能维持 16 到 24 小时。

现在,能够通过发送准备好位图的图像到打印机实现打印一切(甚至纯文本),因为打印机能够更好地控制格式。许多打印机驱动程序根本不使用文本模式,即使打印机能够做到这一点。

绘图仪

绘图仪是一种用于印刷的矢量图形计算机打印设备。过去,绘图仪被广泛用于电脑辅助设计应用等领域,虽然它们一般被具有广泛格式的传统的打印机取代,而现在仍普遍称这些具有广泛格式的打印机为"绘图仪",但是在技术上并非如此。

笔式绘图仪通过在纸张的表面移动钢笔或其他工具来进行印刷。这意味着,绘图仪限于印制线条,而不是其他打印机那样的光栅图形。笔式绘图仪可以绘制复杂的线条包括文字,但由于钢笔的机械运动绘制的速度比较慢。笔式绘图仪通常不能建立一个稳固的色彩区域,但可以通过绘制大量的紧密有规律排列的线条形成一个区域。当计算机的内存昂贵和处理器能力非常有限时,若要生产非常大的图纸或彩色高分辨率的基于矢量的插图,使用笔式绘图仪是最快的方法。

不同于其他类型的打印机,笔式绘图仪的速度是由笔速和加速度而不是页面打印速度测量的。笔式绘图仪的速度主要是受限于笔的类型,所以笔的选择是绘图仪输出速度的关键因素。的确,最现代化的笔式绘图仪能够控制回转速度,这与目前正在使用的笔型有关。

有许多类型的绘图笔,其中一些已不再大量生产。技术用笔的笔尖常常被使用,其中有许多可以被翻新作为手动制图钢笔使用。早期的惠普平板绘图仪及细砂轮绘图仪使用的是细小的专有纤维或塑料的一次性钢笔笔尖。

相片光盘

相片光盘是由柯达公司 1992 年启动设计的将照片数字化并将其存储于光盘的系统,能够容纳近 100 个高品质的图像,扫描和打印幻灯片需要使用特殊的专有编码。The Beige Book 中定义了相片光盘,并符合该 CD-ROM XA 和交互式光盘规格。它们的目的是要在交互式光盘播放器上、相片光盘播放器(例如苹果公司的 PowerCD)或装有合适软件的计算机上播放,该系统未能获得消费者使用的部分原因是它的专有性。在扫描仪的成本迅速下降,和大多数家用个人电脑缺少 CD-ROM 驱动器的情况下,该照片光盘系统由于其高质量电影扫描且低成本的特征,在专业的摄影师之中取得了公平的评价,因为在此之前,那些希望将自己的电影图片数字化的影像专业人士被迫支付更高的费用取得透明胶片电影底片扫描。照片 CD 改为图片 CD,同样出自柯达。

柯达专业摄影大师的 CD 光盘可以拍摄 25 张最大分辨率为 6144×4096 的图片(其中,每个文件包括 6 种分辨率,从基数 1/16 到 64)。如果需要最高分辨率的图片,那么这种类型的相片光盘可用于拍摄 120 胶片,画幅比为 4∶5,当然也适用于小分辨率电影。(见表 3-3)

表 3-3　柯达专业摄影大师的 CD 光盘的变体

名称	分辨率 (像素×像素)	大小 (Mpx)	大小 (兆)	典型应用
Base/16	128×192	0.025	0.07	预览（打印目录，缩略图）
Base/4	256×384	0.098	0.28	网页
Base	512×768	0.393	1.13	计算机屏幕，电视，网络
4 Base	1024×1536	1.573	4.50	高清电视屏幕
16 Base	2048×3072	6.291	18.00	打印达 20×30 厘米
64 Base	4096×6144	25.166	72.00	专业打印，版前印刷，存档（可选）

对于实际使用来说，任何照片光盘的图片要转换为现代格式如 JPEG、TIFF 或 PNG。无论是商业的或免费或开源的，即便现在有许许多多的图片转换程序，大多是只有基本、低分辨率（通常只有基数为 1 的分辨率，512×768）的转换。

Exercises

1. What are the differences between the vector and raster images?
2. What formats do you know about digital images?
3. How to capture digital images with digital camera?
4. What kinds of scanners do you know?
5. Distinguish different kinds of printers.

专业英语常见的语法现象

专业英语的语法特点可以归纳为客观、准确和精练，所以在专业英语中经常出现如下的语法现象。

一、动名词

动名词的作用相当于名词，它在句子中可作主语和宾语。它可以取代时间从句或简化时间从句。例如：

1. Reading is a good habit. 动名词在句中做主语。
2. I enjoy working with you. 动名词在句子中做动词宾语。
3. I am interested in reading. 动名词在句子中做介词宾语。

在专业英语中，动名词的应用相当普遍。它可以令句子精练。例如：通常的表达形式为：

4. Before it is executed, the program should be loaded into main memory.
5. When you use the mouse to click a button, you can select an option from a list.

相应地用动名词来表示的精练形式为：

Before being executed, the program should be loaded into main memory.
By using the mouse to click a button, you can select an option from a list.

二、分词短语

通过使用过去分词可以取代被动语态的关系从句；使用现在分词可以取代主动语态的关系从句。

1. 现在分词短语一般做形容词用，可修饰动作的发出者，有主动的意义。可译成"……的……"，此时多做定语，在意思上和一个定语从句差不多。例如：

A digital image is a representation of a two-dimensional image using ones and zeros (binary).

2. 现在分词短语还可以作状语，用来表示方式、目的、条件、结果和背景等；有时可以表示伴随状态。例如：

A lossless algorithm might, for example, look for a recurring pattern in the file, and replace each occurrence with a short abbreviation, thereby cutting the file size. 现在分词作状语，表示目的和结果。

Modern scanners may be considered the successors of early telephotography and fax input devices, consisting of a rotating drum with a single photo detector at a standard speed of 60 or 120 rpm (later models up to 240 rpm). 现在分词作状语，表伴随状态。

3. 过去分词短语一般做形容词用，可修饰动作的对象。如：

Better algorithms search the image to find an optimum set of 256 colors.

三、不定式

在专业英语中，不定式短语可以大量地用作状语或定语。当然，它也可以替换表示目的、功能的状态从句。例如：

① What is the process? It lays the individual for work and for life in general.

可以表示为：The process is usually to lay one color at a time using a ribbon that has color panels.

② What is another way to get more speed out of a computer? It is to have multiple processors.

可以表示为：Another way to get more speed out of a computer is to have multiple processors.

四、被动语态

被动语态在专业英语中用得非常频繁，这主要有两个原因：一是专业文章中在描写行为或状态本身，注重客观事实或道理，所以由谁或由什么行为或状态作为主体就显得不那么重要了。例如：

① The Adobe Photoshop CS4 workspace is arranged to help you focus on creating and editing images.

② Printers are routinely classified by the technology they employ; numerous such technologies have been developed over the years.

被动语态使用频繁的另外一个原因是便于向后扩展句子,构成更长的句子,以便于对问题做出更精确的描述,但又不至于把句子弄得头重脚轻。例如:

The original QWERTY keyboard was invented to minimize collisions between keys that were frequently struck.

五、其他现象

在专业英语中,一些其他的常用短语也经常出现。

1. 在专业英语中,要对概念或术语下定义时,我们常用以下短语。

① in contrast 表对比,相比之下,如:A lossless algorithm might, for example, look for a recurring pattern in the file, and replace each occurrence with a short abbreviation, thereby cutting the file size. In contrast, a lossy algorithm might store color information at a lower resolution than the image itself, since the eye is not so sensitive to changes in color of a small distance.

② refer to,如:In the past, plotters were widely used in applications such as computer-aided design, though they have generally been replaced with wide-format conventional printers, and it is now commonplace to refer to such wide-format printers as "plotters," even though they technically aren't.

2. 专业英语中,"主语+be 形容词+to 名词"的结构是很常见的。它用于对某一事物、概念或论点加以定论、叙述。

① be necessary to,如:It is necessary to examine the efficiency of the new design.

② be adapted to,如:A living thing is adapted to a special environment.

Chapter 4   Digital Audio

▲ Knowledge Objectives

When you have completed this chapter, you will be able to:
- Know the history of digital audio and the digital audio technologies.
- Compare and contrast different formats of digital audio.
- Choose suited method to get digital audio from various ways.
- Master the basic procedures of processing of digital audio.
- Tell how to output digital audio.

▲ Professional Terms

batch process	批处理
bit stream	比特流,数码流
codec	编解码器
compression	压缩
digital audio processing	数字音频处理
digital audio	数字音频
digital recording	数字录音
downmix	混音
DVD-audio	DVD-音频
electrical recording	电子录音
fade in	淡入
fade out	淡出
lossless compression	无损压缩
magnetic tape recording	磁带录音
multi-track	多轨
phonograph	留声机
pulse-code	脉冲编码
sound effects	音效
telegraphone	电话录音机
transistor	半导体收音机

Part 1　Outline of Digital Audio[①]

Digital audio uses pulse-code modulation and digital signals for sound reproduction. This includes analog-to-digital conversion (ADC), digital-to-analog conversion (DAC), storage, and transmission. In effect, the system commonly referred to as digital is in fact a discrete-time, discrete-level analog of a previous electrical analog. While modern systems can be quite subtle in their methods, the primary usefulness of a digital system is the ability to store, retrieve and transmit signals without any loss of quality.

Digital audio has emerged because of its usefulness in the recording, manipulation, mass-production, and distribution of sound. Modern distribution of music across the Internet via online stores depends on digital recording and digital compression algorithms. Distribution of audio as data files rather than as physical objects has significantly reduced the cost of distribution.

In an analog audio system, sounds begin as physical waveforms in the air, are transformed into an electrical representation of the waveform, via a transducer (for example, a microphone), and are stored or transmitted. To be re-created into sound, the process is reversed, through amplification and then conversion back into physical waveforms via a loudspeaker. Although its nature may change, analog audio's fundamental wave-like characteristics remain the same during its storage, transformation, duplication, and amplification.

Analog audio signals are susceptible to noise and distortion, unavoidable due to the innate characteristics of electronic circuits and associated devices. In the case of purely analog recording and reproduction, numerous opportunities for the introduction of noise and distortion exist throughout the entire process. When audio is digitized, distortion and noise are introduced only by the stages that precede conversion to digital format, and by the stages that follow conversion back to analog.

The digital audio chain begins when an analog audio signal is first sampled, and then (for pulse-code modulation, the usual form of digital audio) it is converted into binary signals—'on/off' pulses—which are stored as binary electronic, magnetic, or optical signals, rather than as continuous time, continuous level electronic or electromechanical signals [1]. This signal may then be further encoded to allow correction of any errors that might occur in the storage or transmission of the signal; however this encoding is for error correction, and is not strictly part of the digital audio process. This "channel coding" is essential to the ability of broadcast or recorded digital system to avoid loss of bit accuracy. The discrete time and level of the binary signal allow a decoder to recreate the analog signal upon replay. An example of a

---

① http://en.wikipedia.org/wiki/Digital_audio

channel code is Eight to Fourteen Bit Modulation as used in the audio Compact Disc (CD).

Digital audio technologies

Digital audio broadcasting:
- Digital Audio Broadcasting (DAB)
- HD Radio
- Digital Radio Mondiale (DRM)
- In-band on-channel (IBOC)

Storage technologies:
- Digital audio player
- Digital Audio Tape (DAT)
- Compact Disc (CD)
- DVD Audio
- Minidisc
- Super Audio CD
- Various audio file formats

Part 2 Formats of Digital Audio[①]

An audio file format is a file format for storing audio data on a computer system. It can be a raw bit stream, but it is usually a container format or an audio data format with defined storage layer.

The general approach towards storing digital audio is to sample the audio voltage which, on playback, would correspond to a certain level of signal in an individual channel with a certain resolution—the number of bits per sample—in regular intervals (forming the sample rate) [2]. This data can then be stored uncompressed, or compressed to reduce the file size.

It is important to distinguish between a file format and a codec. A codec performs the encoding and decoding of the raw audio data while the data itself is stored in a file with a specific audio file format. Most of the publicly documented audio file formats can be created with one of two or more encoders or codecs. Although most audio file formats support only one type of audio data (created with an audio coder), a multimedia container format (as MKV or AVI) may support multiple types of audio and video data.

There are three major groups of audio file formats:
- **Uncompressed formats: WAV, AIFF, AU or raw header-less PCM**

There is one major uncompressed audio format, PCM, which is usually stored as .wav on

---

① http://en.wikipedia.org/wiki/Audio_file_format

Windows or as .aiff on Mac OS. WAV and AIFF are flexible file formats designed to store more or less any combination of sampling rates or bitrates. This makes them suitable file formats for storing and archiving an original recording. There is another uncompressed audio format which is .cda (Audio CD Track). CDA is from a music CD and is 0% compressed.

The AIFF format is based on the IFF format. The WAV format is based on the RIFF file format, which is similar to the IFF format.

BWF (Broadcast Wave Format) is a standard audio format created by the European Broadcasting Union as a successor to WAV. BWF allows metadata to be stored in the file. See European Broadcasting Union: Specification of the Broadcast Wave Format (EBU Technical document 3285, July 1997). This is the primary recording format used in many professional audio workstations in the television and film industry. BWF files include a standardized Timestamp reference which allows for easy synchronization with a separate picture element. Stand-alone, file based, multi-track recorders from Sound Device, Zaxcom, HHB USA, Fostex, and Aaton all use BWF as their preferred format.

- **Lossless compression: FLAC, APE, WavPack, Monkey's Audio**

A lossless compressed format requires much more processing time than an uncompressed format but is more efficient in space usage.

Uncompressed audio formats encode both sound and silence with the same number of bits per unit of time. Encoding an uncompressed minute of absolute silence produces a file of the same size as encoding an uncompressed minute of symphonic orchestra music. In a lossless compressed format, however, the music would occupy a marginally smaller file and the silence takes up almost no space at all.

Lossless compression formats (such as the most widespread FLAC, WavPack, Monkey's Audio, and ALAC/Apple Lossless) provide a compression ratio of about 2:1. Development in lossless compression formats aims to reduce processing time while maintaining a good compression ratio.

- **Lossy compression: MP3, ACC, lossy WAV**

Lossy compression is a data encoding method which discards (loses) some of the data, in order to achieve its goal, with the result that decompressing the data yields content that is different from the original, though similar enough to be useful in some way. Lossy compression is most commonly used to compress multimedia data (audio, video, still images), especially in applications such as streaming media and internet telephony.

Part 3 Capture of Digital Audio[①]

Electrical Recording

Sound recording began as a mechanical process and remained so until the early 1920s (with the exception of the 1899 Telegraphone) when a string of groundbreaking inventions in the field of electronics revolutionized sound recording and the young recording industry [3]. These included sound transducers such as microphones and loudspeakers, and various electronic devices such as the mixing desk, designed for the amplification and modification of electrical sound signals.

After the Edison phonograph itself, arguably the most significant advances in sound recording were the electronic systems invented by two American scientists between 1900 and 1924. In 1906 Lee De Forest invented the "Audion" triode vacuum-tube, electronic valve, which could greatly amplify weak electrical signals, (one early use was to amplify long distance telephone in 1915) which became the basis of all subsequent electrical sound systems until the invention of the transistor. The valve was quickly followed by the invention of the Regenerative circuit, Super-Regenerative circuit and the Superheterodyne receiver circuit, all of which were invented and patented by the young electronics genius Edwin Armstrong between 1914 and 1922. Armstrong's inventions made higher fidelity electrical sound recording and reproduction a practical reality, facilitating the development of the electronic amplifier and many other devices; after 1925 these systems had become standard in the recording and radio industry.

While Armstrong published studies about the fundamental operation of the triode vacuum tube before World War I, inventors like Orlando R. Marsh and his Marsh Laboratories, as well as scientists at Bell Telephone Laboratories, achieved their own understanding about the triode and were utilizing the Audion as a repeater in weak telephone circuits. By 1925 it was possible to place a long distance telephone call with these repeaters between New York and San Francisco in 20 minutes, both parties being clearly heard. With this technical prowess, Joseph P. Maxfield and Henry C. Harrison from Bell Telephone Laboratories were skilled in using mechanical analogs of electrical circuits and applied these principles to sound recording and reproduction. They were ready to demonstrate their results by 1924 using the Wente condenser microphone and the vacuum tube amplifier to drive the "rubber line" wax recorder to cut a master audio disc.

Meanwhile, radio continued to develop. Armstrong's groundbreaking inventions (including FM radio) also made possible the broadcasting of long-range, high-quality radio transmissions of voice and music. The importance of Armstrong's Superheterodyne circuit cannot be over-estimated — it is the central component of almost all analog amplification and both analog

---

[①] http://en.wikipedia.org/wiki/Sound_recording#Electrical_recording

and digital radio-frequency transmitter and receiver devices to this day.

Magnetic Tape Recording

Magnetic tape brought about sweeping changes in both radio and the recording industry. Sound could be recorded, erased and re-recorded on the same tape many times, sounds could be duplicated from tape to tape with only minor loss of quality, and recordings could now be very precisely edited by physically cutting the tape and rejoining it. Within a few years of the introduction of the first commercial tape recorder, the Ampex 200 model, launched in 1948, American musician-inventor Les Paul had invented the first multitrack tape recorder, bringing about another technical revolution in the recording industry. Tape made possible the first sound recordings totally created by electronic means.

Magnetic tape was invented for recording sound by Fritz Pfleumer in 1928 in Germany, based on the invention of magnetic wire recording by Valdemar Poulsen in 1898. Pfleumer's invention used an iron (III) oxide ($Fe2O3$) powder coating on a long strip of paper. This invention was further developed by the German electronics company AEG, which manufactured the recording machines and BASF, which manufactured the tape. In 1933, working for AEG, Eduard Schuller developed the ring shaped tape head. Previous head designs were needle shaped and tended to shred the tape. An important discovery made in this period was the technique of AC biasing which improved the fidelity of the recorded audio signal by increasing the effective linearity of the recording medium.

A wide variety of recorders and formats have developed since, most significantly reel-to-reel and Compact Cassette(Figure 4-1).

Magnetic tape has been used for sound recording for more than 75 years. Tape revolutionized both the radio broadcast and music recording industries. It did this by giving artists and producers the power to record and re-record audio with minimal loss in quality as well as edit and rearrange recordings with ease. The alternative recording technologies of the era, transcription discs and wire recorders, could not provide anywhere near this level of quality and functionality. Since some early refinements improved the fidelity of the reproduced sound, magnetic tape has been the highest quality analog sound recording medium available. Despite this, as of 2007, magnetic tape is largely being replaced by digital systems for most sound recording purposes.

Figure 4-1 A Typical Compact Cassette

Digital Recording

The invention of digital sound recording and later the compact disc in 1982 brought significant improvements in the durability of consumer recordings.

The most recent and revolutionary developments have been in digital recording, with the development of various uncompressed and compressed digital audio file formats, processors capable and fast enough to convert the digital data to sound in real time, and inexpensive mass storage[4]. This generated a new type of portable digital audio player. The minidisc player, using ATRAC(Adaptive Transform Acoustic Coding (ATRAC) is a family of proprietary audio compression algorithms developed by Sony) compression on small, cheap, re-writeable discs was introduced in the 1990s but became obsolescent as solid-state non-volatile flash memory(Flash memory is a non-volatile computer storage technology that can be electrically erased and reprogrammed. It is primarily used in memory cards, USB flash drives, and solid-state drives for general storage and transfer of data between computers and other digital products) dropped in price. As technologies which increase the amount of data that can be stored on a single medium, such as Super Audio CD, DVD-A, Blu-ray Disc and HD DVD become available, longer programs of higher quality fit onto a single disc. Sound files are readily downloaded from the Internet and other sources, and copied onto computers and digital audio players. Digital audio technology is used in all areas of audio, from casual use of music files of moderate quality to the most demanding professional applications. New applications such as internet radio and podcasting have appeared.

Technological developments in recording and editing have transformed the record, movie and television industries in recent decades. Audio editing became practicable with the invention of magnetic tape recording, but digital audio and cheap mass storage allows computers to edit audio files quickly, easily, and cheaply. Today, the process of making a recording is separated into tracking, mixing and mastering. Multitrack recording makes it possible to capture signals from several microphones, or from different 'takes' to tape or disc, with maximized headroom and quality, allowing previously unavailable flexibility in the mixing and mastering stages for editing, level balancing, compressing and limiting, adding effects such as reverberation, equalisation, flanging, and much more.

Libraries of Sound Effects

There are kinds of Sound Libraries, such as SoundDogs, Google Music, Baidu MP3 and so on. Searching from these sites we can get Digital Audio what we need.

> **Sounddogs.com**(Figure 4-2)[①]

Figure 4-2 Homepage of Sounddogs.com

———————————

[①] http://en.wikipedia.org/wiki/Sounddogs

Chapter 4 Digital Audio | 89

It is a commercial online library of sound effects. As of 2010, 500,000 sound effects and production music tracks are available for immediate download or on hard drive or CD. Downloads are in the following formats: AIFF, WAV, and MP3. Their website began providing service in May, 1997. Sounddogs.com is based in Los Angeles, California, with offices in Canada, Argentina, and Uruguay.

> **Google Music**①(Figure 4-3)

Figure 4-3   Google Music Library

A site containing links to a large archive of Chinese pop music (principally Cantopop and Mandopop), including audio streaming over Google's own player, legal lyric downloads, and in most cases legal MP3 downloads. The archive is provided by Top100.cn (i.e. this service does not search the whole Internet) and is only available in mainland China. It is intended to rival the similar, but potentially illegal service provided by Baidu.

> **Baidu MP3 Search**②(Figure 4-4)

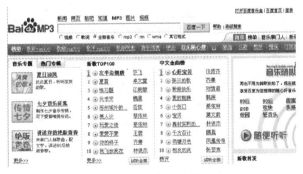

Figure 4-4   Baidu MP3 Library

It provides algorithm-generated links to songs and other multimedia files provided by Internet content providers. Baidu locates file formats such as MP3, WMA and SWF. The multimedia search feature is mainly used in searches for Chinese pop music.

---

① http://en.wikipedia.org/wiki/Google_Music
② http://en.wikipedia.org/wiki/Baidu

Part 4　Digital Audio Processing[①]

1. Cool Edit Pro Overview

Cool Edit Pro is an advanced multi track sound editing program for Windows. It has the following (but not limited too) main capabilities:

* Sound Filters via DSPE (Digital Signal Processing Effect).
* Multi track function: Up to 64 simultaneous tracks.
* Accepts plug-ins to expand its capability.
* Ability to create batch process files.

2. Record From a CD

(i) Setup the Windows Mixer:

Before you begin, you must setup the Windows Mixer to record from the input of the CD.

① Go to the Options menu; choose "Windows Mixer." (Figure 4-5)

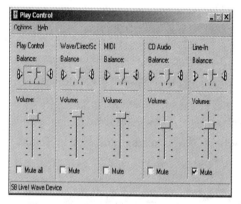

Figure 4-5　Windows Mixer (Play Control)

② Go to the Options menu, and then choose "Properties." (Figure 4-6)

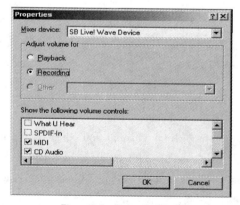

Figure 4-6　Properties Menu

[①] http://www.oscr.arizona.edu/downloads/tutorials/archive/CoolEdit_User.pdf

③ In the properties menu choose "Recording", and then press "OK".

④ In the new dialog box, make sure that "CD Recording" is checked. (Figure 4-7)

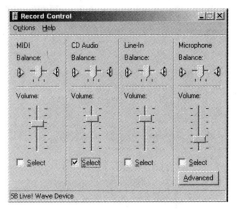

Figure 4-7   Record Control

⑤ Because you will be receiving an analog signal, it's recommended to not have the volume control at its highest setting for the CD Audio. Else you have a chance of having the sound recorded at too high a volume.

⑥ Exit out of this menu.

(ii) **Playing and Recording**

We will now choose the track we want to record, and then record that track.

① First we will create a new sound in the Single track mode. Go to the File menu, and choose "New".

② A dialog box will appear, make sure it is checked to stereo, 16 bit, and 44100khz. Then push "OK". (Figure 4-8)

Figure 4-8   New Waveform

③ A new blank single track will be created. Please insert the Audio CD. Programs like Windows Media Player may try to start. Exit out of these.

④ Make sure the CD Audio menu is enabled. To enable if it is not, go to the View menu, and then choose "Show CD Player". (Figure 4-9)

Figure 4-9　CD Player

⑤ The CD Player should display the number of tracks on the CD. Click on Track 1.

⑥ If you double click on Track 1, or Press Play on the CD Player. The CD will start playing.

⑦ Hit the stop button.

⑧ Go above the CD player and hit the Record (Figure 4-10) button on the playback menu.

Figure 4-10　Record

⑨ A context menu will appear "Recording Time" (Figure 4-11). Set its parameters to "No Time Limit", and "Right Away", and then hit "OK".

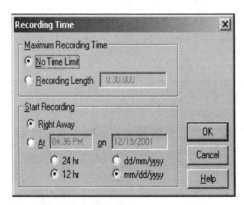

Figure 4-11　Recording Time

⑩ Quickly start jump back to the CD Menu, and press play.

⑪ Let the CD play for a few seconds. Then hit the Stop button on the CD player.

⑫ Jump to the Record button on the Playback menu, and also hit stop.

We can see the Resulting recording. (Figure 4-12)

Chapter 4 Digital Audio

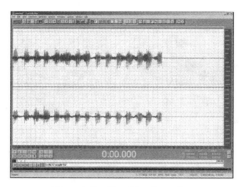

Figure 4-12   Resulting Recording

⑬ You can playback what you have by pressing the spacebar, or by hitting the Play button on the Playback menu.

3. Open and Edit a Track 15 min

We will now open a small file in the Single track vie, edit and save it.

(ⅰ) **Open a File**

① Open the sound file "moo. wav". (Figure 4-13)

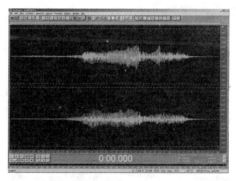

Figure 4-13   The File "moo. wav" Opened in Cool

② Make sure you are in the single track mode.

③ Go to the File menu, open, from the list choose 'Windows PCM (*wav).

④ Go to the directory where the media is stored and open moo. wav.

(ⅱ) **Normalize the File**

We will now normalize the audio selection. Normalize ill read the maximum volume of the sound find, and increases the volume so that the maximum volume of the sound is increased without causing distortion.

① Go to the Edit menu and then choose "Select Entire Wave". At this point your wave file should be displayed reversed.

② Go to the Transform menu, "Amplitude", then "Normalize". (Figure 4-14)

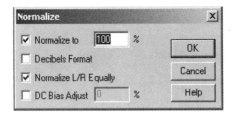

Figure 4-14 Normalize

③ In the Normalize change the 100% to 95% and then hit "OK". (Figure 4-15 and Figure 4-16)

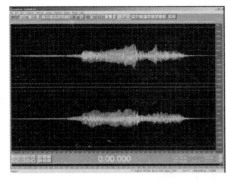

Figure 4-15 Before

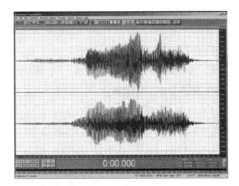

Figure 4-16 After

(iii) Select and Modify

We will now Select and Modify a portion of the file and put add a filter to this portion.

① In the track window, choose an area then click and drag to the left. The area you do this too will become highlighted. (Figure 4-17)

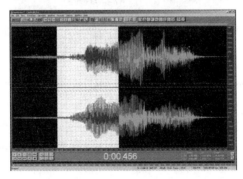

Figure 4-17 Example Selection

② Go to the Transform menu, "Time Pitch" then choose Pitch Bender. In the Pitch Bender Menu(Figure 4-18) choose "Squirrley". Hit "OK" and the filter will be applied to the selection

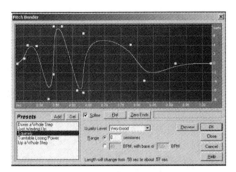

Figure 4-18　Pitch Bender

(ⅳ) **Fade Out**

The last item we will do to this wave is Fade Out.

① We will use a different method to choose the area we want. On the interface down below the displayed wave in the lower right is the Current Position/Track. (Figure 4-19)

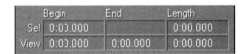

Figure 4-19　Current Position/Track

② Click in the "Begin" area and put "0∶01.448". Click on the "End" area and put 0∶02.146. You will now see that then end of the sound file has been selected.

③ Go to the Transform menu. "Amplitude"-"Amplify" (Figure 4-20). Then choose the second tab "Fade".

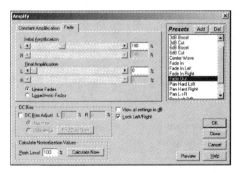

Figure 4-20　Amplify Menu

④ Scroll down to "Fade Out" and then hit "OK". The sound file should now fade out.

(ⅴ) **Save**

We now will save the file before closing it.

① Go to the File Menu, and then go to "Save As" (Figure 4-21), in the pop up window save it in the same directory and name it "moo0.wav". Click "Save".

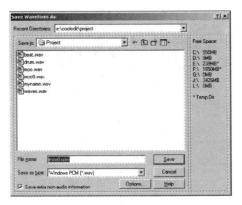

Figure 4-21 Save As

4. Open and Edit a Multi Track 20 min

(i) **Open**(Figure 4-22)

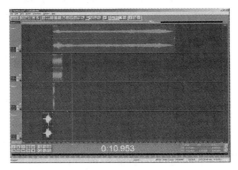

Figure 4-22 Open Sound Files in Multi Track

① First make sure you're in the Multi track mode. Then go to the File menu, open, from the list choose 'Windows PCM (*wav).

② Open the following files, "beat.wav", "drum.wav", "moo0.wav", and "waves.wav". As you will see none of the wave files are displayed. This is because they have opened up in the single track mode.

③ To now Import the movies into multi track go the track and right click on it. The context menu should appear.

④ In the context menu, go to "Insert", and then from the drop down list choose "waves.wav". The sound will open in the first track starting in the position your sound file was at.

⑤ Go down to track 2. Right click again and choose "beat.wav".

⑥ Track 3 choose "drum.wav".

⑦ Track 4 is "moo0.wav".

(ⅱ) **Moving** (Figure 4-23)

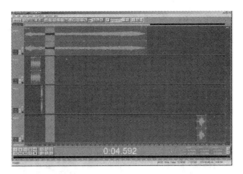

Figure 4-23 Sound Files Placed

We will now move the tracks around to align them to play at certain places.

① Left click on "waves. wav" in track 1. This will select it.

② Right click on the sound and drag to the left. As you can see the sound file moves along the timeline.

③ Flush it at the beginning.

④ Depending if snapping is on move track 2, "beat. wav" to just after the initial rise of the waves sound file (about 5 seconds in).

⑤ Move track 3, "drum. wav", so that it begins right after track 2 ends (again if snapping is enabled.

⑥ Move track 4 "moo0. wav" out of the way (IE to the right) for now.

(ⅲ) **Loop Duplication**

To create the rhythm for this work, we will loop/repeat some of the sounds...

① Left click on "beat. wav" in track 2. Then right click on it. From the context menu choose "Loop Duplicate" (Figure 4-24).

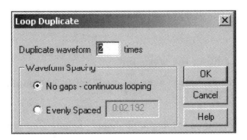

Figure 4-24 Loop Duplicate

② In the dialogue box tell it to repeat 10 times without any gaps. Hit "OK" then. The track will repeat itself 10 times.

③ Double left click on track 2. This will take you to single track mode. Notice that the length of the track is 2.192.

④ Go back to multi track mode by clicking the switch button in the upper left corner.

⑤ Back in Multi Track left click on track 3 "drum. wav". Again choose loop duplicate.

This time however check "Evenly Spaced", and enter 2.192. Click "OK" (Figure 4-25).

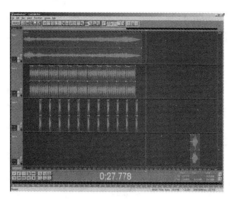

Figure 4-25 Sound Files Duplicated

⑥ On track 3, the last repeat of the sound file "drum.wav" is not needed. Go and click on this instance and hit "Delete" on your keyboard.

⑦ Go to the third instance of "drum.wav" again choose loop duplicate upon right clicking on it and repeat 10 times, but the gaps this time put "1.096". Hit "OK" (Figure 4-26).

Figure 4-26 Finalized Loop Editing

(ⅳ) Editing

We will now complete editing the wave file.

① In track 4 move "moo0.wav" over to it aligns in the middle of the tracks you have created.

② Click on the last instance of track 2 beat. Depending on the tools available open through the View menu, you should have a green line going across the top of the track. Left click on this bar and drag down until the right. This is the volume bar, and will fade-out the last instance of this sound. (Figure 4-27)

Chapter 4 Digital Audio | 99

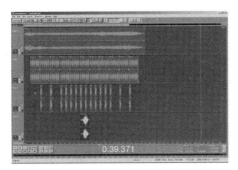

Figure 4-27　Finalized Version

(ⅴ) **Mix Down/Saving**

The final step is to mix down the file and then save it.

① Go to the Edit menu, and then choose "Mix Down", and then "All Waves". Mix Down Menu

② A new Single track will be created that is all the waves from the multi track saved in one stereo file. Click on the File menu, and "Save As". Choose Windows PCM for the file format, then "final. wav" as the file name. (Figure 4-28)

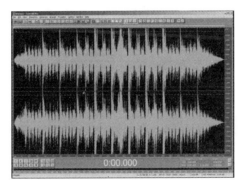

Figure 4-28　Final Mixed File

Part 5　Output of Digital Audio

Audio CD[1] is an umbrella term that refers to many standards of means of playing back audio on a CD.

Compact Discs[2]

A Compact Disc (also known as a CD) (Figure 4-29) is an optical disc used to store digital data, originally developed for storing digital audio. The CD, available on the market since

---

[1]　http://en. wikipedia. org/wiki/Audio_CD

[2]　http://en. wikipedia. org/wiki/Compact_discs

Figure 4-29 The closely spaced tracks on the readable surface of a Compact Disc cause light to diffract into a full visible color spectrum.

late 1982, remains the standard playback medium for commercial audio recordings to the present day.

A Compact Disc is made from a 1.2 mm thick disc of almost pure polycarbonate plastic and weighs approximately 16 grams. A thin layer of aluminum or, more rarely, gold is applied to the surface to make it reflective, and is protected by a film of lacquer. The lacquer is normally spin coated directly on top of the reflective layer. On top of that surface, the label print is applied. Common printing methods for CDs are screen-printing and offset printing.

Table 4-1 Novelty shaped CDs are available in a number of shapes and sizes, and are mostly used for marketing.

Table 4-1 The Shapes and Sizes of CDs

Physical size	Audio Capacity	CD-ROM Data Capacity	Note
12 cm	74—80 min	650—703 MB	Standard size
8 cm	21—24 min	185—210 MB	Mini-CD size (Figure 4-21)
	~6 min	~55 MB	"Business card" size

CD data is stored as a series of tiny indentations (pits), encoded in a tightly packed spiral track molded into the top of the polycarbonate layer. The areas between pits are known as "lands". Each pit is approximately 100 nm deep by 500 nm wide, and varies from 850 nm to 3.5 μm in length.

The spacing between the tracks, the pitch, is 1.6 μm. A CD is read by focusing a 780 nm wavelength (near infrared) semiconductor laser through the bottom of the polycarbonate layer. The change in height between pits and lands results in a difference in intensity in the light reflected. By measuring the intensity change with a photodiode, the data can be read from the disc.

The pits and lands themselves do not directly represent the zeros and ones of binary data. Instead, Non-return-to-zero, inverted (NRZI) encoding is used: a change from pit to land or land to pit indicates a one, while no change indicates a zero. This in turn is decoded by reversing the Eight-to-Fourteen Modulation used in mastering the disc, and then reversing the Cross-Interleaved Reed-Solomon Coding, finally revealing the raw data stored on the disc.

While CDs are significantly more durable than earlier audio formats, they are susceptible to damage from daily usage and environmental factors. Pits are much closer to the label side of a disc, so that defects and dirt on the clear side can be out of focus during playback. Discs consequently suffer more damage because of defects such as scratches on the label side, whereas clear-side scratches can be repaired by refilling them with plastic of similar index of refraction, or by careful polishing. Early music CDs were known to suffer from "CD rot" or "laser rot" where the internal reflective layer itself degrades. When this occurs the CD may become unplayable.

The digital data on a CD begins at the center of the disc and proceeds outwards to the edge, which allows adaptation to the different size formats available. Standard CDs are available in two sizes. By far the most common is 120 mm in diameter, with a 74 or 80-minute audio capacity and a 650 or 700 MB data capacity. This diameter has also been adopted by later formats, including Super Audio CD, DVD, HD DVD, and Blu-ray Disc. 80 mm discs ("Mini CDs") (Figure 4-30) were originally designed for CD singles and can hold up to 21 minutes of music or 184 MB of data but never really became popular.

Figure 4-30 A Mini-CD is 8 Centimeters in Diameter

Today nearly all singles are released on 120 mm CDs, which is called a Maxi single.

The technology was later adapted and expanded to include data storage (CD-ROM), write-once audio and data storage (CD-R), rewritable media (CD-RW), Super Audio CD (SACD), Video Compact Discs (VCD), Super Video Compact Discs (SVCD), PhotoCD, PictureCD, CD-i, and Enhanced CD. CD-ROMs and CD-Rs remain widely used technologies in the computer industry. The CD and its extensions have been extremely successful: in 2004, worldwide sales of CD audio, CD-ROM, and CD-R reached about 30 billion discs. By 2007, 200 billion CDs had been sold worldwide.

DVD-audio[①]

DVD-Audio (commonly abbreviated as DVD-A) is a digital format for delivering high-fidelity audio content on a DVD. DVD-Audio is not intended to be a video delivery format and is not the same as video DVDs containing concert films or music videos. The first discs entered the marketplace in 2000. DVD-Audio was in a format war with Super Audio CD (SACD), another format for delivering high-fidelity audio content. Neither has gained a strong position in the U.S. marketplace.

DVD-Audio offers many possible configurations of audio channels, ranging from single-channel mono to 5.1-channel surround sound(Table 4-2), at various sampling frequencies and sample rates. (The ".1" denotes a Low-frequency effects channel (LFE) for bass and/or special audio effects.)

---

① http://en.wikipedia.org/wiki/DVD-audio

Compared to the compact disc, the much higher capacity DVD format enables the inclusion of either:

- Considerably more music (with respect to total running time and quantity of songs) or
- Far higher audio quality, reflected by higher linear sampling rates and
- Higher bit-per-sample resolution, and/or Additional channels for spatial sound reproduction.

Audio on a DVD-Audio disc can be stored in many different bit depth/sampling rate/channel combinations: (Table 4-2)

Table 4-2 Different Bit Depth/Sampling Rate/Channel Combinations

	16-, 20-or 24-bit depth					
	44.1 kHz	48 kHz	88.2 kHz	96 kHz	176.4 kHz	192 kHz
Mono (1.0)	Yes	Yes	Yes	Yes	Yes	Yes
Stereo (2.0)	Yes	Yes	Yes	Yes	Yes	Yes
Stereo (2.1)	Yes	Yes	Yes	Yes	No	No
Stereo + mono surround (3.0 or 3.1)	Yes	Yes	Yes	Yes	No	No
Quad (4.0 or 4.1)	Yes	Yes	Yes	Yes	No	No
3-stereo (3.0 or 3.1)	Yes	Yes	Yes	Yes	No	No
3-stereo + mono surround (4.0 or 4.1)	Yes	Yes	Yes	Yes	No	No
Full surround (5.0 or 5.1)	Yes	Yes	Yes	Yes	No	No

Different bit depth/sampling rate/channel combinations can be used on a single disc. For instance, a DVD-Audio disc may contain a 96 kHz/24-bit 5.1-channel audio track as well as a 192 kHz/24-bit stereo audio track. Also, the channels of a track can be split into two groups stored at different resolutions. For example, the front speakers could be 96/24, while the surrounds are 48/20.

Audio is stored on the disc in Linear PCM (Linear pulse code modulation (LPCM) is a method of encoding audio information digitally. The term also refers collectively to formats using this method of encoding. The term Pulse-code modulation (PCM), though strictly more general, is often used to describe data encoded as LPCM.) format, which is either uncompressed or losslessly compressed with Meridian Lossless Packing. The maximum permissible total bit rate is 9.6 Megabits per second. Channel/resolution combinations that would exceed this need to be compressed. In uncompressed modes, it is possible to get up to 96/16 or 48/24 in 5.1, and 192/24 in stereo. To store 5.1 tracks in 88.2/20, 88.2/24, 96/20 or 96/24 MLP encoding is mandatory.

The LFE (The low-frequency effect (LFE) channel is the name of an audio track specifically intended for deep, low-pitched sounds ranging from 3-120 Hz.) channel is actually full range, and can be recorded at the same resolution as the other channels. This permits it to be used instead as an extra main channel, for example as a "height" speaker above the listening position; this has been done on some releases. Such usage is non-standard, and will often require special set-up by the end-user.

If no native stereo audio exists on the disc, the DVD-Audio player may be able to downmix the 5.1-channel audio to two-channel stereo audio if the listener does not have a surround sound setup (provided that the coefficients were set in the stream at authoring). Downmixing can only be done to two-channel stereo, not to other configurations, such as 4.0 quad. DVD-Audio may also feature menus, text subtitles, still images and video, plus in high end authoring systems it is also possible to link directly into a Video_TS folder that might contain video tracks, as well as PCM stereo and other "bonus" features.

Since the DVD-Audio format is a member of the DVD family, a single disc can have multiple layers, and even two sides that contain audio and video material. A common configuration is a single-sided DVD with content in both the DVD-Video (VIDEO_TS) and DVD-Audio (AUDIO_TS) directories. The high-resolution, Packed PCM audio encoded using MLP is only playable by DVD players containing DVD-Audio decoding capability. DVD-Video content, which can include LPCM, Dolby or DTS material, and even video, makes the disc compatible with all DVD players [4]. Other disc configurations may consist of double layer DVDs (DVD-9) or two-sided discs (DVD-10, DVD-14 or DVD-18). Some labels have released two-sided DVD titles that contain DVD-Audio content on one side and DVD-Video content on the other, the Classic Records HDAD being one such example.

New Words

discrete-time　离散时间
retrieve　*v.* 检索
transducer　*n.* 传感器,变频器;变换器
timestamp　*n.* 时间戳
triode vacuum-tube　三级真空管
polycarbonate　*n.* 聚碳酸酯
aluminum　*n.* 铝,铝质
lacquer　*n.* 漆;(固定发型的)发蜡,定型剂;头发定型剂,喷发胶
　　　　　vt. 涂漆于,给(木制品或金属)涂漆;给(头发)喷发胶
Megabit　*n.* 兆比特
configuration　*n.* 配置

Notes

[1] The digital audio chain begins when an analog audio signal is first sampled, and then (for pulse-code modulation, the usual form of digital audio) it is converted into binary signals—'on/off' pulses—which are stored as binary electronic, magnetic, or optical signals, rather than as continuous time, continuous level electronic or electromechanical signals.

译文:数字音频转换链首先是模拟音频信号取样,然后(一般的数字音频格式脉冲编码调制)转换成二进制信号——"开、关"脉冲,存储为二进制电子信号、磁信号或光信号,

而不是连续的时间信号、连续电子能级信号或机电式信号。

- the digital audio chain begins when an analog audio signal is first sampled... when 引导时间状语从句,也就是模拟信号取样时数字音频转换链开始。
- 'on/off' pulses—which are stored as binary electronic... which 引导定语从句,指代二进制信号,"开、关"脉冲作为插入语解释二进制信号的存在形式。
- rather than 而不是,连词

[2] The general approach towards storing digital audio is to sample the audio voltage which, on playback, would correspond to a certain level of signal in an individual channel with a certain resolution—the number of bits per sample—in regular intervals (forming the sample rate).

译文:数字音频存储的一般方法是音频电压抽样,播放时对应于具有特定分辨率的通道中的某个等级的信号,在固定的时间间隔每个采样的位数形成采样率。

- ... to sample the audio voltage which, on playback, would correspond to a... which 引导定语从句,修饰 the audio voltage。
- correspond to 相应

[3] Sound recording began as a mechanical process and remained so until the early 1920s (with the exception of the 1899 Telegraphone) when a string of groundbreaking inventions in the field of electronics revolutionized sound recording and the young recording industry.

译文:除了1899年录音电话机的出现,录音一直是机械操作的过程,直到20世纪20年代初,电子领域一连串突破性的发明为录音和新兴的唱片业带来了革命性的变化。

- Sound recording began as a mechanical process and remained so... remain so 依然是这样,so 在此是代词,指代录音是一个机械过程。
- until the early 1920s 直到20世纪20年代初,until 引导时间状语。
- the early 1920s when a string of groundbreaking inventions... when 指代20世纪20年代初,引导时间状语从句,译为"在那时"。
- with the exception of... 除……之外

[4] The most recent and revolutionary developments have been in digital recording, with the development of various uncompressed and compressed digital audio file formats, processors capable and fast enough to convert the digital data to sound in real time, and inexpensive mass storage.

译文:随着各种压缩和非压缩数字音频文件格式的发展,数字化录音经历着最新、最革命的发展:能够快速实时将数据转换为数字声音的处理器及廉价的大容量存储。

- with the development of various uncompressed and compressed digital audio file formats... 随着各种压缩和非压缩数字音频文件格式的发展,在此作为插入语,翻译时可放到前面。
- have been 是现在完成时的标志,指的是已经完成和实现的数字录音中最新的最革命的发展。
- in real time 实时

Selected Translation

Part 3

数字音频的获取

电子录音

直到 20 世纪 20 年代初，录音一直是机械操作的过程（而 1899 年录音电话机则是例外）。电子领域一连串突破性的发明对录音和新兴的唱片业带来了革命性的变化。这些变化包括声音传感器：如麦克风和扬声器；各种电子设备，如用来放大声音信号的调音台和用于电子改造声音信号的调音台。

在爱迪生发明留声机之后，可以说在录音领域最重要的进展是 1900 年至 1924 年间由两个美国科学家发明的电子系统。1906 年，李·德·弗雷斯特发明了"三极管"——三极真空管，能够大幅度扩大微弱电子信号的电子阀（电子阀的早期应用是在 1915 年时改进长途电话），后来成为所有电子声音系统的基础直到晶体管的发明。紧接着是由再生电路、超再生电路、超外差收音机接收器电路，所有这些都由年轻的电子学天才埃德温·阿姆斯特朗在 1914 年到 1922 年之间发明并获得专利。阿姆斯特朗的发明提出更高保真度的录音和对现实的再现，促进了电子放大器和许多其他设备的发展。1925 年后，这些系统成为唱片和广播行业的标准。

就在第一次世界大战前阿姆斯特朗发表了对三极真空管基本操作的研究成果之时，发明家奥兰多·R.玛希和他的实验室成员，以及在贝尔电话实验室的科学家，使用三极管作为弱电话线路的中继器。到 1925 年，有可能将此中继器用于纽约和旧金山长途电话，并且在 20 分钟内双方将清楚地听到对方。有了这项技术，来自贝尔电话实验室的约瑟夫·马克思菲尔德和亨利·C.哈里森擅长电路的人工模拟，他们在录音和复制中应用这些原则。他们准备于 1924 年演示他们的研究成果——使用温特冷凝器麦克风和真空管放大器来驱动"橡胶线"同心橡胶管蜡录音以驱动主音频光盘。

与此同时，无线电继续发展。阿姆斯特朗的突破性的发明（包括调频广播）也为远程广播和语音、音乐的高品质无线传输提供了可能。阿姆斯特朗发明的超外差电路的重要性没有被高估——因为直到今天这几乎是所有模拟放大、模拟和数字无线电频率发射器和接收器装置的核心组成部分。

磁带录音

磁带带来了广播和录音产业界广泛的变化。声音可以在同一磁带上被记录、擦除和多次重复录音，声音可以实现磁带到磁带的复制但是质量只有轻微损失，现在唱片可以被很精确地通过完全地剪切和重组进行编辑。在第一个商业录音机引进的几年里，1948 年启动的 Ampex 200 model（第一部磁带录音机），美国音乐家、发明家莱斯·保罗发明了第一个多轨录音机，给唱片业带来了另一场技术革命。磁带使完全通过电子手段首次录音成为可能。

1928 年，弗里茨·波弗劳姆在 1898 年瓦尔德马·普尔生发明的磁线录音的基础上于德国发明了用磁带记录声音。波弗劳姆的发明使用了铁的氧化物（Fe_2O_3）粉末涂纸层。这项发明由生产录音设备的德国电子公司 AEG 和生产磁带的 BASF 公司进一步发展。1933 年,在 AEG 公司工作的爱德华·舒勒开发了环形磁头,前头部设计成针状以切断磁带。这一时期的重要发现是交流偏置技术,它通过增加记录介质的有效线性改进了录制的音频信号的保真度。

自从各种录音机形式发展以来,最显著的是卷到卷式和压缩盒式录音机。

磁带用于录音已超过 75 年,磁带为电台广播和音乐唱片业都带来了革命性的变革,即它给予艺术家和制作者以记录和重新录制音频并实现最小质量损失以及轻松编辑和重新安排录音的能力。现代可供选择的记录技术(转录光碟和金属盘录音机)无法提供接近这一水平的质量和功能。自从一些早期的改进提高了复制的声音的保真度,磁带一直是最高质量记录模拟声音的介质。尽管如此,截至 2007 年,绝大多数的录音均使用数字录音系统并在很大程度上取代了磁带。

数字录音

1982 年,数字化录音机和随后光盘的发明为消费记录的持久保持带来了显著的改善。

随着各种压缩和非压缩数字音频文件格式的发展,数字化录音经历着最新、最革命的发展:能够快速实时将数字数据转换为声音的处理器及廉价的大容量存储。这产生了一种新型的便携式数字音频播放器。1990 年,该迷你型播放机,在小型、价格便宜、可重写的光盘中引入自适应声学转换编码(ATRAC 是由索尼公司专有的音频压缩算法),但是随着固态非易失性闪速存储器的出现(闪存是一种非易失性的计算机存储技术,可以电子擦除和重新编码。它主要用于记忆卡、USB 闪存驱动器)和固态驱动器的价格下降而逐渐过时。随着技术的提高,可以将大量的数据存储在一个单一的媒介中,例如超级音频光盘、音频 DVD、蓝光光盘和高清 DVD,更多的数据和更高质量的文件能够压缩到单一的光盘上。声音文件可随时从互联网或其他来源下载,并复制到电脑和数码音频播放器。从中等品质的音乐文件到苛刻的专业应用,数字音频技术可用于音频的各个领域。新的应用,如互联网广播和播客已经出现。

近几十年,录音和录音编辑技术的发展改变了唱片、电影和电视行业。随着磁带记录的发明,音频编辑具有了可操作性,而数字音频和廉价的大容量存储使得电脑能够快速、方便、便宜地编辑音频文件。今天,录音制作过程包括跟踪、混合和后期编辑。多轨录音使人们从多个麦克风或从不同的声音载体(如磁带或光盘)捕捉声音信号成为可能,并使得声音信号的处理能力和质量达到最大化,从而使混合和后期编辑阶段原先不能灵活使用的编辑、水平均衡、压缩和限制等操作以及添上如混响、均衡、镶边等效果成为可能。

音效库

不同种类的音效库,如 SoundDogs、谷歌音乐、百度 MP3 等。在这些网站中搜索我们可以获得所需的数字音频。

➢ Sounddogs.com

Sounddogs.com 是一个商业性的在线音效库,2010 500 000 种音效和音乐曲目能够迅速下载到硬盘或 CD。下载的格式有:AIFF、WAV 和 MP3。网站于 1997 年 5 月开始提供服务。该网站以洛杉矶、加利福尼亚为根据地,在加拿大、阿根廷、乌拉圭设有办公室。

➢ 谷歌音乐

谷歌音乐中有一个链接是大型的中国流行音乐库(主要是粤语流行音乐和华语流行音乐),包括在谷歌自身的播放器中播放的音频、歌词下载,而且在大多数情况下是合法的 MP3 下载。该音乐库是由 Top100.cn(本服务不搜索整个互联网)提供的,而且只能在中国大陆使用。

➢ 百度 MP3 搜索

百度 MP3 搜索提供算法生成与歌曲和由互联网内容提供商提供的多媒体文件的链接。百度搜索可以搜到的文件格式有 MP3、WMA 和 SWF 等。多媒体搜索功能主要用于搜索中国流行音乐。

Exercises

1. What are the differences between the analogy and digital audio?
2. How many major groups of audio file formats and which formats are included in each group?
3. Where can we capture digital audios?
4. What are the main capabilities of Cool Edit Pro?
5. How can we output digital audio?

数的表示与读法

一、数的读法

表示数目多少的数字叫做基数。如 0(zero)、1(one)、19(nineteen)、20(twenty)等。其读法有一些基本规则:

1. 21—99 的基数,先说"几十",再说"几",中间加连字号。如 24(twenty-three)。
2. 101—999 的基数,先说"几百",再加 and,再加末位数。如 156(a/one hundred and fifty-six);但也有不用 and 的情况,如 850 可以读作 eight hundred fifty。
3. 1,000 以上的数,先从后向前数,每三位数加一",",第一个","前为 thousand,第二个","前为 million,第三个","前为 billion(美式)或 thousand million(英式)。如

    1,001   one thousand and one
    284,304   two hundred and eighty-four thousand three hundred and four
    20,654,693   twenty million six hundred and fifty-four thousand six hundred and ninety-three
    850,000,000 eight hundred and fifty million

4. 幂次的读法,如 10^{18} 读作 one followed by eighteen zeros。
5. 注意:hundred、thousand、million、billion、trillion 等词一般是单数形式。如 two hundred、three million、five trillion。

二、序数的读法

表示顺序的数字称为序数,如第一、第二、第三等。序数词一般以与之相应的基数词加词尾 th 构成,如 fourth(第四),但也有特别的地方,主要表现在以下几方面:

1. one—first; two—second; three—third; five—fifth; eight—eighth; nine—ninth; twelve—twelfth 等。

2. 以 -ty 结尾的词,要先变 y 为 i,再加 -eth,如:twenty—twentieth; forty—fortieth 等。

3. 以 one、two、three、five、eight、nine 收尾的序数词,要按照第一条办法变,如

thirty-one—thirty-first   eighty-two—eighty-second
fifty-three—fifty-third   ninety-five—ninety-fifth
two hundred and fifty-nine   two hundred and fifty-ninth

4. 序数词有时用缩略形式,如:first(1st); second(2nd); fourth(4th); twenty-third(23rd); two hundred and thirty-fifth(235th)。

5. 序数词表示顺序时,前面常加定冠词,如:The First World War, the third lesson。

三、分数的读法

分数由分子、分母和分数线组成。在英语中,一般用基数词代表分子,序数词代表分母,除了分子是"1"的情况外,序数词都要用复数。如:

$\frac{1}{2}$ One half

$\frac{1}{3}$ One third

$\frac{3}{5}$ Three fifth

$\frac{1}{29}$ One twenty-ninths

$\frac{3}{178}$ Three over one hundred seventy-eight

$4\frac{2}{7}$ Four and two-sevenths

$45\frac{23}{89}$ Forty-five and twenty-three over eighty-nine

当然,还有一些其他的读法,如 $\frac{1}{2}$(one by two 或者 one over two)。

四、小数的读法

小数由三部分组成,即整数位区、小数位区和小数点。整数部分按照基数读,小数部分的表达需分别读出每个数,小数点读作 point。

1. 整数位区不为零的小数称为混合小数。其读法是整数区按照整数的读法,小数点之后的数字按照小数的读法。如 3.576,读作 three point five seven six。又如 2,050.0357,

读作 two thousand and fifty point zero three five seven。

2. 若小数的整数位为零，如 0.45，读作 zero point four five 或 point four five。

3. 若小数是 0.1、0.01、0.001 等，则可读作 one tenth、one hundredth、one thousandth 或 point one、point zero one、point zero zero one。

4. 小数可分为非循环小数和循环小数。如 0.37 读作 zero point three seven recurring；0.2537 读作 zero point two five thirty-seven recurring。

5. 小数有时候需要作四舍五入的近似，如要把 483579 四舍五入到万位，即可得 480,000，英文中读法为：Round off 483,579 to nearest ten thousand。

常用的数学名词

在数字媒体学科文献中，虽然用到数学表达式不多，但当我们在阅读遇到时，大多数不知不觉都会变成汉语语调，例如 $f=1/2\pi$、$\sqrt{LC}$ 如何读才合适？特别在参加演讲、谈判与学术活动中就显得特别重要。因此，有必要了解对基本数字、数学表达式和符号的英语表达。

由于数学学科本身就是一个大的基础学科，包含的内容极为广泛，如数学专业就有数学专业英语，我们在此仅仅总结最基础的数学词汇供大家参考。

一、数的分类

复数、虚数	complex numbers and pure imaginary numbers
实数	real numbers
有理数、无理数	relational numbers and irrational numbers
分数、小数	rractions and decimals
自然数、零	natural numbers and zero
整数、负整数	integers and negatives of natural numbers
奇数、偶数	odd numbers and even
基数、序数	cardinal and ordinal numbers
近似数	approximate numbers
有效数	significant digits

二、常见的数学名词

加法	addition	比例	proportion
减法	subtraction	幂	powers
乘法	multiplication	对数	logarithms
除法	division	根	roots

根号	radical sign	开方	root-extracting
符号	sign	函数	function
括号	the signs of grouping	区间	intervals
小括号（ ）	the parenthesis	矩阵	matrix
中括号 [ ]	the bracket	定义	definition
大括号	the brace	定理	theorem
排列	permutations	引理	lemma
组合	combinations	线、角	line and angle
微分	differentials	相交线、平行线	intersecting line and parallel line
积分	integrals		
等号	signs of equality	三角形、四边形与多边形	triangles, quadrilateral and polygons
不等号	signs of inequality		
小于	be less than	矩形、菱形与正方形	rectangles, lozenges and squares
大于	be greater than		
方程	equation	圆、弧	circle and arc
不等式	inequality	周长	perimeter
多项式	polynomial	面积	area
绝对值	absolute value	直径	diameter
乘方	powers	体积	volume

数学公式的表示与读法

一、基本运算符号

A + B = C	A plus B equals C
A − B = C	A minus B equals C
A × B = C	A multiplied by B equals C
A / B = C	A divided by B equals C
A : B	The ratio of A to B
A : B = C : D	A is to B of A to B as C is to D
0.3%	Zero point three percent
x^2	x squared
x^3	x cubed
x^4	x to the fourth power
$x^{\frac{1}{2}}$	x to the one-half power
$e = 1.6 \times 10^{-19}$	e equals one point six multiplied by ten to minus nineteenth power
$\sqrt{x}$	The square root of x

$\sqrt[3]{x}$	The cube of x
$\sqrt[x]{x}$	The nth root of x
A = B	A equals B
A ≡ B	A is identical with B; A is equivalent to B
A ≠ B	A is not equal to B
A ≈ B	A be approximately equal to B
A > B	A is greater than B
A < B	A is less than B
A ≥ B	A is greater than or equal to B
A ≪ B	A is far less than B

二、简单函数

f(x)	Function of x
f(x) = ax^2 + bx + c	The function of x equals a times the square of x plus b times x plus c
|a| = b	The absolute value of a equals that of b
Max f(x)	The maximum value of f(x)
Min f(x)	The minimum value of f(x)
$a_n \to \infty$	A sub n approaches / tends to infinity
lim b	The limit of b
$\lim_{n \to \infty} S_n = \frac{1}{3}$	The limit of Sn as n gets arbitrarily large is one third
(A + B)C	The quantity A plus B times C
$\frac{x^5 + A}{(x^2 + B)^2}$	x to the fifth power plus A over (divided by) the quantity x squared plus B, to the two-thirds power
logx	Log of x
log$_2$x	Log of x to the base two

Chapter 5 Digital Video

▲ Knowledge Objectives

When you have completed this unit, you will be able to:
- Define digital video.
- List the formats of digital video.
- State the capture, processing and output of digital video.

▲ Professional Terms

bitmap	位图
compatibility	兼容性
DVE	数字特技
horizontal	水平的
interlaced scan	隔行扫描
LCD	液晶显示屏
object-oriented	面向对象的
optical disc	光盘
pixel	像素
progressive scan	逐行扫描
resolution	分辨率
sensor	传感器
TBC	时基校正器
vertical	垂直的,直立的

Part 1 Outline of Digital Video[1]

Digital video is a type of video recording system that works by using a digital rather than an analog video signal. The terms camera, video camera, and camcorder are used interchangeably in this article.

---

[1] http://en.wikipedia.org/wiki/Digital_video

History

Starting in the late 1970s to the early 1980s, several types of video production equipment such as time base correctors (TBC) and digital video effects (DVE) units (two of the latter being the Ampex ADO, and the NEC DVE) were introduced that were operated by taking a standard analog video input and digitizing it internally[1]. This made it easier to either correct or enhance the video signal, as in the case of a TBC, or to manipulate and add effects to the video, in the case of a DVE unit. The digitized and processed clip from these units would then be converted back to standard analog video.

Later on in the 1970s, manufacturers of professional video broadcast equipment, such as Bosch (through their Fernseh division), RCA, and Ampex developed prototype digital videotape recorders in their research and development labs. Bosch's machine used a modified 1 "Type B transport, and recorded an early form of CCIR 601 digital video. None of these machines from these manufacturers were ever marketed commercially, however.

Digital video was first introduced commercially in 1986 with the Sony D-1 format, which recorded an uncompressed standard definition component video signal in digital form instead of the high-band analog forms that had been commonplace until then[2]. Due to the expense, D-1 was used primarily by large television networks. It would eventually be replaced by cheaper systems using compressed data, most notably Sony's Digital Betacam, still heavily used as a field recording format by professional television producers that made it in studios at their company[3].

One of the first digital video products to run on personal computers was PACo: The PICS Animation Compiler from The Company of Science & Art in Providence, RI, which was developed starting in 1990 and first shipped in May 1991. PACo could stream unlimited-length video with synchronized sound from a single file on CD-ROM. Creation required a Mac; playback was possible on Macs, PCs, and Sun Sparcstations. In 1992, Bernard Luskin, Philips Interactive Media, and Eric Doctorow, Paramount Worldwide Video, successfully put the first fifty videos in digital MPEG 1 on CD, developed the packaging and launched movies on CD, leading to advancing versions of MPEG, and to DVD.

QuickTime, Apple Computer's architecture for time-based and streaming data formats appeared in June, 1991. Initial consumer-level content creation tools were crude, requiring an analog video source to be digitized to a computer-readable format. While low-quality at first, consumer digital video increased rapidly in quality, first with the introduction of playback standards such as MPEG-1 and MPEG-2 (adopted for use in television transmission and DVD media), and then the introduction of the DV tape format allowing recording direct to digital data and simplifying the editing process, allowing non-linear editing systems to be deployed cheaply and widely on desktop computers with no external playback/recording equipment needed[4]. The widespread adoption of digital video has also drastically reduced the bandwidth needed for a high definition television signal (with HDV and AVCHD, as well as several commercial variants such as DVCPRO-HD, all using less bandwidth than a standard definition analog signal) and Tapeless camcorders based on flash memory and often a variant of MPEG-4[5].

Overview of Basic Properties

Digital video comprises a series of orthogonal bitmap digital images displayed in rapid succession at a constant rate. In the context of video these images are called frames. We measure the rate at which frames are displayed in frames per second (FPS).

Since every frame is an orthogonal bitmap digital image it comprises a raster of pixels. If it has a width of W pixels and a height of H pixels we say that the frame size is W × H.

Pixels have only one property, their color. The color of a pixel is represented by a fixed amount of bits. The more bits the more subtle variations of colors we can reproduce. This is called the color depth (CD) of the video.

An example video can have a duration (T) of 1 hour (3600 sec), a frame size of 640 × 480 (W × H) at a color depth of 24 bits and a frame rate of 25 fps. This example video has the following properties:

pixels per frame = 640 * 480 = 307,200

bits per frame = 307,200 * 24 = 7,372,800 = 7.37 Mbits

bit rate (BR) = 7.37 * 25 = 184.25 Mbits/sec

video size (VS)[3] = 184 Mbits/sec * 3600 sec = 662,400 Mbits = 82,800 Mbytes = 82.8 Gbytes

The most important properties are bit rate and video size. The formulas relating those two with all other properties are:

BR = W * H * CD * FPS

VS = BR * T = W * H * CD * FPS * T

(units are: BR in bits/sec, W and H in pixels, CD in bits, VS in bits, T in seconds)

While some secondary formulas are:

pixels per frame = W * H

pixels per second = W * H * FPS

bits per frame = W * H * CD

Technical Overview

Digital video cameras come in two different image capture formats: interlaced and progressive scan. Interlaced cameras record the image in alternating sets of lines: the odd-numbered lines are scanned, and then the even-numbered lines are scanned, then the odd-numbered lines are scanned again, and so on. One set of odd or even lines is referred to as a "field", and a consecutive pairing of two fields of opposite parity is called a frame.

A progressive scanning digital video camera records each frame as distinct, with both fields being identical. Thus, interlaced video captures twice as many fields per second as progressive video does when both operate at the same number of frames per second.

Progressive scan camcorders are generally more desirable because of the similarities they share with film. They both record frames progressively, which results in a crisper image. They can both shoot at 24 frames per second, which results in motion strobing (blurring of the subject when fast movement occurs). Thus, progressive scanning video cameras tend to be more expensive than their interlaced counterparts. (Note that even though the digital video format only allows for 29.97 interlaced frames per second [or 25 for PAL], 24 frames per second progressive video is possible through a technique called 3:2 pulldown)

Standard film stocks such as 16 mm and 35 mm record at 24 frames per second. For video, there are two frame rate standards: NTSC, and PAL, which shoot at 30/1.001 (about 29.97) frames per second and 25 frames per second, respectively.

Digital video can be copied with no degradation in quality. No matter how many generations a digital source is copied, it will be as clear as the original first generation of digital footage.

Digital video can be processed and edited on an NLE, or non-linear editing station, a device built exclusively to edit video and audio. These frequently can import from analog as well as digital sources, but are not intended to do anything other than edit videos. Digital video can also be edited on a personal computer which has the proper hardware and software. Using an NLE station, digital video can be manipulated to follow an order, or sequence, of video clips.

More and more, videos are edited on readily available, increasingly affordable hardware and software. Even large budget films, such as Cold Mountain, have been edited entirely on Apple's Final Cut Pro.

Regardless of software, digital video is generally edited on a setup with ample disk space. Digital video applied with standard DV/DVCPRO compression takes up about 250 megabytes per minute or 13 gigabytes per hour.

Digital video has a significantly lower cost than 35 mm film, as the digital tapes can be erased and re-recorded multiple times. Although the quality of images can degrade minimally each time a section of digital video tape is viewed or re-recorded, as is the case with MiniDv tapes, the tape stock itself is very inexpensive — about $3 for a 60 minute MiniDV tape, in bulk, as of December, 2005. Digital video also allows footage to be viewed on location without the expensive chemical processing required by film. By comparison, 35 mm film stock costs about $1000 per minute, including processing.

Digital video is used outside of movie making. Digital television (including higher quality HDTV) started to spread in most developed countries in early 2000s. Digital video is also used in modern mobile phones and video conferencing systems. Digital video is also used for Internet distribution of media, including streaming video and peer-to-peer movie distribution.

Many types of video compression exist for serving digital video over the internet, and onto DVDs. Although digital technique allows for a wide variety of edit effects, most common is the hard cut and an editable video format like DV-video allows repeated cutting without loss of quality, because any compression across frames is lossless. While DV video is not compressed beyond its own codec while editing, the file sizes that result are not practical for delivery onto optical discs or over the internet, with codecs such as the Windows Media format, MPEG2, MPEG4, Real Media, the more recent H.264, and the Sorenson media codec. Probably the most widely used formats for delivering video over the internet are MPEG4 and Windows Media, while MPEG2 is used almost exclusively for DVDs, providing an exceptional image in minimal size but resulting in a high level of CPU consumption to decompress[6].

While still images can have any number of pixels the video community defines one standard for resolution after the other and notwithstanding the devices use incompatible resolutions and insist on their resolution and rescale a video several times from the sensor to the LCD. Anamorph still images are the result of technical limitations while anamorph videos can be result of standardization aberrations. As of 2007, the highest resolution demonstrated for digital video generation is 33 megapixels (7680 x 4320) at 60 frames per second ("UHDV"), though this has only been demonstrated in special laboratory settings. The highest speed is attained in industrial and scientific high speed cameras that are capable of filming 1024x1024 video at up to 1 million frames per second for brief periods of recording.

Part 2   Formats of Digital Video[①]

Digital video is becoming a more important player for custom installers. The growth of media centers, movie downloads and other digital media make it a necessity for integrators to understand the various types of digital video formats available today.

In this primer from TechLore, we take a look at seven of the most frequently-encountered video formats circulating the web and the digital home entertainment circuit: MPG, AVI, MOV, ASF, WMV, RM and FLV (Figure 5-1).

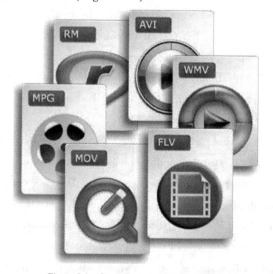

Figure 5-1   Some Formats of Digital Video

---

① http://www.cepro.com/article/the_ultimate_guide_to_digital_video_formats/D1/

MPG (MPEG)

MPG stands for Moving Picture Experts Group (driven by Microsoft's early need to force every file into a three-letter extensionbox, MPEG has evolved by dropping the "E" to become MPG). So, technically, MPG is more of a title than a file format. Even so, it has shifted in meaning as the file extension standards created by that group as well.

MPG is very popular in the video world. And there are a number of MPG formats that you should consider-all with different purposes. With MPEG-1 you get poor video quality, in some situations, no better than VHS. The next generation of MPEG technology is MPEG-2, which is used by most TV stations. MPEG-2 technology is also the compression format behind DVD, as well as the ATSC standard for broadcast HDTV. However, it's best to focus on the most recent evolution of the format: MPEG-4 (commonly known as MP4 or m4v). This format deals with a much better picture quality.

MPEG-4 absorbs many of the features of MPEG-1 and MPEG-2 and other related standards, and adds new features such as (extended) VRML support for 3D rendering, object-oriented composite files (including audio, video and VRML objects), support for externally-specified Digital Rights Management and various types of interactivity.

It is also streamable and supports most multimedia content. It is used by iTunes and with the iPod, as well as often being the most commonly used file format for sharing videos over the Internet.

AVI

The acronym AVI comes from Audio Video Interleave. AVI is not complex in its storage or operations, making it the "go to" video format, with the ability to be played on most any media player.

It is often used as a container video format by compression codecs such as Xvid and Divx. AVI is so versatile, that it can be a container for practically any video file. It was created by Microsoft. However, you need to make sure you are running the right codec, or you won't get the video quality, audio quality, or both (depending on what the problem is and which codec you don't have).

Despite its limitations and the availability of more modern container formats (such as QuickTime and MP4), AVI remains popular among file-sharing communities, due to its high compatibility with existing video editing and playback software like WMP.

MOV

The MOV file extension was created by Apple as a means to store and play video files. MOV files are often used to store videos due to its awesome compression ability. Videos created from a number of digital cameras are automatically stored in MOV format.

MOV is compatible with both Windows and Mac platforms. However, this file can only be played on QuickTime Player. It can be converted to another file format, but that can be a pain.

ASF

ASF (short for Advanced Systems Format) is similar to AVI in that it was created by Microsoft and is a container format which makes use of various codecs as a means of file compression.

ASF files can only be played using WMP, which can be a pain for those who use another media player, such as RealPlayer (RP) or iTunes.

ASF is most often used for steaming media, because you can begin viewing the video before it has completed streaming. For those who have no use for ASF, but have too many ASFs as files, try Total Movie Converter to transform your ASF file to another type you are more prone to use.

WMV

Very similar to ASF, WMV (Windows Media Video) is for all practical purposes an ASF file, only with a specific codec—the WMV codec.

So don't try to run this file extension on anything other than WMP or RealPlayer-it will probably fail miserably. WMV files, although not as high in video quality as a MP4 in my opinion, are still not too shabby.

They are arguably the most popular and widely used streaming media format on the Internet (maybe neck and neck presently with FLV).

Real Media

One of the other media players out there is RealPlayer (RP), which we have touched on in the previous section. RP has a specific file extension which runs exclusively on its player. RealVideo is usually paired with RealAudio and packaged in a RealMedia (.rm) container.

RealMedia is suitable for use as a streaming media format, which is viewed while it is being sent over the network. Streaming video can be used to watch live television, since it does not require downloading the video in advance.

FLV

When you click on a Web page and see a video playing on that page (whether it be an intro video, advertisement, or entertaining video), you are seeing a FLV in action. Flash videos are viewed on the Internet using Adobe Flash Player.

Flash videos are composed of complex codecs, but the video quality is very good (especially Adobe Flash Player 9) if you have an up-to-date PC or notebook. Also, if you happen to have a fairly slow Internet connection, the video quality will suffer because the FLV file is transferred through the Web to your computer bit by bit, literally.

On the other hand, FLV files work fairly good streaming over the web, and can be played by pretty much any media player created. Adobe Flash Player is practically universally accepted.

Part 3　Capture of Digital Video

DV[①]

DV is the abbreviation of Digital Video. Compared with traditional video camera, the big-

---

① http://baike.baidu.com/view/5529.htm

Chapter 5 Digital Video 119

gest difference of them is that DV have a screen allowing users to browse pictures in time. It is called a digital camera screen. It is generally Liquid Crystal Display (LCD). Currently the size of the LCD of digital cameras is 2.5 or 3 inches. It is very expensive and fragile, so it usually need maintenance work and users must be careful when using (Figure 5-2).

Figure 5-2   The Panasonic Camera Using Disc as Storage Medium

Compared with analog camera, DV has some prominent characteristics, such as high resolution, more pure color, nondestructive copy, small in size and light in weight and so on.

According to a storage medium, DV can be divided roughly into four categories: Hard Disk, Disc, DV Band and Memory Card.

Video Library[1]

Video Library collects thousands of different types of Videos and is easy to be searched, such as Yahoo video library (Figure 5-3).

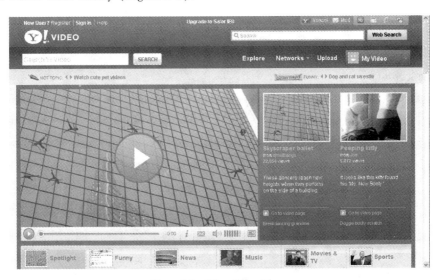

Figure 5-3   Yahoo Video Library

---

[1] http://video.google.cn/? hl = zh-CN&tab = wv

HyperCam 3 [1]

Figure 5-4   HyperCam 3

HyperCam 3 is a new version of the famous HyperCam, being jointly developed with Hyperionics LLC. It is an advanced utility for capturing screen actions and saving them as .AVI files. Though HyperCam may be used just for grabbing a movie or game, it has been chiefly acknowledged as an excellent tool for creating video presentations, tutorials or demo-clips. Stylish, intuitive and user-friendly interface, pre-defined hot-keys for recording actions, built-in video editor, comprehensive text notes workflow, various settings, command line interface, small installation size and more than affordable price—that is what makes HyperCam 3 a must-have tool (Figure 5-4).

Features:

- Saving captured data to AVI files
- Encoding video/audio with codecs presented on PC
- Editing captured AVI files with K-Frame accuracy (trim and join)
- Comprehensive screen notes workflow

Part 4   Processing of Digital Video

VideoStudio [2]

VideoStudio follows a step-by-step paradigm that lets you easily capture, edit, and share your video. VideoStudio also offers more than a hundred transition effects, professional titling capabilities and simple soundtrack creation tools. Learn in seconds, create in minutes.

To make a movie production, first capture footage from a camcorder or another video source. You can then trim the captured videos, arrange their order, apply transitions, and add overlays, animated titles, voiceover narration, and background music. These elements are organized in separate tracks. Changes to one track do not affect other tracks (Figure 5-5).

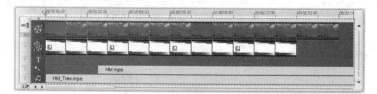

Figure 5-5   Components of a Project as Displayed in Timeline View

---

[1] http://www.solveigmm.com/? Products&id = HyperCam
[2] http://www.ulead.com/vs/vstudio.pdf

A movie production is in the form of a VideoStudio project file (* . VSP), which contains information on the path location of the clips and how the movie has been put together. After you have finished your movie production, you can burn it to a VCD, DVD, HD DVD or record the movie back to your camcorder. You can also output your movie as a video file for playback on the computer. VideoStudio uses the information in the video project file to combine all the elements in your movie into a video file. This process is called rendering.

1. Getting Started

When you run VideoStudio, a startup screen appears which allows you to choose between the following video editing modes:

(i) **VideoStudio Editor** (Figure 5-6) gives you the full editing features of VideoStudio. It provides you total control over the movie production process, from adding clips, titles, effects, overlays, and music to making the final movie on disc or other medium.

Figure 5-6 VideoStudio Editor

(ii) **Movie Wizard** (Figure 5-7) is ideal for users who are new to video editing. It guides you through the movie production process in three quick, easy steps.

Figure 5-7　Movie Wizard

(iii) **DV-to-DVD Wizard** (Figure 5-8) allows you to capture video, add a theme template to it, then burn it onto a disc.

Figure 5-8　DV-to-DVD Wizard

2. Capture

The bulk of video work involves working with raw footage. Transferring footage from a source device to the computer involves a process called capturing.

When capturing, video data is transferred from a source (usually a video camera) through a capture card to the computer's hard drive (Figure 5-9).

Figure 5-9   The Capture Devices of Video

VideoStudio lets you from DV or HDV camcorders, analog camcorders, VCRs, and television. The steps on how to capture is similar for all types of video sources except for the available capture settings in the Capture Video Options Panel that can be selected for each type of source.

In addition to video, VideoStudio also allows you to capture still images. The image format can be BMP or JPEG, and the size depends on its source video. To choose your image format, click File: Preferences. In the Preferences dialog box click the Capture tab and set the format.

3. Edit

The Edit Step is where you arrange, edit and trim the video clips used in your project. In this step, you can apply fade-in/fade-out effects to the existing audio of a video clip, multi-trim or split video, and adjust a clip's playback speed. You can also choose from a wide selection of video filters to apply to your clips.

4. Effect

Transition effects make your movie smoothly change from one scene to the next. They are applied between clips in the Video Track and their attributes can be modified in the Options Panel. Effective use of this feature can add a professional touch to your movie (Figure 5-10 to Figure 5-12).

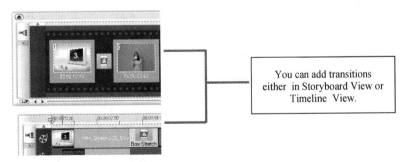

Figure 5-10   Adding Transitions

Figure 5-11   The Flashback Transition

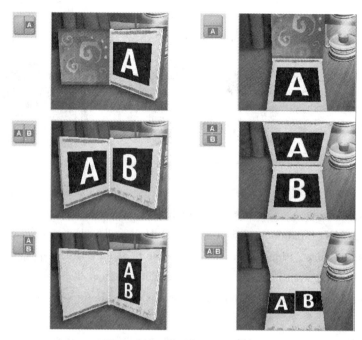

Figure 5-12　The Album Transition

Figure 5-13　The Mask Transitions

5. Overlay

The Overlay Step allows you to add overlay clips to combine with your videos in the Video Track. Use an overlay clip to create a picture-in-picture effect or add a lower-third graphic to create more professional-looking movie productions.

Drag media files to the Overlay Track on the Timeline to add them as overlay clips for your project (Figure 5-14).

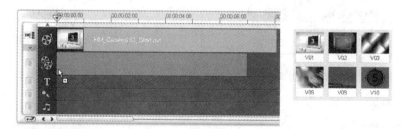

Figure 5-14　Overlay Clips

(i) Title

While a picture may be worth a thousand words, the text in your video production (i.e., subtitles, opening and closing credits, etc.) adds to the clarity and comprehensibility of your movie. In VideoStudio's Title Step, create professional-looking titles, complete with special effects, in minutes.

(ii) **Adding text**

Ulead VideoStudio allows you to add text either in multiple text boxes or in a single text box. Using multiple text boxes gives you the flexibility to position the different words of your text anywhere on the video frame and allows you to arrange the stacking order of the text. Use a single text box when you are creating opening titles and end credits for your projects.

If you switch to Single title before adding to the Timeline the multiple text that you entered, only the selected text or the first text that you typed in (when no text box is selected) will be retained. The other text boxes will be removed and the Text backdrop option will be disabled.

(iii) **Modifying text attributes**

Modify the attributes of your text, such as font face, style, size, and more, by using the available settings in the Options Panel.

More options allow you to set the style and alignment, apply a Border, Shadow and Transparency and add a Text backdrop to your text (Figure 5-15).

Figure 5-15　Modifying Text Attributes

(iv) **Audio**

Sounds are one of the elements that determine the success of your video production. VideoStudio's Audio Step allows you to add both narration and music to your project.

The Audio Step consists of two tracks: Voice and Music. Insert your narrations on the Voice Track and your background music or sound effects on the Music Track.

6. Share

Render your project into a video file format that is suitable for your audience or purpose. You can export the rendered video file as a Web page, multimedia greeting card, or send it to a friend by e-mail. All these and more can be done in VideoStudio's Share Step.

A DVD authoring wizard is also integrated in this step, enabling you to directly burn your project as a DVD, SVCD, or VCD.

Premiere

Adobe Premiere Pro is a high-performance toolset that takes video and audio production to a new level, giving you a professional edge. Delivering frame-accurate control for short-and long-format projects, Adobe Premiere Pro enables you to produce precise results every time.

1. Create projects in a streamlined user interface

Adobe Premiere Pro allows you to arrange clips, view media, and create motion paths with unprecedented ease. In addition, nested timelines allow new methods of displaying footage for complex projects. The capture controls, keyframing features, and media management tools allow you maximum flexibility with your media projects (Figure 5-16).

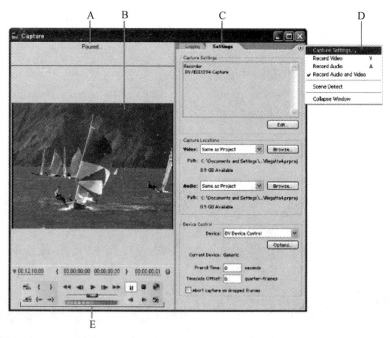

Figure 5-16 Capture window A. Status area B. Preview panel C. Tabs D. Window menu E. Device controls

2. Create projects as part of a larger workflow

Adobe Premiere Pro works with leading Adobe tools such as Adobe After Effects, Adobe Photoshop, and Adobe Encore DVD. It also works effortlessly with processors and video hardware. You can import and export your projects in a variety of formats to suit your needs.

3. Work with enhanced audio capabilities

Take advantage of powerful new audio controls and built-in ASIO and VST support to make your audio punch like never before.

4. Powerful new audio controls

Import and export the highest quality 24-bit, 96 KHz audio files. Edit audio clips at the subframe, audio-sample level with precision up to 1/96,000 of a second with 32-bit floating-point mathematical precision—for example, to remove small pops and crackles. Create and work with multichannel audio to produce surround-sound and other multichannel audio effects.

Record professional voiceovers directly to a timeline as it plays back.

For example, an effect can be applied pre-fader or post-fader, which determines whether the effect is applied before or after the track's fader is applied. Effects are pre-fader by default. Changes you make to effects properties over time can be recorded using the automation options or specified in the Timeline window by using track keyframes (Figure 5-17).

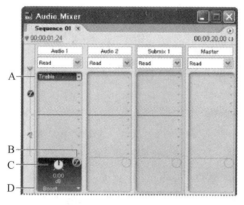

Figure 5-17 Applying Effects to Audio Tracks

5. VST (Virtual Studio Technology) compatibility

Sweeten audio with 17 powerful industry-standard VST plug-ins that come with Adobe Premiere Pro, including Reverb, EQ, Pitch Shift, Dynamics, DeNoiser, and Multiband-Compressor. New VST plug-in support enables you to expand your audio toolkit and use your favorite VST plug-ins with Adobe Premiere Pro. Improve effects and mixing workflow and processing efficiency using sends and submixes.

For example, a submix is a track that combines audio signals routed to it from specific audio tracks or track sends in the same sequence. A submix is an intermediate step between audio tracks and the master track. Submixes are useful when you want to work with a number of audio tracks in the same way. For example, you can use a submix to apply identical audio and effect settings to three tracks of a five-track sequence. Submixes can help make the best use of your computer's processing power by allowing you to apply one instance of an effect instead of multiple instances (Figure 5-18).

Figure 5-18 Choosing a Submix Type in the Audio Mixer Window

6. ASIO (Audio Stream Input/Output) compatibility

Access the multichannel capabilities in a new generation of high-quality sound cards through built-in ASIO support in Adobe Premiere Pro. For information on ASIO, see Setting a track's input source.

For example, when you enable recording for a track, the track can record from the Input/Output Device channel selected in the Audio Hardware Preferences dialog box. This dialog box includes the ASIO Settings button, which lets you enable audio inputs connected to your computer. You can use the track input pop-up menu to choose which channel is routed to a particular track.

7. Adjust color values with ease

Use native YUV processing and three-point color correction to adjust your colors to the needs of your project.

(i) Native YUV processing

Preserve the color values of original DV and other source footage—and improve application performance by avoiding color conversions—with native support for YUV processing.

(ii) Three-point color correction

Make sure shots match, and correct exposure, color-balance, and other jarring errors caused by lighting, cameras, and environment with the new color correction filters in Adobe Premiere Pro. Adjust the hue, saturation, and lightness for highlights, midtones, and shadows; replace a color throughout a clip with a single selection; and more. Use built-in waveforms and vectorscopes to make sure that clips share the same color spectrum and that your color adjustments fall within legal broadcast limits. The Color Corrector uses 32-bit floating-point mathematical precision.

8. Edit with precision

Take advantage of Adobe Premiere Pro's ability to apply transitions to multiple clips. Move clips around easily and work with multiple edit points at once. Then preview how your rendered footage will look before actually rendering it.

(i) Take advantage of editing improvements

Apply transitions on any video track, and automatically apply default transitions to overlapping clips. Overwrite, as well as insert, clips in a single move by dragging and dropping them on a timeline. Remove a group of clips from one area—closing the open gap with a ripple delete—and insert them in another area in a single action. Select and trim multiple edit points at once. Copy and paste noncontiguous clip selections. View live updates in the Trim window, which shows an edit in progress as you're adjusting the clip. Toggle between video-frame-accurate and audio-sample-accurate editing with a single click.

For example, whether you drag clips or use Monitor window controls, you can choose to perform an insert edit or overlay edit. In an insert edit, adding a clip to the sequence forces any clips later in time to shift forward to accommodate the new clip. An insert edit can be compared to splicing a shot into a film sequence. In an overlay edit, adding a clip replaces any frames already in the sequence at the new clip's destination. Overlay edits can be compared to videotape editing, in which you can record over existing material (Figure 5-19 to Figure 5-20).

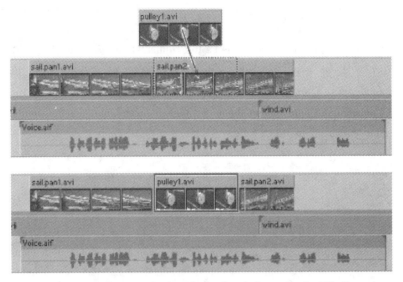

Figure 5-19 Clips before an Overlay Edit (top) and after an Overlay Edit (bottom)

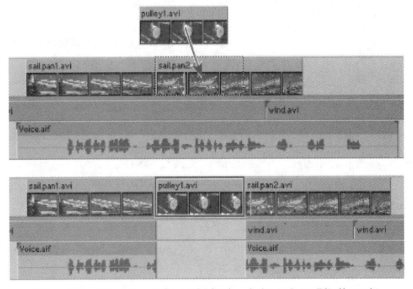

Figure 5-20 Clips before an Insert Edit (top) and after an Insert Edit (bottom)

(ii) **Render-free editing experience**

Play back full-resolution frames, including titles, transitions, effects, motion paths, and color correction on two channels, on screen or on an external video monitor with no additional hardware support required. This new render-free editing experience enables you to see exactly how your work will look, so you can make more rapid edit decisions and ultimately deliver files more quickly.

For example, when you set the Program view's Quality setting to Automatic, Adobe Premiere Pro dynamically adjusts video quality and frame rate in order to preview the sequence in real time. During particularly complex sections of the sequence, or when using a system with inadequate resources, the playback quality degrades gracefully.

Areas that can't be played at the project's full frame rate are indicated by a red line in the time ruler. To play these areas, you can set the time ruler's work area bar over the red preview indicator and render a preview file. This renders the segment as a new file on the hard drive, which Adobe Premiere Pro can play at the project's full frame rate. In the timeline, rendered areas are marked with a green line (Figure 5-21).

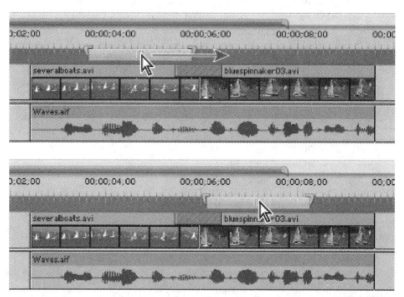

Figure 5-21　Grabbing the Work Area Bar (above) and Dragging it over the Section to Preview (below)

9. Work easily with digital video and export to DVD

Edit DV footage easily and export projects directly to DVD from Adobe Premiere Pro.

(i) **Enhanced DV device control**

Use the new scene-detection controls in Adobe Premiere Pro to divide raw DV footage into scene-based clips. Then, after assembling your rough cut, batch-capture full-resolution versions of only the clips you need.

You can use Adobe Premiere Pro and device control to simplify and automate video capture and to export sequences to tape. Device control lets you precisely control the device and view its source video directly from Adobe Premiere Pro, instead of operating both Adobe Premiere Pro and the controls on the device. With device control, you can use the Capture window to log each clip and then record all logged clips automatically. You can use device control to capture video from or export video to analog or digital video decks or cameras that support device control. Adobe Premiere Pro includes built-in support for DV device control.

(ii) Direct export to DVD

Export projects directly and burn DVDs for distribution of high-quality video content. If a compatible DVD writer is connected to your computer, you can create a DVD directly from a sequence. Adobe Premiere Pro makes the best use of the space available on a DVD by automatically balancing properties such as bitrate and image quality. A DVD you create using Adobe Premiere Pro automatically plays back from the beginning of the disc when inserted in a DVD player. If you want viewers to control the DVD by using a menu of chapters, you must use a DVD authoring program, such as Adobe Encore DVD. Nevertheless, you can still prepare the video using Adobe Premiere Pro and export it in a standard DVD format for use in an authoring program.

Part 5 Output of Digital Video

VCD[①]

Video CD (abbreviated as VCD, and also known as View CD, Compact Disc digital video) is a standard digital format for storing video on a Compact Disc. VCDs are playable in dedicated VCD players, most DVD-Video players, personal computers, and some video game consoles.

The VCD standard was created in 1993 by Sony, Philips, Matsushita, and JVC and is referred to as the White Book standard. In a VCD, the audio and video streams are multiplexed in an MPEG program stream (MPEG-PS) container.

Video CDs are not popular in the US, Canada, Europe, Middle East & Northern parts of Africa, so its support is limited among mainstream software. Windows Media Player prior to version 9 and Quicktime player do not support playing VCD directly, though they can play the DAT files (stored under \MPEGAV for video and audio data) reliably. Windows Vista added native support of VCD like DVD-Video and can launch preferred application upon inserting.

VCD has some similar formats, such as CD-i Digital Video, XVCD, KVCD and DVCD.

1. CD-i Digital Video

Shortly before the advent of White Book VCD, Philips started releasing movies in the Green Book CD-i format. While these used a similar format (MPEG-1), due to minor differences between the standards these discs are not compatible with VCD players. Philips' CD-i players with the Full Motion Video MPEG-1 decoder cartridge would play both formats. Only a few CD-i DV titles were released before the company switched to proper VCD format for publishing movies.

---

① http://en.wikipedia.org/wiki/VCD

2. XVCD

XVCD (eXtended Video CD) is the name generally given to any format that stores MPEG-1 video on a compact disc in Mode 2/XA, at VCD resolution, but does not strictly follow the VCD standard.

A normal VCD is encoded to MPEG-1 at a constant bit rate (CBR), so all scenes are required to use exactly the same data rate, regardless of complexity. However, video on an XVCD is typically encoded at a variable bit rate (VBR), so complex scenes can use a much higher data rate for a short time, while simpler scenes will use lower data rates.

To further reduce the data rate without significantly reducing quality, the size of the GOP can be increased, a different MPEG-1 quantization matrix can be used, the maximum data rate can be exceeded, and the bit rate of the MP2 audio can be reduced (or even the use of MP3 audio instead of MP2 audio). These changes can be advantageous for those who want to either maximize video quality, or use fewer discs.

3. KVCD

KVCD (K Video Compression Dynamics) is a XVCD variant that requires the use of a proprietary-quantization matrix, available for non-commercial use. KVCD is notable because the specification recommends a non-standard resolution of 528×480 or 528×576. KVCD discs encoded at this resolution are only playable by computers with CD-ROM drives, and a small number of DVD players. KVCDs of commercial films are commonly distributed as disc images on peer-to-peer networks.

4. DVCD

DVCD or Double VCD is a method to accommodate longer videos on a CD. A non-standard CD is overburned to include up to 100 minutes of video. However, some CD-ROM drives and players have problems reading these CDs, mostly because the groove spacing is outside specifications and the player's laser servo is unable to track it.

VCD's growth has slowed in areas that can afford DVD-Video, which offers most of the same advantages, as well as better picture quality (higher resolution with fewer digital compression artifacts) due to its larger storage capacity. However, VCD has simultaneously seen significant new growth in emerging economies like India, Indonesia, South America and Africa as a low-cost alternative to DVD. As of 2004, the worldwide popularity of VCD was increasing.

DVD[①]

DVD, also known as Digital Video Disc or Digital Versatile Disc, is an optical disc storage media format, and was invented and developed by Philips, Sony, Toshiba, and Time Warner in 1995. Its main uses are video and data storage. DVDs are of the same dimensions as compact discs (CDs), but are capable of storing more than six times as much data.

---

① http://en.wikipedia.org/wiki/DVD

Variations of the term DVD often indicate the way data is stored on the discs: DVD-ROM (read only memory) has data that can only be read and not written; DVD-R and DVD + R (recordable) can record data only once, and then function as a DVD-ROM; DVD-RW (rewritable), DVD + RW, and DVD-RAM (random access memory) can all record and erase data multiple times. The wavelength used by standard DVD lasers is 650 nm; thus, the light has a red color.

DVD uses 650 nm wavelength laser diode light as opposed to 780 nm for CD. This permits a smaller pit to be etched on the media surface compared to CDs (0.74 μm for DVD versus 1.6 μm for CD), allowing for a DVD's increased storage capacity.

In comparison, Blu-ray, the successor to the DVD format, uses a wavelength of 405 nm, and one dual-layer disc has a 50 GB storage capacity.

Writing speeds for DVD were 1×, that is, 1350 kB/s (1,318 KiB/s), in the first drives and media models. More recent models, at 18× or 20×, have 18 or 20 times that speed. Note that for CD drives, 1× means 153.6 kB/s (150 KiB/s), approximately one ninth as fast.

DVD-Video and DVD-Audio discs refer to properly formatted and structured video and audio content, respectively. Other types of DVDs, including those with video content, may be referred to as DVD Data discs.

1. DVD Recordable and Rewritable

HP initially developed recordable DVD media from the need to store data for backup and transport.

DVD recordables are now also used for consumer audio and video recording. Three formats were developed: DVD-R/RW (hyphen), DVD + R/RW (plus), and DVD-RAM. DVD-R is available in two formats, General (650 nm) and Authoring (635 nm), where Authoring discs may be recorded with encrypted content but General discs may not.

Although most DVD writers can nowadays write the DVD + R/RW and DVD-R/RW formats (usually denoted by "DVD ± RW" and/or the existence of both the DVD Forum logo and the DVD + RW Alliance logo), the "plus" and the "dash" formats use different writing specifications. Most DVD readers and players will play both kinds of discs, although older models can have trouble with the "plus" variants.

2. Dual-layer recording

Dual-layer recording (sometimes also known as double-layer recording) allows DVD-R and DVD + R discs to store significantly more data—up to 8.54 gigabytes per disc, compared with 4.7 gigabytes for single-layer discs. Along with this, DVD-DL's have slower write speeds as compared to ordinary DVD's and when played on a DVD player, a slight transition can be seen between the layers. DVD-R DL was developed for the DVD Forum by Pioneer Corporation; DVD + R DL was developed for the DVD + RW Alliance by Philips and Mitsubishi Kagaku Media (MKM).

A dual-layer disc differs from its usual DVD counterpart by employing a second physical layer within the disc itself. The drive with dual-layer capability accesses the second layer by shining the laser through the first semitransparent layer. In some DVD players, the layer change can exhibit a noticeable pause, up to several seconds. This caused some viewers to worry that their dual-layer discs were damaged or defective, with the end result that studios began listing a standard message explaining the dual-layer pausing effect on all dual-layer disc packaging.

DVD recordable discs supporting this technology are backward-compatible with some existing DVD players and DVD-ROM drives. Many current DVD recorders support dual-layer technology, and the price is now comparable to that of single-layer drives, although the blank media remain more expensive. The recording speeds reached by dual-layer media are still well below those of single-layer media.

There are two modes for dual-layer orientation. With Parallel Track Path (PTP), used on DVD-ROM, both layers start at the inside diameter (ID) and end at the outside diameter (OD) with the lead-out. With Opposite Track Path (OTP), used on many Digital Video Discs, the lower layer starts at the ID and the upper layer starts at the OD, where the other layer ends; they share one lead-in and one lead-out. However, some DVDs also use a parallel track, such as those authored episodically, as in a disc with several separate episodes of a TV series—where more often than not, the layer change is in-between titles and therefore would not need to be authored in the opposite track path fashion.

New Words

analog   *n.* 类似物;模拟 *adj.* 有长短针的;模拟的
interchangeably   *adv.* 可交换地
prototype   *n.* 原型;标准,模范
synchronized   *adj.* 同步化的;同步的
drastically   *adv.* 彻底地;激烈地
orthogonal   *adj.* 正交的;直角的 *n.* 正交直线
crisper   *adj.* 明快的,清晰的;干净利落的;干脆的
counterparts   *n.* 副本;配对物;极相似的人或物
degradation   *n.* 降格,降级;退化;堕落
ample   *adj.* 丰富的;足够的;宽敞的
incompatible   *adj.* 矛盾的;不相容的;不能同时成立的
intuitive   *adj.* 直觉的;凭直觉获知的
abbreviate   *v.* 缩写;节略
dimensions   *n.* 规模,大小
etymology   *n.* 语源,语源学

diameter   *n.* 直径

Notes

[1]   Starting in the late 1970s to the early 1980s, several types of video production equipment, such as time base correctors (TBC) and digital video effects (DVE) units (two of the latter being the Ampex ADO, and the NEC DVE) were introduced that operated by taking a standard analog video input and digitizing it internally.

译文：从 20 世纪 70 年代末到 20 世纪 80 年代初，通过采用标准的模拟视频输入并在内部对其进行数字化处理，人们提出了几种类型的视频生产设备，如：时基校正器（TBC）和数字特效（DVE）（Ampex ADO、NEC DVE 属于后者）。

- Such as time base correctors (TBC) and digital video effects (DVE) units (two of the latter being the Ampex ADO, and the NEC DVE) 作为 several types of video production equipment 的定语从句。

[2]   Digital video was first introduced commercially in 1986 with the Sony D-1 format, which recorded an uncompressed standard definition component video signal in digital form instead of the high-band analog forms that had been commonplace until then.

译文：伴随着索尼 D-1 格式的出现，数字视频于 1986 年首次在商业上被采用。它是以数字形式录制的一种未压缩格式标准定义组件的视频信号，与当时已经司空见惯的高频模拟形式不同。

- Which recorded an uncompressed standard definition component video signal in digital form instead of the high-band analog forms that had been commonplace until then 是定语从句。
- instead of 代替；不是……而是……

[3]   It would eventually be replaced by cheaper systems using compressed data, most notably Sony's Digital Betacam, still heavily used as a field recording format by professional television producers that made it in studios at their company.

译文：它最终会被使用压缩数据的廉价系统所取代，其中最著名的是索尼的数字 Betacam 系统，专业的电视节目制作人在他们公司的工作室大量用其来制作现场录音格式。

- by cheaper systems using compressed data 作状语。
- still heavily used as a field recording format by professional television producers that made it in studios at their company 作定语从句。

[4]   While low-quality at first, consumer digital video increased rapidly in quality, first with the introduction of playback standards such as MPEG-1 and MPEG-2 (adopted for use in television transmission and DVD media), and then the introduction of the DV tape format allowing recording direct to digital data and simplifying the editing process, allowing non-linear editing systems to be deployed cheaply and widely on desktop computers with no external playback/recording equipment needed.

译文：虽然一开始质量比较差，但是消费者层次的数字视频的质量迅速地得到了提高，主要体现在 MPEG-1 和 MPEG-2 等录放标准和 DV 磁带格式的引进，使得数字化的数据可以被直接记录，简化了编辑过程，同时也使得非线性编辑系统可以被编译和广泛地应用于台式电脑，而不再需要外部回放/录音设备。

- While low-quality at first 作让步状语从句。

[5] The widespread adoption of digital video has also drastically reduced the bandwidth needed for a high definition television signal (with HDV and AVCHD, as well as several commercial variants such as DVCPRO-HD, all using less bandwidth than a standard definition analog signal) and Tapeless camcorders based on flash memory and often a variant of MPEG-4.

译文： 广泛采用数字视频也大大降低了对高清电视信号的带宽需要（HDV、AVCHD 以及像 DVCPRO-HD 之类的一些商业化变异等，都使用的是比标准定义的模拟信号更少的带宽），并且无带摄影机通常是闪存和 MPEG-4 的一种变体。

- based on flash memory and often a variant of MPEG-4 作 Tapeless camcorders 的定语。

[6] Probably the most widely used formats for delivering video over the internet are MPEG-4 and Windows Media, while MPEG-2 is used almost exclusively for DVDs, providing an exceptional image in minimal size but resulting in a high level of CPU consumption to decompress.

译文： 或许在网络视频传输中 MPEG-4 和 Windows Media 是用得最广泛的两种格式。而大多数情况下 MPEG-2 格式专门用于 DVD，它能以最小的容量提供优质的图片，但会使 CPU（中央处理器）的消耗增大。

- providing an exceptional image in minimal size but resulting in a high level of CPU consumption to decompress 作定语从句。
- result in 导致，结果是

Selected Translation

Part 1

数字视频概述

数字视频是录像系统的一种类型。它采用的是数字视频信号，而不是模拟视频信号。在本文中 camera、video camera 和 camcorder 这几个术语可交替使用。

历史

从 20 世纪 70 年代末到 20 世纪 80 年代初，通过采用标准的模拟视频输入并对其进行数字化处理，人们提出了几种类型的视频生产设备，如时基校正器（TBC）和数字特效（DVE）（Ampex ADO、NEC DVE 属于后者）。这使更正或增强视频信号变得更加容易，例如在 TBC 中来校正或增强视频信号，或在 DVE 中来对视频进行操作或添加特效。经过这些装置数字化处理的视频会转换回标准的模拟视频。

在 20 世纪 70 年代以后，专业视频播放设备的制造商[如 Bosch（通过 Fernseh 部门）、RCA 和 Ampex]，在它们的研究开发实验室研制数码摄像记录仪的样机。Bosch 的机器使用改进过的 1 英寸 B 型的走带装置，并记录早期的 CCIR 601 数字视频。尽管如此，这些设备都未进行商业应用和推广。

伴随着索尼 D-1 格式的出现，数字视频于 1986 年首次在商业上被采用。它是以数字形式录制的一种未压缩格式标准定义组件的视频信号，与当时已经司空见惯的高频模型形式不同。由于索尼 D-1 费用问题，它最初主要用于大电视台。它最终会被使用压缩数据的廉价系统所取代，其中最著名的是索尼的数字 Betacam 系统，专业的电视节目制作人在他们公司的工作室大量用其来制作现场录音。

最早应用于个人电脑的数字视讯产品是 PACo，它主要是用于动态图片的制作，由位于罗德岛州的科学与技术公司生产，于 1990 年开始研制并在 1991 年 5 月份首次推出。PACo 能从一个单一的文件存储的光盘中流动式地接受无限长的视频，并配以同步的声音。创建需要应用苹果的 Macs，而录音重放则可以在 Macs、个人电脑和 Sun Sparcstations 上实现。在 1992 年，美国菲立普斯互动媒介公司的伯纳德·鲁斯金和派拉蒙国际电影公司的埃里克·多克托罗成功地将 50 个 MPEG-1 格式的视频制成了 CD，并推出了相应的包装和电影，这些对 MPEG 格式的改进和 DVD 的产生起到了推动作用。

QuickTime 出现于 1997 年 6 月，是苹果公司开发的一种基于时间和流数据格式的架构。最初用户水平的内容制作工具是粗糙的，需要将模拟的视频资源数字化，变成一种在计算机上可读的格式。虽然一开始质量比较低，但是给用户设计的数字视频的质量迅速地得到了提高，主要体现在 MPEG-1 和 MPEG-2 等录播标准和 DV 带的引进，使得数字化的数据可以被直接记录，简化了编辑过程，同时也使得非线性编辑系统可以被便宜和广泛地应用于台式电脑，而不再需要外部回放/录音设备。广泛地采用数字视频也大大降低了对高清电视信号的带宽需要（AVCHD、HDV 以及像 DVCPRO-HD 之类的一些商业化变体等，都使用的是比标准定义的模拟信号更少的带宽），并且无带摄像机通常是基于闪存和 MPEG-4 的一种变体。

基本性质的综述

数字视频包括一系列的正交位图数字图像，以一种连续的速率快速地呈现。在视频中，这些图像被称为帧。我们需要估量这些帧呈现的速率，即每秒钟呈现多少帧（FPS）。

由于每帧都是一个正交位图数字图像，是由像素的光栅组成的，那么如果它有一个像素宽度 W 和一个像素高度 H，那么我们就认为它的像素大小为 W×H。

像素只有一个属性，那就是颜色。每个像素的颜色都是通过一定的比特数来表示的。比特数越多，我们能够模拟出更多具有细微变化的颜色。我们将其称为视频的颜色深度（CD）。

假如说现在有这样一个视频：持续时间是一个小时（3600 秒），帧的大小是 640×480（W×H），颜色深度是 24 比特，帧的速率是每秒 25 帧。那么该视频就具有以下的一些属性：

- 每帧的像素 = 640 * 480 = 307,200
- 每帧的比特数 = 307,200 * 24 = 7,372,800 = 7.37Mbits
- 比特率（BR）= 7.37 * 25 = 184.25Mbits/sec
- 视频的大小（VS）= 184Mbits/sec * 3600sec = 662,400Mbits = 82,800Mbytes = 82.8Gbytes

其中最重要的属性是比特率和视频的大小。将这两个属性与其他属性联系起来的公式如下：
- BR ＝ W ∗ H ∗ CD ∗ FPS
- VS ＝ BR ∗ T ＝ W ∗ H ∗ CD ∗ FPS ∗ T

（其中它们的单位分别是：BR 为比特/秒；W 和 H 为像素，CD 为比特，VS 为比特，T 为秒）

其他的一些推导公式包括：
- 每帧的像素 ＝ W ∗ H
- 每秒的像素 ＝ W ∗ H ∗ FPS
- 每帧的比特数 ＝ W ∗ H ∗ CD

技术综述

数字摄影机捕捉图像有两个不同的方式：隔行扫描和逐行扫描。隔行扫描是以交替的行来记录图像的：先扫描奇数行，然后再扫描偶数行，再扫描奇数行，如此反复。一组奇数行或偶数行都是指一个"区域"，两个相对应的奇偶行连在一起就叫做一帧。

逐行扫描的数字摄像机将每一帧单独记录下来，对奇偶行的两个区域采用完全相同的处理方式。因此，当隔行扫描和逐行扫描每秒操作相同数目的帧，隔行扫描虽然扫描两次，但是和逐行扫描每秒扫描的区域是一样大的。

由于隔行扫描和电影的相似性，所以具有逐行扫描功能的摄影机通常应用更广。二者的相似性具体体现在它们都是对帧依次进行扫描，以获得清晰的图像；它们都能力争达到 24 帧/秒，导致动态闪烁（当事物快速移动时会变得模糊不清）。因此，对于同一装置来说，逐行扫描比隔行扫描要贵[值得注意的是虽然数字视频格式仅仅允许每秒 29.97 的帧交错（或者对 PAL 来说是 25 帧/秒），所以通过一种叫做 3:2 的抓片技术进行 24 帧/秒的逐行扫描视频是可以实现的]。

像 16 毫米和 35 毫米之类的标准电影每秒钟可记录 24 帧。对视频来说，它有两种帧速率的标准：NTSC 和 PAL，二者的帧速率分别是 30/1.001（约 29.97）帧/秒和 25 帧/秒。

数字视频可以在不降低质量的情况下被复制。无论被复制多少次，它都可以和最初的数字片段一样清晰。

数字视频可以在非线性编辑系统（NLE）上处理和编辑，它是一个专门用来编辑音频和视频的装置。它们可以像导入数字视频一样导入模拟视频，但是除了视频编辑并不打算用于其他任何地方。数字视频也可以在装有适当的软硬件的个人计算机上编辑。使用非线性编辑系统的话，数字视频可以按照视频剪辑的命令或序列来编辑。

随着软硬件的增多，视频编辑变得更加容易。像《冷山》(*Cold Mountain*)之类拥有较大预算的电影，已经完全用苹果公司的 Final Cut Pro 来编辑。

除了软件，数字视频通常需要在拥有足够磁盘空间的设备上进行编辑。采用 DV/DVCPRO 压缩标准的数字视频需要占用的空间为 250Mb/m 或 13Gb/h。

和 35 毫米的电影相比，数字视频有明显较低的成本。这是因为数字磁带可以被多次抹去后重录。虽然一段数码录像每次被观看或转录时图片的质量都会有最低限度的损坏，就像迷你 DV 的录像带，但这种录像带本身并不贵。2005 年 12 月，在批量购买时一个 60 分钟的迷你 DV 录像带大约需要 3 美元。数字视频也允许在拍摄现场观看录像，这样就免去了处理胶片所需的昂贵的化学药品。相比之下,加上处理费用,一台 35 毫米的电影设备每分钟需要花费 1000 美元。

数字视频可用于除了视频制作以外的其他方面。在 21 世纪初,数字电视(包括高质量的 HDTV),就已经开始在大多数发达国家得到应用。数字视频也可用于现代手机和视频会议系统。数字视频也可用作网络发布的媒介,包括流媒体和对等网络的电影发行。

很多类型的视频压缩是为了适应网络和 DVD 上的数字视频而出现的。虽然数字技术能够实现一系列的视频特效,但是最广泛的还是应用于镜头的硬切和可编辑的视频格式,比如 DV 视频格式,允许重复的剪切,而不会损坏其质量。因为对帧做任何压缩都是无损的。

虽然 DV 视频在压缩时并非超越其自身的解码器,但是如果以 Windows Media、MPEG-2、MPEG-4、Real Media、最新的 H. 264 或者是 Sorenson 之类的编码形式,将其最后的文件大小应用于磁盘或者是上传到网络上是不实际的。或许在网络视频传输中 MPEG-4 和 Windows Media 是用的最广泛的两种格式。而大多数情况下 MPEG-2 格式专门用于 DVD,它能以最小的容量提供优质的图片,但压缩时会占用较大的内存。

虽然图片可以有很多像素,但是在视频领域却针对其分辨率定下了一系列的标准。尽管不同的设备使用的是不相容的分辨率,并且其分辨率不容改变,当一个视频从传感器传送到液晶显示器时需要做多次的调整。静态图片的失真是由于技术的限制所致,而视频的失真却是由于标准的偏差所致。自 2007 年起,主要用于数字视频的最高分辨率是 33 兆像素(7680×4320)、60 帧/秒("UHDV"),尽管它还只是在特殊实验室中被使用。通过商业或科学的高速率摄像机可以获得最高的拍摄速度,在拍摄 1024×1024 大小的视频时其速度可达到每秒 1 万帧的短时期记录。

Exercises

1. What are the differences between the interlaced scan and progressive scan?
2. How many formats of digital video? What are they?
3. What are the differences between the DVD and VCD?

专业英语翻译的标准

翻译是一种语言表达法,是译者根据原作者的思想,用本国语言表达出来。这就要求译者必须确切理解和掌握原著的内容和意思,丝毫不可以离开它而主观地发挥译者个人的想法和推测。在确切理解的基础上,译者必须很好地运用本国语言把原文通顺而流畅地表达出来。

随着国际学术交流的日益广泛,专业英语已经受到普遍的重视,掌握一些专业英语的翻译技巧是非常必要的。专业英语作为一种重要的英语文体,与非专业英语文体相比,具有词义多、长句多、被动句多、词性转换多、非谓语动词多、专业性强等特点,这些特点都是由专业文献的内容所决定的。因此,专业英语的翻译也有别于其他英语文体的翻译。

一、翻译人员必须了解相关专业领域的知识

在专业翻译中,要达到融会贯通,必须了解相关的专业,熟练掌握同一事物的中英文表达方式。单纯靠对语言的把握也能传达双方的语言信息,但运用语言的灵活性特别是选词的准确性会受到很大限制。要解决这个问题,翻译人员就要积极主动地熟悉这个专业领域的相关翻译知识。比如,要翻译"conductor"这个词,仅仅把字面意思翻译出来还远远不够,而且有时用词也不够准确。"conductor"在日常生活中的意思是"售票员和乐队指挥",但在电学中却表示导体的意思。因此,了解了专业领域,在翻译过程中对语言的理解能力和翻译质量就会大大提高。

二、专业英语翻译标准

关于翻译的标准,历来提法很多。有的主张"信、达、雅",有的主张"信、顺",有的主张"等值"等等,并曾多次展开过广泛的争论和探讨。但是,从他们的争论中可以看出,有一点是共同的,即一切译文都应包括原文思想内容和译文语言形式这两个方面;简单地说,符合规范的译文语言,确切忠实地表达原作的风格,这就是英语翻译的共同标准。为此,笔者认为,在进行英语翻译时要坚持两条标准:

1. 忠实

译文应忠实于原文,准确地、完整地、科学地表达原文的内容,包括思想、精神与风格。译者不得任意对原文内容加以歪曲、增删、遗漏和篡改。

2. 通顺

译文语言必须通顺,符合规范,用词造句应符合本民族语言的习惯,要用民族的、科学的、大众的语言,以求通顺易懂。不应有文理不通、逐词死译和生硬晦涩等现象。

三、专业英语翻译过程中要体现语言结构特色

1. 大量使用名词化结构

大量使用名词化结构(Nominalization)是专业英语的特点之一。因为专业文体要求行文简洁、表达客观、内容确切、信息量大、强调存在的事实,而非某一行为。如:

A) Archimedes first discovered **the principle that water is displaced** by solid bodies.

B) Archimedes first discovered **the principle of displacement of water** by solid bodies.

译文:阿基米德最先发展固体排水的原理。

前者显然有一个同位语从句。这样的结构出现在一般的英语文章中。但是在专业文章里,你需要将上述结构转换成名词结构。句中 of displacement of water by solid bodies 系名词化结构,一方面简化了同位语从句,另一方强调 displacement 这一事实。

2. 广泛使用被动语句

专业英语中的谓语至少1/3是被动态。这是因为专业文章侧重叙事推理,强调客观准确。第一、二人称使用过多,会造成主观臆断的印象。因此尽量使用第三人称叙述,采用被动语态,如:

A) **You must measure these levels** in a video studio by two instruments, the waveform monitor and the vectorscope.

B) **These levels must be measured** in a video studio by two instruments, the waveform monitor and the vectorscope.

译文：这些水平必须以数字视频的两种设备来测量：波形监视器和矢量显示器。

在一般英文作文中经常使用主动句，但是在专业文章中，以被描叙的事物充当主语更为常见。但在翻译成中文时应将其还原成主动句并且句子的主语一般不译出。

3. 非限定动词的应用和大量使用后置定语

专业文章要求行文简练，结构紧凑，往往使用分词短语代替定语从句或状语从句；使用分词独立结构代替状语从句或并列分句；使用不定式短语代替各种从句；介词+动名词短语代替定语从句或状语从句。这样可缩短句子，又比较醒目。如：

Live dramatic battles in the mass combat action game **based on the new 3D animated film and TV series Star Wars**：The Clone Wars！

译文：在基于新的3D动画电影和电视系列《星球大战：克隆战争》的大型战斗动作游戏里体验令人激动的战争现场。

短语 **based on the new 3D animated film and TV series Star Wars** 代替了定语从句，使句子简洁紧凑。

又如：

Definition：Streaming technology, **also known as streaming media**, lets a user view and hear digitized content-video, sound and animation-as it is being downloaded.

译文：定义：流式技术，也称流式媒体，让用户在下载时看到和听到下载的数字化内容，包括视频图形、声音和动画。

过去分词结构 **also known as streaming media** 做定语，使句子变得简洁。

4. 大量使用常用句型

科技文章中经常使用若干特定的句型，从而形成科技文体区别于其他文体的标志。例如 It—that 结构句型、被动态结构句型、分词短语结构句型、省略句结构句型等。如：

It is evident that a well lubricated bearing turns more easily than a dry one.

译文：显然，润滑好的轴承，比不润滑的轴承容易转动。

5. 为了描叙事物精确，要使用长句

为了表述一个复杂概念，使之逻辑严密，结构紧凑，科技文章中往往出现许多长句。有的长句多达七八个词。如：

Gobi manages a technology and digital media fund and seeks to work with entrepreneurs developing or applying new technologies along the digital media value chain.

这确实是一个很长的句子，但是在对句子进行分析之后，问题就迎刃而解了。

译文：戈比将数字媒体定义为电信、媒体和科技三者融合而生的新型沟通和通信方式。

6. 大量使用复合词与缩略词

大量使用复合词与缩略词是科技文章的特点之一，复合词从过去的双词组合发展到多词组合；缩略词趋向于任意构词，例如某一篇论文的作者可以就仅在该文中使用的术语组成缩略词，这给翻译工作带来一定的困难。如 full-enclosed 全封闭的（双词合成形容词）。

Chapter 6　Electronic Word

▲ **Knowledge Objectives**

When you have completed this unit, you will be able to:
- Define electronic word.
- List the formats of electronic word.
- State the capture, processing and output of electronic word.

▲ **Professional Terms**

binary files	非正式文件
entropy	熵
hard copy	硬拷贝
impact printer	击打式印刷机
inkjet printer	喷墨打印机
membrane keyboard	薄膜键盘
metadata	元数据
print media	平面媒体

Part 1　Outline of Electronic Word[①]

Perhaps the real question for literary study now is not whether our students will be reading Great Traditional Book or Relevant Modern ones in the future, but whether they will be reading books at all. Our first round of technological perturbation, which pitied the codex book and Culture as we know it against commercial television, didn't turn out as badly as we feared. The print media continued to thrive during TV's great expansion period. And literature continued to be taught in American schools and colleges much as before; students read books and wrote papers and exams about them, which the professors then read, marked up (time and zeal permitting), and returned to the students. Compared so other areas of textual communication in the society around us, literary study has felt almost no pressure from changing technology. This grace period has now been ended by the personal computer and its electronic display of what,

---

① Richard A. Lanham, *The Electronic Word*: Democracy, Technology, and The arts, Chapter One, The Electronic Word: Literary Study and the Digital Revolution.

until a new word is invented, we must call "text."

The literary world, having gingerly learned to manipulate pixeled print ("pixels" are "picture elements", the dots that electronically paint the letters onto the computer screen) through word processing, has found personal computer handy engines to produce printed texts about printed texts. But our thinking has not gone much further than that. Meanwhile, the electronic word has been producing profound changes in the outside world. Some of the billions of dollars American business and government spend to train their employees are being spent in redefining the "textbook"—and, almost in passing, the codex book itself—into an interactive multimedia delivery system. Sooner or later, such electronic "texts" will redefine the writing, reading, and professing of literature as well.

This changed status of the word affects entire range of arts and letters. Digitized communication is forcing a radical realignment of the alphabetic end graphic components of ordinary textual communication. In music, notation, creation, and performance have been transformed. Digitization is substantiating the visual arts. This common digital denominator of the arts and letters forces upon us a rhetoric of the arts like none seen before. And the free marketplace in which the arts and letters live and breathe is being transformed as well, for perhaps the most immediate, certainly the most immediately felt, effect of the electronic word has came in the area of intellectual property. After the technology of the printing press enabled the rapid production of multiple copies of a work, copyright law emerged to establish a market for principle text. In a world of electronic word arid image, literally every fundamental principle of that law, and hence of that marketplace, must be renegotiated. But the most fundamental questions posed for literary study by the electronic word emerge where we would last think to seek them, in our fundamental poetics, and we might begin our survey there.

The interactive reader of the electronic word incarnates the responsive reader of whom we make so much. Electronic readers can do all the things that are claimed for them, or choose not to do them. They can genuflect before the text or spit on its altar, add to a text or subtract from it, rearrange it, revise it, suffuse it with commentary. The boundary between creator and critic (another current vexation) simply vanishes. As dogs the analogous boundary between prose and verse, and, as Richard Ziegfeld has pointed out so perceptively, literary works are being created to exploit this radical interactivity. In interactive fiction, the reader determines the story's outcome by controlling its branching of events. Such decisions amount to literary criticism of a sort in the same way that deploring Nlahum Tate's happy ending of King Lear is an act of critical judgement. Suitably embedded in the fiction, a reader's comments about the plot's decision points become part of the fiction itself. The work snowballs into electronic orality, changes and grows as it moves from one screen and keyboard to another.

Are even the classic printed texts safe from such gymnastics? Imagine growing up as an electronic reader, used to the broad interactive enfranchisements just sketched. How would you feel abut Paradise Lost as presented to you in a codex book? Probably you'd prefer to access it from the CD-ROM disk which, in a few years, will contain all the texts you were asked to reader—or even could read—in your undergraduate career. Wouldn't you begin to play games with it? A weapon in your hands after 2,500 years of pompous pedantry about the Great Books, and you not use it? Hey, man, how about some music with this stuff? Let's voice this rascal and see what happens. Add some graphics and graffiti! Print it our in San Francisco for Luoifer, and Gothic for God. Electronic media will change past literary texts as well as future ones. The electronic word, for both literature and literary history, works both ways.

Part 2　Formats of Electronic Word

Text File[①]

A text file (sometimes spelled "textfile"; an old alternate name is "flatfile") is a kind of computer file that is structured as a sequence of lines. A text file exists within a computer file system. The end of a text file is often denoted by placing one or more special characters, known as an end-of-file marker, after the last line in a text file.

"Text file" refers to a type of container, while plain text refers to a type of content. Text files can contain plain text, but they are not limited to such.

At a generic level of description, there are two kinds of computer files: text files and binary files.

1. Data Storage

Because of their simplicity text files are commonly used for storage of information. They avoid some of the problems encountered with other file formats, such as endianness, padding bytes, or differences in the number of bytes in a machine word. Further, when data corruption occurs in a text file, it is often easier to recover and continue processing the remaining contents. A disadvantage of text files is that they usually have low entropy, meaning that the information occupies more storage than is strictly necessary.

A simple text file needs no additional metadata to assist the reader in interpretation, and therefore may contain no data at all, which is a case of zero byte file.

2. Formats

(i) ASCII

The ASCII standard allows ASCII—only text files (unlike most other file types) to be freely interchanged and readable on Unix, Macintosh, Microsoft Windows, DOS, and other systems. These differ in their preferred line ending convention and their interpretation of values outside the ASCII range (their character encoding).

---

① http://en.wikipedia.org/wiki/Text_file

(ii) MIME

Text files usually have the MIME type "text/plain", usually with additional information indicating an encoding. Prior to the advent of Mac OS X, the Mac OS system regarded the content of a file (the data fork) to be a text file when its resource fork indicated that the type of the file was "TEXT". Under the Windows operating system, a file is regarded as a text file if the suffix of the name of the file (the "extension") is "txt". However, many other suffixes are used for text files with specific purposes. For example, source code for computer programs is usually kept in text files that have file name suffixes indicating the programming language in which the source is written.

(iii) TXT

.txt is a filename extension for files consisting of text usually containing very little formatting (ex: no bolding or italics). The precise definition of the .txt format is not specified, but typically matches the format accepted by the system terminal or simple text editor. Files with the .txt extension can easily be read or opened by any program that reads text and, for that reason, are considered universal (or platform independent).

The ASCII character set is the most common format for English-language text files, and is generally assumed to be the default file format in many situations. For accented and other non-ASCII characters, it is necessary to choose a character encoding. In many systems, this is chosen on the basis of the default locale setting on the computer it is read on. Common character encodings include ISO 8859-1 for many European languages.

Because many encodings have only a limited repertoire of characters, they are often only usable to represent text in a limited subset of human languages. Unicode is an attempt to create a common standard for representing all known languages, and most known character sets are subsets of the very large Unicode character set. Although there are multiple character encodings available for Unicode, the most common is UTF-8, which has the advantage being backwards-compatible with ASCII: that is, every ASCII text file is also a UTF-8 text file with identical meaning[1].

(iv) Standard Windows .txt Files

Microsoft MS-DOS and Windows use a common text file format, with each line of text separated by a two character combination: CR and LF, which have ASCII codes 13 and 10[2]. It is common for the last line of text not to be terminated with a CR-LF marker, and many text editors (including Notepad) do not automatically insert one on the last line.

Most Windows text files use a form of ANSI, OEM or Unicode encoding. What Windows terminology calls "ANSI encodings" are usually single-byte ISO-8859 encodings, except for in locales such as Chinese, Japanese and Korean that require double-byte character sets. ANSI encodings were traditionally used as default system locales within Windows, before the transition to Unicode. By contrast, OEM encodings, also known as MS-DOS code pages, were defined by IBM for use in the original IBM PC text mode display system. They typically include graphical and line-drawing characters common in full-screen MS-DOS applications. Newer Windows text files may use a Unicode encoding such as UTF-16LE or UTF-8.

3. Rendering

When opened by a text editor human-readable content is presented to the user. This often consists of the file's plain text visible to the user. Depending on the application, control codes may be rendered either as literal instructions acted upon by the editor, or as visible escape characters that can be edited as plain text. Though there may be plain text in a text file, control characters within the file (especially the end-of-file character) can render the plain text unseen by a particular method.

DOC (computing)[①]

In computing, DOC or doc (an abbreviation of 'document') is a file extension for word processing documents; most commonly for Microsoft Word. Historically, the extension was used for documentation in plain-text format, particularly of programs or computer hardware, on a wide range of operating systems. During the 1980s, WordPerfect used DOC as the extension of their proprietary format. Later, in the 1990s, Microsoft chose to use the DOC extension for their proprietary Microsoft Word word processing formats. The original uses for the extension have largely disappeared from the PC world.

Binary DOC files often contain more text formatting information (as well as scripts and undo information) than files using other document file formats like Rich Text Format and HyperText Markup Language, but are usually less widely compatible.

The header of a Word 97 document begins with the magic number [0xD0 0xCF 0x11] which possibly spells out "DOC Format 11".

The DOC format varies among Microsoft Office Word Formats. Word versions up to 97 used a different format from Microsoft Word version between 97 and 2003.

In Microsoft Office Word 2007 the binary file format was replaced as the default format by the new XML based Office Open XML format. The filename extensions of this format are .docx or .docm.

The DOC format is native to Microsoft Office Word, but other software, such as the free software word processors OpenOffice.org Writer, and AbiWord, can create and read .doc files. Command line programs for Unix-like operating systems which can convert files from the DOC format to plain text or other standard formats include the wv library, which itself is used directly by AbiWord and as a source of ideas and some coding by KWord. Because the .doc file format was a closed specification for many years, inconsistent handling of the format persists and may cause some loss of formatting information when handling the same file with multiple word processing programs.

---

① http://en.wikipedia.org/wiki/DOC_(computing)

The format specification was available from Microsoft on request until February 2008. Following documentation done by Sun and OpenOffice. org, Microsoft released the . DOC format specification under the Microsoft Open Specification Promise.

On the Palm OS, DOC is shorthand for PalmDoc, a completely unrelated format used to encode text files such as ebooks.

PDF

Portable Document Format (PDF) is an open standard for document exchange. The file format created by Adobe Systems in 1993 is used for representing two-dimensional documents in a manner independent of the application software, hardware, and operating system. Each PDF file encapsulates a complete description of a fixed-layout 2D document that includes the text, fonts, images, and 2D vector graphics which compose the documents. Lately, 3D drawings can be embedded to PDF documents with Acrobat 3D using U3D or PRC and various other data formats.

In 1991 Adobe Systems co-founder John Warnock outlined a system called "Camelot", which evolved into the Portable Document Format (PDF) file-format.

Formerly a proprietary format, PDF was officially released as an open standard on July 1, 2008, and published by the International Organization for Standardization as ISO/IEC 32000-1:2008.

(ⅰ) **Technical Foundations**

Anyone may create applications that can read and write PDF files without having to pay royalties to Adobe Systems; Adobe holds patents to PDF, but licenses them for royalty-free use in developing software complying with its PDF specification.

The PDF combines three technologies:

• A subset of the PostScript page description programming language, for generating the layout and graphics.

• A font-embedding/replacement system to allow fonts to travel with the documents.

• A structured storage system to bundle these elements and any associated content into a single file, with data compression where appropriate.

(ⅱ) **Technical Overview**

1. File Structure

A PDF file consists primarily of objects, of which there are eight types:

- Boolean values, representing true or false
- Numbers
- Strings
- Names
- Arrays, ordered collections of objects
- Dictionaries, collections of objects indexed by Names

- Streams, usually containing large amounts of data
- The null object

Objects may be either direct (embedded in another object) or indirect. Indirect objects are numbered with an object number and a generation number. An index table called the xref table gives the byte offset of each indirect object from the start of the file. This design allows for efficient random access to the objects in the file, and also allows for small changes to be made without rewriting the entire file (incremental update). Beginning with PDF version 1.5, indirect objects may also be located in special streams known as object streams. This technique reduces the size of files that have large numbers of small indirect objects and is especially useful for Tagged PDF.

There are two layouts to the PDF files—non-linear (not "optimized") and linear ("optimized"). Non-linear PDF files consume less disk space than their linear counterparts, though they are slower to access because portions of the data required to assemble pages of the document are scattered throughout the PDF file. Linear PDF files (also called "optimized" or "web optimized" PDF files) are constructed in a manner that enables them to be read in a Web browser plugin without waiting for the entire file to download, since they are written to disk in a linear (as in page order) fashion. PDF files may be optimized using Adobe Acrobat software or pdfopt, which is part of GPL Ghostscript.

2. Imaging Model

The basic design of how graphics are represented in PDF is very similar to that of PostScript, except for the use of transparency, which was added in PDF 1.4.

PDF graphics use a device independent Cartesian coordinate system to describe the surface of a page. A PDF page description can use a matrix to scale, rotate, or skew graphical elements. A key concept in PDF is that of the graphics state, which is a collection of graphical parameters that may be changed, saved, and restored by a page description. PDF has (as of version 1.6) 24 graphics state properties, of which some of the most important are:

- The current transformation matrix (CTM), which determines the coordinate system
- The clipping path
- The color space
- The alpha constant, which is a key component of transparency

3. Interactive Elements

PDF files may contain interactive elements such as annotations and form fields. Interactive Forms is a mechanism to add forms to the PDF file format. PDF currently supports two different methods for integrating data and PDF forms. Both formats today coexist in PDF specification:

- AcroForms (also known as Acrobat forms), introduced in the PDF 1.2 format specification and included in all later PDF specifications.
- Adobe XML Forms Architecture (XFA) forms, introduced in the PDF 1.5 format specification. The XFA specification is not included in the PDF specification; it is only refer-

enced as an optional feature. Adobe XFA Forms are not compatible with AcroForms.

4. Logical Structure and Accessibility

A PDF may contain structure information to enable better text extraction and accessibility. When published, PDF/UA, now ISO/AWI 14289, will provide definitive information on how the contents of PDF files are to be tagged with accurate structure information.

Part 3 Capture of Electronic Word

Keyboard Technology[①]

There are many types of keyboards, usually differentiated by the switch technology employed in their operation. Since there are so many switches needed (usually about 80-110) and because they have to be highly reliable, this usually defines the keyboard. The choice of switch technology affects key response (the positive feedback that a key has been pressed) and travel (the distance needed to push the key to enter a character reliably). Newer models use hybrids of various technologies to achieve greater cost savings (Figure 6-1).

Figure 6-1 Keyboard Construction, in Four Layers, of a Typical Notebook Computer Keyboard

1. Membrane Keyboard

There are two types of membrane-based keyboards: Flat-panel membrane keyboards and full-travel membrane keyboards:

Flat-panel membrane keyboards are most often found on appliances like microwave ovens or photocopiers. Generally, flat-panel membrane keyboards do not have much of a "feel", so many machines which use them issue a beep or flash a light when the key is pressed. They are often used in harsh environments where water or leak proofing is desirable. Although used in the early days of the personal computer (on the ZX80, ZX81 and Atari 400), they have been supplanted by the more tactile dome and mechanical switch keyboards. However, membrane

---

① http://en.wikipedia.org/wiki/Keyboard_technology

keyboards with interchangeable key layouts, such as the IntelliKeys and Discover: board are still commonly used by people with physical, visual, or cognitive disabilities as well as people who require assistive technology to access a computer.

Full-travel membrane-based keyboards are the most common computer keyboards today. They have one-piece plastic keytop/switch plungers which press down on a membrane to actuate a contact in an electrical switch matrix.

2. Dome-switch Keyboard

Dome switch keyboards are a hybrid of flat-panel membrane and mechanical keyboards. They bring two circuit board traces together under a rubber or silicone keypad using either metal "dome" switches or polyester formed domes. Both are common switch technologies used in mass market keyboards today. This type of switch technology happens to be most commonly used in handheld controllers, mobile phones, automotive, consumer electronics and medical devices. Dome switch keyboards are also called direct-switch keyboards (Figure 6-2).

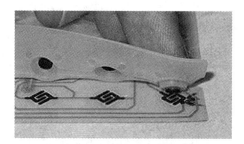

Figure 6-2　How a Dome-switch Keyboard Works: Finger Depresses the Dome to Complete the Circuit Keyboard

3. Scissor-switch Keyboard

A special case of the computer keyboard dome-switch is the scissor-switch. The keys are attached to the keyboard via two plastic pieces that interlock in a "scissor"—like fashion, and snap to the keyboard and the key.

Scissor-switch keyboards are typically slightly more expensive. They are harder to clean (due to the limited movement of the keys and their multiple attachment points) but also less likely to get debris in them as the gaps between the keys are often less (as there is no need for extra room to allow for the 'wiggle' in the key as you would find on a membrane keyboard).

4. Capacitive Keyboard

In this type of keyboard, pressing the key changes the capacitance of a pattern of capacitor pads. Unlike "dome switch" keyboards, the pattern consists of two D-shaped capacitor pads for each switch, printed on a printed circuit board (PC board) and covered by a thin, insulating film of soldermask which plays the role of a dielectric. The mechanism of capacitive switches is very simple, compared to mechanical ones. Its movable part is ended with a flat foam element (of dimensions near to a tablet of Aspirin) finished with aluminium foil below. The opposite side of the switch is a PC board with the capacitor pads.

5. Mechanical-switch Keyboard

Mechanical-switch keyboards use real switches, one under each key. Depending on the construction of the switch, these keyboards have varying responses and travel times. Notable keyboards utilizing this technology are the Apple Extended II, and its modern imitator, the Matias Tactile Pro. These two keyboards use ALPS switches. On PCs, the OmniKey series from Northgate Computers was popular and the line is now carried by Creative Vision Technologies under the Avant brand. Cherry Corporation of Germany also makes mechanical switches used in special purpose and high end keyboards. In India, the TVS Gold mechanical keyboard is very popular despite costing about five times as much as a membrane keyboard.

6. Buckling-spring Keyboard

Many typists prefer buckling-spring keyboards. The buckling spring mechanism (expired U.S. Patent 4,118,611) atop the switch is responsible for the tactile and aural response of the keyboard. This mechanism controls a small hammer that strikes a capacitive or membrane switch.

7. Hall-effect Keyboard

Hall-effect keyboards use magnets and Hall-effect sensors instead of an actual switch. When a key is depressed, it moves a magnet, which is detected by the solid-state sensor. These keyboards are extremely reliable, and are able to accept millions of keystrokes before failing. They are used for ultra-high reliability applications, in locations like nuclear powerplants or aircraft cockpits. They are also sometimes used in industrial environments. These keyboards can be easily made totally waterproof. They also resist large amounts of dust and contaminants. Because a magnet and sensor is required for each key, as well as custom control electronics, they are very expensive.

8. Laser Keyboard

A laser projection device approximately the size of a computer mouse projects the outline of keyboard keys onto a flat surface, such as a table or desk. This type of keyboard is portable enough to be easily used with PDAs and cellphones, and many models have retractable cords and wireless capabilities. However, sudden or accidental disruption of the laser will register unwanted keystrokes. Also, if the laser malfunctions, the whole unit becomes useless, unlike conventional keyboards which can be used even if a variety of parts (such as the keycaps) are removed. This type of keyboard can be frustrating to use since it is susceptible to errors, even in the course of normal typing, and its complete lack of tactile feedback makes it even less user-friendly than the cheapest

Figure 6-3 Most keyboards are rigid, but this foldable keyboard demonstrates one of many variations from the usual.

membrane keyboards.

9. Roll-up Keyboard

Some keyboards are designed out of flexible materials that can roll up in a moderately tight bundle. Normally the external materials are either silicone or polyurethane. It is important to note that although many manufacturers claim that the keyboards are foldable, they cannot be folded without damaging the membrane that holds the circuitry. Typically they are completely sealed in rubber, making them watertight like membrane keyboards. Like membrane keyboards, they are reported to be very hard to get used to, as there is little tactile feedback (Figure 6-3).

Image Scanner[①]

In computing, a scanner is a device that optically scans images, printed text, handwriting, or an object, and converts it to a digital image. Common examples found in offices are variations of the desktop (or flatbed) scanner where the document is placed on a glass window for scanning. Hand-held scanners, where the device is moved by hand, have evolved from text scanning "wands" to 3D scanners used for industrial design, reverse engineering, test and measurement, orthotics, gaming and other applications. Mechanically driven scanners that move the document are typically used for large-format documents, where a flatbed design would be impractical.

Modern scanners typically use a charge-coupled device (CCD) or a Contact Image Sensor (CIS) as the image sensor, whereas older drum scanners use a photomultiplier tube as the image sensor. A rotary scanner, used for high-speed document scanning, is another type of drum scanner, using a CCD array instead of a photomultiplier. Other types of scanners are planetary scanners, which take photographs of books and documents, and 3D scanners, for producing three-dimensional models of objects.

Another category of scanner is digital camera scanners, which are based on the concept of reprographic cameras. Due to increasing resolution and new features such as anti-shake, digital cameras have become an attractive alternative to regular scanners. While still having disadvantages compared to traditional scanners (such as distortion, reflections, shadows, low contrast), digital cameras offer advantages such as speed, portability and gentle digitizing of thick documents without damaging the book spine. New scanning technologies are combining 3D scanners with digital cameras to create full-color, photo-realistic 3D models of objects.

In the biomedical research area, detection devices for DNA microarrays are called scanners as well. These scanners are high-resolution systems (up to 1 μm/ pixel), similar to microscopes. The detection is done via CCD or a photomultiplier tube (PMT).

Scanners typically read red-green-blue color (RGB) data from the array. This data is then

---

① http://en.wikipedia.org/wiki/Image_scanner#Document_processing

processed with some proprietary algorithm to correct for different exposure conditions, and sent to the computer via the device's input/output interface (usually SCSI or bidirectional parallel port in machines pre-dating the USB standard). Color depth varies depending on the scanning array characteristics, but is usually at least 24 bits. High quality models have 48 bits or more color depth. Another qualifying parameter for a scanner is its resolution, measured in pixels per inch (ppi), sometimes more accurately referred to as Samples per inch (spi). Instead of using the scanner's true optical resolution, the only meaningful parameter, manufacturers like to refer to the interpolated resolution, which is much higher thanks to software interpolation. As of 2009, a high-end flatbed scanner can scan up to 5400 ppi and a good drum scanner has an optical resolution of 12,000 ppi.

Manufacturers often claim interpolated resolutions as high as 19,200 ppi; but such numbers carry little meaningful value, because the number of possible interpolated pixels is unlimited and doing so does not increase the level of captured detail.

The size of the file created increases with the square of the resolution; doubling the resolution quadruples the file size. A resolution must be chosen that is within the capabilities of the equipment, preserves sufficient detail, and does not produce a file of excessive size. The file size can be reduced for a given resolution by using "lossy" compression methods such as JPEG, at some cost in quality. If the best possible quality is required lossless compression should be used; reduced-quality files of smaller size can be produced from such an image when required (e.g., image designed to be printed on a full page, and a much smaller file to be displayed as part of a fast-loading web page).

The third important parameter for a scanner is its density range. A high-density range means that the scanner is able to reproduce shadow details and brightness details in one scan.

By combining full-color imagery with 3D models, modern hand-held scanners are able to completely reproduce objects electronically. The addition of 3D color printers enables accurate miniaturization of these objects, with applications across many industries and professions.

Part 4　Processing of Electronic Word[1,2]

Art Fonts Library

Art Library collects many kinds of fonts and is easy to be searched, such as anke-art Fonts and pop art Fonts (Table 6-1).

---

[1] http://cooltext.com/Fonts-anke-art
[2] http://www.2-free.net/pop-art-fonts/

Table 6-1 Art Fonts Library

Type	Name	Sample
anke-art Fonts	Hearts	HEARTS
	Incognitype	Incognitype
	Knuffig	Knuffig
	Wasser	Wasser
Pop Art	Three D	AEGQSABEFSY&248
	Comic	AEGQSABEFSY&248
	Bold Italic	AEGQSABEFSY&248
	Extra	★✷◎←☏💡☎🔫✍
	Volume	AA AA AA AA 💡
	Stencil	AEGQSABEFSY&248

Ulead Cool 3D

COOL 3D Production Studio brings you state of the art 3D capabilities. With its advance modeling tools, plug-ins, as well as video and animation functions, you can achieve optimum results creating your 3D titles. COOL 3D is definitely the smartest way to create 3D to liven up videos, Web pages, and presentations—the possibilities are digitally infinite (Figure 6-4).

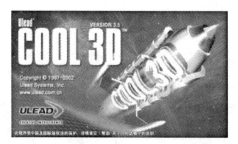

Figure 6-4 COOL 3D

With the intuitive 3D suite you can compose animated titles, mixing them with video and audio. Save your work as a video, or export to popular 3D modeling and animation formats. Whether you go for realism or surrealism, you be in full control of a gallery of art rendering and animation effects—all created to spice up your project. When you begin using COOL 3D, you will soon discover just how far it can take you beyond the basics of 3D design.

What's cool in Ulead COOL 3D Production Studio?

Cutting Edge 3D Art

With Ulead COOL 3D Production Studio, you can conveniently convert text and shapes into dazzling 3D figures as well as import/export. X and .3DS files, work with Lathe and Geometric objects, do Freeform deformation and achieve any 3D titling goal in minutes. Create and edit your work like a pro without the hassle. All you have to do is click away.

Video Support like Nothing Else

You don't have to edit your 3D video clips outside COOL 3D. User-friendly and powerful, COOL 3D allows you to use video files as scene background or object texture and edit the clips right there. It's video support like you've never seen before. COOL 3D gives you the power of many programs, saving you both time and money.

Awesome Effects

Plug-in effects are what make your still or animated title extra special. In COOL 3D, you can give objects a unique backdrop with Background effects, create astonishing 3D text titles with Text and Bevel effects. Or make objects move in special patterns with Object effects, give them a unique flair with Global effects, and enrich your project with Particle effects.

Part 5　Output of Electronic Word

Printer (computing)[①]

In computing, a printer is a peripheral which produces a hard copy (permanent readable text and/or graphics) of documents stored in electronic form, usually on physical print media such as paper or transparencies. Many printers are primarily used as local peripherals, and are attached by a printer cable or, in most newer printers, a USB cable to a computer which serves as a document source. Some printers, commonly known as network printers, have built-in network interfaces, typically wireless and/or Ethernet based, and can serve as a hard copy device for any user on the network. Individual printers are often designed to support both local and network connected users at the same time. In addition, a few modern printers can directly interface to electronic media such as memory cards, or to image capture devices such as digital

---

① http://en.wikipedia.org/wiki/Printer_(computing)

Figure 6-5 A Lexmark Printer

cameras, scanners; some printers are combined with a scanners and/or fax machines in a single unit, and can function as photocopiers. Printers that include non-printing features are sometimes called multifunction printers (MFP), multi-function devices (MFD), or all-in-one (AIO) printers. Most MFPs include printing, scanning, and copying among their features (Figure 6-5).

Consumer and some commercial printers are designed for low-volume, short-turnaround print jobs; requiring virtually no setup time to achieve a hard copy of a given document. However, printers are generally slow devices (30 pages per minute is considered fast; and many inexpensive consumer printers are far slower than that), and the cost per page is actually relatively high. However, this is offset by the on-demand convenience and project management costs being more controllable compared to an out-sourced solution. The printing press remains the machine of choice for high-volume, professional publishing. However, as printers have improved in quality and performance, many jobs which used to be done by professional print shops are now done by users on local printers.

Laser Printer[1]

Figure 6-6 HP LaserJet 4200 Series Printer

A laser printer is a common type of computer printer that rapidly produces high quality text and graphics on plain paper. As with digital photocopiers and multifunction printers (MFPs), laser printers employ a xerographic printing process but differ from analog photocopiers in that the image is produced by the direct scanning of a laser beam across the printer's photoreceptor (Figure 6-6).

A laser beam projects an image of the page to be printed onto an electrically charged rotating drum coated with selenium or, more common in modern printers, organic photoconductors. Photoconductivity removes charge from the areas exposed to light. Dry ink (toner) particles are then electrostatic ally picked up by the drum's charged areas. The drum then prints the image onto paper by direct contact and heat, which fuses the ink to the paper.

Unlike impact printers, laser printer speed can vary widely, and depends on many

---

[1] http://en.wikipedia.org/wiki/Laser_printer

factors, including the graphic intensity of the job being processed. The fastest models can print over 200 monochrome pages per minute (12,000 pages per hour). The fastest color laser printers can print over 100 pages per minute (6000 pages per hour). Very high-speed laser printers are used for mass mailings of personalized documents, such as credit card or utility bills, and are competing with lithography in some commercial applications.

The cost of this technology depends on a combination of factors, including the cost of paper, toner, and infrequent drum replacement, as well as the replacement of other consumables such as the fuser assembly and transfer assembly. Often printers with soft plastic drums can have a very high cost of ownership that does not become apparent until the drum requires replacement.

A duplexing printer (one that prints on both sides of the paper) can halve paper costs and reduce filing volumes. Formerly only available on high-end printers, duplexers are now common on mid-range office printers, though not all printers can accommodate a duplexing unit. Duplexing can also give a slower page-printing speed, because of the longer paper path.

In comparison with the laser printer, most inkjet printers and dot-matrix printers simply take an incoming stream of data and directly imprint it in a slow lurching process that may include pauses as the printer waits for more data. A laser printer is unable to work this way because such a large amount of data needs to output to the printing device in a rapid, continuous process. The printer cannot stop the mechanism precisely enough to wait until more data arrives, without creating a visible gap or misalignment of the dots on the printed page.

Instead the image data is built up and stored in a large bank of memory capable of representing every dot on the page. The requirement to store all dots in memory before printing has traditionally limited laser printers to small fixed paper sizes such as letter or A4. Most laser printers are unable to print continuous banners spanning a sheet of paper two meters long, because there is not enough memory available in the printer to store such a large image before printing begins.

New Words

    plain   *adj.* 平的;朴素的;简单的;清晰的
    endianness   *n.* 字节顺序
    corruption   *n.* 堕落;贪污,腐败
    suffix   *n.* 后缀;下标
    italics   *n.* 斜体字,斜体
    terminal   *n.* 终端机;终点;末端;极限
    repertoire   *n.* 全部节目;计算机指令系统;(美)某人或机器的全部技能
    terminology   *n.* 术语,术语学;用辞
    encapsulate   *vt.* 压缩;将……装入胶囊;将……封进内部
    royalties   *n.* 版税;专利税;王权;皇室

incremental   *adj.* 增加的，增值的
scatter   *vi.* 分散，散开；散射 *vt.* 使散开，使分散；使散射；使散播，使撒播
silicone   *n.* 硅树脂；硅酮
rotary   *adj.* 旋转的，转动的；轮流的
reprographic   *adj.* 复印（术）的；复制（术）的
peripheral   *n.*【计算机】外围设备；辅助设备（如打印机、扫描仪等）
cable   *n.*【电工学】电缆；多芯导线；被覆线
xerographic   *adj.* 静电印刷的
selenium   *n.*［化］硒
lithography   *n.* 平版印刷术，石印术
misalignment   *n.* 不重合；未对准

Notes

[1] Although there are multiple character encodings available for Unicode, the most common is UTF-8, which has the advantage of being backwards-compatible（向下兼容）with ASCII: that is, every ASCII text file is also a UTF-8 text file with identical meaning.

译文：尽管有多种可供 Unicode 使用的字符编码，然而最常见的是 UTF-8。UTF-8 的优势体现在它采用向下兼容的 ASCII：那就是说，每个 ASCII 文本文件也是一个拥有相同的意思的 UTF-8 文本文件。

- which has the advantage of being backwards-compatible with ASCII 是非限制定语从句，修饰先行词 UTF-8。
- available for 可用于……的；对……有效的；能参加……的

[2] Microsoft MS-DOS and Windows use a common text file format, with each line of text separated by a two character combination: CR and LF, which have ASCII codes 13 and 10.

译文：微软的磁盘操作系统和 Windows 系统使用的是一种相同的文本文件格式，每一行文本都可以被分解为两个字符的组合：CR 和 LF，他们的 ASCII 码分别是 13 和 10。

- with each line of text separated by a two character combination: CR and LF, which have ASCII codes 13 and 10 作状语从句，which have ASCII codes 13 and 10 作定语从句。

Selected Translation

Part 5

电子文字的输出

打印机

在计算机系统中，打印机是一种辅助设备。通过它，我们可以得到一份电子文档的硬拷贝（永久性可读的文本或图像），通常都是以纸质或透明胶片等实体作为印刷媒介。起初许多打印机被用作本机的辅助设备并用一根打印电缆（一些新的打印机使用的是

USB 连接线)将其与计算机连接起来,作为文件的来源。有些打印机通常被称为网络打印机,它们拥有内置的网络接口,一般以无线或以太网为基础,任何网络上的用户都可将其作为硬拷贝装置。个人打印机通常能同时支持本机或网络连接的用户。另外,一些现代的打印机可以直接连接电子媒体(如记忆卡)或影像捕获设备(如数码相机、扫描仪)。那些包括除打印以外其他功能的打印机有时被称为多功能打印机(MFP)、多功能设备(MFD),或一体化(AIO)打印机。大部分多功能打印机有打印、扫描和复印功能。

一些用户型的和商业型的打印机是专为低容量和高速率的打印工作而设计的,要求在几乎没有安装时间的情况下完成一份特定文件的硬拷贝。然而,打印机通常是一种缓慢的设备(30页/分钟已被认为是快速的了,而且许多便宜的用户型打印机的速度更加慢),同时每页的成本其实也是比较高的。尽管如此,和外源解决方案相比而言,它提供的按需选择的方便和便于对项目花费的管理的优势使得这一缺点得到了弥补。印刷机仍然是一种可以选择高容量和专业出版的设备。由于打印机的质量和性能有所改善,许多过去经常由专业的打印店做的工作现在由用户在自己的打印机上就可以完成。

激光打印机

激光打印机是一种常见的电脑打印机,能在白纸上迅速地产生高质量的文本和图形。随着数字复印机和多功能打印机(MFP)的出现,激光打印机采用一种和图像影印机不同的静电印刷的打印过程。它的图像是由穿过打印机的感光器的激光光束直接扫描产生的。

激光光束投射到图片页上,采用涂有硒的带电转鼓式印刷或者更多的是使用一种现代打印机使用的有机光导体。光电导性将电荷从该区域移开使其暴露于光下,干燥的油墨粒子(即墨粉)在电鼓指控的区域以静电的方式拾起,然后直接通过接触器和热量电鼓将融合了墨水的图像打印到纸张上。

和击打式印刷机相比,激光打印机的打印速率可以变化较大,其取决于许多因素,包括被处理的图形强度。最快的样机每分钟可以打印的数量超过 200 单色页(12000 页/小时)。而最快的彩色激光打印机每分钟可以打印的数量超过 100 页(6000 页/小时)。高速激光打印机用于个人文件(如信用卡或水电费信息文件)的大规模传送并在一些商业应用方面与平板印刷展开竞争。

这项技术的费用取决于多种因素,包括纸张、墨粉和电鼓更换频率之类的成本,以及其他消耗品的更换,如定影和传输装置。通常采用软塑料鼓的打印机需要很高的成本,而这一点直到鼓需要更换时才能显现出来。

一个双面的打印机可以降低纸张成本和文件归档的数量。从前只有高端打印机可以实现双面打印,如今虽然不是所有打印机都有这种技术,但是在中档办公打印机上却已经很常见了。由于双面打印的纸张路径更长,打印速度会相应减慢。

和激光打印机相比较而言,大多数喷墨打印机和点阵式打印机只会接收数据并以缓慢的速度直接进行打印,有时可能由于打印机要等待更多的数据而需要暂停。激光打印机不能以这种方式工作,因为大量的数据需要以一个快速、持续的过程输出到打印设备。打印机不能在打印纸上没有留下任何可见的横线或失调点的情况下足够准确地使机器停止以等待更多数据的到来。

相反,图像数据建立并保存在一个拥有很大记录容量的卡里面,它能够记录页面上的每一个点。在打印前机器将所有的点以记忆的形式储存,按照惯例这就会将打印纸张限制在较小的范围,如证书或 A4 的大小。大多数的激光打印机不能打印拥有两米长纸张的连续横幅。因为在开始打印之前,打印机没有足够的内存来存储这样大的图像。

Exercises

1. How dose the digital revolution influence literary study?
2. How many formats of electronic word? What are they?

从句的翻译

英语中的从句有定语从句、状语从句、主语从句、表语从句、宾语从句以及同位语从句。翻译英语从句时,应弄清原文的句法结构,根据汉语的特点和表达方式,正确地译出原文的意思。下面根据不同的从句结构,来讨论它们的译法。

一、定语从句翻译法

定语从句的翻译方法较多,一般有三种方法,一是将从句翻译成前置定语,二是从句单独翻译成一句话,三是将定语从句译成状语分句。对每一种方法的解释及说明都是针对本部分的定语从句的翻译而言的。一般来说,限制性定语从句一般采用第一种译法,非限制性定语从句采用第二种译法。以下是几种典型的方法:

1. 合译法:合译法通常用于句式较短的情况,主要以限制性定语从句为主。翻译时,可采用前置法,把定语从句译成带"的"的定语词组,放在被修饰词之前,从而将复合句译成汉语单句。如:

① The earthquake that you were talking about souded shocking.

你们刚才谈论的那场地震好可怕啊。

② Applications of the optical 3D measurement technology based on the digital photography on the reverse engineering and compositions of the digital image process system are introduced.

介绍了基于数字摄影的光学三维测量技术在逆向工程中的应用以及数字图像处理硬件系统的构成。

2. 分译法:分译法是指将主句和从句分开翻译的一种方法,主要用于较长的非限制性定语从句里。采用这种方法可避免句子的冗长和累赘。翻译时,将从句从句子中抽出来单独组成分句,放在主句后面。如:

① Hypermedia refers to computer software that uses elements of text, graphics, video, and audio connected in such a way that the user can easily move within the information.

超媒体是指一种计算机软件,它使用文本、图形、视频及音频等信息元素建立了特别的链接方式,使用户可以方便地在各种媒体间跳转。

② A similar effect is commonly observed in western movies, where the wheels of a stagecoach appear to be rotating more slowly than would be consistent with the coach's forward motion, and sometimes in the wrong direction.

一个类似的效果也常在西部电影中观察到,电影中马车的轮子看上去转得比马车实际向前运动的速度要慢,偶尔还会向相反的方向转动。

③ A pixel is the smallest dot in the system which can be manipulated for its brightness and colour.

像素是该系统内最小的点子,每一像素的明暗和颜色可单独的操纵和调整。

3. 转译法:有些非限制性定语从句,从形式上看它们是定语从句,但它们并不表示先行词的特征和属性,而起状语的作用,这时可根据具体情况,采用转译法,把定语从句译成目的、结果、原因、条件、让步等状语从句。如:

① The strike would prevent the docking of ocean steamships, which require assistance of tugboats.

罢工会使远洋航船不能靠岸,因为他们需要拖船的帮助。(翻译成原因状语从句)

② He wishes to write an article, which will attract public attention to the matter.

他想写一篇文章,以便能引起公众对这件事的关注。(翻译成目的状语从句)

综上所述,定语从句一般要视其含义,与先行词关系的密切程度、长度的不同而采取不同的翻译方法,一般可以将其译成前置定语,独立成分,与先行词等融合在一起,甚至将其译成各种状语分句。

二、状语从句翻译法

在复合句中状语从句通常由连词或起连词作用的词引导,用来修饰主句中的动词、形容词或副词。对于状语从句的翻译,一般情况下按正常语序翻译。如:

① Although Starcom IP lost the telco's digital media account, Starcom Beijing will continue handling China Telecom's offline media planning and buying duties, which it won in March last year.

虽然星传 IP 失去了电信的数字媒体账户,星传北京将继续处理去年三月赢取的中国电信离线媒体计划和购买的业务。

② However, if your visitor has monitor resolutions set to 1600 × 800 and has the browser "maximized", your page will have 500 pixels of blank space on either side of your 600 pixel table.

然而,假如访问者的显示率设定为 1600 × 800,让浏览器呈现最大状态,那么网页就会很难看:600 像素表格的两边会出现 500 像素的空白。(由 if 引导的条件状语从句)

③ As the ceaseless development of technology of digital media confluence, prospective network buys content will be more realistic, more individual and quick.

随着数字媒体融合技术的不断发展,未来网络购物将更具真实感、更加个性化、更加方便快捷。(由 as 引导的伴随状语从句)

④ When spring arrives, high-tech media gadgets, like digital cameras, camcorders and portable digital music players, start to get a workout.

随着春季的到来,像数码相机、便携式摄像机和便携式数码音乐播放器等高科技多媒体产品要大显身手了。(由 when 引导时间状语从句)

⑤ I could understand his point of view, in that I'd been in a similar position.

我能理解他的观点,因为我也有过类似的处境。(In that = because)

⑥ For all that he seems so bad-tempered, I still think he has a very kind nature.

尽管他好像脾气很坏,我仍然认为他心地善良。(for all that 引导让步状语从句,翻译为"尽管……""虽然……")

⑦ Electricity is such an important energy that modern industry couldn't develop without it

电是一种非常重要的能量,没有它,现代化工业就不能发展。(由 such...that... 引导的结果状语从句,译为汉语的并列句)

三、主语从句翻译法

1. "主—谓—宾"结构:以 what、how、whether、that、where、when 引导的主语从句,可以译成"主—谓—宾"结构,从句本身做句子的主语,其余部分按原文顺序译出。如:

① What someone chooses to observe and the way one observes it must, after all, in part be a reflection of experience and of ideas as to what is significant.

某人选择观察的事物和他观察事物的方式在某种程度上终归反映这个人的经历和他关于重大事件的看法。(what 引导的主语从句,翻译成名词"……的事(情)")

② When we will begin to work has not been decided yet.

什么时候开始工作还没决定呢。(when 引的主语从句,直接翻译成"……时候")

2. 分译法:把原来的主语从句从整体结构中分离出来,译成另一个相对独立的单句。如:

① It has been rightly stated that this situation is a threat to international security.

这个局势对国际安全是个威胁,这样的说法是完全正确的。(It 是形式主语,that this situation is a threat to international security 是真正的主语)

② It is my duty that I must teach English well.

我必须教好英语,这是我的职责。

四、表语从句翻译法

大部分情况下可以采用顺译法,间或也可以用逆译法。如:

① That was how they were defeated.

他们就是这样给打败的。(顺译法)

② His view of the press was that the reporters were either for him or against him.

他对新闻界的看法是,记者们不是支持他,就是反对他。(顺译法)

③ Water and food is what the people in the area badly need.

该地区的人们最需要的是水和食品。(逆译法)

五、宾语从句翻译法

翻译宾语从句时一般按原句的顺序即可。当句中有 it 作形式宾语时,it 一般省略不译。如：

① Lagrange argued that trigonometric series were of very limited use.

拉格伦日认为三角级数的应用是非常有限的。

② I don't believe he has seen the film.

我相信他没看过这部电影。

③ It features new cutting-edge functionality that makes enjoying digital media content simple.

它采用新的先进的功能，使欣赏数字媒体内容简单。

④ I took it for granted that he would sign the document.

我认为他当然会在文件上签字。

六、同位语从句翻译法

同位语从句是用来进一步说明从句前面一个名词的具体内容。常见的带同位语从句的名词有：fact、news、promise、truth、belief、idea、answer、information、knowledge、doubt、hope、law、opinion、plan、suggestion、question 等，同位语从句较短小时，翻译时可考虑将其前置；如果较长，则可考虑后置。如：

① The question whether we need it has not yet been considered.

我们是否需要它，这个问题还没有考虑。（从句前置）

② This is a universally accepted principle of international law that the territory sovereignty does not admit of infringement.

一个国家的领土不容侵犯，这是国际法中尽人皆知的准则。（从句前置）

③ In this case, the sampling process corresponds to the fact that moving pictures are a sequence of individual frames with a rate (usually between 18 and 24 frames per second) corresponding to the sampling frequency.

在这种情况下，抽样过程就相当于：活动图像是一串单个的画面，帧频（通常每秒 18 到 24 帧）相当于抽样频率。（顺译法）

④ His criticism was based on his own belief that it was impossible to represent signals with corners using trigonometric series.

他批评的论据是基于自己的信念，即不可能用三角函数级数来表示具有间断点的信号。（从句后置）

Chapter 7 Digital Layout and Design[①]

▲ **Knowledge Objectives**

When you have completed this chapter, you:
- should know about what digital layout and design is and how does it give to birth.
- can briefly tell the history of publishing.
- can identify the equipment of digital layout and design.
- should be able to use some special support programs to aid the layout and design.

▲ **Professional Terms**

camera-ready art	照相制版
codex	古抄本
color calibration	颜色校准
digital layout and design	数字排版和设计
direct digital printing	直接数码印刷
GUI	图形用户界面
newsletter	时事通讯
offset lithography press	平板印刷机
papyrus scroll	古本手卷
resolution	分辨率
rotary press	转轮印刷机
typography	铸排机
wax tablet	蜡版

Part 1 Introduction, Birth

Introduction

Performing digital layout and design on a computer has truly revolutionized the graphic design profession. In its most basic form, page layout programs bring type, graphics, and photographs together in a single document. As long as the information you wish to include is in a file

---

① See *Digital Media—An Introduction*, Chapter 6.

format the program recognizes, it can be used in the design.

The principal element that distinguishes in a digital layout and design program from a sophisticated word processing program is the way it handles type. Unlike a word processing program that processes type in rows of letters (much like a typewriter would), digital layout and design programs see type as blocks of information that can be picked up and moved around, much like designers a few decades ago picked up and moved around cut pieces of printed typography and pasted them to boards (hence, the phrase "cut and paste"). Professional digital layout and design programs offer extensive capabilities for type treatment and layout variables. Text can be wrapped around a curved line or shape, distorted, or skewed, and the spaces between lines of text and even the letters themselves can be adjusted.

Graphic design was once the exclusive province of trained professionals. Today, many programs contain templates, including typestyle information and layouts for a variety of standard design functions, like newsletters or business cards. While not appropriate for the design professional, this is especially helpful to the many users of digital layout and design programs who do not have extensive training in design, but who, with these new tools, are able to design serviceable documents on their own.

The Birth of Digital Layout and Design

The digital revolution in publishing can be traced to the mid-1980s with the production by Aldus Corporation of a new software program called Pagemaker. It was developed for the recently introduced Apple Macintosh computer and fully utilized its GUI to create an extraordinary new tool for designers. The Pagemaker program was able to combine text and graphics in the same document. The combination of the Macintosh and desktop publishing software would allow designers to see pages on the computer screen as they would look when printed. This WYSIWYG capability proved to be of critical importance.

At the same time, computer-printed output took a huge step toward professional quality with the first laser printers. Unlike the then-conventional dot-matrix printers, where text and images were composed of large, quite apparent dots, Apple's Laser Writer printed much sharper and clearer text.

As we have already noted, prior to this development, documents were prepared for publication using traditional and mechanical cut-and-paste techniques. Images were prepared separately, while text was sent out to a professional typesetter using a Compugraphic (one of the earliest) or similar typesetting machine that could set and space the text according to the designer's specifications. It would then be sent to an imagesetter, a machine that would print the text at high resolution (1,200 dpi to 4,000 dpi, depending on the machine being used) to film or on long sheets of photographic paper that were then developed in special chemicals similar to a regular black-and-white photograph. The typesetting machine itself held a group of internal fonts or typefaces that could be printed at a very high resolution to ensure smooth crisp typography. Generally, 1,200 dpi was considered to be typeset quality. The sheets of printed type, or galleys, were cut apart and pasted onto cardboard layout panels along with various graphics or photographs. This camera-ready art would be photographed, stripped, made into plates, and then run on an offset lithography press to create the final printed piece.

With the arrival of digital layout and design programs, a new graphic design environment was born. Type and text could be brought together and combined in the computer. Text styles, the text font, size, and spacing could all be seen on the screen and problems corrected or changed. The relationship of the type to graphics or photos could be adjusted almost endlessly. Changes in composition or content could be completed without having to send out new specifications to a printer, eliminating the once-typical loss in time and money.

Part 2 A Brief History of Publishing

Throughout much of its history, a literate elite has controlled publishing. One can say publishing began with the first form of written, portable communication, the scroll. Scrolls were at first prepared from papyrus, a special kind of reed found in Egypt, which was slit, peeled, and soaked in water. The flattened reeds were laid next to each other, overlapping slightly. A second set of prepared reeds was then laid on top of the first at a ninety—degree angle. Under pressure, the reeds would bond together to form a writing surface. Sections of papyrus were glued together to form the scrolls we are familiar with today (see Figure 7-1). Papyrus has proven to be one of the most durable writing surfaces ever created.

Figure 7-1 Papyrus Scroll Segment from the Egyptian Book of the Dead.

The creation of a smooth writing surface using papyrus matured around 1500 B.C., and revolutionized the process of recording information. Papyrus sheets were the common writing surface for centuries in the Middle East and parts of Europe until being replaced by parchment during the Roman Empire.

Initially papyrus scrolls were used to record religious texts and other important information, although it was not uncommon for more mundane subjects like the sale of a donkey to be duly recorded (see Figure 7-2). Around A.D. 500 the codex (see Figure 7-3), a primitive form of book made of smaller individual sheets of papyrus (and later parchment) became

Chapter 7　Digital Layout and Design　　167

common (see Figure 7-4). This might have happened for several reasons. The codex was not only more economical and convenient to use but also took less space to store. Unlike a scroll, where only one side of the surface could be written upon, the codex was able to use both sides of the writing surface.

Figure 7-2　Papyrus Fragment—Often Used to Record Daily Things

Figure 7-3　This Franco-Flemish book of hours was created on parchment, ca. 1330—1340.

Figure 7-4　A Primitive Codex-Book of Esther Scroll (Hebrew), 8th century

In addition to the codex, wax tablets were used well into the Medieval period. To make a wax tablet, a flat piece of wood was carved out on one side, filled with wax, and smoothed into a flat writing surface. Several of these could be joined together to make a form of notebook. Due to the ease upon which they could be written, they were often used for general personal and business correspondence and quick notes (see Figure 7-5). With the use of a stylus, a scribe could write and record information quickly and, if deemed important, that information was copied to a more permanent material—papyrus roll or parchment codex. The wax tablet was then resurfaced and used again. Wax tablets were used through the eleventh and twelfth centuries until finally being replaced with pen and parchment, a smoother and superior writing surface that came from the smoothly scraped hides of butchered lambs.

These various forms of early writing and publishing are in certain ways similar to today's. We may make notes for publications in a notepad (wax tablet) or even a palm-pilot-type device, and then enter the information to a desktop computer for a more workable form. For permanence, we might decide to publish the work in "codex" form as hard copy on paper (rather than papyrus or parchment, which tend to jam in laser printers).

Figure 7-5 Woman Holding Wax Tablets in the Form of the Codex

Figure 7-6 Reproduction of early books required a scribe to copy the entire text by hand.

Whatever form early books took, they were, by necessary, one-of-a-kind items. During the Middle Ages, for example, if additional copies were needed, then someone (usually a monk or scribe trained in this discipline) would meticulously and laboriously copy each scroll until another had been completed. Waiting for a new copy of a book might take well over a year (see Figure 7-6). Needless to say, early books produced in this fashion were extremely rare and valuable. Most people never saw, much less owned, a book. Libraries or repositories of books were almost always centered in monasteries or in some cases with the nobility. The personal library of a wealthy and educated nobleman might contain no more than two hundred or so books.

The Paper Revolution

Hundreds of years before those in the West were scraping hides to make parchment and painstakingly copying documents one at a time, the Chinese had discovered that a fibrous material like cotton could be mixed with water and heated until it become soft and pliable. Pouring the mixture over fine bamboo screens allowed the water to escape, leaving the cotton fibers nesting together on the surface. This primitive paper was pliable and held ink well. Traditionally, the invention of paper has been attributed to Cai Lun, who lived in the Eastern Han

Dynasty, and presented the new writing surface to Emperor He Di in A.D. 105. However, it is very likely that this primitive form of papermaking was in use several hundred years before that date.

Paper would play a critical role in the history of publishing for two reasons. It was less expensive than silk, an earlier Chinese writing surface, or any of the other materials used around the world. It was also firm enough to stay on the surface of carved, inked, wooden blocks. Long before its invention in the West, the Chinese had discovered that individual blocks of wood or clay could be carved into various symbols, organized together, and used to print copies of documents. As early as A.D. 740, China had its first printed newspaper, and by 1041 the Chinese had developed their own form of movable type.

During the Renaissance, a variety of products, inventions, and technologies began making their way from the East to Europe because of trading. Although the Chinese had been guarding the secret of manufacturing paper, in A.D. 751 when the Tang army was defeated by the Ottoman Turks, a number of papermakers were captured along with the Chinese soldiers. Consequently, papermaking spread to the Arab world. Four centuries later, as a result of the Crusades, papermaking makes its way from the Middle East and Northern Africa to Spain.

The Print Revolution

By the fourteenth century, inexpensive paper was readily available throughout Europe. Fine art printmaking was already in full bloom, but it was not until Johannes Gutenberg's printing press in 1455 that true multiple copies of books became a reality (see Figure 7-7). Gutenberg's most important contribution to publishing was not, however, the printing press. It was actually type founding, the mechanical production of cast type, which made the printing of books possible. By casting the face and body of the type in one operation, Gutenberg was able to cast multiples of the separate types in metal molds. His movable type was designed so that it could be aligned in the manuscript he was printing to form a flow from letter to letter and word to word. This mimicked the hand quality of letterforms used to that point (see Figure 7-8). While movable type was first used in China some 400 years before Gutenberg's printing press, Chinese type was far less durable, being made of clay or wood rather than metal.

Gutenberg's printing press was actually a modified winepress. On it, he assembled rows of type, which were locked into place and inked (see Figure 7-9). Dampened paper was positioned over the inked type and the platen, a kind of pressure plate, was screwed down on top of the paper and type. A lever was used in order to further increase pressure, resulting in firm and even contact between the paper and type. After the impression was made, the press was opened and the paper hung to dry. It was in this manner that Gutenberg's forty-two-line Bible was published in Mainz.

Figure 7-7　First Incunabula with Illustrations, Ulrich Boner's *Der Edelstein*

Figure 7-8　The decoration of this page from a French Book of Hours, ca. 1400, includes a miniature, initials and borders.

Figure 7-9　Gutenberg's Publishing Press

　　This process, while excruciatingly slow by today's standards, dramatically changed the way in which information was disseminated. It was a revolution in every sense of the word, paving the way for sharing culture and knowledge with the general populace instead of limiting it to the ruling classes. It also made spreading the word about new scientific developments during the Renaissance much easier. By 1499, more than 250 cities around Europe were printing documents using some form of Gutenberg's invention.

　　As press became more sophisticated and faster, newspaper were established and published works of fiction were circulated to the world. By the Industrial Revolution, rotary press were developed (see Figure 7-10), capable of making up to 1,000 impressions per hour as compared to Gutenberg's 200-300 impressions per day. In 1886, the Linotype machine (see Figure 7-11), a form of automatic typesetter, replace the tedious job of handsetting type one character at a time, line by line (see Figure 7-12). Using molds of type, it was able to drop a mold of each letter into place using a keyboard to type the letters (see Figure 7-13). The type was then cast line by line instead of character by character (see Figure 7-14).

Figure 7-10　Rotary presses made multiple prints at a greatly increased rate.

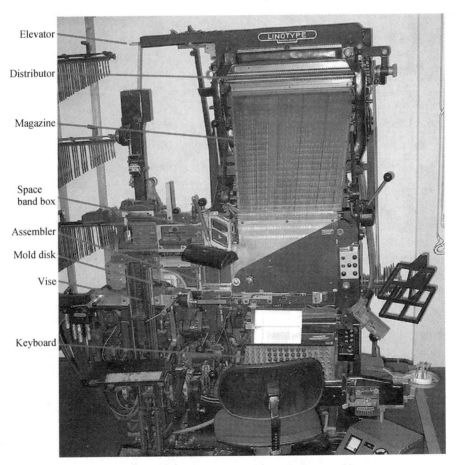

Figure 7-11　Linotype Machines and Some Components of It

Figure 7-12　Matrix Transposition: "NOTINHG RUNS LIKE A DEERE"

Figure 7-13　The Keyboard Used to Type the Letters

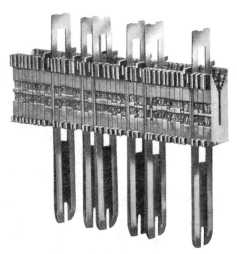

Figure 7-14　An Example of Machine Set Type

　　The evolution of print technology was not only a series of mechanical advances but aesthetic one as well. Type forms and type foundries developed along with the technology, creating different typefaces as the technology evolved. We still recognize the genius of many of this era's type designers. Names like Garamond(1480—1561), Caslon(1692—1766), Baskerville (1706—1775), Bodoni(1740—1813), and Goudy(1865—1947) live on in the names of the fonts they designed.

The Desktop Revolution

　　When the first printed books appeared in the middle of the fifteenth century, they were usually print versions of manuscripts like the Bible and prayer books. In the sixteenth and seventeenth centuries, printed books moved beyond religious tracts to include nonsecular subjects like science, poetry, and drama. As a result, then began to have a powerful impact on European society(see Figure 7-15). By the eighteenth century, independent printers like Benjamin Franklin helped foment revolutions in Europe and America.

Figure 7-15　Martin Luther's writings had a profound impact on German Culture and language, which soon spread throughout Europe.

In the last 200 years, an enormous number of books, periodicals, newspapers, and other forms of publications have been printed on ever-widening subjects. Technology evolved to the point where millions of copies of a particular book or other publication could be printed in a matter of days. Distribution of those books, as well as the change from private subscription to public libraries, guaranteed access to anyone who wished to read. One thing, however, remained constant from the days of ancient imperial China—book publishing remained in the hands of those controlling the technology, or those wealthy enough to purchase access to that technology. However, that changed in the 1980s.

Like the development of movable type and the printing press, desktop publishing or digital layout and design—the ability to combine text and image together within a computer in preparation for printing—has brought the power of publishing within the reach of the nonprofessional. In addition, desktop publishing has established itself as a legitimate force in digital imaging today, forever changing the face of the design world and the publishing industry. Available to anyone who wishes to create designs, newsletters, forms, advertisements, catalogs, and similar kinds of printed matter, it has been applauded by many but often scorned by professionals who see the quantity of publications designed by amateurs rising at the expense of design excellence. Learning a computer program is not the same as having the background and art training necessary to create coherent, visually appealing designs.

Part 3   Digital Layout and Design: The Equipment

Although digital layout and design software was originally produced for the Apple Macintosh computer, the PC has long since caught up with this technology. Whatever format you choose to use—Mac or PC—the programs will have a GUI. Other important components include a scanner for digitizing artwork and a printer for output. An image—editing program is necessary for correcting or modifying images to be placed in a publication, while some form of word processing software is useful in preparing text for long documents.

Of course, the publishing software itself is of prime importance. Although Pagemaker introduced the world to desktop publishing, other software producers quickly entered the field. QuarkXPress (see Figure 7-16) appears to have become the current program of choice in the professional world. Adobe, the current maker of Pagemaker, has created a new

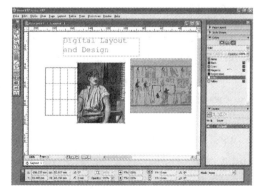

Figure 7-16   Quark XPress Screen with a Variety of Layout Information

digital layout and design program called InDesign that has many of the same features as Quark. Each program offers its own workspace, interface, and depth of features. Still, all digital layout and design software is able to combine text and graphics to create an onscreen display representing a draft of an actual document page complete with both text and graphics.

Input: Scanners

Scanners are often used to digitize photographs or other artwork for use in a desktop publishing program. Scanners can take many forms. The most important element to consider is the scanner's ability to digitize images at the size, resolution, and bit depth you need for the output you intend to use. The resolution of your scan can affect the smoothness of the tonal range of a bitmap image and how clearly detail is depicted. Bit depth can determine the scanner's ability to see subtle variations in similarly colored areas. Depending on your output (laser printer, offset lithography press, direct digital printing), the spi or samples per inch of the scan will need to be adjusted for maximum effectiveness.

It may be tempting to scan at the highest optical resolution your scanner can provide in order to include more data for printing a bitmap image, but that would be as significant a mistake as scanning at too low a resolution. If your scan contains more data than an output device needs, it will simply take longer to print (in the case of desktop printers) or output to film for offset printing, and the quality of your output can be degraded. If your scan is at too low a resolution, the overall quality of your output will be degraded.

In order to include photographs of high quality in publications, film/slide scanners are becoming increasingly important. While not able to deliver the quality of scans originating from professional drum scanners, they can deliver scans that have a greater dynamic range than those of a flatbed scanner. More importantly, by scanning from the original negative or slide, one can avoid the problems that might be associated with scanning from poor, damaged, or out-of-focus prints.

Printers

The exciting thing about desktop publishing is that it can take many forms. Output is determined by need. If simply producing several black-and-white posters for an event is your goal, then a laser or simple inkjet printer (see Figure 7-17) will be sufficient. If color is added to the design, then a higher-quality color inkjet printer or color laser printer is necessary. If more than a few copies are needed, digital files containing your completed design can be delivered to a commercial offset printer. While greater information is available about various kinds of printers in Chapter 3 of "Digital Media—An Introduction", you will find that most designers use desktop printers to create relatively inexpensive proofs, in order to give clients a clear idea of what the finished piece will look like prior to going to press. High-quality desktop inkjet printers are now available that can print pieces up to $16'' \times 20''$ so that full bleed proofs, showing what a print would look like if an image goes right to the edge of the paper, are possible.

Having a printer that can show you the final output can help you spot problems that even WYSIWYG on your computer monitor might not make obvious.

Figure 7-17 Oversize Print from a Large Format Inkjet Printer

Color Calibration

How can you know that the images, colors, and gradations you see on the computer screen are the same as those that will be printed? The answer is accurate color calibration. However, searching for that has often been compared to a search for the Holy Grail. Color modes and a description of color gamut will be reviewed in Chapter 3 of "Digital Media—An Introduction", but an awareness of color calibration is of critical important to anyone attempting to print from a file composed on a personal computer.

There are a variety of software applications that can help designers calibrate their system. The most readily available system for both PC and Macintosh is the Adobe Gamma control panel (see Figure 7-18). This simple tool makes it easy to adjust gray values on the monitor in order to eliminate color casts that might affect the color balance of your work. Some desktop programs offer their own calibration systems, such as Pagemaker's Kodak Monitor Installer which creates ICC (International Color Consortium) or ICM (which is Windows' version of ICC) profiles for use in color-managed applications that support the Kodak Color Management System.

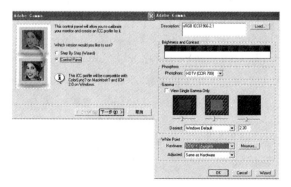

Figure 7-18 Basic monitor calibration can be accomplished through the Adobe color control panel.

For very critical work there are also hardware solutions that will physically measure color and density on your monitor and then compare it to printed output and suggest changes in your system to bring the two closer together. While the importance of accurate colors on a screen cannot be overestimated, neither can the difficulty in achieving them. Even the color temperature of the light in the room we are using to view prints can affect our sense of accuracy in determining color fidelity.

Part 4 Support Programs

Desktop publishing requires the coordination of work in several programs. You will find these programs covered in greater detail elsewhere in this book. However, the brief descriptions given here will serve to illustrate how work completed in other specialized programs can be brought together within a desktop publishing program to create a publication design.

Image—Editing Programs

While many desktop publishing programs can scan an image directly, it will come into the program as an uncorrected raw image. Desktop publishing programs are limited in their ability to adjust and correct images. This is usually left to more powerful image-editing programs, like PhotoShop. Image-editing programs have the ability to do rather sophisticated color correction and can also crop an image to the exact specifications needed. Image-editing programs also have the ability (along with the scanner) to determine the resolution of the image in terms of file size, print dimensions, and dots per inch. In addition, a good image-editing programs can save an image in a variety of formats. While a tagged image file format (TIFF) is often used due to its portability and universal recognition, a professional image-editing program can also create EPS or encapsulated PostScript files. The EPS file format can contain both vector and bitmap graphics and is supported by all page-layout programs so that PostScript language artwork can be transferred between applications.

Word Processing Programs

While text can certainly be entered directly into a digital-layout-and-design program, this is often awkward for long documents like books or reports that will require multiple pages. Because we are familiar with word processing programs and can work more quickly with them, it makes sense to type and edit most of the information we need directly into a word processing program and then later import the text into the digital layout and design program. This is also allows clients to provide editable data, which can save time and streamline workflow.

Vector-Based Illustration Programs

A vector-based (resolution independent graphic) illustration program uses mathematically defined shapes made of lines and curves rather than raster or bitmap images that use a grid of small squares known as pixels to represent images. Vectors, which describe graphics according to their geometric characteristics, are very useful for cleaning up line scans (crisp one-bit black-and-white images with no gray values) and especially for converting raster scans of logos and other simple objects to vector images. While the quality of raster or bitmap images will change depending upon the number of pixels in the image, vector images are not dependent upon resolution and can be resized without a loss in quality. Most importantly, vector-based programs can create EPS files of vector-based images for use in digital layout and design programs.

New Words

  sophisticate *n.* 久经世故的人;精通者 *vt.* 弄复杂;使变得世故;曲解 *vi.* 诡辩
  specification *n.* 规格;说明书;详述
  papyrus *n.* 纸莎草;纸莎草纸
  parchment *n.* 羊皮纸;羊皮纸文稿
  mundane *adj.* 世俗的,平凡的;世界的,宇宙的
  meticulously *adv.* 细致地;一丝不苟地;拘泥地
  clay *n.* 粘土;泥土;肉体;似黏土的东西 *vt.* 用黏土处理
  excruciatingly *adv.* 极其痛苦地;难以忍受地
  circulated *adj.* 流通的
  manuscript *n.* 手稿;原稿 *adj.* 手写的
  legitimate *adj.* 合法的;正当的;合理的;正统的 *vt.* 使合法;认为正当
  gradations *n.* 层次(gradation 的复数);分级;渐变

Notes

[1] While not appropriate for the design professional, this is especially helpful to many users of digital layout and design programs who do not have extensive training in design, but who, with these new tools, are able to design serviceable documents on their own.

译文:虽然不适用于专业设计,它对众多数字排版和设计程序用户来说却特别有用,他们虽然没有经过广泛设计训练,但是能够使用这些新工具靠自己独立设计有用的文档。

While not appropriate for the design professional 是一个转折条件状语从句。

由两个 who 引导的定语从句,who do not have extensive training in design, but who, with these new tools, are able to design serviceable documents on their own 修饰先行词 many users,在这二个 who 引导的从句中 with these new tools 作伴随状语。

[2] Available to anyone who wishes to create designs, newsletters, forms, advertisements, catalogs, and similar kinds of printed matter, it has been applauded by many but often scorned by professionals who see the quantity of publications designed by amateurs rising at the

expense of design excellence.

译文: 桌面出版系统对于任何想要创作设计、时事通讯、表格、广告、目录和一些相似类型印刷品的人来说都是可用的,大多数人都对此表示赞同,但是却常被专业人士嘲笑,他们认为业余人士设计的出版物的数量上的增加是以牺牲优秀设计为代价的。

Available to anyone who wishes to create designs, newsletters, forms, advertisements, catalogs, and similar kinds of printed matter 是一个伴随状语,其中由 who 引导的定语从句来修饰先行词 anyone。

后面的句子是主句,定语从句 who see the quantity of publications designed by amateurs rising at the expense of design excellence 修饰先行词 professionals。

at the expense of 意为"以……为代价"。

[3] Still, all digital layout and design software is able to combine text and graphics to create an onscreen display representing a draft of an actual document page complete with both text and graphics.

译文: 并且,所有数字排版和设计软件都可以将文本和图形结合在一起,从而创建屏幕显示,表示带有文本和图形的实际文档页面草稿。

representing a draft of an actual document page complete with both text and graphics 是由现在分词引导的定语从句,修饰先行词 onscreen display。

[4] While greater information is available about various kinds of printers in Chapter 3, you will find that most designers use desktop printers to create relatively inexpensive proofs, in order to give clients a clear idea of what the finished piece will look like prior to going to press.

译文: 虽然在第 3 章大量地介绍了各种各样的打印机,但您会发现大多数设计师为了在进行打印之前让客户清楚地了解所完成的作品效果,会使用台式打印机打印一份相对廉价的稿子。

While 意为"虽然",表示转折。

to create relatively inexpensive proofs 动词不定式表示目的。

what the finished piece will look like prior to going to press 是由 what 引导的宾语补足语。

Selected Translation

Part 2

出版业历史简介

一群受过教育的精英分子控制了出版业的大部分历史。可以说出版业始于最初形式的写作、便携式通信的卷轴。卷轴最初是由在埃及发现的一种特殊芦苇——纸草制备而成的,先将纸草裂开、去皮、浸泡在水中,把展平的芦苇一个挨一个铺平,稍微有点交叠。然后将第二套芦苇以 90 度的角度放在第一套芦苇的上面。在压力的作用下,芦苇结合在一起形成书写材料。把纸草粘合在一起就形成了今天我们所熟悉的卷轴。纸草被证明是曾经创造的最耐用的书写材料之一。

大约在公元前1500年,利用纸草制备光滑书写材料的创作开始成熟,并且改革了记录信息的过程。几个世纪以来,纸草薄片在中东和部分欧洲国家都是普遍的书写材料,直到罗马帝国时被羊皮纸所取代。

虽然像出售驴子这样的日常事件被适当的记录也并不罕见,但是最初古本手卷是用来记录宗教事件和其他一些重要的信息的。公元500年左右,古典抄本更为常见,它最初是由单个的小一点儿的纸草片作成的,后来用的是羊皮纸。古典抄本不仅用起来经济、方便,而且占用存储空间小。卷轴只有一面可以书写,和卷轴不一样,古典抄本的两面都可以被用来书写。

除了古典抄本,蜡版也在中世纪得到很好的运用。在一块扁平的木块一面雕刻,灌上蜡油,将蜡油弄平滑以形成平整的书写材料,这样就形成了蜡版。一些蜡版结合在一起就形成了记事本。由于可以在上面轻松地书写,它们常被用于普通个人、商业通信和快速记录。随着铁笔的运用,抄写员可以更快地书写和记录信息,如果信息很重要,可以将信息抄写在更为持久的材料上——纸草卷册或者是羊皮纸抄本。蜡版铺设新表面后又可以被重新利用。公元11世纪到12世纪,蜡版一直都在被使用,直到最后被钢笔和羊皮纸取代,羊皮纸来自被屠杀的小羊身上平滑的兽皮,是一种更为光滑和优质的书写材料。

在某些方面,这些早期的书写和出版的各种形式和今天的形式类似。我们现在可以在触摸类型的设备(以前是蜡板)上为出版物作注释,然后将信息输入电脑以获得更具操作性的形式。为了获取持久性,我们可能会将作品以古抄本的形式复制在纸上(而不是印在易让激光打印机堵塞的纸草或羊皮纸上)。

不管早期的书籍采取何种形式,它们都必然是每种类型只有一个的。例如在中世纪,如果需要副本,一些人(通常是一个僧侣或经过训练的专业抄写员)会细致地手工抄写每个卷轴,直到完成一个副本。等待一个书的新副本往往要花上一年以上的时间。不用说,照这样生产的早期书本极其罕见和珍贵。大多数人从没见过书,拥有书的人就更少了。图书馆或者是存放图书的储藏室几乎总是以寺庙为主或者在某些情况下属于贵族。一个富有的、受过教育的贵族的个人图书馆可能只拥有不超过200册左右的书籍。

纸业革命

数百年前,当西方采用剥下来的兽皮做成羊皮纸,人们煞费苦心地抄写文档,一次只抄写一本时,中国人就已经发现了一种类似棉花的纤维材料,它可以和水混合,然后加热,直到变得柔韧。将这种混合物向优质的竹筛上倾倒过滤掉水分,留下棉纤维覆盖在竹筛表面。这种原始的纸张很柔韧,并且能够很好地吸收墨水。传统上,纸的发明归功于东汉时期的蔡伦,他在公元105年将这种新的书写材料呈送给和帝。但是,极有可能在这之前几百年,最初的造纸形式已经开始运用。

纸张在出版业历史上扮演着重要的角色有两个原因。纸张比中国早些时候用的书写材料丝绸,或者是世界各地运用的其他任何一种材料都要便宜。纸张还足够结实,可以放在墨水涂染的木质雕刻印版上。在西方发明纸张之前很久,中国人已经发现,个别木块或粘土可以被雕刻成各种各样的符号,将它们组合在一起可以被用来打印文档的副本。早在公元740年,中国就有了第一份印刷的报纸,到1041年中国人就发明了活字印刷。

文艺复兴时期,由于贸易,各种各样的产品、发明、技术开始从东方传播到欧洲。虽然中国人保守了造纸的秘密,但是在公元751年当唐朝军队被土耳其人打败后,大量的造纸工人和中国士兵一起被俘获。结果,造纸业传到阿拉伯。四个世纪以后,由于十字军东征,造纸业从中东和南美传到西班牙。

印刷革命

到14世纪,廉价的纸张已经普及整个欧洲。版画复制的精细工艺已经达到全盛时期,但是直到1455年约翰尼斯·古登堡的印刷机的出现才使真正的大量书籍的副本复印成为现实。但是实际上古登堡对出版业最重要的贡献不是打印机,而是铸字机,它是一种烧铸模板的机械化产品,使打印书本成为可能。通过在操作过程中烧铸字面和字体,古登堡可以在金属模具中烧铸各种各样的字体。他设计的活字印刷是为了能够排列他所打印的原稿,以形成一连串的字母和单词。它模仿了适合这种情况信纸的手写特性。然而活字印刷大约在古登堡的印刷机400年前就在中国首次使用,但中国的模板是由粘土或木头作成的,远远不够耐用。

古登堡的打印机实际上是一个改进的葡萄榨汁机。他在上面安装几行字样,将它们固定在一个地方并蘸上墨水。将潮湿的纸张放在蘸有墨水的字样上,用一种压板式的滚筒压过纸张和字样。控杆被用来进一步地增加压力,致使纸张和字样更紧密地结合在一起。在压过之后,打开印刷机将纸张晾干。古登堡就是以这种方法将42行圣经在美因茨出版的。

虽然这种方法和今天的标准来看非常地慢,但是它戏剧性地改变了信息传播的方式。在各种意义上,它都是对文字的改革,铺平了与平民共享文化和知识的道路,而不是将它限制于统治阶级。它也使文艺复兴时期,有关新科学发展的消息传播起来更容易。到1499年,欧洲各地250多个城市运用古登堡发明的一些形式来打印文档。

随着印刷机变得更先进,速度越来越快,以小说作品为基础出版的报纸在世界范围内流通。到了工业革命时期,转轮印刷机得到了发展,和古登堡的印刷机每天压印200—300次相比,它可以每小时压印多达1000次压印。1886年,一种自动排字机——莱诺铸排机代替了每次逐行打入一个字母的沉闷的排字工作。使用字样铸模,通过键盘输入字母能够使每个字母的字样顺利进入指定位置。然后字样被逐行逐行地烧铸,而不是逐字逐字地烧铸。

印刷技术的改进不仅仅是一系列机械的进步,而且还有审美方面的进步。字样形式和字样铸模也和技术一起发展,当技术进步的时候就创造了不同的字体。我们还要承认这个时代许多的字样设计师的天才。像加拉蒙(1480—1561)、卡斯龙(1692—1766)、巴斯克维尔(1706—1775)、博多尼(1740—1813)和高迪(1865—1947)这样的名字永远活在他们所设计的字体的名字之中。

桌面革命

15世纪中期,当第一批印刷书籍出现时,它们通常是以像圣经和祈祷书为原稿的印刷版本。在16、17世纪,印刷书籍走出宗教的范围,向科学、诗歌和戏剧之类超凡脱俗的主题发展。结果,对欧洲社会产生了强有力的影响。到了18世纪,像本杰明·富兰克林之类的独立作家挑起了欧洲和美洲的革命。

在最近的 200 年中,大量的书籍、期刊、报纸以及其他形式的更广主题范围内的出版物被印刷。技术发展到今天这种程度,一本特定的书或者是其他的出版物的成千上万的副本可以在几天之内印刷完成。这些书的分配,和从私人订阅到公共图书馆的改变一样,保证了任何想要阅读的人的使用权。但是,自从中国帝制时期以来有一件事一直保持不变——书籍出版权掌控在掌握技术的人或者是足够富有支付得起这种技术的人的手里。不过,这种处境在 20 世纪 80 年代得到改善。

和可活动字体和印刷机的发展一样,桌面出版系统或者是数字化排版和设计(能够将文字和图像在电脑里合成为印刷作准备)已经将出版的权力带给非专业人士。除此之外,现在桌面出版系统也使它自身成为数字图像领域一股合法的力量,不断地改变设计界和出版产业的面貌。桌面出版系统对于任何想要创作设计、时事通讯、表格、广告、目录和一些相似类型印刷品的人来说都是可用的,大多数人都对此表示赞同,但是却常被专业人士嘲笑,他们认为业余人士设计的出版物的数量上的增加是以牺牲优秀设计为代价的。学习计算机程序并不等同于拥有了创作连贯、外观上造型优美的设计的背景和艺术培训。

Exercises

1. Introduce digital layout and design on your own words.
2. Distinguish the different kinds of equipments used for digital layout and design.
3. Use the support programs to design a project whatever you are favorite.
4. Design a mock-up for a new postage stamp. Celebrating a native animal from a particular nation, to be submitted to their postal service. Scan an image, then size and crop it to fill a 2″ × 3″ rectangle. Label the image in italics, add the country's name in normal style, and write the value of the stamp in bold style.

被动句与长句的翻译

被动句的翻译

被动语态被广泛应用于英语中,当着重指出动作的承受者或不必说明谁是动作的执行者时,就用被动语态。尤其是在科技英语中,被动语态用得相当多,常把事物的名称作为主语放在突出的位置上,用被动语态表述有关的动作或状态。而在汉语中被动句却不如英语中使用得频繁。因此,在翻译英语文章时,英语的被动语态一般都译成汉语的主动句式,只有在特别强调被动动作或特别突出被动者时才译成汉语被动句式或无主句。很多被动的动作往往借助于主动语态或具有被动意义的单词来表达。英语被动句译为汉语主动句时,主语可以是原句的主语,可以是 by 后面的名词或代词,也可以是原句中隐藏的动作执行者。被动语态的译法主要有以下几种形式:

一、译成汉语被动句

英译汉时，汉语也有用被动形式来表达的情况。这时通常看重被动的动作。在把英语被动句译成汉语被动句时，我们常常使用"被"、"受到"、"遭到"、"得到"、"让"、"给"、"把"、"使"、"由"等措词。如：

① If the signal is transmitted by analog techniques, the received signal will be severely corrupted by noise.

如果用模拟技术进行信号传输，那么接收到的信号将要受到噪声的严重破坏。

② It is more likely that print will be used as a supplementary medium in most telecommunications—based systems, and better ways of communicating information through print will be investigated and incorporated into the design of study guides and other print—based media.

打印机将更有可能在大部分基于电信的系统中被用作补充媒体，而且通过打印而传递信息的这种较好方式将被审查并成为学习指导书和其他基于打印的媒体的设计中去。

③ His many contributions—in particular, those concerned with the series and transform that carry his name—are made even more impressive by the circumstances under which he worked.

他当时进行研究所处的境遇使他的许多贡献（特别是以他的名字命名的级数和变换）给人留下了极深的印象。

二、译成汉语主动

直接将原文的被动语态按主动语态译成汉语的主动句。这类句子有的是英语中形式上是被动句，但意义上是主动的句子；有的则是英语从习惯来说要用被动语态表达，而汉语习惯于用主动语态来表达的句子。如：

① The machine will be repaired tomorrow.

这台机器明天修理。（不必译作：这台机器明天被修理。）

② The experiment will be finished in a month.

这项实验将在一个月后完成。（不必译作：这项实验将在一个月后被完成。）

③ A signal is called a digital signal if its time is discretized and its amplitude is quantized.

时间上离散，幅值上量化的信号称为数字信号。

④ Signals are presented mathematically as functions of one or more independent variables.

在数学上，信号可以表示为一个或多个变量的函数。

⑤ This reliability can further be improved by using error—detecting and error—correcting codes.

利用检错和纠错编码能进一步提高可靠性。

⑥ This organ is situated at the base of the brain.

该器官位于脑底。

⑦ It is well-known that paper was first made in China.

众所周知，纸最初是在中国发明的。

在"it is (has been) + p.p + that."句型中,it 引导的被动语态常有固定的用法:

It is assumed that:人们认为

It is said that:据说

It is learned that:据闻

It is supposed that:据推测

It is considered that:据估计

It is believed that:人们认为

It is reported that:据报道

It is well-known that:众所周知

It is asserted that:有人断言

It can't be denied that:不可否认

It must be admitted that:必须承认

It must be pointed that:必须指出

三、译成汉语的加强语句

当英语被动句不是强调被动的动作,而只是强调或肯定某一事实或行为的存在时,通常可用"是……的"或"为所"等句式来翻译此类句子。如

① These computers were made in Xinhua Company.

这些电子计算机是新华公司制造的。

② The project was completed last year.

这个项目是去年完成的。

③ The cakes which have just been cooked are made of corn.

刚做好的蛋糕是玉米做的。

四、译成汉语的无主句

在科技英语中,在讲述什么事情时往往是强调如何去做,而不介意谁去做。对于这一类被动句的翻译,我们可以译为汉语无主句。

① Now the heart can be safely opened and its valves repaired.

现在可以安全地打开心脏,并对心脏瓣膜进行修复。

② This instrument must be handled with great care.

必须仔细操作这台仪器。

总之,在翻译英语被动语态语句时,不能固守原句,要灵活地采用多种翻译技巧,使译文既在内容上忠实于原文,又符合汉语的表达方式。

长句的翻译

英语习惯于用长句表达比较复杂的概念,而汉语则不同,常常使用若干短句,并列表达思想。长句在科技英语文章中出现得极为频繁,一般来说,造成长句的原因有三方面:

1. 修饰语过多;

2. 并列成分多;

3. 语言结构层次多。

在翻译长句时,首先不要因为句子太长而产生畏惧心理,因为无论是多么复杂的句子,它都是由一些基本的成分组成的。其次要弄清英语原文的句法结构,找出整个句子的中心内容及其各层意思,然后分析几层意思之间的相互逻辑关系,再按照汉语的特点和表达方式,正确地译出原文的意思,不必拘泥于原文的形式。

分析长句的结构应考虑以下几个方面:

1. 找出全句的主语、谓语和宾语,从整体上把握句子的结构。

2. 找出句中从句的引导词,分析从句的功能。例如,是否为主语从句、宾语从句、表语从句等,若是状语,它是表示原因、结果,还是表示条件,等等。

3. 分析词、短语和从句之间的相互关系,例如,定语从句所修饰的先行词是哪一个等。

4. 注意插入语等其他成分。

5. 注意分析句子中是否有固定词组或固定搭配。

在翻译英语长句的时候,要特别注意英语和汉语之间的差异,长句要恰当地断成长度适中、合乎汉语习惯的句子。长句的翻译是难点也是重点,关键是首先找出句子的骨架,即主、谓、宾语,然后再将其他修饰成分嵌入框架。如果英文句子内容符合汉语规则,则可自前而后依序译出;如果句子内容顺序不符合汉语规则,可根据逻辑关系从后向前译出;如果不便用一句话表达,可将句子重新组织,按逻辑关系分成两个或数个短句。只要能完整准确地传达原意,即使没有拘泥于原文结构,也是正确的。下面通过几个例子加以说明。

① It is a device which converts analog signals (such as sound or voice from microphone), to digital data so that the signal can be processed by a digital circuit such as a digital signal processor.

结构分析:弄清该句的句法结构是翻译此句的关键,根据句子结构和语意分析,这个句子是由 which 引导的定语从句,主句为 It is a device,从句的结构比较复杂,在从句中 so that 引导目的状语,另外要注意的是这个句子要译成汉语的主动句。

参考译文:该转换器将模拟信号(如麦克风传出的话音信号)转换成数字信号后,送入诸如数字信号处理器这样的的数字线路进行处理。

② Even with the differences between print and digital media, some universal information design principles—indifferent to language, culture, or time—help maximize the effectiveness of any information display.

结构分析:在这个句子中,with 引导伴随状语,indifferent to language, culture, or time 作为前置的条件状语,然后按中文的语序来翻译就可以了。

参考译文:虽然印刷媒体和数字媒体存在不同,但是有一些通用的信息设计原则,不管语言、文化或者时间是否不同都可以提高信息表现的最大效果。

③ The Master of Digital Media is a flexible program that can be either studied on-campus, fully online or a combination of both depending on your preference.

结构分析:本句由 that 引导定语从句,either...or...意为"要么……要么……"。

参考译文:精通数字媒体技术是一个灵活的过程,可以在校园里学习,可以完全在线学,或根据你的偏好将两种方式结合。

④ The property described in the preceding paragraph would not be particularly useful, unless it were true that a large class of interesting functions could be represented by linear combinations of complex exponentials.

结构分析:此句 unless 意为:"如果不,除非",根据汉语的表达习惯,译文的表达顺序与原文正好相反。

参考译文:除非很多有用信号都能用复指数函数的线性组合来表示,否则上面所讨论的性质就不是特别有用。

⑤ This is separate from the structural design of a web site, which provides a framework into which the content is inserted, and the presentation of a site, which involves graphic design.

结构分析:此句中包含两个 which 引导的非限制性定语从句,其中第一个非限制性定语从句中包含由介词+which 引导的定语从句。将整个句子的结构理顺后,整个句子就好理解了。

参考译文:这与网站的结构设计是分开的,网站的结构设计提供了一个内容可以嵌入进的框架,以及一个站点的外观,包括绘画设计。

⑥ After several other attempts to have his work accepted and published by the Institute de France, Fourier undertook the writing of another version of his work, which appeared as the text "The Analytical Theory of Heat".

结构分析:根据句子结构和语意分析,这个句子可分成4段:状语(After…)+嵌套在状语中的后置定语(to have…)+主句(Fourier undertook…)+定语从句(which…)。从语意上讲,主句讲的是结果,从句说的是细节。根据汉语的表达习惯,译文的表达顺序与原文相同。

参考译文:为了使研究成果能被法兰西研究院接受并发表,在经过了几次尝试之后,傅立叶把他的成果以另一种方式呈现在《热的分析理论》这本书中。

⑦ You already learned about the missing font support in XNA and you know that using bitmap fonts is the only option to display text in XNA (apart from using some custom 3D font rendering maybe).

结构分析:此句中, that 引导的是宾语从句,using 是现在分词作名词性结构,using bitmap fonts 作主语成分,using some custom 3D font 和介词 apart from 构成介宾结构,rendering 现在分词作后置定语。根据汉语的表达习惯,译文的表达顺序与原文相同。

参考译文:你已经知道了在 XNA 中没有字体支持,而且位图字体是现在唯一的显示文本的方法(除了渲染一些3D字体外)。

⑧ Science moves forward, they say, not so much through the insights of great men of genius as because of more ordinary things like improved techniques and tools.

结构分析:此句中的主要结构涉及 not so much…as… 的固定表达,意为:"与其说……不如说……"。

参考译文:他们说,科学的发展与其说是借助伟大天才的真知灼见,不如说是由于改进了技术和工具等更为普通的事物。

英汉语序的对比与翻译

英译汉、汉译英的翻译方法和技巧是建立在英汉两种语言语句结构和语序的对比之上的。翻译的本质是不同思维方式的转换,思维的方式决定着语言的表达形式。西方民族的思维形式是重在分析,这种思维形式使西方人惯于"由一列多"的思维,句子结构以主语和谓语为核心,统摄各种短语和从句,结构复杂,形成了"树杈形"的句式结构;而东方民族思维形式是重在综合,这种思维形式使中国人注重整体和和谐,强调"从多而一"的思维形式,句子结构以动词为中心,以时间顺序为语序链,形成"流水型"的句式结构。

例如:He had flown yesterday from Beijing where he spent his vocation after finishing the meeting he had taken part in in Tianjin.

他本来在天津开会,会议一结束,他就上北京去度假了,昨天才坐飞机回来。

从以上句子来看,汉语句子以动词为关键词,以时间顺序为语序链;而英语句子则以主要动词为谓语,以分词、介词、不定式、动名词或介词等短语(或从句)表示汉语中相应动词的语义和动作的先后顺序。汉语的几个短句往往可以译成一个由英语关联词及各种短语联接在一起的一个英语长句。因此翻译时,必须按照东西方民族思维方式的特点,调整语句结构,以符合英汉语的表达习惯。

从语言上看,英语句子结构复杂,多长句;汉语多短句。英语多用被动,汉语多用主动。英语多变化,汉语多重复。英语较抽象,汉语较具体。如:

There is no race of men anywhere on earth so backward that it has no language, no set of speech sounds by which the people communicate with one another.

在世界上的任何种族,不论其多么落后,都有自己的语言,都有人们用以交流的语言体系。

从语序上看,英汉语句中的主要成分主语、谓语、宾语或表语的词序基本上是一致的,但各种定语的位置,各种状语的次序和从句的次序在英、汉语言中则有同有异。下面分别加以说明。

一、定语语序的对比

1. 形容词、分词作定语。英语中,形容词和分词作定语通常放在所修饰的名词之前,但在有些情况下,如修饰 some、any、every、nobody、nothing、noone 时,形容词必须后置。而在汉语中形容词作定语一般都前置。例如:

We were pleased at the inspiring news.(前置)
听到这个鼓舞人心的消息我们很高兴。(前置)
The excited people rushed into the building.(前置)
激动的人们冲进了这幢大楼。(前置)
I've got something important to tell you.(后置)
我有重要的事要告诉你。(前置)
He was the only person awake at the moment.(后置)
他是那时唯一醒着的人。(前置)

2. 短语作定语。英语中,修饰名词的短语一般放在名词之后,而汉语则往往反之,例如:

The next train to arrive was from New York.(不定式作定语,后置)

下一列到站的火车是从纽约开来的。(前置)

There was no time to think.(不定式作定语,后置)

已经没有时间考虑了。(后置)

The man standing by the window is our teacher.(分词短语作定语,后置)

站在窗户旁的那位男士是我们的老师。(前置)

二、状语语序的对比

英语中状语短语可放在被修饰的动词之前或之后,译成汉语时则大多数放在被修饰的动词之前。例如:

He is sleeping in the bedroom.(位于动词之后)

他正在卧室里睡觉。(位于动词之前)

英语中时间状语、地点状语的排列一般是从小到大,而汉语中则是从大到小。例如:

Fourier was born on March 21, 1768, in Auxerre, France.

傅立叶1768年3月21日生于法国奥克斯雷市。

三、从句语序的对比

英语复合句中,从句的位置比较灵活,可以放在主句之前,也可以放在主句之后。而汉语中,通常是从句在前,主句在后。如对于时间状语从句,一般是按时间的先后来描述,对于原因状语从句,一般是原因在前,结果在后。例如:

I went out for a walk after I had my dinner.(后置)

After I had my dinner, I went out for a walk.(前置)

我吃了晚饭后出去散步。(前置)

I will go on with the work when I come back tomorrow.(后置)

我明天回来时会继续干这份工作的。(前置)

I haven't seen him since I came here.(后置)

我来这儿后还没见过他呢。(前置)

He had to stay in bed because he was ill.(后置)

因为他病了,他只好呆在床上。(前置)

根据汉英句子语序特点和表达习惯,采取一些必要的手段来调整语句的顺序,在翻译当中是必要的,因此,只有了解汉英两种语言语序的不同,才能在汉英互译时,以符合汉英语言的表达形式进行翻译。

Chapter 8 2D Animation

▲ **Knowledge Objectives**

When you have completed this chapter, you should be able to:
- Know about traditional animation's processing and relative technique.
- Can master the main formats of animation and tell the relation and differences between them.
- Can choose the suitable method to capture traditional animations with various ways.
- Be able to operate some special software to process different file formats animations.

▲ **Professional Terms**

animatic	动画影像分镜
animator	动画师
cel animation	赛璐珞动画
clean-up animators	清稿动画师
Color Mixer	彩色混合器
inbetweener	补间动画师
Lempel-Ziv Walch(LZW)	压缩格式
soundtrack	音轨
story reel	故事轴
storyboard	分镜头
videomatics	影像分镜

Part 1 Outline of Traditional Animation[1]

Traditional animation, also referred to as classical animation, cel animation, or hand-drawn animation, is the oldest and historically and the most popular form of animation. In a traditionally-animated cartoon, each frame is drawn by hand. The term "traditional animation" is often used in contrast with the now more commonly used computer animation. Following is the simple introduce of the process of traditional Animation.

---

[1] http://en.wikipedia.org/wiki/Traditional_animation

Storyboards

Traditionally-animated productions, just like other forms of animation, usually begin life as a storyboard, which is a script of sorts written with images as well as words, similar to a giant comic strip. The images allow the animation team to plan the flow of the plot and the composition of the imagery. The storyboard artists will have regular meetings with the director, and may have to redraw or "re-board" a sequence many times before it meets final approval.

Voice Recording

Before true animation begins, a preliminary soundtrack or "scratch track" is recorded, so that the animation may be more precisely synchronized to the soundtrack. Given the slow, methodical manner in which traditional animation is produced, it is almost always easier to synchronize animation to a pre-existing soundtrack than it is to synchronize a soundtrack to pre-existing animation. A completed cartoon soundtrack will feature music, sound effects, and dialogue performed by voice actors. However, the scratch track used during animation typically contains just the voices, any vocal songs that the characters must sing along to, and temporary musical score tracks; the final score and sound effects are added in post-production.

In the case of most pre-1930 sound animated cartoons, the sound was post-synched; that is, the sound track was recorded after the film elements were finished by watching the film and performing the dialogue, music, and sound effects required. Some studios, most notably Fleischer Studios, continued to post-synch their cartoons through most of the 1930s, which allowed for the presence of the "muttered ad-libs" present in many Popeye the Sailor and Betty Boop cartoons.

Animatic

Often, an animatic or story reel is made after the soundtrack is created, but before full animation begins. An animatic typically consists of pictures of the storyboard synchronized with the soundtrack. This allows the animators and directors to work out any script and timing issues that may exist with the current storyboard. The storyboard and soundtrack are amended if necessary, and a new animatic may be created and reviewed with the director until the storyboard is perfected. Editing the film at the animatic stage prevents the animation of scenes that would be edited out of the film; as traditional animation is a very expensive and time-consuming process, creating scenes that will eventually be edited out of the completed cartoon is strictly avoided.

In the mid 1970s, these were known as videomatics and used primarily for test commercial projects.

Advertising agencies today employ the use of animatics to test their commercials before they are made into full up spots. Animatics use drawn artwork, with moving pieces (for example, an arm that reaches for a product, or a head that turns). Video storyboards are similar to animatics, but do not have moving pieces. Photomatics are another option when creating test spots, but instead of using drawn artwork, there is a shoot in which hundreds of digital photographs are taken. The large amount of images to choose from may make the process of creating a test commercial a bit easier, as opposed to creating an animatic, because changes to drawn art take time and money. Photomatics generally cost more than animatics, as they require a shoot and on-camera talent.

Design and Timing

Once the animatic has been approved, it and the storyboards are sent to the design departments. Character designers prepare model sheets for all important characters and props in the film. These model sheets will show how a character or object looks from a variety of angles with a variety of poses and expressions, so that all artists working on the project can deliver consistent work. Sometimes, small statues known as maquettes may be produced, so that an animator can see what a character looks like in three dimensions. At the same time, the background stylists will do similar work for the settings and locations in the project, and the art directors and color stylists will determine the art style and color schemes to be used.

While design is going on, the timing director (who in many cases will be the main director) takes the animatic and analyzes exactly what poses, drawings, and lip movements will be needed on what frames. An exposure sheet (or X-sheet for short) is created; this is a printed table that breaks down the action, dialogue, and sound frame-by-frame as a guide for the animators. If a film is based more strongly on music, a bar sheet may be prepared in addition to or instead of an X-sheet. Bar sheets show the relationship between the on-screen action, the dialogue, and the actual musical notation used in the score.

Animation

Once the Animatic is finally approved by the director, animation begins.

In the traditional animation process, animators will begin by drawing sequences of animation on sheets of transparent paper perforated to fit the peg bars in their desks, often using colored pencils, one picture or "frame" at a time. A key animator or lead animator will draw the key drawings in a scene, using the character layouts as a guide. The key animator draws enough of the frames to get across the major points of the action; in a sequence of a character jumping across a gap, the key animator may draw a frame of the character as he is about to leap, two or more frames as the character is flying through the air, and the frame for the character landing on the other side of the gap.

Timing is important for the animators drawing these frames; each frame must match exactly what is going on in the soundtrack at the moment the frame will appear, or else the discrepancy between sound and visual will be distracting to the audience. For example, in high-budget productions, extensive effort is given in making sure a speaking character's mouth matches in shape the sound that character's actor is producing as he or she speaks.

While working on a scene, a key animator will usually prepare a pencil test of the scene. A pencil test is a preliminary version of the final animated scene; the pencil drawings are quickly photographed or scanned and synced with the necessary soundtracks. This allows the animation to be reviewed and improved upon before passing the work on to his assistant animators, who will add details and some of the missing frames in the scene. The work of the assistant animators is reviewed, pencil-tested, and corrected until the lead animator is ready to meet with the director and have his scene sweatboxed, or reviewed by the director, producer, and other key creative team members. Similar to the storyboarding stage, an animator may be required to re-do a scene many times before the director will approve it.

In high-budget animated productions, often each major character will have an animator or group of animators solely dedicated to drawing that character. The group will be made up of one supervising animator, a small group of key animators, and a larger group of assistant animators. For scenes where two characters interact, the key animators for both characters will decide which character is "leading" the scene, and that character will be drawn first. The second character will be animated to react to and support the actions of the "leading" character.

Once the key animation is approved, the lead animator forwards the scene on to the clean-up department, made up of the clean-up animators and the inbetweeners. The clean-up animators take the lead and assistant animators' drawings and trace them onto a new sheet of paper, taking care in including all of the details present on the original model sheets, so that it appears that one person animated the entire film. The inbetweeners will draw in whatever frames are still missing in between the other animators' drawings. This procedure is called tweening. The resulting drawings are again pencil-tested and sweatboxed until they meet approval.

At each stage during pencil animation, approved artwork is spliced into the Leica reel.

This process is the same for both character animation and special effects animation, which on most high-budget productions are done in separate departments. Effects animators animate anything that moves and is not a character, including props, vehicles, machinery and phenomena such as fire, rain, and explosions. Sometimes, instead of drawings, a number of special processes are used to produce special effects in animated films; rain, for example, has been created in Disney animated films since the late-1930s by filming slow-motion footage of water in front of a black background, with the resulting film superimposed over the animation.

Backgrounds

While the animation is being done, the background artists will paint the sets over which the action of each animated sequence will take place. These backgrounds are generally done in gouache or acrylic paint, although some animated productions have used backgrounds done in watercolor, oil paint, or even crayon. Background artists follow very closely the work of the background layout artists and color stylists (which is usually compiled into a workbook for their use), so that the resulting backgrounds are harmonious in tone with the character designs.

Know about the simple process of traditional animation, then let's learn something about the relative technique of traditional animation.

Xerography

Applied to animation by Ub Iwerks at the Walt Disney studio during the late 1950s, the electrostatic copying technique called xerography allowed the drawings to be copied directly onto the cels, eliminating much of the "inking" portion of the ink-and-paint process. This saved time and money, and it also made it possible to put in more details and to control the size of the xeroxed objects and characters (this replaced the little known, and seldom used, photographic lines technique at Disney, used to reduce the size of animation when needed). At first it resulted in a sketchier look, but the technique was improved upon over time.

The xerographic method was first tested by Disney in a few scenes of Sleeping Beauty, and was first fully used in the short film Goliath II, while the first feature entirely using this process was One Hundred and One Dalmatians (1961). The graphic style of this film was strongly influenced by the process. Some hand inking was still used together with xerography in this and subsequent films when distinct colored lines were needed. Later, colored toners became available, and several distinct line colors could be used, even simultaneously. For instance, in The Rescuers the characters outlines are gray. White and blue toners were used for special effects, such as snow and water.

The APT Process

Invented by Dave Spencer for the 1985 Disney film The Black Cauldron, the APT (Animation Photo Transfer) process was a technique for transferring the animators' art onto cels. Basically, the process was a modification of a repro-photographic process; the artists' work were photographed on high-contrast "litho" film, and the image on the resulting negative was then transferred to a cel covered with a layer of light sensitive dye. The cel was exposed through the negative. Chemicals were then used to remove the unexposed portion. Small and delicate details were still inked by hand if needed. Spencer received an Academy Award for Technical Achievement for developing this process.

Computers and Traditional Animation

The methods mentioned above describe the techniques of an animation process that originally depended on cels in its final stages, but painted cels are rare today as the computer moves into the animation studio, and the outline drawings are usually scanned into the computer and filled with digital paint instead of being transferred to cels and then colored by hand. The drawings are composited in a computer program on many transparent "layers" much the same way as they are with cels, and made into a sequence of images which may then be transferred onto film or converted to a digital video format.

It is now also possible for animators to draw directly into a computer using a graphics tablet, Cintiq or a similar device, where the outline drawings are done in a similar manner as they would be on paper. The Goofy short How To Hook Up Your Home Theater (2007) represented Disney's first project based on the paperless technology available today. Some of the advantages are the possibility and potential of controlling the size of the drawings while working on them, drawing directly on a multiplane background and eliminating the need of photographing line tests and scanning.

Though traditional animation is now commonly done with computers, it is important to differentiate computer-assisted traditional animation from 3D computer animation, such as Toy Story and ReBoot. However, often traditional animation and 3D computer animation will be used together, as in Don Bluth's Titan A. E. and Disney's Tarzan and Treasure Planet. Most anime still use traditional animation today. DreamWorks executive Jeffrey Katzenberg coined the term "tradigital animation" to describe films produced by his studio which incorporated elements of traditional and computer animation equally, such as Spirit: Stallion of the Cimarron and Sinbad: Legend of the Seven Seas.

Interestingly, many modern video games such as Viewtiful Joe, The Legend of Zelda: The Wind Waker and others use "cel-shading" animation filters to make their full 3D animation appear as though it were drawn in a traditional cel style. This technique was also used in the animated movie Appleseed, and cel-shaded 3D animation is typically integrated with cel animation in Disney films and in many television shows, such as the Fox animated series Futurama.

Special Effects Animation

Besides traditional animated characters, objects and backgrounds, many other techniques are used to create special elements such as smoke, lightning and "magic", and to give the animation in general a distinct visual appearance.

Notable examples can be found in movies such as Fantasia, Wizards, The Lord of the Rings, The Little Mermaid, The Secret of NIMH and The Thief and the Cobbler. Today the special effects are mostly done with computers, but earlier they had to be done by hand. To produce these effects, the animators used different techniques, such as drybrush, airbrush, charcoal, grease pencil, backlit animation or, during shooting, the cameraman used multiple exposures with diffusing screens, filters or gels. For instance, the Nutcracker Suite segment in Fantasia has a fairy sequence where stippled cels are used, creating a soft pastel look.

Part 2　Formats of 2D Animation

It mainly contains three formats of 2D Animation, which are SWF, GIF and EXE.

SWF [1] (see Table 8-1)

Table 8-1　Some Properties of the File Format SWF

Filename extension	.swf
Internet media type	application/x-shockwave-flash
Developed by	FutureWave Software later taken over by Macromedia and Adobe Systems
Type of format	Vector graphic animation

The file format SWF, has variably stood for "Small Web Format" or "Shockwave Flash". It is a partially open repository for multimedia and vector graphics, originating with FutureWave Software and then coming under the control of Adobe. Intended to be small enough for publication on the web, SWF files can contain animations or applets of varying degrees of interactivity and function.

SWF currently functions as the dominant format for displaying "animated" vector graphics on the Web. It may also be used for programs, commonly games, using ActionScript.

SWF files can be generated from within several Adobe products: Flash, Flex Builder (an IDE), as well as through MXMLC, a command line application compiler which is part of the freely available Flex SDK. Other than Adobe products, SWFs can be built with open source Motion-Twin ActionScript 2 Compiler (MTASC), the open source Ming library, the free software suite SWFTools, the proprietary SWiSH Max2. There are also various third party programs that can produce files in this format, such as Multimedia Fusion 2, Captivate, SWiSH Max or BannerSnack.

History of SWF

FutureWave Software, a small company later acquired by Macromedia, originally defined the file format with one primary objective: to create small files for displaying entertaining animations. The idea was to have a format which could be reused by a player running on any system and which would work with slower network connections.

Adobe acquired Macromedia in 2005.

On May 1, 2008, Adobe dropped its licensing restrictions on the SWF format specifications, as part of the Open Screen Project. However, Rob Savoye, a member of the Gnash development team, has pointed to some parts of the Flash format which remain closed. On July 1, 2008, Adobe released code which allowed the Google and Yahoo search-engines to crawl and index SWF files.

Description

Originally limited to presenting vector-based objects and images in a simple sequential

---

[1] http://en.wikipedia.org/wiki/Swf

manner, the format in its later versions allows audio (since Flash 3), video (since Flash 6) and many different possible forms of interaction with the end-user. Once created, SWF files can be played by the Adobe Flash Player, working either as a browser plugin or as a stand-alone player. SWF files can also be encapsulated with the player, creating a self-running SWF movie called a "projector".

Adobe makes available plugins, such as Adobe Flash Player and Adobe Integrated Runtime, to play SWF files in web browsers on many desktop operating systems, including Microsoft Windows, Apple Mac OS X, and Linux on the x86 architecture. As of 2007 intensive development had taken place on Gnash, a free-software implementation of a SWF player. Another FOSS implementation is Swfdec.

Based on an independent study conducted by Millward Brown, over 99% of Web users now have an SWF plugin installed, with around 90% having the latest version of the Flash Player.

Sony PlayStation Portable consoles can play limited SWF files in Sony's web browser, beginning with firmware version 2.71. Both the Nintendo Wii and the Sony PS3 consoles can run SWF files through their Internet browsers.

Also many mobile phones support flash as standard, such as Nokia.

Licensing

Adobe makes available a partial specification of SWF. The document is claimed to be missing "huge amounts" of information needed to completely implement SWF, omitting specifications for RTMP and Sorenson Spark. However, the RTMP specification was released publicly in June 2009, and the Sorenson Spark codec is not Adobe's property. Until May 1, 2008, implementing software that plays SWF was disallowed by the specification's license. On that date, as part of its Open Screen Project, Adobe dropped all such restrictions on the SWF and FLV formats. However, the SWF specification was released under a very restrictive license.

This manual may not be copied, photocopied, reproduced, translated, or converted to any electronic or machine-readable form in whole or in part without written approval from Adobe Systems Incorporated.

As a result, some believe that coordinating with developers of an SWF implementation is made more difficult because the document cannot be easily shared. However, because the document can be directly downloaded from the Adobe web site by anyone wishing to read it, the impact of that restriction may be inconsequential.

Implementing software which creates SWF files has always been permitted, on the condition that the resulting files render "error free in the latest publicly available version of Adobe Flash Player."

GNU has started developing a free software SWF player called Gnash under the GNU General Public License (GPL). Another player is the GNU LGPL Swfdec. However, GNU does not provide financial support for either project.

Scaleform GFx is a commercial alternative SWF player that features full hardware acceleration using the GPU and has high conformance up to Flash 8 and AS2. Scaleform GFx is licensed as a game middleware solution and used by many PC and console 3D games for user interfaces, HUDs, mini games, and video playback.

GIF (Graphics Interchange Format) (see Table 8-2)[1]

Table 8-2 Some Properties of the File Format GIF

Graphics Interchange Format	
Filename extension	.gif
Internet media type	image/gif
Type code	GIF GIFf
Uniform Type Identifier	com.compuserve.gif
Magic number	GIF87a/GIF89a
Developed by	CompuServe
Type of format	Raster graphics image format

The Graphics Interchange Format (GIF) is a bitmap image format that was introduced by CompuServe in 1987 and has since come into widespread usage on the World Wide Web due to its wide support and portability.

The format supports up to 8 bits per pixel thus allowing a single image to reference a palette of up to 256 distinct colors. The colors are chosen from the 24-bit RGB color space. It also supports animations and allows a separate palette of 256 colors for each frame. The color limitation makes the GIF format unsuitable for reproducing color photographs and other images with continuous color, but it is well-suited for simpler images such as graphics or logos with solid areas of color.

GIF images are compressed using the Lempel-Ziv-Welch (LZW) lossless data compression technique to reduce the file size without degrading the visual quality. This compression technique was patented in 1985. Controversy over the licensing agreement between the patent holder, Unisys, and CompuServe in 1994 spurred the development of the Portable Network Graphics (PNG) standard; since then all the relevant patents have expired.

History of GIF

CompuServe introduced the GIF format in 1987 to provide a color image format for their file downloading areas, replacing their earlier run-length encoding (RLE) format, which was black and white only. GIF became popular because it used LZW data compression, which was

---

[1] http://en.wikipedia.org/wiki/Gif

more efficient than the run-length encoding that formats such as PCX and MacPaint used, and fairly large images could therefore be downloaded in a reasonably short time, even with very slow modems.

The original version of the GIF format was called 87a. In 1989, CompuServe devised an enhanced version, called 89a that added support for animation delays (multiple images in a stream were already supported in 87a), transparent background colors, and storage of application-specific metadata. The 89a specification also supports incorporating text labels as text (not embedding them in the graphical data), but as there is little control over display fonts, this feature is not widely used. The two versions can be distinguished by looking at the first six bytes of the file (the "magic number" or "signature"), which, when interpreted as ASCII, read "GIF87a" and "GIF89a", respectively.

GIF was one of the first two image formats commonly used on Web sites, the other being the black and white XBM. JPEG came later with the Mosaic browser.

The feature of storing multiple images in one file, accompanied by control data, is used extensively on the Web to produce simple animations. The optional interlacing feature, which stores image scan lines out of order in such a fashion that even a partially downloaded image was somewhat recognizable, also helped GIF's popularity, as a user could abort the download if it was not what was required.

Usage

- GIFs are suitable for sharp-edged line art (such as logos) with a limited number of colors. This takes advantage of the format's lossless compression, which favors flat areas of uniform color with well defined edges (in contrast to JPEG, which favors smooth gradients and softer images).
- GIFs can also be used to store low-color sprite data for games.
- GIFs can be used for small animations and low-resolution film clips.
- In view of the general limitation on the GIF image palette to 256 colors, it is not usually used as a format for digital photography. Digital photographers use image file formats capable of reproducing a greater range of colors, such as TIFF, RAW or the lossy JPEG, which is more suitable for compressing photographs.
- The PNG format is a popular alternative to GIF images since it uses better compression techniques and does not have a limit of 256 colors, but PNGs do not support animations. The MNG and APNG formats, both derived from PNG, support animations, but are not widely used.

Palettes

GIF is palette-based (see Figure 8-1): the colors used in an image (a frame) in the file have their RGB values defined in a palette table that can hold up to 256 entries, and the data

Figure 8-1 An example of a GIF image saved with a 'web-safe' palette and dithered using the Floyd-Steinberg method. Note that due to the reduced number of colors in the image, there are severe display issues.

for the image refer to the colors by their indexes (0—255) in the palette table. The color definitions in the palette can be drawn from a color space of millions of shades (2^{24} shades, 8 bits for each primary), but the maximum number of colors a frame can use is 256. This limitation seemed reasonable when GIF was developed because few people could afford the hardware to display more colors simultaneously. Simple graphics, line drawings, cartoons, and grey-scale photographs typically need fewer than 256 colors.

As a further refinement, each frame can designate one index as a "transparent background color": any pixel assigned this index takes on the color of the pixel in the same position from the background, which may have been determined by a previous frame of animation.

Many techniques, collectively called dithering, have been developed to approximate a wider range of colors with a small color palette by using pixels of two or more colors to approximate in-between colors. These techniques sacrifice spatial resolution to approximate deeper color resolution. While not part of the GIF specification, dithering can of course be used in images subsequently encoded as GIF images. This is often not an ideal solution for GIF images, both because the loss of spatial resolution typically makes an image look fuzzy on the screen, and because the dithering patterns often interfere with the compressibility of the image data, working against GIF's main purpose.

In the early days of graphical web browsers, graphics cards with 8-bit buffers (allowing only 256 colors) were common and it was fairly common to make GIF images using the websafe palette. This ensured predictable display, but severely limited the choice of colors. Now that 32-bit graphics cards, which support 24-bit color, are the norm, palettes can be populated with the optimum colors for individual images.

A small color table may suffice for small images, and keeping the color table small allows the file to be downloaded faster. Both the 87a and 89a specifications allow color tables of 2^n colors for any n from 1 through 8. Most graphics applications will read and display GIF images with any of these table sizes; but some do not support all sizes when creating images. Tables of 2, 16, and 256 colors are widely supported.

Example GIF File

Sample image (see Figure 8-2), 3 pixels wide by 5 high.

Chapter 8 2D Animation

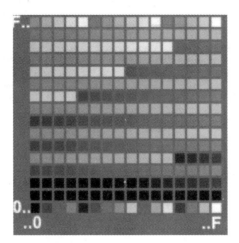

Figure 8-2 Bytes D_h to $30C_h$ Define a Palette of 256 Colors.

Microsoft's Paint program saves a small black and white image as the following GIF file (see Figure 8-3). Paint does not make optimal use of the GIF format; due to the unnecessarily large color table and symbol width, this GIF file is not an efficient representation of the 15-pixel image (illustrated enlarged above).

```
byte#   hexadecimal      text or
(hex)                    value       Meaning
-----   -----------      --------    -------
000:    47 49 46
        38 39 61         GIF89a      Header
                                     Logical Screen Descriptor
006:    03 00            3           - canvas width in pixels
008:    05 00            5           - canvas height in pixels
00A:    F7                           - GCT follows (256 colors at 3 x 8 bits/primary)
00B:    00               0           - background color #0
00C:    00                           - default pixel aspect ratio
                         R    G   B  Global Color Table
00D:    00 00 00         0    0   0  - color #0 black
010:    80 00 00         128  0   0  - color #1 dark red ("maroon")
  :       :                             :
085:    00 00 00         0    0   0  - color #40 black
  :       :                             :
30A:    FF FF FF         255 255 255 - color #255 white
30D:    21 F9                        Graphic Control Extension (Sentinel '!' + GCE label F9)
30F:    04                           - 4 bytes of extension data
310:    01                           - a transparent color index is indicated
311:    00 00                        - delay for animation: no delay
313:    10               16          - color #16 is transparent
314:    00                           - end (empty sub-block)
315:    2C                           Image Descriptor (Sentinel ',')
316:    00 00 00 00      (0,0)       - NW corner of image is at (0,0) of canvas
31A:    03 00 05 00      (3,5)       - and is 3x5 (i.e., fills the full canvas)
31E:    00                           - other characteristics (e.g., no local color table)
31F:    08               8           LZW min. code size (symbol width)
320:    0B               11          11 bytes LZW encoded image data follow
321:    00 51 FC 1B 28 70 A0 C1 83 01 01
32C:    00                           - end (empty sub-block)
32D:    3B                           Trailer (Sentinel ';')
```

Figure 8-3 Microsoft's Paint Program Saves a Small Black and White Image

Image Coding

The image pixel colors, scanned horizontally from top left, are converted by LZW encoding to codes that are then mapped into bytes for storing in the file. For the sample image above the reversible mapping between 9-bit codes and bytes is shown below (see Figure 8-4).

9-bit (hex)	binary	Bytes (hex)
100	00000000	00
028	01010000|1	51
0FF	111111|00	FC
103	00011|011	1B
102	0010|1000	28
103	011|10000	70
106	10|100000	A0
107	1|1000001	C1
	10000011	83
101	00000001	01
	0000000|1	01

Figure 8-4　Coding of the sample image.

A slight compression is evident: pixel colors defined initially by 15 bytes are exactly represented by 12 code bytes including control codes. The encoding process that produces the 9-bit codes is shown below (see Figure 8-5). A local string accumulates pixel color numbers from the palette, with no output action as long as the local string can be found in a code table. There is special treatment of the first two pixels that arrive before the table grows from its initial size by additions of strings. After each output code, the local string is initialized to the latest pixel color (that could not be included in the output code).

For clarity the table is shown in Figure 8-5 as being built of strings of increasing length. That scheme can function but the table consumes an unpredictable amount of memory. Memory can be saved in practice by noting that each new string to be stored consists of a previously stored string augmented by one character. It is economical to store at each address only two words: an existing address and one character.

```
                        Table            9-bit
                        string --> code  code   Action
                           #0 | 000h            Initialize root table of 9-bit codes
                      palette |   :
                       colors |   :
                         #255 | 0FFh
                          clr | 100h
                          end | 101h
                                          100h   Clear
Pixel              Local
color  Palette     string
BLACK  #40         28                     028h   1st pixel always to output
WHITE  #255        FF                            String found in table
                   28 FF        | 102h           Always add 1st string to table
                   FF                            Initialize local string
WHITE  #255        FF FF                         String not found in table
                                           0FFh  - output code for previous string
                   FF FF        | 103h           - add latest string to table
                   FF                            - initialize local string
WHITE  #255        FF FF                         String found in table
BLACK  #40         FF FF 28                      String not found in table
                                           103h  - output code for previous string
                   FF FF 28     | 104h           - add latest string to table
                   28                            - initialize local string
WHITE  #255        28 FF                         String found in table
WHITE  #255        28 FF FF                      String not found in table
                                           102h  - output code for previous string
                   28 FF FF     | 105h           - add latest string to table
                   FF                            - initialize local string
WHITE  #255        FF FF                         String found in table
WHITE  #255        FF FF FF                      String not found in table
                                           103h  - output code for previous string
                   FF FF FF     | 106h           - add latest string to table
                   FF                            - initialize local string
WHITE  #255        FF FF                         String found in table
WHITE  #255        FF FF FF                      String found in table
WHITE  #255        FF FF FF FF                   String not found in table
                                           106h  - output code for previous string
                   FF FF FF FF  | 107h           - add latest string to table
                   FF                            - initialize local string
WHITE  #255        FF FF                         String found in table
WHITE  #255        FF FF FF                      String found in table
WHITE  #255        FF FF FF FF                   String found in table
                                                 No more pixels
                                           107h  - output code for last string
                                           101h  End
```

Figure 8-5　The Encoding Process that Produces the 9-bit Codes

The LZW algorithm requires a search of the table for each pixel. A linear search through up to 4096 addresses would make the coding slow. In practice the codes can be stored in order of numerical value; this allows each search to be done by a SAR (Successive Approximation Register, as used in some ADCs), with only 12 magnitude comparisons. For this efficiency an extra table is needed to convert between codes and actual memory addresses; the extra table upkeeping is needed only when a new code is stored which happens at much less than pixel rate.

Image Decoding

Decoding begins by mapping the stored bytes back to 9-bit codes. These are decoded to recover the pixel colors as shown below (see Figure 8-6). A table identical to the one used in the encoder is built by adding strings by this rule:

```
code        code    code  --> string   Palette color   Action
100h                000h  | #0                         Initialize root table of 9-bit codes
                     :    | palette
                     :    | colors
                    0FFh  | #255
                    100h  | clr
                    101h  | end
028h                                   #40   BLACK     Decode 1st pixel
0FFh        028h                                       Incoming code found in table
                                       #255  WHITE     - output string from table
                    102h  | 28 FF                      - add to table
103h        0FFh                                       Incoming code not found in table
                    103h  | FF FF                      - add to table
                                                       - output string from table
                                       #255  WHITE
                                       #255  WHITE
102h        103h                                       Incoming code found in table
                                                       - output string from table
                                       #40   BLACK
                                       #255  WHITE
                    104h  | FF FF 28
103h        102h                                       - add to table
                                                       Incoming code found in table
                                                       - output string from table
                                       #255  WHITE
                                       #255  WHITE
                    105h  | 28 FF FF                   - add to table
106h        103h                                       Incoming code not found in table
                    106h  | FF FF FF                   - add to table
                                                       - output string from table
                                       #255  WHITE
                                       #255  WHITE
                                       #255  WHITE
107h        106h                                       Incoming code not found in table
                    107h  | FF FF FF FF                - add to table
                                                       - output string from table
                                       #255  WHITE
                                       #255  WHITE
                                       #255  WHITE
                                       #255  WHITE
101h                                                   End
```

Figure 8-6   Decoded means to recover the pixel colors.

Is incoming code found in table?

YES: add string for local code followed by first byte of string for incoming code.

NO: add string for local code followed by copy of its own first byte.

LZW Code Lengths

Shorter code lengths can be used for palettes smaller than the 256 colors in the example. If the palette is only 64 colors (so color indexes are 6 bits wide), the symbols can range from 0 to 63, and the symbol width can be taken to be 6 bits, with codes starting at 7 bits. In fact, the symbol width need not match the palette size: as long as the values decoded are always less than the number of colors in the palette, the symbols can be any width from 2 to 8, and the palette size any power of 2 from 2 to 256. For example, if only the first four colors (values 0 to 3) of the palette are used, the symbols can taken to be 2 bits wide with codes starting at 3 bits.

Conversely, the symbol width could be set at 8, even if only values 0 and 1 are used; these data would only require a 2-color table. Although there would be no point in encoding the file that way, something similar typically happens for bi-color images: the minimum symbol width is 2, even if only values 0 and 1 are used.

The code table initially contains codes that are one bit longer than the symbol size in order to accommodate the two special codes clr and end and codes for strings that are added during the process. When the table is full the code length increases to give space for more strings, up to a maximum code 4095 = FFF(hex). As the decoder builds its table it tracks these increases in code length and it is able to unpack incoming bytes accordingly.

EXE[①]

EXE is the common filename extension denoting an executable file (a program) in the DOS, OpenVMS, Microsoft Windows, Symbian, and OS/2 operating systems. Besides the executable program, many EXE files contain other components called resources, such as bitmaps and icons which the executable program may use for its graphical user interface.

There are several main executable file formats:

- **DOS**

16-bit DOS MZ executable: The original DOS executable file format, these can be identified by the letters "MZ" at the beginning of the file in ASCII.

16-bit New Executable: Introduced with Multitasking MS-DOS 4.0, these can be identified by the "NE" in ASCII. These never became popular or useful for DOS and cannot be run by any other version of DOS, but can usually be run by 32-bit Windows and OS/2 versions.

- **OS/2**

32-bit Linear Executable: Introduced with OS/2 2.0, these can be identified by the "LX" in ASCII. These can only be run by OS/2 2.0 and higher. They are also used by some DOS extenders.

Mixed 16/32-bit Linear Executable: Introduced with OS/2 2.0, these can be identified by the "LE" in ASCII. This format is not used for OS/2 applications anymore, but instead for VxD drivers under Windows 3.x and Windows 9x, and by some DOS extenders.

- **Windows**

32-bit Portable Executable: Introduced with Windows NT, these are the most complex and can be identified by the "PE" in ASCII (although not at the beginning, these files also begin with "MZ"). These can be run by all versions of Windows NT, and also Windows 95 and higher, partially also in DOS using HX DOS Extender. They are also used in BeOS R3, although the format used by BeOS somewhat violates the PE specification as it doesn't specify a

---

① http://en.wikipedia.org/wiki/EXE

correct subsystem.

64-bit Portable Executable: Introduced by 64-bit versions of Windows, these are PE files with a CPU type corresponding to a 64-bit instruction set such as x86-64 or IA-64. These can only be run by 64-bit editions of Microsoft Windows running on machines with the CPU type specified in the file.

- **Other EXE Formats**

Besides these, there are also many custom EXE formats, such as W3 (a collection of LE files, only used in WIN386.EXE), W4 (a compressed collection of LE files, only used in VMM32.VXD), DL, MP, P2, P3 (last three used by Phar Lap extenders), and probably more.

When a 16-bit or 32-bit Windows executable is run by Windows, execution starts at either the NE or the PE, and ignores the MZ code. On the other hand, DOS cannot (except using HX DOS Extender, supports PE files only) execute these files. To prevent DOS from crashing, all Windows executable files should and usually do start with a "working" DOS program called a stub, simply displaying the message "This program cannot be run in DOS mode" (or similar). A few dual-mode programs (MZ-NE or MZ-PE) (such as regedit and some older WinZIP self extractors) include a more functional DOS section.

Part 3   Capture of 2D Animation

Create the Animation[①]

There are two major forms of animation: 2D (hand-drawn, or computer assisted) and 3D (CGI). This page focuses on 2D animation.

The overall capture of creating a 2D animation is divided into three parts: pre-production, production, and post-production.

1. Pre-Production

Pre-production involves establishing the plot of the completed animation. Because each shot in animation is so labor-intensive, it's imperative to get shots right during pre-production. Re-animating a shot (because a character uses knowledge not gained until later in the story, for example) is very expensive, especially compared to live-action filming.

Most animations are storyboarded, in which the main action in each scene is drawn in a comic book-like form. Storyboards are usually pasted on large foam-core or posterboard sheets, which can be quickly read through by the staff. During pre-production, the staff reviews the storyboard for consistency, and parts of the storyboard may be redrawn multiple times.

---

① http://en.wikiversity.org/wiki/2D_Animation_process

In North America, the dialog for the animation is recorded during pre-production. It's then provided to the animators so they can draw mouth movements to precisely match the dialog spoken by the actors. In other parts of the world (most notably in Asia), the dialog is recorded during production as the actors follow along with the rough animation.

2. Production

Each shot in a 2D animation involves multiple single drawings of characters (although some computer programs such as 'Anime Studio', can create characters much like puppets, which can be posed at different keyframes, and the computer moves the character between those keyframes). To demonstrate the concept, think of a still camera that can take many photographs in rapid succession. Imagine aiming that camera at a person and taking many quick photographs as the person walks towards you. Each photograph corresponds to an individual drawing in an animation.

A shot may contain only one drawing (especially in "limited animation" forms like anime), but usually contain about ten to twenty drawings. These drawings are divided into "keys" and "in-betweens." Keys are important drawings that convey the extremes of the character's movement—the first drawing is almost always a key—while in-betweens (or "tweens") are the remaining, less important drawings in the shot.

Figure 8-7 An Inked Drawing

Typically, each drawing begins with a sketch, in pencil, of the character's pose. This drawing is then cleaned up in ink (see Figure 8-7), though this is not always done; Disney went through a period in which this step was skipped, as is most clearly visible in the original 101 Dalmations. Skipping the inking step was thought to make the animation look more vibrant and alive, but critics and audiences didn't like the look.

This is the point at which computers often step in. Some companies' hand-ink each drawing, writing over the cleaned pencil lines with a pen. Others—especially studios whose artists can draw very clean pencil lines—will scan the pencils directly into the computer, then ink the drawing digitally (see Figure 8-8).

Figure 8-8 A Colored Key Cel

The drawing is now considered a "cel." Before computers, the drawing would now be photocopied onto a sheet of clear celluoid or acetate, then hand-painted. This created a "cel," which was placed on top of a background painting and filmed with the click of a film camera. Cels are still highly prized by collectors, though few true cels remain. Many of those on the market are reproductions.

Today, the digital cels are colored on a computer. Meanwhile, a background is drawn (on the computer, or hand-drawn and scanned). The background is imported into an animation program, and each cel is layered onto the background in succession. This is then saved on the computer as a single video file.

In practice, the keys are usually drawn by a top animator, and these are then scanned and assembled into a "rough cut" of the shot while the keys are given to a junior animator, who will draw the tweens (see Figure 8-9). The film can then be assembled during production, and junior animators can be directed in small adjustments to improve the flow of each shot and scene. In Asia, this is typically when dialog is recorded, so that the junior animators can match the tweens to the vocal performance.

Figure 8-9　A Colored Tween

3. Post-Production

Even after all the tweens have been colored and added to the animation, the film is far from complete. There's still music and sound effects to be added, as well as visual effects (glows, hazes, etc.). The animation also may need to be edited in the more traditional film sense; shots cut slightly short or held longer, even scenes cut entirely. It's said that one famous anime series (Gundam Seed) changed its ending when the primary actor broke down during recording, and new animation was hastily drawn, colored, and incorporated into the final minutes of the show.

Animation Library[①]

Animation library is a big database that collects thousands of different types of animations and you can also search the animation you are exactly interested in. Animation library are wide varieties. Some are drawn by hand, and others are made by computer cartographic software.

You can find the free libraries that contain various of animations, such as the following library (see Figure 8-10).

---

① http://www.animationlibrary.com/

Figure 8-10　The World's Largest Animation Collection

There is also special animation library (see Figure 8-11) for children who can be attracted firmly by colorful and interesting animations.

Figure 8-11　Special Animation Library for Children Which Contains Various of Interesting Animations

Part 4 Processing

Flash

Flash is an authoring tool that lets you create anything from a simple animation to a complex, interactive web application such as an online store. You can make your Flash applications media rich by adding pictures, sound, and video. Flash includes many features that make it powerful but easy to use, such as drag-and-drop user interface components, built-in behaviors that add ActionScript to your document, and special effects that you can add to objects.

1. Create a Motion Tween

You create a motion tween by defining properties for an instance, a grouped object, or text in a starting keyframe, and then changing the object's properties in a subsequent keyframe. Flash creates the animation from one keyframe to the next in the frames between the keyframes.

To create a motion tween, you'll take an instance of a tire symbol and make it appears to bounce.

① In the Timeline (Window→Timeline), double-click the Layer 1 title and type **TireAnim.** Press Enter (Windows) or Return (Macintosh) to rename the layer.

② With the TireAnim layer still selected, drag the Tire movie clip from the Library window to the Stage, positioning it above the tire shadow.

③ Use the Selection tool to reposition the tire (see Figure 8-12), if necessary.

④ With the Selection tool still selected, in the TireAnim layer, select Frame 30. Then press F6 to insert a keyframe.

⑤ Select Frame 15 and press F6 to add another keyframe.

⑥ With the playhead still on Frame 15, press Shift to move the tire in a straight line, and drag the tire up (see Figure 8-13).

⑦ In the TireAnim layer, select any frame between Frames 2 and 14. In the Property inspector, select Motion from the Tween pop-up menu. An arrow appears in the Timeline between the two keyframes.

⑧ Select any frame between Frames 16 and 29. Again, use the Tween pop-up menu in the Property inspector to select Motion.

⑨ Select File→Save to save your changes.

 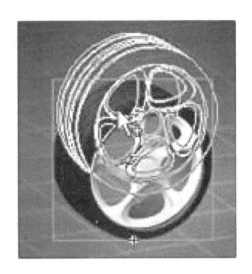

Figure 8-12　Use the Selection Tool to Reposition the Tire　　　　Figure 8-13　Drag the Tire up Straightly

2. Create a Shape Tween

With shape tweening, you specify attributes for a shape in one keyframe, and then modify the shape or draw another shape in a subsequent keyframe. As with motion tweening, Flash creates the animation in the frames between the keyframes.

You'll now set up a tween for the tire's shadow so that as the tire bounces, the shadow moves and fades.

① Click the ShadowAnim layer to select it.

② Select Frame 30 and press F6 to insert a keyframe; then select Frame 15 and press F6 to insert a keyframe.

③ With the playhead on Frame 15, select the Selection tool. Drag the tire shadow slightly up and to the right(see Figure 8-14).

④ With Frame 15 still selected, select the Eyedropper tool in the Tools panel, and then click the shadow object.

If the Color Mixer (see Figure 8-15) is not already open, select Window > Color Mixer to open it, and change the Alpha value from 25% to 10%.

⑤ Click the pop-up menu control in the upper-right side of the Color Mixer and select Close Panel.

⑥ Select any frame between Frames 2 and 14 on the ShadowAnim layer. In the Property inspector, select Shape from the Tween pop-up menu.

⑦ On the ShadowAnim layer, select any frame between Frames 16 and 29. Again, use the Tween pop-up menu in the Property inspector to select Shape.

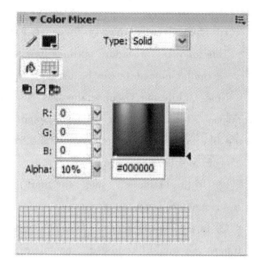

Figure 8-14　Drag the Tire Shadow Slightly up and to the Right

Figure 8-15　Reset the Alpha Value.

Gif Animator

Ulead GIF Animator is the only program you need to create great looking animations. Whether you are creating animations for the Web, presentations, and multimedia files or simply just want to impress your friends, GIF Animator provides you with all the necessary tools.

The Object Tweening function in GIF Animator helps generate the animation for you. With just a series of clicks your animation is done, it does not get easier than that.

The multitude of editing tools such as the Paintbrush, Eyedropper, Fill, and Selection tools gives you the ability to further edit and enhance your images.

Creating animated text banners for your Web pages is a snap with the Banner Text function.

There are various video filters and video effects that you can use for your animations to make them more interesting and unique.

Tweening is a method for creating or updating intermediate frames between two frames containing the same objects but with different attributes—either different positions or transparency. By doing this, the objects appear to be moving or fading when the animation is played.

1. Preparing for Tweening:

The following procedure outlines how to prepare for position tweening; however, a similar procedure can be used for transparency tweening.

① In order to prepare your objects for position tweening, you should first decide which frames you will use for the start and end frames.

② Position the objects in the start frame the way you would like them to appear before the movement begins.

③ Position the objects in the end frame the way you would like them to appear when the movement ceases.

2. Then Creating Newly Tweened Frames:

This following procedure outlines how to insert tweened frames into your animation; however, a similar procedure can be used for updating intermediate frames.

Note: While the Tween dialog box is open, you can select frames and/or objects in the workspace, Frame Panel or Object Manager Panel. It is to say that you can adjust what you would like to tween or select intermediate frames that you would like to update.

① Select Frame: Tween.

② On the Frame tab, select the Start and End Key Frames by entering the frame numbers in the respective boxes.

③ In the How to generate frames section, select Insert frames and then define the number of frames you would like to use to complete the tweening. A larger number of frames will create a smoother animation, but will also increase the file size.

④ Enter a value in the Frame delay box, which will define the duration each frame will be displayed in 1/100th of a second.

⑤ On the Objects tab, select to tween objects→all showing objects or Currently objects selected.

⑥ Select Object attribute to tween→position and/or transparency.

⑦ Click Start Preview to preview the animation in the workspace and the Frame Panel. Click Stop Preview when done.

⑧ Click OK when you are satisfied.

New Words

preliminary   *n.* 初步行动,准备,初步措施 *adj.* 初步的,开始的,预备的

maquette   *n.* 初步设计的模型;设计草图

discrepancy   *n.* 不符;矛盾;相差

inbetweener   *n.* 中间画动画师;中间画画手

diffuse   *adj.* 弥漫的;散开的 *vt.* 扩散;传播 *vi.* 传播;四散

repository   *n.* 贮藏室(博物馆,资源丰富地区)

standalone   *n.* 独立的电脑,单机 *adj.* 单独的

plugin   *n.* 插件;相关插件

encapsulate   *v.* 装入胶囊,封进内部,压缩

coordinate   *n.* 同等的人物,同位格 *adj.* 同等的,等位的 *v.* 协调,整合,综合[计算机]坐标

restriction   *n.* 限制,约束 *vi.* 结果,(作为结果)发生

acceleration   *n.* 加速,促进;加速度

optimal   *adj.* 最佳的,最理想的

specification　　n. 规格；说明书；详述
labor-intensive　　a. 劳动密集型的
horizontally　　adv. 水平地；地平地
correspond to　　相当于……，符合于……
imperative　　adj. 必要的，势在必行的；命令的；紧急的　n. 需要；命令；祈使语气；规则
subsequent　　adj. 后来的，随后的

Notes

[1] Given the slow, methodical manner in which traditional animation is produced, it is almost always easier to synchronize animation to a pre-existing soundtrack than it is to synchronize a soundtrack to pre-existing animation.

译文：考虑到传统动画片缓慢但有系统的处理方法，用动画去同步影片中出现的各种音乐声音等效果总是比用声音去同步动画来得容易。

Given the slow, methodical manner in which traditional animation is produced 是条件状语。其中 given 是介词，意为"考虑到……"。

it is almost always easier to synchronize animation to a pre-existing soundtrack than it is to synchronize a soundtrack to pre-existing animation 是比较句，将用动画同步声音和用声音同步动画来进行比较，在这个句子中，两个 it 都是形式主语，其中前一个 it 指代不定式 to synchronize animation to a pre-existing soundtrack，后一个 it 指代不定式 to synchronize a soundtrack to pre-existing animation，在这两句中不定式作真正的主语。

[2] For example, in high-budget productions, extensive effort is given in making sure a speaking character's mouth matches in shape the sound that character's actor is producing as he or she speaks.

译文：例如，为了保证动画角色说话时的唇形和它的配音演员配的声音相吻合，在高预算产品中会倾注大量的劳力和财力。

在这个句子中 in high-budget productions 作为状语，并将它前置。

extensive effort is given in making sure a speaking character's mouth matches in shape the sound that character's actor is producing as he or she speaks. 这是一个被动句，making 现在分词引导目的状语从句，在这个从句中 as he or she speaks 作为时间状语。

[3] Originally limited to presenting vector-based objects and images in a simple sequential manner, the format in its later versions allows audio (since Flash 3), video (since Flash 6) and many different possible forms of interaction with the end-user.

译文：起初，动画的格式被限于只能以一种简单有序的方法呈现基于矢量的对象和图像，在后来的版本中，动画的格式中有音频（从 Flash 3 后）、视频（从 Flash 6 后）以及许多和用户终端交互的不同的可能形式。

limited to 意为"被限于……"，过去分词作伴随状语。

Allow 意为"允许，准许"，在这里可以理解为"有，拥有"的意思。

[4] Tweening is a method for creating or updating intermediate frames between two

frames containing the same objects but with different attributes—either different positions or transparency.

译文:补间动画是对两个关键帧之间的中间帧进行创作和更新的一种方法,这两个关键帧具有相同的对象但是对象的属性不同,要么所放置的位置不同,要么透明度不同。

For 引导目的状语,在状语中现在分词 containing 作伴随状语修饰 two frames,either different positions or transparency 作限制性定语,修饰 different attributes。

Either…or…意为"两者之一,要么……要么……"。

Selected Translation

Part 4

二维动画处理

Flash

Flash 是一种软件著作工具,用它创作的动画可以小到简单的动画,大到一个复杂的、有交互功能的网络运用,比如网上书店。你可以将图片、声音、视频添加到 Flash 运用中。Flash 包含很多功能强大但易于使用者操作的特色产品,像拖放用户界面的组件、添加脚本语言到文件中的内置行为还有可以对对象实施的一些特效。

1. 创作一个动作补间动画

你可以通过定义属性来创作一个补间动画,比如首个关键帧里有一组对象或者文本,然后在随后的关键帧里改变对象的属性。Flash 可以在两个关键帧之间创建动画。

以制作一个看起来像弹起来的轮胎为实例来说明怎样创建补间动画。步骤如下。

① 重命名图层:在时间轴里(可以单击窗口→时间轴来打开时间轴)双击图层 1 标题输入"**TireAnim**"。如果是 Windows 用户按 Enter 确定,如果是 Macintosh 用户按返回键即可。

② 选中图层"TireAnim",将轮胎的影片片断从元件库中拖放到舞台中,放到阴影的上面。

③ 如果有必要运用"选择工具"移动轮胎,重新放置它的位置。

④ 仍然选中"选择工具"在图层"TireAnim"里选择第 30 帧,然后按 F6 插入一个新的关键帧。

⑤ 选择第 15 帧,然后按 F6 插入另一个新的关键帧。

⑥ 将播放头放在第 15 帧,按 Shift 键的同时向上拖动轮胎,使它沿直线向上移动。

⑦ 在图层"TireAnim"里,选择第 2 到 14 帧间的任何一帧。在属性监视器中,在补间动画的下拉菜单中选择补间动画。这时在时间轴中,这两个关键帧之间会出现一个箭头。

⑧ 选择第 16 到 29 间的任何一帧,如上步所示,在属性监视器中,运用补间动画的下拉菜单来选择动画。

⑨ 保存文件:在菜单栏中选择文件→保存以此来保存文件。

2. 创作一个形状补间动画

在制作形状补间动画时,在一个关键帧中首先指定一个形状的属性,然后在后面的一个关键帧里修改形状或者是再画另一个形状,和制作动画补间动画的过程相似。Flash可以在两个关键帧之间创建动画。

现在来制作一个轮胎的阴影"ShadowAnim",这样当轮胎弹起来的时候阴影就会跟着移动和消褪。

① 点击"ShadowAnim"这个图层以此来选中这个图层。

② 选择第 30 帧,按 F6 插入一个新的关键帧,然后选择第 15 帧,也按 F6 插入一个新的关键帧。

③ 将播放头放在第 15 帧,选中"选择工具"。将轮胎阴影竖直向上移动再向右移动。

④ 仍然选中第 15 帧,在工具箱中选择吸管工具然后单击阴影对象。

如果色彩混合器没有打开,选择窗口色彩混合器选项来调出色彩混合器窗口,将初始值 25% 重新设置成 10%。

⑤ 点击色彩混合器右上方菜单控制按钮来关闭色彩混合器面板。

⑥ 在"ShadowAnim"图层中选择第 2 到 14 帧之间的任意一个帧。在属性监视器中,在补间动画的下拉菜单中选择"形状补间"。

⑦ 在"ShadowAnim"图层中选择第 16 到 29 帧之间的任意一个帧,同上,在属性监视器中,在补间动画的下拉菜单中选择"形状补间"。

Gif 动画

Ulead GIF Animator 软件是制作界面美观的动画的不二选择,不管你制作动画是为了网络运用、展示、多媒体文件应用还是只是简单地想给你的朋友留下印象,GIF Animator 软件会为你提供全部必要的工具。

GIF Animator 中的补间动画功能能够帮你管理动画,管理起来再简单不过了,你只需要设置好你的动画的一系列链接就可以了。

GIF Animator 有很多编辑工具,比如笔刷、滴管、填充和选择工具等,拥有这些工具你能够进行深加工以此来完善你的动画。

运用带有标题文本功能的按钮可以创建应用于网络上的动态文本标题。

GIF Animator 还有各种各样的视频滤镜和视频特效,在动画中运用这些工具,你的动画会变得更有趣,更具特色。

补间动画是对两个关键帧之间的中间帧进行创作和更新的一种方法,这两个关键帧具有相同的对象但是对象的属性不同,要么所放置的位置不同,要么透明度不同。这样做的话,当播放动画的时候,对象就会看起来在移动或者是在消褪。

1. 制作补间动画的准备工作:

以下的步骤概括了怎样为位置不同的形状补间动画作准备,透明度不同的形状补间动画的准备工作的步骤和这个相似。

① 为了给位置不同的形状补间动画准备对象,首先你得决定以哪一帧作为开始帧和结尾帧。

② 在运动开始之前，以你喜欢的一种呈现方式将对象放置在开始帧中。

③ 在运动开始之前，以你喜欢的一种呈现方式将对象放置在结尾帧中。

2. 接着创建新的补间动画帧：

以下的步骤概括了怎样在你的动画中插入帧，而更新中间帧具有相似的步骤。

注意：当动画对话框打开的时候，你可以在工作区、帧面板或者对象管理面板中选择帧或者对象，也可以同时选中两者，也就是说你可以调整你想要制作动画的帧或者是选择你想要更新的中间帧。

① 选择帧：动画。

② 在帧的标签中选择开始关键帧和结束关键帧，在对话框中输入各自对应的帧数就可以了。

③ 在怎样管理帧这一部分，选择"插入帧"然后确定你想要完成动画的帧的数目。大量的帧可以创建播放流畅的动画，但同时也会增大文件的容量。

④ 在帧延时对话框中输入一个值，它会定义在播放时在 1% 秒内每个帧的持续时间。

⑤ 在对象标签中的"对象对于动画"选项中"都可见"或"仅当前可见"。

⑥ 在"对象对于动画的属性"选项下选择"位置"或"透明度"，也可两者都选。

⑦ 在工作区和帧面板中，点击"开始预览"来预览动画，预览完后点击"停止预览"即可。

⑧ 当你对动画满意的时候点击"OK"即可。

Exercises

1. Describe the outline of traditional animation and tell the relationship between traditional animation and 2D animation.

2. How many kinds of formats are there for 2D animation? And can you distinguish the differences between them?

3. How to process 2D animation with various of formats?

4. Create an animation with the topic you like.

文献检索简介

文献信息检索是指从任何文献信息集合中查出所需信息的活动、过程和方法。广义的文献信息检索还包括文献信息存储，两者又往往合并称为"文献信息存储与检索"。当然，对于信息用户来说，信息检索仅指信息的查找过程。

一、文献检索的意义

1. 充分利用已有的文献信息资源,避免重复劳动。

科学研究具有继承和创造两重性,科学研究的两重性要求科研人员在探索未知或从事研究工作之前,应该尽可能地占有与之相关的资料、情报。研究人员在开始研究某一课题前,必须利用科学的文献信息检索方法来了解课题的进展情况,在前人的研究基础上进行研究。可以说一项科研成果中95%是别人的,5%是个人创造的。科研人员只有通过查找文献信息,这样才能做到心中有数,防止重复研究,将有限的时间和精力用于创造性的研究中。

2. 缩短查找文献信息的时间,提高科研效率。

目前文献信息的数量和类型增加十分迅速,科研人员不可能将世界上所有的文献都阅读完。据美国科学基金会统计,一个科研人员花费在查找和消化科技资料上的时间占全部科研时间的51%,计划思考占8%,实验研究占32%,书面总结占9%。如果科研人员掌握好科学的文献信息检索方法,就可以缩短查阅文献的时间,获取更多的文献信息,提高科研效率。

3. 促进专业学习,实现终身学习。

掌握了科学的文献信息检索方法,可以把学生引导到超越教学大纲的更广的知识领域中去,促进学生的专业学习。在当代社会,人们需要终生学习,不断更新知识,才能适应社会发展的需求,掌握了科学的文献信息检索方法,在研究实践和生产实践中根据需要查找文献信息,就可以无师自通,很快找到一条吸取和利用大量新知识的捷径。

二、国内检索系统

目前我国高校和科研机构一般根据自己的专业设置和科研需要购置了不同的数据库,下面是常见和常用的一些数据库。

《中国期刊网全文数据库》(http://www.cnki.edu.cn);

《万方数据资源系统》(http://www.wfdata.com.cn);

《重庆维普中文科技期刊数据库》(http://www.cqvip.com.cn);

《中国专利数据库》(http://www.sipo.gov.cn);

《中国生物医学文献数据库》(http://cbm.imicams.ac.cn);

《中国科技论文在线》(http://www.paper.edu.cn);

《国家科技成果网》(http://www.nast.org.cn);

《国家科技图书文献中心》(http://www.nstl.gov.cn)。

三、国际著名的六大检索系统

1. 美国《科学引文索引》(Science Citation Index,简称 SCI)。

2. 美国《工程索引》(Eingineering Index,简称 Ei)。

3. 美国《化学文摘》(Chemical Abstracts,简称 CA)。CA 报道的化学化工文献量占全世界化学化工文献总量的98%左右,是当今世界上最负盛名、收录最全、应用最为广泛的查找化学化工文献大型检索工具。

4. 英国《科学文摘》(Science Abstracts，简称 SA)、《物理文摘》(Physics Abstracts，简称 PA)、《电子与电气文摘》(Electrical Engineering & Electronics Abstracts，简称 EEA)、《计算机与控制文摘》(Computers and Control Abstracts，简称 CCA)、《信息技术》(Information Technology，简称 IT)。

5. 俄罗斯《文摘杂志》(Abstract Journals，简称 AJ)。

6. 日本《科学技术文献速报》，现扩充为大型数据库"日本科学技术情报中心"(Japan Information Center Science and Technology，简称 JICST)。

文献检索方法简介

文献检索是科学研究工作中的一个重要步骤，它贯穿研究的全过程。文献不仅为选题提供依据，选题以后必须围绕选题广泛地查阅文献资料，能否正确掌握文献检索方法，关系到研究的过程、质量以及能否出成果，因此必须掌握文献检索的技能。了解和掌握文献的分类及其特点，是迅速有效地查找所需信息的必要前提。

一、文献的类型

一级文献，即原始文献，是由亲自经历事件的人所提供的各种形式的材料和各种原著。这种文献是我们搞好研究的第一手资料，对研究工作有很大的价值。

二级文献，指对一级文献加工整理而成的系统化、条理化的文献资料。如索引、书目、文摘以及类似内容的各种数据库等。

三级文献，指在二级文献的基础上对一级文献进行分类后，经过加工、整理而成的带有个人观点的文献资料。如数据手册、年鉴、动态综述述评等。

二、检索文献的步骤

1. 分析研究课题。在检索之前先要分析检索的课题，一要分析主题内容，弄清课题的关键问题所在，确定检索的学科范围；二要分析文献类型，不同类型的文献各具特色，根据自己的检索需要确定检索文献类型范围；三要确定检索的时间范围；四要分析已知的检索线索，逐步扩大。

2. 确定检索工具。正确地确定检索工具，能使我们在浩瀚的文献海洋中畅游无阻，从而以最简捷的方法，迅速、准确地获得研究所需的文献信息。几种检索工具：

索引：把文献的一些特征，如书目、篇名、作者以及文献中出现的人名、地名、概念、词语等组织起来，按一定的顺序(字母或笔画)排列，供人检索。

文摘：它概括地介绍原文献的内容，简短的摘要，使人们不必看全文就可以大致了解文章的内容，是一种使用广泛的检索工具。如《新华文摘》、《教育文摘》等。

书目：它将各种图书按内容或不同学科分类编制成目录，如《全国总书目》。

参考性与资料性工具书：它的范围很广，如辞典、百科全书、年鉴等。

计算机和互联网:可以通过搜索引擎等对文献进行查询。

3. 确定检索方法。常用的检索方法主要有:

顺序查找法:从课题研究的起始年代开始往后顺时查找,直到近期为止,这种方法查全率高,但费时。

回溯查找法:这是利用某一篇论文(或专著)后面所附的参考资料为线索,跟踪追查的方法。这种查找方法针对性更强、直接、效率高。

计算机检索:计算机以其强大的数据处理和存储能力成为当今最为理想的信息检索工具。计算机检索有以下优点:检索速度快,检索范围大。它可以同时对跨越几年甚至几十年的数据做检索;检索途径多。计算机的数据库能提供十几种甚至几十种的检索工具,还可以使用逻辑的方法把它们组合起来使用,非常灵活;可以同时检索多个数据库。计算机可以把几个数据库同时打开供检索,并且可以去掉其中重复的数据;可以立刻得到原文。由于早期的检索系统大多提供索引、文摘等二级文献,有时我们不得不再去寻找原文即一级文献。现在使用计算机全文检索系统,当场就能看到全文,并且根据需要还可以打印出来。

三、计算机的检索方式

当前广泛使用的计算机检索包括:联机检索、光盘检索和国际互联网检索。

联机检索(online retrieval)是指用户利用计算机终端设备,通过通信线路,从信息中心的计算机(主机)数据库中检索出所需要的信息的过程。它允许用户以人机对话、联机会话这样交互的方式(interactive)直接访问系统及数据库,检索是实时(real time)、在线(online)进行的。用户的提问一旦传到主机被接收后,机器便立刻执行检索运算,很快将检索结果传送到用户终端,用户可反复修改检索式,最后获得较满意的检索结果。联机检索能远程登录到国内外检索系统。大型检索系统不仅数据库多,而且数据库的文献报道量大,高达有数以百万条记录,数据更新及时,系统检索点多,组合方式多样,输出形式、输出方式多样。用户容易得到最新、最准确和最完全的检索效果。

基于Web方式的联机检索使用WWW浏览器在Windows界面下交互作业,给用户揭示到一篇篇文章的信息,有很强的直观性,也可以检索多媒体信息。Web版数据库检索大量采用超文本。超文本(hypertext)的内容排列是非线性的,它按知识(信息)单元及其关系建立起知识结构网络,如具有图形、画面的信息又称作超媒体(hypermedia)。超文本(媒体)的检索是通过超文本链接(hyperlink)来实现的。其形式有的在网页的文字处有下划线,或以图标方式标志,用户点击(point—and—click)这些标志便能进入到与此信息相关的下一页,在该页面上通过超文本链接进入再一个页面,超文本起信息导向作用。这样,用户从一个页面转向另外一个页面的控制过程中获取自己所需要的信息。

Web版文献数据库检索在采用超文本的基础上又将命令检索、菜单检索方式融合其中,交互使用,集各种检索机制为一体。许多大型国际联机检索系统在互联网上开设了自己的站点,提供用户检索服务。

Chapter 9 3D Animation

▲ **Knowledge Objectives**

When you have completed this unit, you will be able to:
- Define computer animation.
- Explain the principle of making computer animation.
- Learn computer animation development equipments.
- Know main formats of computer animation.
- State methods to capture 3D animation.
- Learn some software to make 3D animation.

▲ **Professional Terms**

CGI	计算机成像/电脑产生的影像
computer screen	计算机显示屏
digital video	数字视频/数字录像
facial animation	面部动画
persistence of vision	视觉暂留
skeletal animation	骨骼动画
stop motion animation	定格动画

Part 1 Outline of 3D Animation[①]

Computer Animation

Computer animation (or CGI animation) is the art of creating moving images with the use of computers. It is a subfield of computer graphics and animation. Increasingly it is created by means of 3D computer graphics, though 2D computer graphics are still widely used for stylistic, low bandwidth, and faster real-time rendering needs. Sometimes the target of the animation is the computer itself, but sometimes the target is another medium, such as film. It is also referred to as CGI (computer-generated imagery or computer-generated imaging), especially when used in films. (Figure 9-1)

To create the illusion of movement, an image is displayed on the computer screen and

---

① http://en.wikipedia.org/wiki/Computer_animation

repeatedly replaced by a new image that is similar to the previous image, but advanced slightly in the time domain (usually at a rate of 24 or 30 frames/second). This technique is identical to how the illusion of movement is achieved with television and motion pictures.

Computer animation is essentially a digital successor to the art of stop motion animation of 3D models and frame-by-frame animation of 2D illustrations. For 3D animations, objects (models) are built on the computer monitor and 3D figures

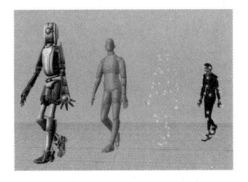

Figure 9-1　An Example of Computer Animation Which is Produced in the "Motion Capture" Technique

are rigged with a virtual skeleton. For 2D figure animations, separate objects (illustrations) and separate transparent layers are used, with or without a virtual skeleton. Then the limbs, eyes, mouth, clothes, etc. of the figure are moved by the animator on key frames. The differences in appearance between key frames are automatically calculated by the computer in a process known as tweening or morphing. Finally, the animation is rendered.

For 3D animations, all frames must be rendered after modeling is complete. For 2D vector animations, the rendering process is the key frame illustration process, while tweened frames are rendered as needed. For pre-recorded presentations, the rendered frames are transferred to a different format or medium such as film or digital video. The frames may also be rendered in real time as they are presented to the end-user audience. Low bandwidth animations transmitted via the internet (e.g. 2D Flash) often use software on the end-users computer to render in real time as an alternative to streaming or pre-loaded high bandwidth animations.

Explanation

To trick the eye and brain into thinking they are seeing a smoothly moving object, the pictures should be drawn at around 12 frames per second (frame/s) or faster (a frame is one complete image). With rates above 70 frames/s no improvement in realism or smoothness is perceivable due to the way the eye and brain process images. At rates below 12 frame/s most people can detect jerkiness associated with the drawing of new images which detracts from the illusion of realistic movement. Conventional hand-drawn cartoon animation often uses 15 frames/s in order to save on the number of drawings needed, but this is usually accepted because of the stylized nature of cartoons. Because it produces more realistic imagery computer animation demands higher frame rates to reinforce this realism.

The reason no jerkiness is seen at higher speeds is due to "persistence of vision." From moment to moment, the eye and brain working together actually store whatever one looks at for a fraction of a second, and automatically "smooth out" minor jumps. Movie film seen in theaters in the United States runs at 24 frames per second, which is sufficient to create this illusion of continuous movement.

Methods of Animating Virtual Characters

In most 3D computer animation systems, an animator creates a simplified representation of a character's anatomy, analogous to a skeleton or stick figure. The position of each segment of the skeletal model is defined by animation variables, or Avars. In human and animal characters, many parts of the skeletal model correspond to actual bones, but skeletal animation is also used to animate other things, such as facial features (though other methods for facial animation exist). The character "Woody" in Toy Story, for example, uses 700 Avars, including 100 Avars in the face. The computer does not usually render the skeletal model directly (it is invisible), but uses the skeletal model to compute the exact position and orientation of the character, which is eventually rendered into an image. Thus by changing the values of Avars over time, the animator creates motion by making the character move from frame to frame.

There are several methods for generating the Avar values to obtain realistic motion. Traditionally, animators manipulate the Avars directly. Rather than set Avars for every frame, they usually set Avars at strategic points (frames) in time and let the computer interpolate or 'tween' between them, a process called keyframing. Keyframing puts control in the hands of the animator, and has roots in hand-drawn traditional animation.

In contrast, a newer method called motion capture makes use of live action. When computer animation is driven by motion capture, real performers act out the scene as if they were the character to be animated. His or her motion is recorded to a computer using video cameras and markers, and that performance is then applied to the animated character.

Each method has their advantages, games and films are using either or both of these methods in productions. Keyframe animation can produce motions that would be difficult or impossible to act out, while motion capture can reproduce the subtleties of a particular actor. For example, in the 2006 film Pirates of the Caribbean: Dead Man's Chest, actor Bill Nighy provided the performance for the character Davy Jones. Even though Nighy himself doesn't appear in the film, the movie benefited from his performance by recording the nuances of his body language, posture, facial expressions, etc. Thus motion capture is appropriate in situations where believable, realistic behavior and action is required, but the types of characters required exceed what can be done through conventional costuming.

Computer Animation Development Equipment

Computer animation can be created with a computer and animation software. Some impressive animation can be achieved even with basic programs; however the rendering can take a lot of time on an ordinary home computer. Because of this, video game animators tend to use low resolution, low polygon count renders, such that the graphics can be rendered in real time on a home computer. Photorealistic animation would be impractical in this context.

Professional animators of movies, television, and video sequences on computer games make photorealistic animation with high detail. This level of quality for movie animation would take tens to hundreds of years to create on a home computer. Many powerful workstation computers are used instead. Graphics workstation computers use two to four processors, and thus are a lot more powerful than a home computer, and are specialized for rendering. A large number of workstations (known as a render farm) are networked together to effectively act as a giant computer. The result is a computer-animated movie that can be completed in about one to five years (this process is not comprised solely of rendering, however). A workstation typically costs $2,000 to $16,000, with the more expensive stations being able to render much faster, due to the more technologically advanced hardware that they contain. Pixar's Renderman is rendering software which is widely used as the movie animation industry standard, in competition with Mental Ray. It can be bought at the official Pixar website for about $3,500. It will work on Linux, Mac OS X, and Microsoft Windows based graphics workstations along with an animation program such as Maya and Softimage XSI. Professionals also use digital movie cameras, motion capture or performance capture, bluescreens, film editing software, props, and other tools for movie animation.

The Future

One open challenge in computer animation is a photorealistic animation of humans. Currently, most computer-animated movies show animal characters (A Bug's Life, Finding Nemo, Ratatouille, Newt, Ice Age, Over the Hedge), fantasy characters (Monsters Inc., Shrek, Teenage Mutant Ninja Turtles 4, Monsters vs. Aliens), anthropomorphic machines (Cars, WALL-E, Robots) or cartoon-like humans (The Incredibles, Despicable Me, Up). The movie Final Fantasy: The Spirits Within is often cited as the first computer-generated movie to attempt to show realistic-looking humans. However, due to the enormous complexity of the human body, human motion, and human biomechanics, realistic simulation of humans remains largely an open problem. Another problem is the distasteful psychological response to viewing nearly perfect animation of humans, known as "the uncanny valley." It is one of the "holy grails" of computer animation. Eventually, the goal is to create software where the animator can generate a movie sequence showing a photorealistic human character, undergoing physically-plausible motion, together with clothes, photorealistic hair, a complicated natural background, and possibly interacting with other simulated human characters. This could be done in a way that the viewer is no longer able to tell if a particular movie sequence is computer-generated, or created using real actors in front of movie cameras. Complete human realism is not likely to happen very soon, and when it does it may have major repercussions for the film industry.

For the moment it looks like three dimensional computer animations can be divided into two main directions: photorealistic and non-photorealistic rendering. Photorealistic computer animation can itself be divided into two subcategories: real photorealism (where performance capture is used in the creation of the virtual human characters) and stylized photorealism. Real photorealism is what Final Fantasy tried to achieve and will in the future most likely have the ability to give us live action fantasy features as The Dark Crystal without having to use advanced puppetry and animatronics, while Antz is an example on stylistic photorealism (in the future stylized photorealism will be able to replace traditional stop motion animation as in Corpse Bride). None of them mentioned are perfected as of yet, but the progress continues.

The non-photorealistic/cartoonish direction is more like an extension of traditional animation, an attempt to make the animation look like a three dimensional version of a cartoon, still using and perfecting the main principles of animation articulated by Disney's Nine Old Men, such as squash and stretch.

While a single frame from a photorealistic computer-animated feature will look like a photo if done right, a single frame from a cartoonish computer-animated feature will look like a painting.

Amateur Animation

The popularity of sites such as Newgrounds, which allows members to upload their own movies for others to view, has created a growing community of what are often considered amateur computer animators. With many free utilities available and programs such as Windows Movie Maker or iMovie, which are included in the operating system, anyone with the tools and a creative mind can have their animation viewed by thousands. Many high end animation software options are also available on a trial basis, allowing for educational and non-commercial development with certain restrictions. Several free and open source animation software applications exist as well, Blender as an example. One way to create amateur animation is using the GIF format, which can be uploaded and seen on the web easily.

Architectural Animation

Architects use services from animation companies to create 3-dimensional models for both the customers and builders. It can be more accurate than traditional drawings. Architectural animation can also be used to see the possible relationship the building in relation to the environment and its surrounding buildings.

Part 2   Formats of 3D Animation

AVI[1,2]

Audio Video Interleave, known by its acronym AVI, is a multimedia container format introduced by Microsoft in November 1992 as part of its Video for Windows technology. AVI files can contain both audio and video data in a file container that allows synchronous audio-with-video playback. Like the DVD video format, AVI files support multiple streaming audio and video, although these features are seldom used. Most AVI files also use the file format extensions developed by the Matrox OpenDML group in February 1996. These files are suppor-

---

① http://en.wikipedia.org/wiki/Audio_Video_Interleave
② http://www.cepro.com/article/the_ultimate_guide_to_digital_video_formats/D1/

ted by Microsoft, and are unofficially called "AVI 2.0".

AVI is a derivative of the Resource Interchange File Format (RIFF), (Figure 9-2), which divides a file's data into blocks, or "chunks." Each "chunk" is identified by a FourCC tag. An AVI file takes the form of a single chunk in a RIFF formatted file, which is then subdivided into two mandatory "chunks" and one optional "chunk".

. The first sub-chunk is identified by the "hdrl" tag. This sub-chunk is the file header and contains metadata about the video, such as its width, height and frame rate. The second sub-chunk is identified by the "movi" tag. This chunk contains the actual audio/visual data that make up the AVI movie. The third optional sub-chunk is identified by the "idx1" tag which indexes the offsets of the data chunks within the file.

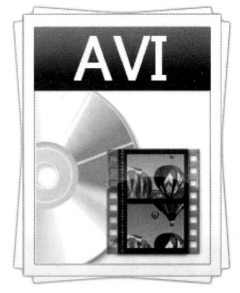

Figure 9-2　An Icon of AVI Format

By way of the RIFF format, the audio/visual data contained in the "movi" chunk can be encoded or decoded by software called a codec, which is an abbreviation for coder/decoder. Upon creation of the file, the codec translates between raw data and the compressed data format used inside the chunk. An AVI file may carry audio/visual data inside the chunks in virtually any compression scheme, including Full Frame (Uncompressed), Intel Real Time (Indeo), Cinepak, Motion JPEG, Editable MPEG, VDOWave, ClearVideo / RealVideo, QPEG, and MPEG-4 Video.

AVI is considered by some to be an outdated container format. There is significant overhead when used with popular MPEG-4 codecs, increasing file size more than necessary. Also the container has no native support for modern MPEG-4 features like B-Frames.

AVI files also do not contain pixel aspect ratio information—meaning that many players, including WMP, render all AVI files with square pixels. Therefore, the frame appears stretched or squeezed horizontally when the file is played back.

Despite its limitations and the availability of more modern container formats such as MP4, AVI remains popular among file-sharing communities, due to its high compatibility with existing video editing and playback software like WMP.

MOV[①,②]

The MOV file extension was created by Apple as a means to store and play video files.

---

① http://www.cepro.com/article/the_ultimate_guide_to_digital_video_formats/D2/

② http://en.wikipedia.org/wiki/QuickTime_File_Format

MOV files are often used to store videos due to its awesome compression ability. Videos created from a number of digital cameras are automatically stored in MOV format.

MOV is compatible with both Windows and Mac platforms. However, this file can only be played on QuickTime Player. It can be converted to another file format, but that can be a pain.

The format specifies a multimedia container file that contains one or more tracks, each of which stores a particular type of data: audio, video, effects, or text. Each track either contains a digitally-encoded media stream or a data reference to the media stream located in another file. Tracks are maintained in a hierarchical data structure consisting of objects called atoms. An atom can be a parent to other atoms or it can contain media or edit data, but it cannot do both.

The ability to contain abstract data references for the media data, and the separation of the media data from the media offsets and the track edit lists means that QuickTime is particularly suited for editing, as it is capable of importing and editing in place (without data copying). Other later-developed media container formats such as Microsoft's Advanced Systems Format or the Matroska and Ogg containers lack this abstraction, and require all media data to be rewritten after editing.

WMV[①]

Windows Media Video (WMV) is a compressed video compression format for several proprietary codecs developed by Microsoft. The original video format, known as WMV, was originally designed for Internet streaming applications, as a competitor to RealVideo. The other formats, such as WMV Screen and WMV Image, cater for specialized content. Through standardization from the Society of Motion Picture and Television Engineers (SMPTE), WMV 9 has gained adoption for physical-delivery formats such as HD DVD and Blu-ray Disc.

A WMV file is in most circumstances encapsulated in the Advanced Systems Format (ASF) container format, the file extension. WMV typically describes ASF files that use Windows Media Video codecs. The audio codec used in conjunction with Windows Media Video is typically some version of Windows Media Audio, or in rarer cases, the deprecated Sipro ACELP. net audio codec. Microsoft recommends that ASF files containing non-Windows Media codecs use the generic.

Although WMV is generally packed into the ASF container format, it can also be put into the AVI or Matroska container format. The resulting files have the. AVI and. MKV file extensions, respectively. WMV can be stored in an AVI file when using the WMV 9 Video Compression Manager (VCM) codec implementation. Another common way to store WMV in an AVI file is to use the VirtualDub encoder.

Software that can play WMV files includes Windows Media Player, RealPlayer, MPlayer,

---

① http://en.wikipedia.org/wiki/WMV

The KMPlayer and VLC Media Player.

But WMV has been the subject of numerous complaints from users and the press. Users dislike the digital rights management system which is sometimes attached to WMV files. The loss of the ability to restore licenses for WMV files in the Windows Media Player 11 was not positively received. In addition, the Microsoft Zune does not support the standard Windows Media DRM system, rendering protected WMV files unplayable.

MPG[41]

MPG stands for Moving Picture Experts Group, driven by Microsoft's early need to force every file into a three-letter extension box, MPEG has evolved by dropping the "E" to become MPG.

So, technically, MPG is more of a title than a file format. Even so, it has shifted in meaning as the file extension standards created by that group as well.

MPG is very popular in the video world. And there are a number of MPG formats that you should consider—all with different purposes.

MPG video pioneered digital distribution of video on the Internet and disc. Thus, it works with everything. With MPEG-1 you get poor video quality, in some situations, no better than VHS.

The next generation of MPEG technology is MPEG-2, which is used by most TV stations. MPEG-2 technology is also the compression format behind DVD, as well as the ATSC standard for broadcast HDTV. So, don't think MPEG-2 is going away anytime soon.

However, it's best to focus on the most recent evolution of the format: MPEG-4, commonly known as MP4 or m4v. This format deals with a much better picture quality.

Think Blu-ray or HD-DVD quality high-definition video, with an even better compression ratio.

MPEG-4 absorbs many of the features of MPEG-1 and MPEG-2 and other related standards, and adds new features such as extended VRML support for 3D rendering, object-oriented composite files, including audio, video and VRML objects, support for externally-specified Digital Rights Management and various types of interactivity.

It is also streamable and supports most multimedia content. It is used by iTunes and with the iPod, as well as often being the most commonly used file format for sharing videos over the Internet.

MPEG-4 is still a developing standard and is divided into a number of parts. Unfortunately, the companies promoting MPEG-4 compatibility do not always clearly state which "part" level compatibility.

The key parts to be aware of are MPEG-4 part 2 (MPEG-4 SP/ASP, used by codecs such as DivX, Xvid, Nero Digital and 3ivx and by Quicktime 6) and MPEG-4 part 10 (MPEG-4 AVC/H.264, used by the x264 codec, by Nero Digital AVC, by Quicktime 7, and by next-gen DVD formats like HD DVD and Blu-ray Disc).

Another version of MPEG-4 is 3GP. A growing number of mobile and smart phones have a video recording option. Most store the files as a 3GP file.

They can then be transferred from phone to phone or over the Internet. 3GP files can be played on QuickTime Player and RealPlayer, but not on WMP.

Part 3　Capture 3D Animation

Produce[①]

How to make 3D animation?

① Promotion—to make the 3D series trailer, which combines AD promotion and fun story into 3D animation production. That must be the best demo of the CG shot and 3D AD.

Figure 9-3　3D Animation Promotion[②]

② Concept—It is a pre-production in professional animation workflow, which covers 2D design based on the animation script includes scenes/background, sculpt, prop, and style orientation, the stage will provide reference for coming 3D production. (Figure 9-4)

---

① http://www.vrtiger.com/wedo/1.html
② http://www.bergen.edu/pages/5076.asp

Chapter 9　3D Animation

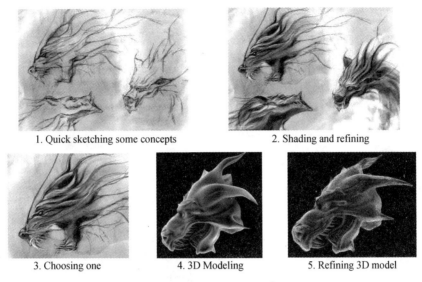

1. Quick sketching some concepts　　2. Shading and refining

3. Choosing one　　4. 3D Modeling　　5. Refining 3D model

Figure 9-4　Concept Design①

③ Sub-story board—To hand draw the main shots and explain the camera movements and scenarios based on the writing script for later 3D production reference. (Figure 9-5)

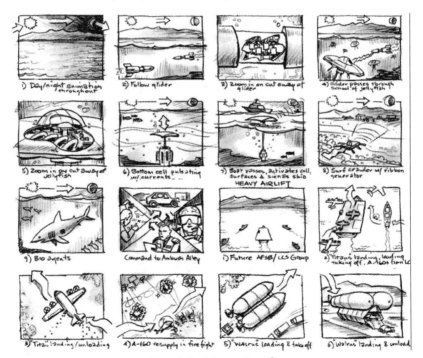

Figure 9-5　Sub-story Board②

④ 3D rough modeling—the animators use the 3D software to make the rough model of

---

①　http://en.wikipedia.org/wiki/Concept_art
②　http://storyboards.greghigh.com/3DAnimation.jpg

scenes, sculpt, and prop; this is a preparation for layout. (Figure 9-6)

1. Rough modeling of a vase   2. The effect after modified and rendered

Figure 9-6　3D Rough Modeling①

⑤ 3D layout storyboard—based on the 3D rough model and sub-storyboard, the animator produces a 3D layout. In the step, the animator sets the camera position, basic animation, and shot timing by professional software. (Figure 9-7)

Figure 9-7　3D Layout Storyboard②

⑥ 3D sculpt modeling/scene background/Prop modeling—According to the Comprehensive advice by client, Executive Producer, and director, the animator will refine the 3D

---

① http://www.3dmax8.com/3dmax/article/2008/0902/article_251.html
② http://www.3dworldmag.com/page/3dworld?entry = mini_short_cuts_paper_plane

models, which will be all actors in the final animation. (Figure 9-8)

Figure 9-8   3D Sculpt Modeling and Scene Background①

⑦ Texturing—According to the Comprehensive advice by client, Executive Producer, and director, to do the 3D model decoration by setting up the color, texture, material, this is the essential part in the animation workflow. (Figure 9-9)

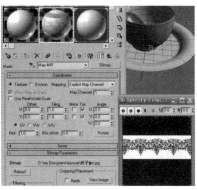 

1. Set texture maps   2. The effect after rendered

Figure 9-9   Texturing②

⑧ Skinning—According to story scenario, to set up of the transform, movement on main characters, the step is a preparation for animator's job and to provide the solution for animation. (Figure 9-10)

---

① http://www.3dmax8.com/3dmax/article/2008/0812/article_66.html
② http://www.3dmax8.com/3dmax/2009/0224/2758_3.html

Figure 9-10　Skinning①

⑨ 3D sub-storyboard—Referring to the script and 2D sub-storyboard, the animator produces the performance animation for each shot according to the Layout shot and timing. (Figure 9-11)

Figure 9-11　3D Sub-storyboard②

---

① http://www.freshwap.net/ae6/dl/rpc+plugins+3ds+max+9
② http://en.wikiversity.org/wiki/LessonPage:3D_Storyboard_FrameForge:Kinsuji

⑩ Lighting—According to the style orientation, the lighting division is responsible for lightening up the scenes, drawing refining, material further adjusting, and control the rendering atmosphere of each shot. (Figure 9-12)

Figure 9-12　Lighting①

⑪ 3D VFX—According to specific story, the effect division would produce the water, smoke, fog, fire, light in the 3D software (Maya). (Figure 9-13)

Figure 9-13　3D VFX in Maya②

⑫ Layer rendering/composition—After the animation and lighting production, the rendering worker will do the layer rendering based on the synthesis division's opinion, and provide the layer and channel for coming workflow. (Figure 9-14)

---

①　http://www.3dmax8.com/3dmax/caizhi/2008/1005/article_207.html
②　http://3d.fevte.com/maya/dh/dh-14697.html

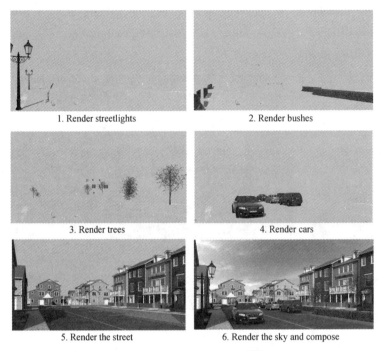

Figure 9-14　Layer Rendering①②

⑬ Dub and music—Based on the script requirement, the dub division would provide appropriate sound effect and background music for each shot.

⑭ Editing—the post-production worker uses the rendered video to compose a full video, and customize into different version for various demand based on client, executive producer and director.

3D Model Library

Model is the main subject to create an animation. Besides creating by yourself in the 3D animation software, you can also download various models from the Internet directly. For example, use some 3D plant models (Figure 9-15) and modify, then you can built a garden in 3DS MAX.

Figure 9-15　3D Plant Models③

---

① http://www.3dmax8.com/3dmax/2010/0616/3392_2.html
② http://www.3dmax8.com/3dmax/2010/0616/3392_3.html
③ http://www.3lian.com/psd/3d/

There are some 3D models of 3D model library in the Internet. (Figure 9-16, 9-17, 9-18)

Small gun　　　　　　　Machine gun　　　　　　　Battery

Figure 9-16　3D military models

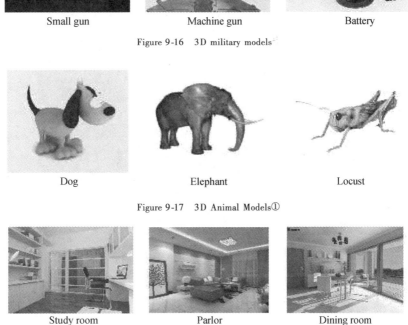

Dog　　　　　　　Elephant　　　　　　　Locust

Figure 9-17　3D Animal Models①

Study room　　　　　　　Parlor　　　　　　　Dining room

Figure 9-18　3D Indoor Models②

Part 4　Process 3D Animation

3DS MAX③,④

With 3ds Max, you can create 3D places and characters, objects and subjects of any type. You can arrange them in settings and environments to build the scenes for your movie or game or visualization. You can animate the characters, set them in motion, make them speak, sing and dance, or kick and fight. Then, shoot movies of the whole virtual thing.

You can use 3ds Max to visualize designs of real things that will actually be built, such as buildings and machines.

Once you've installed 3ds Max, you open it from the Start menu, or use any other Win-

---

① http://www.3lian.com/psd/3d/01/0106/index_2.html
② http://www.3lian.com/psd/3d/01/0108/index_2.html
③ http://images.autodesk.com/adsk/files/3dsmax8tutorialsvol1.pdf
④ http://images.autodesk.com/adsk/files/3ds_max_2011_help.pdf

dows method. The figure below shows the application window with a scene file loaded. (Figure 9-19)

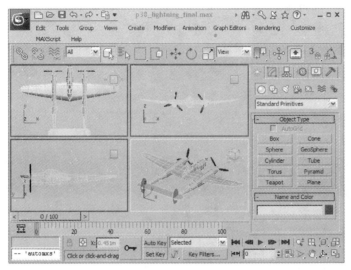

Figure 9-19   The Application Window with a Scene File Loaded

3ds Max is a single-document application, meaning you can work on only one scene at a time. You can run 3ds Max several times and open a different scene in each instance, but doing so requires a lot of RAM. For best performance, open only one instance and work on one scene at a time.

1. Modeling Objects

You model and animate objects in the viewports, whose layout is configurable. You can start with a variety of 3D geometric primitives. You can also use 2D shapes as the basis for lofted or extruded objects. You can convert objects to a variety of editable surface types, which you can then model further by pulling vertices and using other tools. (Figure 9-20)

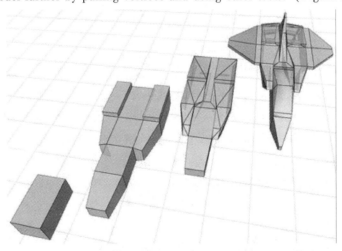

Figure 9-20   Plane Models

Another modeling tool is to apply modifiers to objects. Modifiers can change object geometry. Bend and Twist are examples of modifiers.

Modeling, editing, and animation tools are available in the command panels and toolbar.

2. Material Design

You design materials using the Material Editor, which appears in its own window. You use the Material Editor to create realistic materials by defining hierarchies of surface characteristics. The surface characteristics can represent static materials, or be animated. (Figure 9-21)

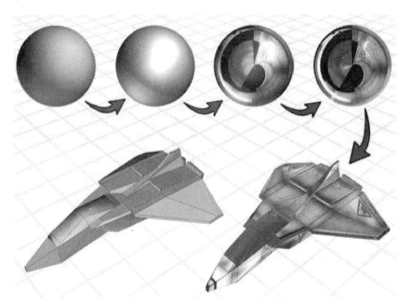

Figure 9-21 Design Materials

3. Lights and Cameras

You create lights with various properties to illuminate your scene. The lights can cast shadows, project images, and create volumetric effects for atmospheric lighting. Physically-based lights let you use real-world lighting data in your scenes and Radiosity provides incredibly accurate light simulation in renderings. (Figure 9-22)

The cameras you create have real-world controls for lens length, field of view, and motion control such as truck, dolly, and pan.

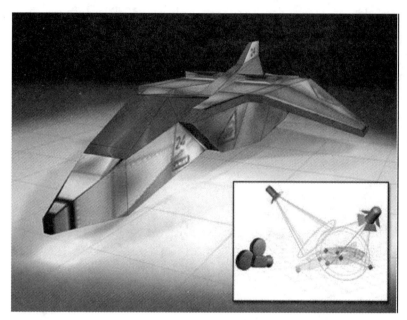

Figure 9-22   Lights and Cameras

4. Animation

You can begin animating your scene at any time by turning on the Auto Key button. Turn the button off to return to modeling. You can also perform animated modeling effects by animating the parameters of objects in your scene. (Figure 9-23)

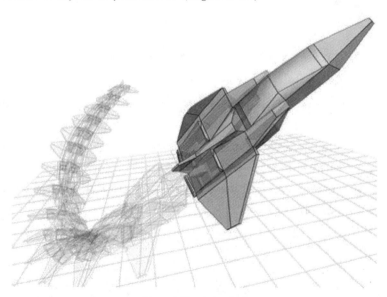

Figure 9-23   Animating

When the Auto Key button is on, 3ds Max automatically records the movement, rotation, and scale changes you make, not as changes to a static scene, but as *keys* on certain *frames* that represent time. You can also animate many parameters to make lights and cameras change over time, and preview your animation directly in the 3ds Max viewports.

You can use Track View to control animation. Track View is a floating window where you edit animation keys, set up animation controllers, or edit motion curves for your animated effects.

5. Rendering

Rendering adds color and shading to your scene. The renderers available with 3ds Max include features such as selective ray tracing, analytical antialiasing, motion blur, volumetric lighting, and environmental effects. (Figure 9-24)

Figure 9-24   Rendering

When you use the default scanline render, a radiosity solution can provide accurate light simulation in renderings, including the ambient lighting that results from reflected light. When you use the mental ray renderer, a comparable effect is provided by global illumination.

If your workstation is part of a network, network rendering can distribute rendering jobs over multiple workstations.

With Video Post, you can also composite the scene with animations stored on disk.

6. The 3ds Max Window

Most of the main window is occupied by the viewports, where you view and work with your scene. The remaining areas of the window hold controls and show status information. (Figure 9-25)

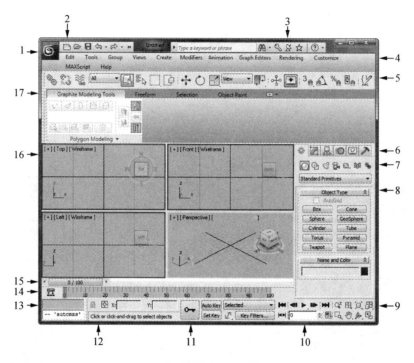

1. Application button
3. InfoCenter
5. Main toolbar
7. Object categories (Create panel)
9. Viewport navigation controls
11. Animation keying controls
13. MAXScript mini-listener
15. Time slider
17. Modeling ribbon

2. Quick Access toolbar
4. Menu bar
6. Command panel tabs
8. Rollout
10. Animation playback controls
12. Prompt line and status bar controls
14. Track bar
16. Viewports

Figure 9-25　The 3ds Max Window

One of the most important aspects of using 3ds Max is its versatility. Many program functions are available from multiple user-interface elements. For example, you can open Track View for animation control from the Main toolbar as well as the Graph Editors menu, but the easiest way to get to a specific object's track in Track View is to right-click the object, and then chooses Track View Selected from the quad menu.

You can customize the user interface in a variety of ways: by adding keyboard shortcuts, moving toolbars and command panels around, creating new toolbars and tool buttons, and even recording scripts into toolbar buttons.

MAXScript lets you create and use custom commands in the built-in scripting language. For more information, access the MAXScript Help from the Help menu.

7. A Typical Project Workflow

These topics explain the basic procedures for creating scenes:

(i) Setting Up Your Scene

You start with a new unnamed scene when you open 3ds Max. You can also start a new scene at any time by choosing New or Reset from the Application menu.

① Choosing a Unit Display

You choose a system of unit display on the Units Setup dialog. Choose from Metric, Standard US, and Generic methods, or design a custom measuring system. You can switch between different systems of unit display at any time.

② Setting the System Unit

The System Unit setting, in the Units Setup dialog, determines how 3ds Max relates to distance information you input to your scene. The setting also determines the range for round-off error. Consider changing the system unit value only when you model very large or very small scenes.

③ Setting Grid Spacing

Set spacing for the visible grid in the Grid And Snap Settings dialog→Home Grid panel. You can change grid spacing at any time.

④ Setting the Viewport Display

The default four viewports in 3ds Max represent an efficient and popular screen layout. Set options in the Viewport Configuration dialog to change viewport layout and display properties. (Figure 9-26)

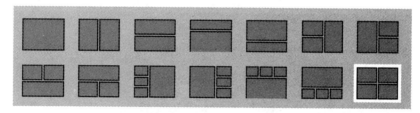

Figure 9-26　Viewport Layout Options

⑤ Saving Scenes

Save your scene frequently to protect yourself from mistakes and loss of work.

(ii) **Modeling Objects**

You model objects in your scene by creating standard objects, such as 3D geometry and 2D shapes, and then applying modifiers to those objects. 3ds Max includes a wide range of standard objects and modifiers. (Figure 9-27)

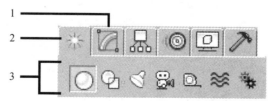

1. Modify panel　　2. Create panel　　3. Object categories

Figure 9-27　Standard Objects and Modifiers

① Creating Objects

You create objects by clicking an object category and type on the Create panel and then clicking or dragging in a viewport to define the object's creation parameters. 3ds Max organizes the Create panel into these basic categories: Geometry, Shapes, Lights, Cameras, Helpers, Space Warps, and Systems. Each category contains multiple subcategories from which you can choose.

You can also create objects from the Create menu by choosing an object category and type and then clicking or dragging in a viewport to define the object's creation parameters. 3ds Max organizes the Create menu into these basic categories: Standard Primitives, Extended Primitives, AEC Objects, Compound, Particles, Patch Grids, NURBS, Dynamics, Shapes, Lights, Cameras, Helpers, Space Warps, and Systems.

② Selecting and Positioning Objects

You select objects by clicking or dragging a region around them. You can also select objects by name or other properties such as color or object category.

After selecting objects, you position them in your scene using the transform tools Move, Rotate, and Scale. Use alignment tools to precisely position objects.

③ Modifying Objects

You sculpt and edit objects into their final form by applying modifiers from the Modify panel. The modifiers you apply to an object are stored in a stack. You can go back at any time and change the effect of the modifier, or remove it from the object.

(iii) Using Materials

You use the Material Editor to design materials and maps to control the appearance of object surfaces. Maps can also be used to control the appearance of environmental effects such as lighting, fog, and the background. (Figure 9-28)

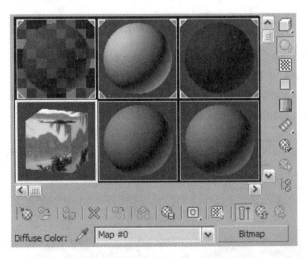

Figure 9-28　Varieties of Materials in the Material Editor's Sample Slots

① Basic Material Properties

You set basic material properties to control such surface characteristics as default color, shininess, and level of opacity. You can create realistic, single-color materials using just the basic properties.

② Using Maps

You extend the realism of materials by applying maps to control surface properties such as texture, bumpiness, opacity, and reflection. Most of the basic properties can be enhanced with a map. Any image file, such as one you might create in a paint program, can be used as a map, or you can choose procedural maps that create patterns based on parameters you set.

3ds Max also includes a raytrace material and map for creating accurate reflections and refraction.

③ Viewing Materials in the Scene

You can view the effect of materials on objects in a shaded viewport, but the display is just an approximation of the final effect. Render your scene to view materials accurately.

(ⅳ) **Placing Lights and Cameras**

You place lights and cameras to complete your scene in much the same way lights and cameras are placed on a movie set prior to filming.

Figure 9-29 Lights and Cameras Placed to Compose a Scene

Figure 9-30 The Resulting Scene

① Default Lighting

Default lighting evenly illuminates the entire scene. Such lighting is useful while modeling, but it is not especially artistic or realistic.

② Placing Lights

You create and place lights from the Lights category of the Create panel or menu when you are ready to get more specific about the lighting in your scene.

3ds Max includes the following standard light types: omni, spot, and directional lights. You can set a light to any color and even animate the color to simulate dimming or color-shifting lights. All of these lights can cast shadows, project maps, and use volumetric effects.

③ Photometric Lights

Photometric lights provide you with the ability to work more accurately and intuitively using real-world lighting units (lumens and candelas). Photometric lights also support industry-standard photometric file formats (IES, CIBSE, LTLI) so that you can model the characteristics of real-world manufactured luminaires, or even drag ready-to-use luminaires from the Web. Used in conjunction with the 3ds Max radiosity solution, photometric lights let you evaluate more accurately (both physically and quantitatively) the lighting performance of your scene.

Photometric lights are available from the Create panel→Lights drop-down list.

④ Daylight System

The Daylight system combines sunlight and skylight to create a unified system that follows the geographically correct angle and movement of the sun over the earth at a given location. You can choose location, date, time, and compass orientation. You can also animate the date and time. This system is suitable for shadow studies of proposed and existing structures.

⑤ Viewing Lighting Effects in the Scene

When you place lights in a scene, the default lighting turns off and the scene is illuminated only by the lights you create. The illumination you see in a viewport is just an approximation of the true lighting. Render your scene to view lighting accurately.

⑥ Placing Cameras

You create and place cameras from the Cameras category of the Create panel. Cameras define viewpoints for rendering, and you can animate cameras to produce cinematic effects such as dollies and truck shots.

You can also create a camera automatically from a Perspective viewport by using the Create Camera from View command found on the Views menu. Just adjust your Perspective viewport until you like it, and then choose Views→Create Camera From View. 3ds Max creates a camera and replaces the Perspective viewport with a Camera viewport showing the same perspective.

(v) **Animating Your Scene**

You can animate almost anything in your scene. Click the Auto Key button to enable automatic animation creation, drag the time slider, and make changes in your scene to create animated effects.

① Controlling Time

3ds Max starts each new scene with 100 frames for animation. Frames are a way of measuring time, and you move through time by dragging the time slider. You can also open the Time Configuration dialog to set the number of frames used by your scene and the speed at which the frames are displayed.

② Animating Transforms and Parameters

While the Auto Key button is on, 3ds Max creates an animation key whenever you transform an object or change a parameter. To animate a parameter over a range of frames, specify the values at the first and last frames of the range. 3ds Max calculates the values for all of the frames in between.

③ Editing Animation

You edit your animation by opening the Track View window or by changing options on the Motion panel. Track View is like a spreadsheet that displays animation keys along a time line. You edit the animation by changing the keys.

Track View has two modes. You can display the animation as a series of function curves that graphically show how a value changes over time in the Curve Editor mode. Alternatively, you can display your animation as a sequence of keys or ranges on a grid in the Dope Sheet mode.

(vi) **Rendering Your Scene**

Use the rendering features to define an environment and to produce the final output from your scene. (Figure 9-31)

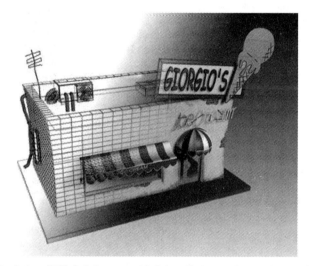

Figure 9-31 Rendering, "Fills In" Geometry with Color, Shadow, Lighting Effects, and So On

① Defining Environments and Backgrounds

Rarely do you want to render your scene against the default background color. Open the Environment And Effects dialog→Environment panel to define a background for your scene, or to set up effects such as fog.

② Setting Rendering Options

To set the size and quality of your final output, you can choose from many options on the Render Setup dialog. You have full control over professional grade film and video properties as well as effects such as reflection, antialiasing, shadow properties, and motion blur.

③ Rendering Images and Animation

You render a single image by setting the renderer to render one frame of your animation.

You specify what type of image file to produce and where 3ds Max stores the file.

Rendering an animation is the same as rendering a single image except that you set the renderer to render a sequence of frames. You can choose to render an animation to multiple single frame files or to popular animation formats such as AVI or MOV.

Maya[①]

Autodesk Maya, one of the world's leading software applications for 3D digital animation and visual effects. Maya provides a comprehensive suite of tools for your 3D content creation work ranging from modeling, animation, and dynamics through to painting and rendering to name but a few. (Figure 9-32)

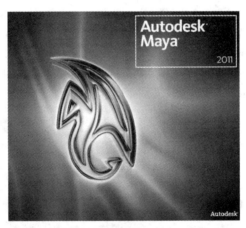

Figure 9-32 The Icon of Maya

With Maya, you can create and edit 3D models in a variety of modeling formats and animate your models using Maya's suite of animation tools. Maya also provides a range of tools to allow you to render your animated 3D scenes to achieve photo realistic imagery and animated visual effects.

You can create convincing visual simulations using Maya dynamics and nDynamics tools. Using Maya® Fluid Effects™, you can simulate and render viscous fluids, atmospheric, pyrotechnic, and ocean effects. Maya® nCloth™ lets you create simulations of fabric and clothing, while Maya® nParticles™ can be used to simulate a wide range of effects including liquids, clouds, smoke, spray, and dust. Other Maya dynamic simulation tools include Maya® Fur™, Maya® Hair™, and Maya® Artisan™ brush tools.

---

① http://images.autodesk.com/adsk/files/gettingstartedmaya2011.pdf

Chapter 9 3D Animation

1. The User Interface Overview[①] (Figure 9-33)

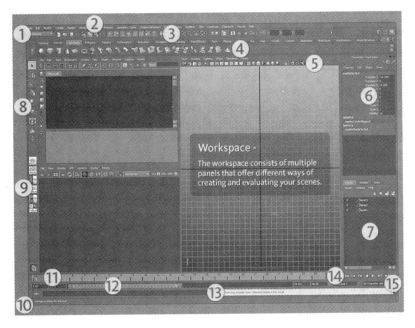

1. Menu Sets
2. Menus
3. Status Line
4. Shelf
5. Panel Toolbar
6. Channel Box
7. Layers
8. QWERTY Tool Box
9. Quick Layout Buttons
10. Help Line
11. Time Slider
12. Range Slider
13. Command Line
14. Playback
15. Anim/Character

Figure 9-33 The User Interface of Maya

2. Working in Maya[②]

Maya is the premier application for creating compelling 3D digital content, including models, animation, visual effects, games, and simulations.

The work you do in Maya generally falls into these categories:

(i) Creating models

Polygons, NURBS, and subdivision surfaces are different object types with different ways of modeling. Each has its own strengths, and different artists prefer working with different types.

Polygons let you model a surface by building up and reshaping a number of simple surface facets.

NURBS let you easily create smooth, curving surfaces with high-level control.

Subdivision surfaces let you edit surfaces at a high level with minimum overhead data,

---

① http://download.autodesk.com/us/maya/ADSK_Maya_UIOverview_2011.png

② http://download.autodesk.com/us/maya/2011help/index.html

while still letting you work with subsections of the surface as if they were made from polygons.

(ii) Character rigging

Most animations involve "characters," articulated models such as a person, an animal, robot, or anything else that moves by articulation. Maya lets you define internal skeletons for characters and bind skin to them to create realistic movement with deformation.

(iii) Animation

Just about everything you can think of in Maya is keyable or able to be animated.

(iv) Dynamics, fluids, and other simulated effects

Maya includes a comprehensive suite of tools for simulating real world effects such as fire, explosions, fluids, hair and fur, the physics of colliding objects, and more.

(v) Painting and paint effects

Maya includes an incredible system for using a graphics tablet (or the mouse) to paint 2D canvases, paint directly on 3D models, paint to create geometry, scriptable paint, and virtually limitless other possibilities.

(vi) Lighting, shading, and rendering

When you want to render a still image or movie of you scene or animation, you can create them using your choice of renderers.

3. Animation in Maya[28]

Maya animation provides you with the powerful tools you need to bring the characters and objects in your scenes to life. These tools give you the freedom to animate any attribute of an object and the control you need to successfully transform joints and bones, IK handles, and models over time.

Types of animation in Maya:

(i) Keyframe animation

Keyframe animation lets you transform objects or skeletons over time by setting keyframes. For example, you can keyframe the joints and IK handles of a character's arm to create an animation of its arm waving.

(ii) Driven key animation

Driven key animation lets you link and drive the attributes of one object with those of another object by setting driven keys. For example, you can key a character's X and Z translations as Driver attributes and a door model's Y rotation as the Driven attribute to create an animation of a character and a swinging door.

(iii) Nonlinear animation

Nonlinear animation lets you split, duplicate, and blend animation clips to achieve the motion effects that you want. For example, you can use nonlinear animation to create a looping walk cycle for one of your characters.

(iv) Path animation

Path animation lets you set a curve as an animation path for an object. When you attach an object to a motion path, it follows the curve during its animation. For example, when you assign a car model to a motion path that follows a road in your scene, the car follows the road when you play the animation.

(v) **Motion capture animation**

Motion capture animation lets you use imported motion capture data to apply realistic motion to the characters in your scene. For example, you can use the captured motion of a horse to animate the skeleton of a quadruped model.

(vi) **Layered animation**

Layered animation lets you create and blend animation on separate layers. You can modify an animation sequence on layers without permanently altering the original, or simply organize your keyframe animation onto layers.

(vii) **Dynamic animation**

Dynamic animation lets you create realistic motion using the rules of physics to simulate natural forces. For example, you can use Maya® Dynamics to create effects such as sparks spraying from a welding torch or hail falling from the sky.

(viii) **Expressions**

Expressions are instructions that you can type to animate attributes. For example, you can write an expression formula that animates the flapping of a bird's wings.

New Words

bandwidth   *n.* 带宽;频带宽度
render   *vt.* 着色;表达,描绘,渲染
frame   *n.* 帧
keyframing   关键帧
tween   *prep.* 在两者之间 *adv.* 中间地 *vt.* 补间
tweening   中间计算;补间
morphing   *n.* 图像变形技术;变形
vector   *n.* 矢量;航线
jerkiness   *n.* 急动;痉挛;不平稳
anatomy   *n.* 解剖;分析;构造;骨骼
analogous   *adj.* 类似的;模拟的
Avar animation variable   动画变量
interpolate   *vi.* 插入;修改
nuance   *n.* (颜色、音调、表情、措词等的)细微差别
polygon   *n.* 多边形;多角形物体
photorealistic   *adj.* 逼真的;相片般真实的 *n.* 真实感;仿真
performance capture   绩效捕捉;高性能捕捉
anthropomorphic   *adj.* 拟人化的

holy grail （传说中耶稣在最后晚餐时用的）圣杯,圣盘;必杀技
repercussion   n. ［常用复数］反应,影响
subcategory   n. 子范畴;亚类
puppetry   n. 木偶(戏);傀儡;机械刻板的动作
squash   vt. 镇压;把……压扁;vi. 受挤压;发出挤压声;挤入 n. 挤压
acronym   n. 首字母缩略词
synchronous   adj. 同步的;同时的
mandatory   adj. 强制的;托管的;命令的
metadata   n. 元数据
abbreviation   n. 缩写;缩写词
codec   n. 编码解码器;多媒体数字信号编解码器
awesome   adj. 可怕的,引起敬畏的;令人难忘的;极好的
hierarchical   adj. 分层的;等级体系的
encapsulated   adj. 密封的;压缩的
arguably   adv. 可论证地;可能,大概
pioneer   vt. 开创;倡导;提倡
versatility   n. 多功能性;多才多艺;用途广泛

Notes

［1］ At rates below 12 frame/s most people can detect jerkiness associated with the drawing of new images which detracts from the illusion of realistic movement.

译文:当速度低于12帧每秒以下时,大多数人能够觉察到由绘制新图片所引起的跳跃,这就干扰了真实运动的假象。

- associated with the drawing of new images 是一个宾语补足语,修饰 jerkiness。
- which detracts from the illusion of realistic movement 是一个定语从句,也修饰 jerkiness。
- associate with 与…有关,与…有联系;联合。

［2］ Thus motion capture is appropriate in situations where believable, realistic behavior and action is required, but the types of characters required exceed what can be done through conventional costuming.

译文:因此,必须具有可信的、有现实感的行为和动作的情况下,动作捕捉才是合适的。但是这种类型的角色所必需的要求超过了通过传统道具所能做到的。

- where believable, realistic behavior and action is required 是一个定语从句,修饰 situations。
- what can be done through conventional costuming 是一个宾语从句。

［3］ This could be done in a way that the viewer is no longer able to tell if a particular movie sequence is computer-generated, or created using real actors in front of movie cameras.

译文:这就在某种程度上可以使观众不再能够辨别出一个特定的运动序列是由计算机产生的还是真实的演员在摄像机前面表演得到的。

• that the viewer is no longer able to tell if a particular movie sequence is computer-generated, or created using real actors in front of movie cameras 是一个主语从句，修饰 This，但是这个句子本身又是个由两个并列的从句 a particular movie sequence is computer-generated 和 created using real actors in front of movie cameras 组成的。

Selected Translation

Part 1

三维动画概述

计算机动画

计算机动画（又称为计算机成像动画），是一种通过使用计算机来制作动画的艺术。它是计算机图形和动画的一个子领域。虽然为了满足格式上的、低宽带和更快的实时渲染的需求，二维计算机图形仍然被广泛地使用着，但计算机动画开始越来越多地借助于三维计算机图形。有时候动画指向的就是计算机本身，有时候则是其他媒体，例如电影。它也被称为计算机成像或者电脑产生的影像，尤其是在电影中使用的时候。

为了制造运动上的假象，画面显示在计算机屏幕上，然后很快被一副和前面的画面相似但是稍微在时间上移动了一些（通常是以 24 或 30 帧每秒的速度）的新画面所代替。这种技术和电视以及电影里制造运动的假象的原理是一样的。

三维计算机动画本质上是基于三维模型和逐帧的二维动画图例的定格动画的数字化继承者。三维动画中的对象（或模型）创建在计算机显示器上，而三维人物是通过一个虚拟的骨架来操纵的。二维数字动画使用单独的对象（或图例）和单独的透明图层，有时候也带有虚拟骨架，有时候又没有。然后人物形象的四肢、眼睛、嘴巴和衣服等的移动是通过设置关键帧动画来完成的。关键帧之间的差异是通过计算机自动计算来完成的，这个过程称为补间或者变形。最后，渲染动画。

对于三维动画，在完成建模之后必须渲染所有的帧。对于二维矢量动画，渲染过程就是关键帧形成图像的过程，同时补间帧也需要被渲染。为了预录制的展示，渲染之后的帧就会被转换成不同的格式或媒体，例如电影或者数字视频。这些帧也可能会被实时渲染呈现给终端用户的观众。通过因特网传输的低带宽动画（例如二维 flash 动画）经常使用终端用户计算机上的软件进行实时渲染来作为一种可替代的流或者预先载入的高带宽动画。

计算机动画说明

要成功地欺骗眼睛和大脑，使它们觉得自己正在看一个平滑运动的物体，图片更换的速度必须达到大约 12 帧每秒以上（一帧就是一幅完整的图片）。当速度达到 70 帧每秒的时候，由于眼睛和大脑处理图像的方式，真实感和平滑度就不能再得到改善了。当速度低于 12 帧每秒以下时，大多数人能够觉察到由绘制新图片所引起的跳跃，这就干扰了真实运动的假象。传统手工绘制的卡通片经常使用 15 帧每秒的速度以节约所需绘制的图画数量，但是由于卡通片的风格，这通常是可以接受的。因为计算机动画能产生更多真实的意象，就要求有更高的帧频率来增强这种真实感。

在高频率的速度时没有跳跃感的原因是"视觉暂留"。时时刻刻，眼睛和大脑一起工作,实际上把任何所看到的景象只存储几分之一秒,然后自动"平滑掉"一些小跳跃。在美国,人们在电影院里看到的电影是以24帧每秒的速度运行的,这就足以产生连续运动的假象。

制作虚拟人物动画的方法

在大多数三维计算机动画系统中,一名动画师创造一个人物解剖模型的简化表示,类似于一具骨架或者人物线条画。骨骼模型每一部分的位置是通过动画变量来定义的。在人类和动物角色中,骨骼模型的许多部分符合实际的骨头,但是骨骼动画也用来制作其他动画,例如面部特征的动画(尽管已经有其他的制作面部动画的方法)。例如,在《玩具总动员》中"Woody"这个角色,就是用了700个动画变量,包括100个在面部的动画变量。计算机常常不是直接渲染骨骼模型(它是不可见的),但是使用骨骼模型来计算角色的确切位置和方向,最终渲染成一幅图像。因此通过随时间的推移来改变动画变量值的方法,动画师通过逐帧移动角色来创建动画。

有好几种方法可以产生动画变量来获得具有真实感的运动。传统上,动画师直接操作动画变量。而不是为每一帧设置动画变量,他们常常及时在重要位置(帧)设置动画变量,并且让计算机插入(帧)或者在帧之间补间,这个方法叫做设置关键帧。关键帧的设置由动画师控制,它来源于手工绘制传统动画的方法。

与此相反,一种新的称为动作捕捉的方法利用的是真人活动。当计算机动画由动作捕捉驱动时,真实的表演者在场外行动就像他们是制作的动画中的角色。他(或她)的运动被摄像机记录在计算机中并标记下来,然后这些表演行为将会用在动画角色中。

每一种方法都有它们的长处,在游戏和电影的制作中正在使用这些方法。关键帧动画能够产生那些很困难或者不可能表演出来的运动,而动作捕捉能够复制某一个特定演员的细微动作。例如,在2006年的电影《加勒比海盗2:亡灵宝藏》中,演员比尔·奈伊为戴维·琼斯这个角色做了一系列的动作表演以供捕捉。尽管奈伊自己并不在电影中出现,这部电影却得益于所记录的他在表演中的身体语言、姿势、面部表情等的细微差别。因此,必须具有可信的、有现实感的行为和动作的情况下,动作捕捉才是合适的。但是这种类型的角色所必需的要求超过了通过传统道具所能做到的。

计算机动画的开发设备

计算机动画能够用计算机和动画软件来制作。有些给人印象深刻的动画能够用基本程序来完成。但是在普通的家用电脑上渲染会花很长时间。正因为如此,视频游戏动画倾向于低分辨率、低多边形数的渲染,这样图形就可以在家用电脑上进行实时渲染。而仿真动画在这种情形下是不现实的。

制作电影、电视和在电脑游戏中的视频序列的专业动画师采用高细节层次的仿真动画。这种质量水平的电影动画在家用电脑上可能要花几十到几百年来制作。很多强大的工作站就被用来制作这种动画。图形工作站使用两到四个处理器,这样就比家用电脑强大得多并且特别适合用于渲染。大量的工作站(被称为渲染农场)组合起来,可以像一个巨型计算机那样有效率地工作。这样一部计算机动画电影可以在一到五年内完成(当然这个过程不只是包括渲染)。一个工作站通常价值2000美元到16000美元,较昂贵的工作站能提供更快的渲染服务,因为它们拥有在技术上更先进的硬件。Pixar's Renderman是一个作为电影动画的行业标准而广泛运用的渲染软件,在渲染器上很有竞争力。

它可以以大约 3500 美元的价钱在 Pixar 官方网页上购买。它能在 Linux、Mac OS X 和 Microsoft Windows 系统上运行基于图形工作站的动画程序，例如 Maya 和 Softimage XSI。专业人员也采用数字摄像机、动作捕获或者绩效捕获、蓝屏、影片编辑软件、小道具以及其他工具来制作电影动画。

未来

计算机动画里一个开放性的挑战是人物的仿真动画。目前，大多数计算机动画电影展示的是动物角色（例如《虫虫危机》《海底总动员》《料理鼠王》《纽特》《冰河世纪》《篱笆墙外》）、幻想角色（例如《怪兽公司》《怪物史莱克》《忍者神龟 4》《怪兽大战外星人》）、拟人化的机械（例如《汽车总动员》《机器人瓦力》《机器人历险记》）或者卡通人物（例如《超人特工队》《卑鄙的我》《飞屋环游记》）。电影的最终幻想是：内在精神经常被第一代由电脑生成的电影引用，这种电影试图展示看起来逼真的人类。然而，由于人体结构、人体运动和人体生物力学极大的复杂性，人体现实仿真很大程度上依然是一个公开的问题。另一个问题是令人讨厌的心理反应，就是观看近乎完美的人类动画，被称为恐怖谷理论。它是计算机动画的权威指南之一。最后，我们的目标是创建软件，利用这些软件动画师可以生成一个表现仿真人物角色的运动序列，感受穿着衣服以及带有真实感的头发、复杂的自然背景的类似真实人体的运动，并且可能和其他的模拟人物角色相互作用。这就在某种程度上可以使观众不再能够辨别出一个特定的运动序列是由计算机产生的还是真实的演员在摄像机前面表演得到的。完全的人类真实感还不太可能很快实现，当能够实现的时候，这可能主要影响到电影业。

目前似乎三维计算机动画能够被分成两个主要的方向：仿真和非真实感渲染。仿真计算机动画本身就可以分为两个子部分：真实感仿真（在创建虚拟人物角色时采用的是高性能捕捉）和风格化仿真。真实感的仿真是《最终幻想》试图达到的，并且在未来最有可能呈现给我们像《夜魔水晶》中的那种具有真实人物活动的幻想特征而不必使用先进的木偶戏和动画技术。《小蚁雄兵》就是一个风格化仿真的例子。（在未来，风格化仿真将可能取代《僵尸新娘》中的那种传统定格动画。）

非真实感或者卡通方向更可能像是传统动画的一个扩展，是一种制作类似三维卡通版的动画的尝试，这种动画仍然使用和完善被迪斯尼九大元老（动画师）明确表述过的动画主要原则，例如挤压和拉伸。

在一个仿真计算机动画放映时单独的一帧看起来会像是一张照片，如果这样看的话。而在卡通计算机动画放映时单独的一帧看起来则会像是一幅图画。

业余动画

Newgrounds 等网站允许会员上传他们自己的电影以供其他人观看，这些网站的流行创造了一个不断增长的业余动画师的社区。由于有许多免费可用的工具和类似 Windows Movie Maker 和 iMovie 这样包含在开放系统中的程序，任何使用这些工具和有创造思维的人都可以让数千观众看到他们的动画。许多高端动画软件的选择也常常会是一个允许教育和非商业化开发并有一定使用限制的试用版。也存在几个免费的开源动画软件应用程序，Blender 就是一个例子。一种创作业余动画的方法是使用 GIF 格式，这种格式很容易在网络上上传和看到。

建筑动画

建筑师使用从动画公司得到的服务来为客户和施工人员创作三维模型。这样的模型比传统绘画更准确。建筑动画也可以用来查看建筑与周围的环境以及与它周围的其他建筑之间可能的关系。

Exercises

1. Please explain the following professional terms：

① CGI animation

② Persistence of vision

③ Skeletal animation

2. Short answers：

① Please reference some other documents and state possible developing trends of computer animation?

② What are the basic procedures for creating scenes in 3DS Max?

3. Practice：

① Learn 3DS MAX or Maya to make some animations.

互联网上常用的数字媒体技术专业资源

数字媒体技术专业旨在培养兼具技术素质和艺术素质的现代艺术设计人才，与数字媒体艺术专业相比，本专业略注重技术素质的培养，可适应新媒体艺术创作、网络多媒体制作、广告、影视动画、大众传媒、房地产业的演示动画片制作工作。

数字媒体技术专业主要包括：影视、动画、游戏、网站这四个方面，因此互联网上常用的该专业的文献资源主要也包括这四个方面，或者是综合了这四个方面的网络资源。

在互联网上常用的数字媒体技术资源有下面一些：

1. 传媒类网址

国家广播电影电视总局：http://www.sarft.gov.cn/

中华人民共和国新闻出版总署：http://www.gapp.gov.cn/cms/html/21/index.html

中华传媒网：http://info.mediachina.net/news/index.php

京华传媒网：http://www.jhcm.com/

传媒学术网：http://academic.mediachina.net/

华文报刊网：http://www.chinesebk.com/

中华电视网：http://www.chinatv-net.com/

中国传媒咨询网：http://www.gotton.cn/

中国网络传播网：http://www.diffuse.cn/

中国广告网：http://www.cnad.com/

传媒中国网：http://www.mediach.com/html/index.html

2. 影视、动画类网址
中国影视广告网:http://www.cftvc.com/
中国电影家协会:http://www.cfa.org.cn/
中国电视艺术家协会:http://www.ctaa.org.cn/
中国电视艺术网:http://www.tv1958.com/tv/
中国动漫资源网:http://www.51cacg.com/
中国动画网:http://www.chinanim.com/
迪斯尼中国官方网站:http://www.disney.cn/
中华轩:http://www.sinodoor.com/
3. 游戏类网址
GameRes 游戏开发资源网:http://www.gameres.com/
中国游戏中心:http://www.chinagames.net/
中国 IT 实验室—游戏开发:http://game.chinaitlab.com/
戏游网:http://www.gamers.com/
游戏开发者:http://www.chinadogame.com.cn/
云世界:http://edu.gamfe.com/
硅谷动力—游戏开发者:http://games.enet.com.cn/zhuanti/school/
4. 网站设计开发类网址
W3 school:http://www.w3school.com.cn/
WEB 开发教程:http://www.sosodz.com/
建站交流资讯平台:http://www.websbook.com/
A5 下载:http://down.admin5.com/
网页教学网:http://www.webjx.com/
网页特效代码:http://www.jscode.cn/
5. 综合类网站
中国地区高校数字媒体专业网站:http://www.cndmt.org/index.htm
中国数字影视门户:http://www.zgszysmh.cn/

数字媒体技术专业论文投稿期刊

数字媒体技术专业涵盖的范围非常广泛,因此该专业论文可以根据内容的侧重点不同投稿到不同方向的期刊。

例如:《电影文学》《当代电影》《电影艺术》《中国电视》《电视研究》《电影评价》《大众摄影》《中国摄影》《现代传播》《当代传播》《国际新闻界》《中国记者》《新闻记者》《新闻与传播研究》《新闻战线》《新闻界》《中国广播电视学刊》《电子学报》《通信学报》《计算机学报》《软件学报》《计算机科学》《计算机工程与应用》《计算机应用》《计算机应用与软件》《微型计算机》《计算机与网络》等。

Chapter 10　Virtual Reality

▲ Knowledge Objectives

When you have completed this unit, you will be able to:
- Define virtual reality.
- State the history of virtual reality.
- Describe application areas of virtual reality.
- To sketch out social implications of virtual reality.

▲ Professional Terms

artificial reality	人工现实
augmented reality	扩增实境/增强现实
cyberspace	网络空间/赛博空间
force feedback	力反馈
VR	虚拟现实

Part 1　Terminology, Concepts and Timeline[①]

Virtual reality (VR) is a term that applies to computer-simulated environments that can simulate places in the real world, as well as in imaginary worlds. Most current virtual reality environments are primarily visual experiences, displayed either on a computer screen or through special stereoscopic displays, but some simulations include additional sensory information, such as sound through speakers or headphones. Some advanced, haptic systems now include tactile information, generally known as force feedback, in medical and gaming applications.

Users can interact with a virtual environment or a virtual artifact (VA) either through the use of standard input devices such as a keyboard and mouse, or through multimodal devices such as a wired glove and omnidirectional treadmills. The simulated environment can be similar to the real world—for example, in simulations for pilot or combat training—or it can differ significantly from reality, such as in VR games. In practice, it is currently very difficult to create a high-fidelity virtual reality experience, due largely to technical limitations on processing

---

① http://en.wikipedia.org/wiki/Virtual_reality#Background

power, image resolution, and communication bandwidth; however, the technology's proponents hope that such limitations will be overcome as processor, imaging, and data communication technologies become more powerful and cost-effective over time. (Figure 10-1)

Figure 10-1   U. S. Navy Personnel Using a VR Parachute Trainer

Virtual reality is often used to describe a wide variety of applications commonly associated with immersive, highly visual, 3D environments. The development of CAD software, graphics hardware acceleration, head mounted displays, data gloves, and miniaturization have helped popularize the notion. In the book *The Metaphysics of Virtual Reality* by Michael R. Heim, seven different concepts of virtual reality are identified: simulation, interaction, artificiality, immersion, telepresence, full-body immersion, and network communication. (Figure 10-2)

Figure 10-2   World Skin (1997), Maurice Benayoun's Virtual Reality Interactive Installation

Terminology and Concepts

The term "artificial reality", coined by Myron Krueger, has been in use since the 1970s; however, the origin of the term "virtual reality" can be traced back to the French playwright, poet, actor, and director Antonin Artaud. In his book *The Theatre and Its Double* (1938), Artaud described theatre as "a virtual reality, in which characters, objects, and images take on the phantasmagoric force of alchemy's visionary internal dramas". It has been used in *The Judas Mandala* (1982), a science-fiction novel by Damien Broderick, where the context of use is somewhat different from that defined above. The earliest use cited by the Oxford English Dictionary is in a 1987 article titled "Virtual reality", but the article is not about VR technology.

The concept of virtual reality was popularized in mass media by movies such as Brainstorm and The Lawnmower Man. The VR research boom of the 1990s was accompanied by the non-fiction book *Virtual Reality* (1991) by Howard Rheingold. The book served to demystify the subject, making it more accessible to less technical researchers and enthusiasts, with an impact similar to that which his book *The Virtual Community* had on virtual community research lines closely related to VR. *Multimedia: from Wagner to Virtual Reality*, edited by Randall Packer and Ken Jordan and first published in 2001, explores the term and its history from an avant-garde perspective. Philosophical implications of the concept of VR are systematically discussed in the book *Get Real: A Philosophical Adventure in Virtual Reality* (1998) by Philip Zhai, wherein the idea of VR is pushed to its logical extreme and ultimate possibility. According to Zhai, virtual reality could be made to have an ontological status equal to that of actual reality.

Timeline

Virtual reality can trace its roots to the 1860s, when 360-degree art through panoramic murals began to appear. An example of this would be Baldassare Peruzzi's piece titled, *Sala Delle Prospettive*.① (Figure 10-3) In the 1920s, vehicle simulators were introduced. Morton Heilig wrote in the 1950s of an "Experience Theatre" that could encompass all the senses in an effective manner, thus drawing the viewer into the onscreen activity. He built a prototype of his vision dubbed the Sensorama in 1962, along with five short films to be displayed in it while engaging multiple senses (sight, sound, smell, and touch). Predating digital computing, the Sensorama was a mechanical device, which reportedly still functions today. Around this time, Douglas Englebart uses computer screens as both input and output devices. In 1966, Tom Furness introduces a visual flight stimulator for the Air Force. In 1968, Ivan Sutherland, with the help of his student Bob Sproull, created what is widely considered to be the first virtual reality and augmented reality (AR) head mounted display (HMD) system. It was primitive both in terms of user interface and realism, and the HMD to be worn by the user was so heavy it had to be suspended from the ceiling. The formidable appearance of the device inspired its name, The Sword of Damocles. Also notable among the earlier hypermedia and

Figure 10-3 Sala Delle Prospettive

---

① http://www.elite-view.com/html/Museum_Art_The_High_Renaissance/id-103673.html

virtual reality systems was the Aspen Movie Map, which was created at MIT in 1977. The program was a crude virtual simulation of Aspen, Colorado in which users could wander the streets in one of three modes: summer, winter, and polygons. The first two were based on photographs—the researchers actually photographed every possible movement through the city's street grid in both seasons—and the third was a basic 3D model of the city. In the late 1980s, the term "virtual reality" was popularized by Jaron Lanier, one of the modern pioneers of the field. Lanier had founded the company VPL Research in 1985, which developed and built some of the seminal "goggles and gloves" systems of that decade. In 1991, Antonio Medina, a MIT graduate and NASA scientist, designed a virtual reality system to "drive" Mars rovers from Earth in apparent real time despite the substantial delay of Mars-Earth-Mars signals. The system, termed "Computer-Simulated Teleoperation" as published by Rand, is an extension of virtual reality.

Part 2 Application Areas[①]

The potential for virtual reality as an entertainment medium is apparent. Instead of manipulating computerized images of two boxers or a car race, the virtual playground allows the user to experience the event. Disney World's Epcot Center houses a virtual reality system.

Most entertainment applications of the present day are visually based. Virtual reality will allow players of the future to experience a variety of tactile events. For example, in a simulated boxing match, virtual reality users would bob and weave, and throw, land, and receive punches in return.

Virtual reality also has practical applications in business, manufacturing, and medicine. Already, the National Aeronautics and Space Administration (NASA) has developed a virtual wind tunnel to test aerodynamics shape. Virtual reality holds promise for discovering the most efficient manufacturing conditions by allowing planners to evaluate the actual physical motions and strength needed to complete a job. For example, the McDonnell-Douglas Corporation is using virtual reality to explore the use of different materials and tools in building the F-18 E/F aircraft. The study of people in relation to their environments (ergonomics) may also be revolutionized by trials in cyberspace. Engineers at the Volvo car company use virtual reality to test various designs for the dashboard configuration from the perspective of the user.

In medicine, virtual reality systems are being developed to help surgeons plan and practice delicate surgical procedures. Philip Green, a researcher at SRI International, has developed a telemanipulator, a special remote-controlled robot, to be used in surgery. Such surgery was performed in 2002 by a physician in Halifax, Nova Scotia, on a patient located hundreds

---

① http://science.jrank.org/pages/7198/Virtual-Reality-Applications-virtual-reality.html

of miles away. Using instruments connected to a computer, the operation was performed cyberspace, while the computer sent signals to direct the telemanipulator.

Virtual reality may even have applications in psychiatry. For example, someone with acrophobia (a fear of heights) may be treated by having the patient stand atop virtual skyscrapers or soar through the air like a bird.

Part 3　Social Implication (1)[①]

Fiction Books

Many science fiction books and movies have imagined characters being "trapped in virtual reality".

A comprehensive and specific fictional model for virtual reality was published in 1935 in the short story Pygmalion's Spectacles by Stanley G. Weinbaum. In the story, the main character, Dan Burke, meets an elfin professor, Albert Ludwig, who has invented "a movie that gives one sight and sound, taste, smell, and touch. You are in the story, you speak to the shadows (characters) and they reply, and instead of being on a screen, the story is all about you, and you are in it." A more modern work to use this idea was Daniel F. Galouye's novel Simulacron-3, which was made into a German teleplay titled *Welt am Draht* ("World on a Wire") in 1973. Other science fiction books have promoted the idea of virtual reality as a partial, but not total, substitution for the misery of reality, or have touted it as a method for creating breathtaking virtual worlds in which one may escape from Earth. They are not aware of this, because their minds exist within a shared, idealized virtual world known as Dream Earth, where they grow up, live, and die, never knowing the world they live in is but a dream.

Stanislaw Lem wrote a short story in early 1960 called "*dziwne skrzynie profesora Corcorana*", in which he presented a scientist who devised a completely artificial virtual reality. Among the beings trapped inside his created virtual world, there is also a scientist, who also devised such machines creating another level of virtual world. The Piers Anthony novel Killobyte follows the story of a paralyzed cop trapped in a virtual reality game by a hacker, whom he must stop to save a fellow trapped player slowly succumbing to insulin shock. This novel toys with the idea of both the potential positive therapeutic uses, such as allowing the paralyzed to experience the illusion of movement while stimulating unused muscles, as well as virtual realities' dangers. Vernor Vinge's *True Names*, published in 1981, imagines a virtual world which is probably the first to represent a metaverse. In the story, characters interact with each other in a complete world, where they own homes and are represented using avatars. This type of virtual world was later to be realized as Second Life, which was launched in 2003.

---

① http://en.wikipedia.org/wiki/Virtual_reality#Impact

Other popular fictional works that use the concept of virtual reality include William Gibson's *Neuromancer* which defined the concept of cyberspace, Neal Stephenson's *Snow Crash*, in which he made extensive reference to the term avatar to describe one's representation in a virtual world, and Rudy Rucker's *The Hacker and the Ants*, in which programmer Jerzy Rugby uses VR for robot design and testing.

Television

Perhaps the earliest example of virtual reality on television is the Doctor Who serial "The Deadly Assassin". This story, first broadcast in 1976, introduced a dream-like computer-generated reality, known as the Matrix. The first major American television series to showcase virtual reality was *Star Trek: The Next Generation*. Several episodes featured a holodeck, a virtual reality facility that enabled its users to recreate and experience anything they wanted. One difference from current virtual reality technology, however, was that replicators, force fields, holograms, and transporters were used to actually recreate and place objects in the holodeck, rather than illusions of physical objects, as is done today.

Cult British BBC2 sci-fi series Red Dwarf featured a virtual reality game titled "Better Than Life", in which the main characters had spent many years connected. Virtual reality has also been featured in other Red Dwarf episodes, including "Back to Reality", where venom from the despair squid caused the characters to believe that all of their experiences on Red Dwarf had been part of a VR simulation. Other episodes that feature virtual reality include "Gunmen of the Apocalypse", "Stoke Me a Clipper", "Blue", "Beyond a Joke", and "Back in the Red".

The popular hack multimedia franchise is based on a virtual reality MMORPG dubbed "The World" The French animated series *Code Lyoko* is based on the virtual world of *Lyoko* and the Internet. The virtual world is accessed by large scanners which use an atomic process, and breaks down the atoms of the person inside, digitizes them, and recreates an incarnation on *Lyoko*.

Motion Pictures

Steven Lisberger's 1982 movie *TRON* was the first mainstream Hollywood picture to explore the idea of virtual reality. One year later, it would be fully expanded in the Natalie Wood film Brainstorm. One of the non-science fiction movies that uses VR as a story driver is 1994's *Disclosure*, starring Michael Douglas and based on the Michael Crichton book of the same name. A VR headset is used as a navigating device for a prototype computer filing system. James Cameron's *Avatar* depicts a time when people's consciousness are virtually transported into biologically grown avatars.

Games

In 1991, Virtuality (originally W Industries) licensed the Amiga 3000 for use in their VR machines, and released a VR gaming system called the 1000CS. This was a stand-up immersive HMD platform with a tracked 3D joystick. The system featured several VR games including *Dactyl Nightmare*, *Legend Quest*, *Hero*, and *Grid Busters*. The Aura Interactor Virtual Reality Game Wear is a chest and back harness through which the player can feel punches, explosions, kicks, uppercuts, slam-dunks, crashes, and bodyblows. It works with the Sega Genesis and Super Nintendo Entertainment System.

Figure 10-4　Classic Virtual Reality HMD with Glove

In the *Mage*: *The Ascension role-playing game*, the mage tradition of the Virtual Adepts is presented as the creators of VR. The Adepts' ultimate objective is to move into virtual reality, scrapping their physical bodies in favour of improved virtual ones. Also, the hack series centers on a virtual reality video game. This shows the potentially dangerous side of virtual reality, demonstrating the adverse effects on human health and possible viruses, including a comatose state which some players assume. Metal Gear Solid bases heavily on VR usage, either as a part of the plot (notably Metal Gear Solid 2), or simply to guide the players through training sessions. (Figure 10-4)

Part 4　Social Implication (2)

Radio

In 2009, British digital radio station BBC Radio 7 broadcasted Planet B, a science-fiction drama set in a virtual world. *Planet B* is the largest ever commission for an original drama programme.

Fine Art

David Em was the first fine artist to create navigable virtual worlds in the 1970s. His early work was done on mainframes at III, JPL, and Caltech. Jeffrey Shaw explored the potential of VR in fine arts with early works like *Legible City* (1989), *Virtual Museum* (1991), and *Golden Calf* (1994). Canadian artist Char Davies created immersive VR art pieces Osmose (1995) and Ephémère (1998). Maurice Benayoun's work introduced metaphorical, philosophical or political content, combining VR, network, generation and intelligent agents, in works like *Is God Flat* (1994), *The Tunnel under the Atlantic* (1995), and *World Skin* (1997). Other pioneering artists working in VR have included Luc Courchesne, Rita Addison, Knowbotic Research, Rebecca Allen, Perry Hoberman, Jacki Morie, and Brenda Laurel. All mentioned artists are documented in the Database of Virtual Art.

Marketing

A side effect of the chic image that has been cultivated for virtual reality in the media is that advertising and merchandise have been associated with VR over the years to take advantage of the buzz. This is often seen in product tie-ins with cross-media properties, especially gaming licenses, with varying degrees of success. The NES Power Glove by Mattel from the 1980s was an early example, as well as the U-Force and the Sega Activator. TV commercials featuring VR have also been made for other products, however, such as Nike's "Virtual Andre" in 1997, featuring a teenager playing tennis using a goggle and gloves system against a computer.

Therapeutic Uses

The primary use of VR in a therapeutic role is its application to various forms of exposure therapy, ranging from phobia treatments to newer approaches to treating PTSD. A very basic VR simulation with simple sight and sound models has been shown to be invaluable in phobia treatment, like zoophobia, and acrophobia, as a step between basic exposure therapy such as the use of simulacra and true exposure. A much more recent application is being piloted by the U.S. Navy to use a much more complex simulation to immerse veterans suffering from PTSD in simulations of urban combat settings. Much as in phobia treatment, exposure to the subject of the trauma or fear leads to desensitization, and a significant reduction in symptoms.

Other research fields in which the use of virtual reality is being explored are physical medicine, rehabilitation, physical therapy, and occupational therapy. In adult rehabilitation, a variety of virtual reality applications are currently being evaluated within upper and lower limb motor rehabilitation for individuals recovering from stroke or spinal cord injury. In pediatrics, the use of virtual reality is being evaluated to promote movement abilities, navigational abilities, or social skills in children with cerebral palsy, acquired brain injury, or other disabilities. Research evidence is emerging rapidly in the field of virtual reality for therapeutic uses. A number of recent reviews published in peer-reviewed journals have summarized the current evidence for the use of Virtual Reality within pediatric and adult rehabilitation. One such review concluded that the field is potentially promising.

New Words

stereoscopic *adj.* 立体的;有立体感的
haptic *adj.* 触觉的
tactile *adj.* 触觉的,有触觉的;能触知的
artifact *n.* 人工制品;手工艺品
multimodal *adj.* 多峰的;多模式的
omnidirectional *adj.* 全方向的
treadmill *n.* 踏车,跑步机;单调的工作
high-fidelity *n.* 高保真;高保真度
telepresence *n.* 临场感

demystify vt. 使非神秘化;阐明;启发
accessible adj. 易接近的;可进入的;可理解的
panoramic adj. 全景的
mural adj. 墙壁的 n. 壁画;壁饰
prototype n. 原型;标准,模范
head mounted display 头盔式现实器
formidable adj. 强大的;可怕的;令人敬畏的;艰难的
goggle n. 护目镜
teleoperation n. 遥操作;远程操作
telemanipulator n. 遥控装置
manipulate vt. 操纵;操作;巧妙地处理;修改,篡改
NASA 美国国家航空航天局
wind tunnel 风洞
aerodynamics n. 气体力学;航空动力学
ergonomics n. 工效学;人类工程学
SRI International 斯坦福国际研究所
acrophobia n. 恐高症
elfin n. 小精灵;淘气鬼;矮人
tout vt. 吹捧,兜售;劝诱;侦查
paralyzed adj. 瘫痪的;麻痹的
succumb vi. 屈服;听任;被压垮
insulin shock 胰岛素休克
metaverse n. 虚拟实境
avatar n. 具体化;神化之身
holodeck n. 全息甲板;全景操作平台
replicator n. 复制基因;[计]重复符
force field n. 力场;(科幻小说中的)(无形的)力障碍区
hologram n. 全息照相;全息图
venom n. 毒液;恶意
squid n. 鱿鱼;乌贼,枪乌贼
franchise n. 特权;公民权;经销权;管辖权
uppercut vi. 击上钩拳,用上钩拳击 n. 上钩拳
slam-dunk n. (篮球)扣篮;作大投入;大笔回报
comatose adj. 昏迷的;昏睡状态的;麻木的;怠惰的
metaphorical adj. 比喻性的;隐喻性的
chic adj. 别致的 n. 时髦;别致的款式
simulacrum n. 像;幻影;影[复]simulacra
trauma n. 创伤(由心理创伤造成精神上的异常)

desensitization　　*n.* 脱敏(现象);感觉迟钝
rehabilitation　　*n.* 复原;康复;改造,再教育

Notes

[1] The VR research boom of the 1990s was accompanied by the non-fiction book *Virtual Reality* (1991) by Howard Rheingold. The book served to demystify the subject, making it more accessible to less technical researchers and enthusiasts, with an impact similar to that which his book *The Virtual Community* had on virtual community research lines closely related to VR.

译文:随着霍华德·瑞恩高德在1991年出版的《虚拟现实》的畅销,虚拟现实技术在20世纪90年代逐渐兴起。该书有助于使这一事物去神秘化,使之更容易被不懂得该技术的研究人员和爱好者接受。这种影响就和该作者的《虚拟社区》一书使得对虚拟社区的研究路线与虚拟现实紧密相关是相似的。

- be accompanied by 伴随有(附有,带有);相伴而生;随…而来。
- accessible 易接近的;可理解的。
- closely related to 与…密切相关,与…紧密联系。
- making it more accessible to less technical researchers and enthusiasts 是一个动名词短语做插入语,是对 The book served to demystify the subject 的补充说明。
- that which his book *The Virtual Community* had on virtual community research lines closely related to VR,其中 that 指代前面的 impact,which 引导后面的定语从句。

[2] This novel toys with the idea of both the potential positive therapeutic uses, such as allowing the paralyzed to experience the illusion of movement while stimulating unused muscles, as well as virtual realities' dangers.

译文:这部小说没有认真地考虑(虚拟现实的)潜在的积极治疗用途——例如通过刺激瘫痪病人未活动的肌肉来让他们体验运动的错觉,以及虚拟现实的危险因素。

- toy with 不是很认真地考虑;轻率地对待。
- such as allowing the paralyzed to experience the illusion of movement while stimulating unused muscles 是一个插入语,用来修饰 the potential positive therapeutic uses。
- the potential positive therapeutic uses 和 virtual realities' dangers 是两个并列的宾语,是 idea 所指内容的两个部分。

[3] A side effect of the chic image that has been cultivated for virtual reality in the media is that advertising and merchandise have been associated with VR over the years to take advantage of the buzz.

译文:在媒体中为虚拟现实创建的别致的图形有一个附带的作用,即多年以来广告业和商业已经与虚拟现实相联系并且将它利用得如火如荼。

- that has been cultivated for virtual reality in the media 是定语从句,修饰 the chic image。
- that advertising and merchandise have been associated with VR over the years to take advantage of the buzz 是一个宾语从句。

Selected Translation

Part 1

术语、概念和发展历史

虚拟现实(VR)是一个适用于计算机模拟环境的术语,可以模拟真实世界和虚拟世界中的环境。现在大多数的虚拟现实环境都主要是视觉体验,是通过计算机屏幕或者特殊的立体显示设备来显示的,但是一些仿真中包含了其他感觉处理,比如从音响和耳机中获得声音。现在一些高级的触觉系统中包含了触觉信息,一般也叫做力反馈,在医学和游戏领域中会应用到。

通过使用标准输入设备例如键盘和鼠标,或者通过多模式设备例如一只有线手套,或者通过全方位跑步机,用户就能够与虚拟环境进行交互。虚拟环境能和现实世界相类似,例如飞行仿真和作战训练,也能与现实世界明显不同,例如在虚拟游戏中。实际上,目前还很难创造一个高逼真的虚拟现实环境,这主要是由于技术上的一些限制造成的,包括计算机的处理能力、图像分辨率和通信带宽。然而,该技术的支持者希望随着时间的推移,处理器、图像和数据通信技术会变得更加强大并且具有成本效益,这些限制将会被克服。

虚拟现实常常被用来描述成广泛多样的与沉浸感、高度可视化、三维环境有关的应用。CAD 软件的开发、图形硬件加速、头盔式显示器、数据手套和微型化帮助推广了虚拟现实这个概念。麦克·汉姆在他的《虚拟现实的形而上学》这本书里定义了虚拟现实的七个不同的概念:仿真、交互作用、人工、沉浸、远程操作、全身沉浸和网络通信。

术语和概念

"人工现实"这个术语是由迈伦·克鲁格创造的,从 20 世纪 70 年代就开始使用了。然而,"虚拟现实"这一术语的起源能够追溯到法国剧作家、诗人、演员和导演安东尼·阿尔托。在他的《戏剧及其重影》(1938),阿尔托将戏剧描述成"一个虚拟的现实,在这个虚拟的现实中,人物、物体和图片呈现出幻影般的国内戏剧中炼金术的幻想力。"这个术语已经被用在《护法法师》(1982)中,这是达米安·布拉德里克的一部科幻小说,在这部小说里,这一术语的使用范围与上面定义的有所不同。"虚拟现实"一词在牛津英语字典里最早是被引用在 1987 年的一篇文章里,但是那篇文章并不是关于虚拟现实技术的。虚拟现实的概念在大众媒体里是通过电影来普及的,例如《头脑风暴》和《锄草人》。20 世纪 90 年代虚拟现实研究的兴起伴随着霍华德·瑞恩高德的非科幻类的书《虚拟现实》(1991)的畅销。该书有助于使这一事物去神秘化,使之更容易被低技术的研究人员和爱好者接受。这种影响就和该作者的《虚拟社区》一书使得对虚拟社区的研究路线与虚拟现实紧密相关是相似的。由兰德尔·帕克和肯·乔丹编辑的《多媒体:从瓦格纳到虚拟现实》在 2001 年首次发行。该书以一种前卫的观点探讨了"虚拟现实"这一术语和它的历史。菲利普·翟的《无中生有:虚拟现实中的哲学探索》(1998)一书系统地讨论了虚拟现实的哲学意蕴,其中虚拟现实的想法被推类至尽(即达到了鼎盛)并终会出现。根据菲利普·翟的观点,虚拟现实可能被赋予了与实际的现实相平等的本体论地位。

发展历史

虚拟现实的根源可以追溯到19世纪60年代,那个时候360度的全景壁画才开始出现。巴达萨尔·佩鲁齐的一幅名为"礼堂透视图"的壁画就是那个时期的一个例子。在20世纪20年代,汽车驾驶模拟器被人所知。莫顿·海利希写下了20世纪50年代的"体验剧院",它以一种有效的方式包含了所有的感觉,这样就把观众都吸引到了屏幕上的活动中。他在1962年创建了一个被称为"传感影院"的视觉原型,随着其中放映的五个短片同时参与多种感觉(视觉、听觉、嗅觉和触觉)。"传感影院"是一个早于数字计算的机械设备,据说在今天还在使用。大约在这个时候,道格拉斯·恩格尔巴特使用计算机屏幕作为输入和输出设备。1966年汤姆·弗尼斯向空军介绍了一种可视的飞行模拟器。1968年伊凡·苏泽兰在他的学生鲍勃·斯普劳尔的帮助下,创建了第一个被广泛认可的虚拟现实和扩增实境头盔式显示器系统。那时用户界面和现实主义这两个术语都很简单原始。头盔式显示器重得必须将它吊在天花板上,这样才能被用户戴在头上。设备强大的外观使它的名字"达摩克利斯之剑"更令人激动。在早期超媒体和虚拟现实系统领域著名的还有白杨树镇电影地图,它是1977年由麻省理工学院创建的。这个程序是一个原始的白杨树镇虚拟仿真系统。在科罗拉多,用户可以以三种模式中的一种在其街上漫游:夏天、冬天和多边形。前两种模式是基于照片的——研究者实际地拍摄在两个季节中每一个可能穿越城市街道的行动;而第三个是这个城市的一个基本的三维模型。在20世纪80年代晚期,"虚拟现实"这个术语被这个领域的现代先驱——杰伦·拉尼尔大众化了。拉尼尔在1985年建立了一个可视化编程语言研究公司,十年来这个公司开发和创建了一些有发展潜能的"护目镜和防护手套"系统。1991年,毕业于麻省理工学院的美国国家航空航天局科学家安东尼奥·梅迪尔设计了一个虚拟现实系统。尽管火星—地球之间的信号存在着大量延时,这个系统可以用来在地球上明显实时地"驾驶"火星漫游者号探测器。兰德公司发布的"计算机仿真远程操作"系统是对虚拟现实的一种扩展。

Exercises

1. What are application areas of virtual reality?
2. How does virtual reality impact our lives? You can reference other articles.
3. Collect some resources related to Virtual Lab and introduce it to your classmates.

科技论文的结构与写作初步

科技资料主要包括科技图书与科技论文。一般而言,图书的篇幅比论文要长得多,通常可分为两大类:专著和普及性读物。专著通常会对某一问题或某一类问题进行深入的探论,所包含的内容往往比较难。普及性读物则是对某一问题较为全面、实用的论述,通常注重实践性。两类图书具有相同的结构:前言、目录、正文、附录、索引和参考文献。本章主要讨论科技论文的结构与写作问题。

科技论文一般包括:报刊科普论文、学术论文、毕业论文、学位论文。科技论文是在科学研究、科学实验的基础上,对自然科学和专业技术领域里的某些现象或问题进行专题研究、分析和阐述,揭示出这些现象和问题的本质及其规律性而撰写成的文章。也就是说,凡是运用概念、判断、推理、论证和反驳等逻辑思维手段,来分析和阐明自然科学原理、定律和各种问题的文章均属科技论文的范畴。

科技论文主要用于科学技术研究及其成果的描述,是研究成果的体现。运用它们进行成果推广、信息交流、促进科学技术的发展。它们的发表标志着研究工作的水平,为社会所公认,载入人类知识宝库,成为人们共享的精神财富。科技论文还是考核科技人员业绩的重要标准。

科技论文一般具备以下五个特点:

1. 学术性。科技论文是科学研究的成果,是客观存在的自然现象及其规律的反映。它要求运用科学的原理和方法,对自然科学领域新问题进行科学分析,严密论证,抽象概括。学术论文的科学性,要求作者在立论上不得带有个人好恶的偏见,不得主观臆造,必须切实地从客观实际出发,从中引出符合实际的结论。在论据上,应尽可能多地参考资料,以最充分的、确凿有力的论据作为立论的依据。在论证时,必须经过周密的思考,进行严谨的论证。可见,学术性是科技论文最基本的特征。

2. 创造性。科技论文不同于教科书和综述性的科学报告,后者的主要任务在于传授知识,能否提出新的内容并不起决定作用,而科技论文则必须有新的内容科学研究是对新知识的探求。创造性是科学研究的生命。学术论文的创造性在于作者要有自己独到的见解,能提出新的观点、新的理论。这是因为科学的本性就是"革命的和非正统的","科学方法主要是发现新现象、制定新理论的一种手段,旧的科学理论就必然会不断地被新理论推翻"。因此,没有创造性,学术论文就没有科学价值。

3. 理论性。学术论文在形式上是属于议论文的,但它与一般议论文不同,它必须是有自己的理论系统的,不能只是材料的罗列,应对大量的事实、材料进行分析、研究,使感性认识上升到理性认识。一般来说,学术论文具有论证色彩,或具有论辩色彩。论文的内容必须符合历史唯物辩证法,符合"实事求是"、"有的放矢"、"既分析又综合"的科学研究方法。

4. 专业性。不同的专业的科技论文的内容和表示形式不尽相同。可将科技论文分为理论型、实验型和描述型三种。理论型论文的主要研究方法是理论分析;实验型论文的主要研究方法是设计实验、实验过程研究和实验结果分析;描述型论文的主要研究方法是描述说明,目的是介绍新发现的事物或现象及其所具有的科学价值,重点说明这一新事物是什么现象或不是什么现象。

5. 平易性。指的是要用通俗易懂的语言表述科学道理,不仅要做到文从字顺,而且要准确、鲜明、和谐、力求生动。即为人所用,不要让别人看不懂。

随着科学技术飞速发展,科技论文大量发表,越来越要求论文作者以规范化、标准化的固定结构模式(即通用型格式)来表达他们的研究过程和成果。这种通用型结构形式,是经过长期实践,人们总结出来的论文写作的表达形式和规律。这种结构形式是最明确、最易令人理解的表达科研成果的好形式,并逐步形成了科学技术报告、学位论文和学

术论文的编写格式。国家标准(GB 7713-87),其通用型基本结构如下:

1. 标题
2. 作者及其工作单位
3. 摘要
4. 引言
5. 正文
6. 结论
7. 致谢
8. 参考文献
9. 附录

英文科技论文的阅读是迅速了解科技与工程动态的必要手段,而英文科技论文的写作是进行国际学术交流必须掌握的技能,也是科技成果得到世界同行认可的最佳方式。在撰写英文科技论文时,除了遵循科技论文的基本要求之外,还需要注意英文国际论文的写作风格。究其原因主要在于中国人和西方人思维方式、文化习惯等方面上的差异,这一点突出的表现在文章的结构与表达上的不同。比如说,中国人行文比较含蓄,因此文章各段之间可能存在不明显的内在关联;而西方人则比较直截了当,他们的文章结构往往一目了然。因此,即使已有一篇现成的中文论文,在其基础上写英文论文时,也不能采用"拿来主义"逐字逐句翻译。

理解与撰写英文科技论文的第一步就是要了解英文科技论文的分类。英文科技论文一般分为:

1. 综述文章(Review paper)
2. 研究论文(Research paper)
3. 简报(brief / Note/ Short article)
4. 评论/回复(Comments / Reply)
5. 书评(Book review)

综述文章一般是对一类在自己研究的基础上的总结,不是情况的罗列,除了对文献的占有之外,对这个问题自己的分析与看法是不可缺少的。究其原因是,已经发表的研究报告,有些是重要的,但大多数是无关紧要的,综述必须能够根据自己的研究经验去粗取精,以便追随研究者参考。如何去粗取精,这就需要比较,在理论的进展、技术的有效,以及应用的条件等方面都需要考虑。此外,问题的演变与发展也是综述必须包括的内容。因此,只有本行业内有较大影响的学者才可能写出较好的综述。

研究论文通常是指对科学领域中的某些现象和问题进行比较系统的研究,以探讨其本质特征及其发展规律等的理论性文章。英文研究论文通常又分为长论文与短论文。本章主要讨论研究论文的结构与写作问题。

简报是传递某方面信息的小论文,具有简洁、精悍、快速、新颖和连续性等特点,一般是某项科学研究的初步进展与新的发现。

评论通常是针对该杂志先前发表的某篇研究论文或简报所做出的评论性文章,且一般是评判性的指出该论文存在的问题与错误之处;而回复则是原论文作者就评论文章指出的问题给出的回复。

理解与撰写英文科技论文的第二步就是要了解推敲科技论文的结构,使之成为西方人利于理解的形式。尽管目前中文科技论文与英文科技论文在论文整体结构上已经趋于一致,但东西方文化的表达与逻辑思维上存在不小差异,特别是科技论文本身的严肃性,即使西方本土大学生也需要科技论文的正规训练。

本章以研究论文为主,简述科技论文的结构与规范。研究论文一般结构如下:

> 标题(Title)
> 摘要(Abstract)
> 关键词(Key Words)
> 正文
>   引言(Introduction)
>   主体(Body)
>   结论(Conclusion)
> 致谢(Acknowledgment)
> 参考文献(Reference)

一、标题(Title)

标题是论文特定内容最恰当、最简明的逻辑组合,即应"以最少数量的单词来充分表述论文的内容"。标题主要有两个作用:(1)吸引读者,题名相当于论文的"标签"(label),读者通常根据标题来考虑是否需要阅读摘要或全文,因此,标题表达不当,就会失去其应有的作用,使读者错过阅读论文的机会。(2)帮助文献追踪或检索。文献检索系统多以题名中的主题词作为线索,因而标题必须准确反映论文的核心内容,否则就有可能产生漏检与错误。因此,不恰当的标题很可能会导致该论文的"丢失",从而失去科技论文本身的意义与潜在价值。

1. 基本要求

(1)准确(Accuracy)

标题要准确地反映论文的内容,不能过于空泛和一般化,也不宜过于烦琐。为确保标题的含义准确,应尽量避免使用非定量的、含义不明的词,并力求用词专业性与专指性。

(2)简洁(Brevity)

标题的用词应该简短、明了,以最少的文字概括尽可能多的内容。题名最好不超过10—12个单词,或100个英文字符;若能用一行文字表达,则尽量不用2行(超过2行可能会削弱读者的印象)。当然,在撰写题名时不能因为追求形式上的简短而忽视对论文内容的反映。题名过于简短,常起不到帮助读者理解论文的作用。另外,还要注意避免题名中词意上的重叠;在内容层次很多的情况下,如果难以简短化,最好采用主、副题名相结合的方法。

（3）清楚（Clarity）

标题要清晰地反映文章的具体内容和特色,明确表明研究工作的独到之处,力求简洁有效、重点突出。为使表达直接、清楚,以便引起读者的注意,尽可能地将表达核心内容的主题词放在标题开头。题名中应慎重使用缩略语,尤其对于有多个解释的缩略语,应严加限制,必要时应在括号中注明全称。对那些全称较长,缩写后已得到科技界公认的才可使用,并且这种使用还应得到相应期刊读者群的认可。

2. 标题的结构

（1）标题的构成

标题常分为词组型标题、动宾型标题、陈述句标题、问句型标题以及带副标题或破折号标题等几种。标题通常由名词、分词与动名词等短语构成。如果确实需要用一个句子表达时,大部分编辑和学者一般都认为标题不应由陈述句构成。一般认为,陈述句容易使标题具有判断式的语意。有时可以用问句作为标题,尤其是在评论论文中,使用具探讨性的疑问句性标题显得比较生动,易引起读者的兴趣,生动且切题。

（2）标题的句法规则

由于标题比句子简短,且无需主、谓、宾,因此词序显得尤为重要。题名最好由最能反映论文核心内容的主题词扩展而成,如果词语间的修饰关系使用不当,就会影响读者正确理解标题的真实含意。例如 Cars blamed for pollution by scientist（科学家造成的污染归罪于汽车）,正确的写法应为 Cars blamed by scientist for pollution（科学家将污染归罪于汽车）。

（3）标题中介词的用法

"with"是标题中常用到的介词。一般而言,汉语中是以名词作形容词的,英语中用对应的名词作形容词就不适合。如当名词用作形容词来修饰另一个名词时,如果前者是后者具有的一部分或者是后者所具有的性质、特点时,常需要前置词"with + 名词"组成的前置词短语作形容词放在所要修饰的名词之后。如"具中国特色的新型机器"应译为"New types of machines with the Chinese characteristics"而不用"Chinese characteristics machines"。

在标题中,常常会遇到"××的××",此处"的"在英语中有两个前置词与之相对应,即"of"和"for"。其中"of"主要表示所有关系,"for"主要表示目的、用途。如 A design method of sliding mode robust controller for uncertain system is presented（提出了一种针对不确定系统的滑模鲁棒控制器设计方法）。

（4）题名中单词的大小写

题名中字母主要有全大写、首字母大写、每个实词首字母大写等三种形式。作者应遵循相应期刊的习惯,对于专有名词首字母、首字母缩略词、德语名词首字母与句号后单词的首字母等在一般情况下均应大写。

总之,科技论文标题撰写的 ABC 是 Accuracy（准确）、Brevity（简洁）与 Clarity（清楚）,此外,要特别注意中英文句法的正确性,尤其是动词分词和介词的使用。对于题名的长度、缩写与字母的大小写等,应注意参考相关期刊的"读者须知"及其近期发表的论文。

二、摘要(Abstract)

摘要是全文的精华,是对一项科学研究工作的研究目的、方法和研究结果的概括与总结。摘要写得好与坏直接关系到论文是否被录用。一般来说,摘要必须回答"研究什么"、"怎么研究"、"得到了什么结果"、"结果说明了什么"等问题。此外,简短精炼是其主要特点,只需简明扼要地将目的、方法、结果和结论分别加以概括即可。

1. 基本要求

摘要首先必须符合格式规范。第二,语言必须规范通顺,准确得体,用词要确切、恰如其分,而且要避免非通用的符号、缩略语、生偏词。另外,摘要的语气要客观,不要作出言过其实的结论。

有相当数量的作者和审稿人认为,科技论文的撰写应使用第三人称、过去时和被动语态。但调查表明,科技论文中被动语态的使用在1920—1970年曾比较流行,但由于主动语态的表达更为准确,且更易阅读,因而目前大多数期刊都提倡使用主动语态。国际知名科技期刊 *Nature*、*Cell* 等尤其如此,其中第一人称和主动语态的使用十分普遍。

(1) 时态以简练为佳

一般现在时:用于说明研究目的、叙述研究内容、描述结果、得出结论、提出建议或讨论等;公认事实、自然规律、永恒真理等也要用一般现在时。

一般过去时:用于叙述过去某一时刻的发现、某一研究过程(实验、观察、调查、医疗等过程)。用一般过去时描述的发现、现象,往往是尚不能确认为自然规律、永恒真理,只是当时情况;所描述的研究过程也明显带有过去时间的痕迹。

现在完成时把过去发生的或过去已完成的事情与现在联系起来,而过去完成时可用来表示过去某一时间以前已经完成的事情,或在一个过去事情完成之前就已完成的另一过去行为。一般较少使用。

(2) 语态要合适

采用何种语态,既要考虑摘要的特点,又要满足表达的需要。一篇摘要很短,尽量不要随便混用,更不要在一个句子里混用。

主动语态:摘要中谓语动词采用主动语态,有助于文字简洁、表达有力。

被动语态:以前强调多用被动语态,理由是科技论文主要是说明事实经过,至于那件事是谁做的,无需一一证明。为强调动作承受者,采用被动语态为好;被动者无关紧要,也必须用强调的事物做主语。

英文摘要的人称:原来摘要的首句多用第三人称 This paper... 等开头,现在倾向于采用更简洁的被动语态或原形动词开头。如:To describe..., To study..., To investigate..., To assess..., To determine...,行文时最好不用第一人称。

(3) 注意事项

冠词:主要是定冠词 the 易被漏用。the 用于表示整个群体、分类、时间、地名以及独一无二的事物、形容词最高级等较易掌握,用于特指时常被漏用。这里有个原则,即当我们用 the 时,听者或读者已经明确我们所指的是什么。

数词:避免用阿拉伯数字作首词。

单复数:一些名词单复数形式不易辨认,从而造成谓语形式出错。

使用短句:长句容易造成语义不清,但使用短句时要避免单调和重复。

2. 内容与结构

从结构与内容来看,摘要一般都包括:

(1) 目的(objectives、purposes):包括研究背景、范围、内容、要解决的问题及解决这一问题的重要性和意义。一般有"论文导向"与"研究导向"两类:

论文导向多使用现在式,如 This paper presents…;研究导向则使用过去式,如 This study investigated…。

(2) 方法(methods and materials):包括材料、手段和过程。

介绍研究或试验过程,常用词汇有:test、study、investigate、examine、experiment、discuss、consider、analyze、analysis 等。

说明研究或试验方法,常用词汇有:measure、estimate、calculate 等。

介绍应用、用途,常用词汇有:use、apply、application 等。

(3) 结论(conclusions):主要结论,研究的价值和意义等。

介绍结论常用词汇有:summary、introduce、conclude 等;展示研究结果常用词汇有:show、result、present 等;陈述论文的论点和作者的观点常用词汇有:suggest、report、present、explain、expect、describe 等;阐明论证用词汇有:support、provide、indicate、identify、find、demonstrate、confirm、clarify 等;推荐和建议用词汇有:suggest、suggestion、recommend、recommendation、propose、necessity、necessary、expect 等。

另外,在摘要中不要用到公式、参考文献等。要始终记住一点,摘要是一个独立的部分,换句话说,别人不看你的文章,只看你的摘要就能了解你的研究工作。

在英文摘要的撰写中,还应注意以下几点:

(1) 力求简捷。如 at a temperature of 250℃ to 300℃→at 250 to 300℃;at a high pressure of 2 kPa→at 2 kPa;has been found to increase→increased;from the experimental results, it can be concluded that→the results show。

(2) 能用名词作定语的尽量不用动名词作定语,能用形容词作定语的尽量不用名词作定语。如 measuring accuracy→measurement accuracy;experiment results→experimental results。

(3) 可直接用名词或名词短语作定语的情况下,要少用 of 句型。如 accuracy of measurement→measurement accuracy;structure of crystal→crystal structure。

(4) 可用动词的情况尽量避免用动词的名词形式。如 Measurement of thickness of plastic sheet was made→Thickness of plastic sheet was measured。

(5) 一个名词不宜用多个前置形容词来修饰,可改用复合词,兼用后置定语。如 thermal oxidation apparent activation energy→Apparent active energy of thermo-oxidation。

(6) 描述作者的工作一般用过去时态(因为工作是在过去做的),但陈述这些工作所得出的结论时,应该用现在时态。

(7) 一般都应使用动词的主动语态,如 B is exceeded by A→A exceeds B。

(8) 尽量用短句。

三、主体(Body)

科技论文是集假说、数据和结论为一体的概括性描述,而论文主体则是研究工作的具体描述。论文主体的撰写一般始于论文提纲。论文提纲是一篇论文的行文计划,是论文目的、假说、内容与结论最清楚的表述形式。

如何起草论文提纲?主要解决三个问题,即 A)为什么我要做这件工作,主要的目的和假设是什么?B)我的研究方法与结果是什么?C)这一结果意味着什么?意义何在?提纲本身应该文字简练、思路完整,如果提纲准备充分,那么正文组织起来就更容易。

一般论文提纲与相对应的主体部分包括引言或相关研究简介(Introduction)、研究方法或者系统制作(Methods)、实验与讨论(Experiment & Discussion)与结论(Conclusion)几个部分。

基本结构及其要求

(1)引言(Introduction)

引言是本项研究的导读,主要包括谁做了什么?做得怎么样?我们做了哪些工作?做得怎样?体现出一篇论文的研究起初和创新要素。应该说外刊论文对于引言的要求是非常高的,可以毫不夸张的说,一个好的引言就相当于文章成功了一半。

要写好引言,最重要的是要保持层次感和逻辑性。

首先,要阐述自己的研究领域,尽量简洁。

其次,相关工作的总结回顾,要把该领域内的过去和现在的状况全面地概括总结出来,不能有丝毫的遗漏,特别是最新的进展和过去经典文献的引用,否则,很可能意味着你做得不够深入或者全面。

再次,分析过去研究的局限性,并且阐明自己研究的创新点。阐述局限性时要客观公正,实事求是。在阐述自己创新点时,要仅仅围绕过去研究的缺陷性来描述,完整而清晰地描述自己的解决思路。中文文章的特点是创新性要多要大,而英文文章的特点恰恰相反:深入系统地解决一到两个问题就算相当不错。

最后,总结性的描述论文的研究内容,作为引言的结尾。

(2)研究方法(Methods)

研究方法部分是描述论文的实践过程,应该按照逻辑思维规律来组织结构,包含材料、内容,应有概念、判断、推理,最终形成观点。通常按照研究对象可分为:以系统为主的研究论文与以方法研究为主的论文。以系统为主的研究论文主要介绍系统的设计或制作;以方法研究为主的论文主要介绍某种研究方法,一般包括实验方法与理论推理两种。由于研究对象的千差万别,难以形成统一的模式,但是它们主要内容一般包括:

- 研究目的

研究目的是正文的开篇,要写得简明扼要,重点突出。先介绍为什么要进行这个研究,通过研究要达到的目的是什么。如果课题涉及面较广,论文只写其某一方面,则要写清本文着重探索哪一方面的问题。并交待探索原因、效果或方法。

- 研究方法

科研课题从开始到成果的全过程,都要运用实验材料、设备以及观察方法。因此,应将选用的材料、设备和实验的方法加以说明,以便他人据此重复验证。

- 研究过程

研究过程主要说明研究的技术路线,以及具体操作步骤。对于实验型研究,主要说明实验条件、实验设备和操作过程;对于理论性研究,主要说明问题的假设、推理工具与推理过程,达到严谨的科学性、逻辑性。

- 实验结果或仿真结果分析与讨论

该部分是整篇论文的核心部分。一切实验成败由此判断,一切推理由此导出,一切议论由此引出。因此,应该充分表达,并且采用表格、图解、照片等附件。要尽量压缩众所周知的评论,突出本研究的新发现,及经过证实的新观点、新见解。这一部分一般应包括:主要原理或概念、实验条件;本研究的结果与他人研究结果的相同或差异;解释因果关系,论证其必然性;提出本研究存在的问题或尚需探索的问题。

此外,研究方法撰写中特别要注意表述的完整性和科学性。

(3) 结论(Conclusion)

该部分是整个研究的总结,是全篇论文的归宿,起着画龙点睛的作用。一般说来,读者选读某篇论文时,先看标题、摘要、前言,再看结论,才能决定阅读与否。因此,结论写作也是很重要的。撰写结论时,不仅对研究的全过程、实验的结果、数据等进一步认真地加以综合分析,准确反映客观事物的本质及其规律,而且,对论证的材料,选用的实例,语言表达的概括性、科学性和逻辑性等方方面面,也都要一一进行总判断、总推理、总评价。同时,撰写时,不是对前面论述结果的简单复述,而要与引言相呼应,与正文其他部分相联系。总之,结论要有说服力,恰如其分。语言要准确、鲜明。结论中,凡归结为一个认识、肯定一种观点、否定一种意见,都要有事实、有根据,不能想当然,不能含糊其词,不能用"大概"、"可能"、"或许"等词语。如果论文得不出结论,也不要硬写。凡不写结论的论文,可对实验结果进行一番深入讨论。

此外,论文结构上,要思路清晰,层次分明,逻辑性强;文字表述上,要语句通顺,通俗易懂,文字简练准确;特别要强调的是,表格与图像图形信息能够达到文字描述所不易达到的效果。表格的优点是能够清晰地展示文章的第一手结果,便于后人在研究时进行引用和对比;图的优点在于能够将数据的变化趋势灵活地表现出来,表达上更为直接和富于感染力。总体上来说,图表应该结合使用,取长补短,使结果的展现更加丰富。

四、其他(Others)

1. 作者的署名顺序

科技论文的作者在享受科技成果和荣誉的同时也承担同样的责任。严谨的科学工作者并不会无原则地分享成果和荣誉,要成为一篇论文的作者,必须对论文的思想和写作有实质性的贡献。只要你的名字在论文作者中,你就要对整篇文章负全部责任。实际上,很多著名学者很后悔成为某些论文的作者;当导师和研究生合作的论文出现问题时,导师无论怎样辩白都是十分无力的,国内学生与导师尤其需要注意。

科技论文作者的署名顺序也需特别注意,许多著名学者也会因为科技论文的署名问题导致合作关系的破灭。通常,署名顺序取决于学科领域与学会的惯例,如在医学界,署名顺序一般根据作者的资历来决定,第一作者一般是实验室主任或者是课题负责人;又如某些领域,作者的署名往往根据作者姓氏顺序来决定。

一般认为文章的成果是属于通讯作者的,说明思路是通讯作者的;而第一作者是最主要的参与者,应该说,通讯作者多数情况和第一作者是同一个人,通讯作者的另一个好处是能和外界建立更广泛的联系,这会大大地提高你在科学界的地位。

现在,大多数作者建议按照作者的贡献来确定作者的署名顺序,因为这样比较公平,也符合 IEEE 与 IEE 的惯例。如果出现争议,建议慷慨分享成果和荣誉,从长期合作的角度出发,某一篇论文的署名顺序并不重要。

大家知道,中国人名与外国人名顺序也有差异,中国人姓在前,名在后;而外国人名在前,姓在后。如中文名字曹晓红,则英文应写成 Xiaohong Cao;有些外国学者了解中国人的姓氏习惯,又有可能把本已经正确的英文名字 Xiaohong Cao 理解成 Xiaohong 为姓氏、Cao 为名字,因此,更多学者建议采用 Xiao-hong Cao。

通常,如果有多个作者,则应在作者姓名的右上角用阿拉伯数字标注明作者所在的单位。由于各国各单位对成果的归属都有较严格的控制,因此,不要使用几个大写字母所组成的完全缩写或简称,单位内部级别按照从小到大的顺序。如:

Xiao-hua Xia[1], Alan S. I. Zinober[2]

[1] Department of Educational Technology, University of Pretoria, South Africa

[2] Department of Applied Mathematics, The University of Sheffield, Sheffield S10 2TN, UK

2. 关键词(Keywords)

关键词是论文的文献检索标识,是表达文献主体概念的自然语言词汇。列出关键词有助于读者对全文的理解,同时便于查阅和检索。

按照 GB7713-87 规定:关键词一般使用名词形式,词数为 3—6 个,以显著的字符另起一行,排在摘要的下方。关键词的选用要语义准确,能概括出论文所要论述的主要内容或中心,要尽可能避免词汇的语义过宽或过窄。

3. 致谢(Acknowledgement)

通常,致谢包含两个主要的内容:第一是表明研究的基金来源,如中国的国家自然科学基金(Nature Science Foundation of China,简称 NSFC)等。写基金的时候一般都要标注清楚基金号(Grant Number),只有这样才算是该项基金的研究成果;第二是对参与人员(没有列在作者中的研究人员)和单位表示感谢,有时候还要添加上对编辑(editor)和匿名审稿人(anonymous reviewers)的感谢,这是一种基本的礼貌。

下面给出几个例子:

• This work is supported by Bogazici University Research Fund (Project No: 99A202).

• This project is supported by Perkins Engines, TRW and EPSRC Grant Reference GR/L42018. The invaluable assistance of our colleague Mr. John Twiddle during the data capture phase of this work is gratefully acknowledged.

• Financial support for the present work was granted by the Iranian Telecommunication Research Center under grant number T500/10177. The authors, hereby, gratefully acknowledge this support.

• We would like to thank an anonymous reviewer for assistance with the proof of Theorem 1. This research was partially supported by the Engineering and Physical Sciences Research Council (EPSRC), United Kingdom, by Grant GR/S41050/01, and partially supported by the RSA-China Scientific Agreement.

下面给出几个中国基金项目的翻译:
• 国家自然科学基金:Chinese National Natural Science Foundation.
• 国家"863 计划"(国家高技术研究发展计划项目):Chinese National Programs for High Technology Research and Development
• 国家"973 项目"(国家基础研究发展规划项目):Key Project of Chinese National Programs for Fundamental Research
• 国家"十五"重点科技攻关项目:The 10th Five Years Key Programs for Science and Technology Development
• 国家杰出青年科学基金:National Science Foundation for Distinguished Young Scholars

4. 参考文献

参考文献重要之点在于格式。不同的杂志对于参考文献的格式要求不一样。作者一般要注意以下几个问题。

作者:有的是简写在前,有的简写在后,有的简写有点,有的简写没有点。

文章:有的要加上引号,有的没有引号。

文章的期刊:有的要简写,有的要全称,有的要斜体,有的则不需要。

文章年和期卷号的顺序:有的是年在前,有的是年在后。

文献的排列顺序:有的是按照字母的顺序,有的则是按照在论文中出现的顺序用阿拉伯数字排序。

下面给出实例如下:
• Tao, C. W., Chan, M.-L., & Lee, T.-T. (2003). Adaptive fuzzy sliding mode controller for linear systems with mismatched time-varying uncertainties. *IEEE Transactions on Systems, Man, and Cybernetics—Part B: Cybernetics*, 33(2), 283-293.
• Harb A. Nonlinear chaos control in a permanent magnet reluctance machine. Chaos, Solitons & Fractals 2004;19(5):1217-24.
• B.K. Yoo, W.C. Ham, Adaptive control of robot manipulator using fuzzy compensator, IEEE Trans. Fuzzy Systems 8 (2000) 186.

以上是一般科技论文参考文献的格式。注意到有些年代写在前面,有些在后面;有些作者写完后用",",有些则用".";有些把页码写全,如 283-293,有些只写初始页码。

• A. J. Koivo, Fundamentals for Control of Robotic Manipulators, *Wiley*, *New York*, 1989.

一般参考书籍的格式,一般写明出版社、地点、年代以及版本号。
• Silpa-Anan C, Brinsmead T, Abdallah S, Zelinsky A. Preliminary experiments in visual servo control for autonomous underwater vehicle. IEEE/RSJ international conference on in-

telligent robotics and systems (IROS); 2001. Available from: http://www.syseng.anu.edu.au/rsl/.

有些参考文献是通过网络获取的,一般作者也应该注明。

此外,有些杂志在标注所应用论文时,还特别要注明文献类别,如专著(monograph,简称 M)、论文集(conference,简称 C)、期刊(journal,简称 J)、学位论文(doctrinal,简称 D)、报告(report,简称 R)、标准(standard,简称 S)与专利(patent,简称 P),具体可以参考中华人民共和国国家标准 UDC 025.32 与 GB 7714-87。

5. 附录

前面已经谈到,适当的表格与图像图形信息能够达到文字描述所不易达到的效果,使得表达上更为直接和富于感染力。一般来说,表格与图像图形应该出现在正文引用部分适当的地方。有时,为了文章的简洁清晰,有时候常常把复杂表述放在文章结尾处附录中,如某定理的公式证明、某方法的详细描述等。

Chapter 11　Multimedia

▲ Knowledge Objectives

When you have completed this unit, you will be able to:
- Understand the meaning and characteristics of multimedia.
- Recognize the types of multimedia and know the formats of each type.
- Understand and state the application of multimedia.
- Be aware of the characteristic, challenge, desirable features and components of multimedia system.

▲ Professional Terms

3D animation	3D 动画
audio	音频
hypermedia	超媒体
interactive multimedia	互动多媒体
multimedia	多媒体
rich media	富媒体
video	视频

Part 1　Introduction to Multimedia

What is Multimedia?[①]

Multimedia is media and content that uses a combination of different content forms. The term can be used as a noun (a medium with multiple content forms) or as an adjective describing a medium as having multiple content forms. The term is used in contrast to media which only use traditional forms of printed or hand-produced material. Multimedia includes a combination of text, audio, still images, animation, video, and interactivity content forms.

Multimedia is usually recorded and played, displayed or accessed by information content processing devices, such as computerized and electronic devices (Figure 11-1), but can also be part of a live performance. *Multimedia* (as an adjective) also describes electronic media

---

① http://en.wikipedia.org/wiki/Multimedia

devices used to store and experience multimedia content. Multimedia is distinguished from mixed media in fine art; by including audio, for example, it has a broader scope. The term "rich media" is synonymous for interactive multimedia. Hypermedia can be considered one particular multimedia application.

Figure 11-1   Multimedia can be Stored or Recorded in Many Kinds of Devices

You can present multimedia by creating presentations which can include text, graphics, video, animation, and sound in the manner you wish. You can setup how your presentation is interactive with a computer keyboard, mouse, and touch screen. Your presentations can be published to be display on the Internet, on a Stand-Along CD, or you can use large plasma screens to present advertisements or information.

Major Characteristics of Multimedia[①]

Multimedia presentations may be viewed in person on stage, transmitted, or played locally with a media player. A broadcast may be a live or recorded multimedia presentation. Broadcasts and recordings can be either analog or digital electronic media technology. Digital online multimedia may be downloaded or streamed. Streaming multimedia may be live or on-demand. Multimedia games may be used in a physical environment with special effects, with multiple users in an online network, or locally with an offline computer, game system, etc. The various formats of technological or digital multimedia may be intended to enhance the users' experience, for example to make it easier and faster to convey information, or in entertainment or art, to transcend everyday experience.

Enhanced levels of interactivity are made possible by combining multiple forms of media content. Online multimedia is increasingly becoming object-oriented and data-driven, enabling applications with collaborative end-user innovation and personalization on multiple forms of content over time. In addition to seeing and hearing, haptic technology enables virtual objects to be felt. Emerging technology involving illusions of taste and smell may also enhance the multimedia experience.

---

① http://en.wikipedia.org/wiki/Multimedia

Part 2　Types of Multimedia

There are many type of multimedia, and we will introduce the common types of multimedia in the following.

Word①

Word is one of the types of multimedia. A word is a unit which is a constituent at the phrase level and above. It is sometimes identifiable according to such criteria as
- being the minimal possible unit in a reply
- having features such as
  - a regular stress pattern
  - phonological changes conditioned by or blocked at word boundaries
- being the largest unit resistant to insertion of new constituents within its boundaries, or
- being the smallest constituent that can be moved within a sentence without making the sentence ungrammatical.

A word is sometimes placed, in a hierarchy of grammatical constituents, above the morpheme level and below the phrase level.

Images②

An image (from Latin imago) is an artifact, for example a two-dimensional picture has a similar appearance to some subject—usually a physical object or a person.

Images may be two-dimensional, such as a photograph, screen display, and as well as a three-dimensional, such as a statue. They may be captured by optical devices—such as cameras, mirrors, lenses, telescopes, microscopes, etc. and natural objects and phenomena, such as the human eye or water surfaces (Figure 11-2).

igure 11-2　Water Lily of Xihu Photographed by a Camera

---

① http://www.sil.org/linguistics/GlossaryOfLinguisticTerms/WhatIsAWord.htm
② http://en.wikipedia.org/wiki/Image_file_formats

The word image is also used in the broader sense of any two-dimensional figure such as a map, a graph, a pie chart, or an abstract painting. In this wider sense, images can also be rendered manually, such as by drawing, painting, carving, rendered automatically by printing or computer graphics technology, or developed by a combination of methods, especially in a pseudo-photograph[1].

A volatile image is one that exists only for a short period of time. This may be a reflection of an object by a mirror, a projection of a camera obscura, or a scene displayed on a cathode ray tube. A fixed image, also called a hard copy, is one that has been recorded on a material object, such as paper or textile by photography or digital processes.

A mental image exists in an individual's mind: something one remembers or imagines. The subject of an image need not be real; it may be an abstract concept, such as a graph, function, or "imaginary" entity. For example, Sigmund Freud claimed to have dreamed purely in aural-images of dialogs. The development of synthetic acoustic technologies and the creation of sound art have led to a consideration of the possibilities of a sound-image made up of irreducible phonic substance beyond linguistic or musicological analysis.

A still image is a single static image, as distinguished from a moving image (see below). This phrase is used in photography, visual media and the computer industry to emphasize that one is not talking about movies, or in very precise or pedantic technical writing. A film still is a photograph taken on the set of a movie or television program during production, used for promotional purposes.

1. Formats of image

Including proprietary types, there are hundreds of image file types. The PNG, JPEG, and GIF formats are most often used to display images on the Internet. We will briefly introduce some common formats of image in the following.

(i) **JPG**

JPG is optimized for photographs and similar continuous tone images that contain many, many colors. It can achieve astounding compression ratios even while maintaining very high image quality. GIF compression is unkind to such images. JPG works by analyzing images and discarding kinds of information that the eye is least likely to notice. It stores information as 24 bit color. Important: the degree of compression of JPG is adjustable. At moderate compression levels of photographic images, it is very difficult for the eye to discern any difference from the original, even at extreme magnification. Compression factors of more than 20 are often quite acceptable. Better graphics programs, such as Paint Shop Pro and Photoshop, allow you to view the image quality and file size as a function of compression level, so that you can conveniently choose the balance between quality and file size.

(ii) **GIF**

GIF creates a table of up to 256 colors from a pool of 16 million. If the image has fewer than 256 colors, GIF can render the image exactly. When the image contains many colors, software that creates the GIF uses any of several algorithms to approximate the colors in the image with the limited palette of 256 colors available. Better algorithms search the image to find an optimum set of 256 colors. Sometimes GIF uses the nearest color to represent each pixel, and sometimes it uses "error diffusion" to adjust the color of nearby pixels to correct for the error in each pixel.

GIF achieves compression in two ways. First, it reduces the number of colors of color-rich images, thereby reducing the number of bits needed per pixel, as just described. Second, it replaces commonly occurring patterns (especially large areas of uniform color) with a short abbreviation: instead of storing "white, white, white, white, white," it stores "5 white."

Thus, GIF is "lossless" only for images with 256 colors or less. For a rich, true color image, GIF may "lose" 99.998% of the colors.

(iii) **BMP**

BMP is an uncompressed proprietary format invented by Microsoft. There is really no reason to ever use this format.

(iv) **TIFF**

TIFF is, in principle, a very flexible format that can be lossless. The details of the image storage algorithm are included as part of the file. In practice, TIFF is used almost exclusively as a lossless image storage format that uses no compression at all. Most graphics programs that use TIFF do not compression. Consequently, file sizes are quite big. (Sometimes a lossless compression algorithm called LZW is used, but it is not universally supported.)

(v) **PNG**

PNG is also a lossless storage format. However, in contrast with common TIFF usage, it looks for patterns in the image that it can use to compress file size. The compression is exactly reversible, so the image is recovered exactly.

(vi) **RAW**

RAW is an image output option available on some digital cameras. Though lossless, it is a factor of three of four smaller than TIFF files of the same image. The disadvantage is that there is a different RAW format for each manufacturer, and so you may have to use the manufacturer's software to view the images. (Some graphics applications can read some manufacturer's RAW formats.)

(vii) **PSD, PSP**

PSD, PSP, etc. are proprietary formats used by graphics programs. Photoshop's files have the PSD extension, while Paint Shop Pro files use PSP. These are the preferred working formats as you edit images in the software, because only the proprietary formats retain all the editing power of the programs. These packages use layers, for example, to build complex images, and layer information may be lost in the nonproprietary formats such as TIFF and JPG. However, be sure to save your end result as a standard TIFF or JPG, or you may not be able to view it in a few years when your software has changed.

Currently, GIF and JPG are the formats used for nearly all web images. PNG is supported by most of the latest generation browsers. TIFF is not widely supported by web browsers, and should be avoided for web use. PNG does everything GIF does, and better, so expect to see PNG replace GIF in the future. PNG will not replace JPG, since JPG is capable of much greater compression of photographic images, even when set for quite minimal loss of quality.

2. When should you use each?

(i) JPG

This is the format of choice for nearly all photographs on the web. You can achieve excellent quality even at rather high compression settings. I also use JPG as the ultimate format for all my digital photographs. If I edit a photo, I will use my software's proprietary format until finished, and then save the result as a JPG.

Digital cameras save in a JPG format by default. Switching to TIFF or RAW improves quality in principle, but the difference is difficult to see. Shooting in TIFF has two disadvantages compared to JPG: fewer photos per memory card, and a longer wait between photographs as the image transfers to the card. I rarely shoot in TIFF mode.

Never use JPG for line art. On images such as these with areas of uniform color with sharp edges, JPG does a poor job. These are tasks for which GIF and PNG are well suited. See JPG vs. GIF for web images.

(ii) GIF

If your image has fewer than 256 colors and contains large areas of uniform color, GIF is your choice. The files will be small yet perfect. Here is an example of an image well-suited for GIF:

Do NOT use GIF for photographic images, since it can contain only 256 colors per image.

(iii) PNG

PNG is of principal value in two applications:

① If you have an image with large areas of exactly uniform color, but contains more than 256 colors, PNG is your choice. Its strategy is similar to that of GIF, but it supports 16 million colors, not just 256.

② If you want to display a photograph exactly without loss on the web, PNG is your choice. Later generation web browsers support PNG, and PNG is the only lossless format that web browsers support.

PNG is superior to GIF. It produces smaller files and allows more colors. PNG also supports partial transparency. Partial transparency can be used for many useful purposes, such as fades and antialiasing of text. Unfortunately, Microsoft's Internet Explorer does not properly support PNG transparency, so for now web authors must avoid using transparency in PNG images.

(iv) TIFF

This is usually the best quality output from a digital camera. Digital cameras often offer around three JPG quality settings plus TIFF. Since JPG always means at least some loss of quality, TIFF means better quality. However, the file size is huge compared to even the best JPG setting, and the advantages may not be noticeable.

A more important use of TIFF is as the working storage format as you edit and manipulate digital images. You do not want to go through several load, edit, save cycles with JPG storage, as the degradation accumulates with each new save. One or two JPG saves at high quality may not be noticeable, but the tenth certainly will be. TIFF is lossless, so there is no degradation associated with saving a TIFF file.

Do NOT use TIFF for web images. They produce big files, and more importantly, most web browsers will not display TIFFs.

Audio[①]

Audio is sound within the acoustic range available to humans. An audio frequency (AF) is an electrical alternating current within the 20 to 20,000 hertz (cycles per second) range that can be used to produce acoustic sound. In computers, audio is the sound system that comes with or can be added to a computer. An audio card contains a special built-in processor and memory for processing audio files and sending them to speakers in the computer. An audio file is a record of captured sound that can be played back. Sound is a sequence of naturally analog signals that are converted to digital signals by the audio card, using a microchip called an analog-to-digital converter (ADC). When sound is played, the digital signals are sent to the speakers where they are converted back to analog signals that generate varied sound.

Audio files are usually compressed for storage or faster transmission. Audio files can be sent in short stand-alone segments—for example, as files in the Wave file format. In order for users to receive sound in real-time for a multimedia effect, listening to music (Figure 11-3), or in order to take part in an audio or video conference, sound must be delivered as streaming sound. More advanced audio cards support wavetable, or precaptured tables of sound. The most popular audio file format today is MP3 (MPEG-1 Audio Layer-3).

Figure 11-3 Listening to the Music

---

① http://www.w3schools.com/media/media_soundformats.asp

1. Formats of audio

Audio can be stored in many different formats. The following are some of the formats.

(i) The MIDI Format

The MIDI (Musical Instrument Digital Interface) is a format for sending music information between electronic music devices like synthesizers and PC sound cards. The MIDI format was developed in 1982 by the music industry. The MIDI format is very flexible and can be used for everything from very simple to real professional music making.

MIDI files do not contain sampled sound, but a set of digital musical instructions (musical notes) that can be interpreted by your PC's sound card. The downside of MIDI is that it cannot record sounds (only notes). Or, to put it another way: It cannot store songs, only tunes. The upside of the MIDI format is that since it contains only instructions (notes), MIDI files can be extremely small. The example above is only 23K in size but it plays for nearly 5 minutes.

The MIDI format is supported by many different software systems over a large range of platforms. MIDI files are supported by all the most popular Internet browsers. Sounds stored in the MIDI format have the extension .mid or .midi.

(ii) The RealAudio Format

The RealAudio format was developed for the Internet by Real Media. The format also supports video. The format allows streaming of audio (on-line music, Internet radio) with low bandwidths. Because of the low bandwidth priority, quality is often reduced. Sounds stored in the RealAudio format have the extension .rm or .ram.

(iii) The AU Format

The AU format is supported by many different software systems over a large range of platforms. Sounds stored in the AU format have the extension .au.

(iv) The AIFF Format

The AIFF (Audio Interchange File Format) was developed by Apple. AIFF files are not cross-platform and the format is not supported by all web browsers. Sounds stored in the AIFF format have the extension .aif or .aiff.

(v) The SND Format

The SND (Sound) was developed by Apple. SND files are not cross-platform and the format is not supported by all web browsers. Sounds stored in the SND format have the extension .snd.

(vi) The WAVE Format

The WAVE (waveform) format is developed by IBM and Microsoft. It is supported by all computers running Windows, and by all the most popular web browsers (except Google Chrome). Sounds stored in the WAVE format have the extension .wav.

(vii) The MP3 Format (MPEG)

MP3 files are actually MPEG files. But the MPEG format was originally developed for video by the Moving Pictures Experts Group. We can say that MP3 files are the sound part of the MPEG video format. MP3 is one of the most popular sound formats for music recording. The MP3 encoding system combines good compression (small files) with high quality. Expect all your future software systems to support it. Sounds stored in the MP3 format have the extension .mp3, or .mpga (for MPG Audio).

2. What Format to Use?

The WAVE format is one of the most popular sound format on the Internet, and it is supported by all popular browsers. If you want recorded sound (music or speech) to be available to all your visitors, you should use the WAVE format. The MP3 format is the new and upcoming format for recorded music. If your website is about recorded music, the MP3 format is the choice of the future.

Video[①]

Video is the technology of electronically capturing, recording, processing, storing, transmitting, and reconstructing a sequence of still images representing scenes in motion (Figure 11-4). Video can be recorded and transmitted in various physical media: in magnetic tape when recorded as PAL or NTSC electric signals by video cameras, or in MPEG-4 or DV digital media when recorded by digital cameras. Quality of video essentially depends on the capturing method and storage used. Digital television (DTV) is a relatively recent format with higher quality than earlier television formats and has become a standard for television video.

Figure 11-4 Video

3D-video, digital video in three dimensions, premiered at the end of 20th century. Six or eight cameras with real-time depth measurement are typically used to capture 3D-video streams. The format of 3D-video is fixed in MPEG-4 Part 16 Animation Framework eXtension (AFX).

In the United Kingdom, Estonia, Australia, Netherlands, Finland, Hungary and New Zealand, the term video is often used informally to refer to both Videocassette recorders and video cassettes.

---

① http://www.w3schools.com/media/media_videoformats.asp

1. Formats of video

Video can be stored in many different formats. The following are some of the formats.

(i) **The AVI Format**

The AVI (Audio Video Interleave) format was developed by Microsoft. The AVI format is supported by all computers running Windows, and by all the most popular web browsers. It is a very common format on the Internet, but not always possible to play on non-Windows computers. Videos stored in the AVI format have the extension .avi.

(ii) **The Windows Media Format**

The Windows Media format is developed by Microsoft. Windows Media is a common format on the Internet, but Windows Media movies cannot be played on non-Windows computer without an extra (free) component installed. Some later Windows Media movies cannot play at all on non-Windows computers because no player is available. Videos stored in the Windows Media format have the extension .wmv.

(iii) **The MPEG Format**

The MPEG (Moving Pictures Expert Group) format is the most popular format on the Internet. It is cross-platform, and supported by all the most popular web browsers. Videos stored in the MPEG format have the extension .mpg or .mpeg.

(iv) **The QuickTime Format**

The QuickTime format is developed by Apple. QuickTime is a common format on the Internet, but QuickTime movies cannot be played on a Windows computer without an extra (free) component installed. Videos stored in the QuickTime format have the extension .mov.

(v) **The RealVideo Format**

The RealVideo format was developed for the Internet by Real Media. The format allows streaming of video (on-line video, Internet TV) with low bandwidths. Because of the low bandwidth priority, quality is often reduced. Videos stored in the RealVideo format have the extension .rm or .ram.

(vi) **The Shockwave (Flash) Format**

The Shockwave format was developed by Macromedia. The Shockwave format requires an extra component to play. This component comes preinstalled with the latest versions of Netscape and Internet Explorer. Videos stored in the Shockwave format have the extension .swf.

Animation[①]

Animation is the rapid display of a sequence of images of 2D or 3D artwork or model positions in order to create an illusion of movement. It is an optical illusion of motion due to the

---

① http://en.wikipedia.org/wiki/Animation

phenomenon of persistence of vision, and can be created and demonstrated in a number of ways. The most common method of presenting animation is as a motion picture or video program, although several other forms of presenting animation also exist.

Animation is both time-consuming and costly to produce. For this reason, most of the animation made for television and film is produced by professorial studios. However, there are also many independent studios. In fact, there are many resources, such as lower-cost animation programs and distribution networks, which make the work of the independent animator much easier than it was in the past.

When animation is used for films or movies, each frame is produced on an individual basis. Frames can be produced using computers or photographs of images that are either drawn or painted. Frames can also be generated by altering a model unit in small ways and using a special camera to take pictures of the results. No matter what method is used, the film or movie that results fools the eye into seeing continuous movement.

Persistence of vision is often projected as the reason the eyes can be fooled into seeing continuous movement that isn't really happening. Basically, the brain and the eyes cooperate, storing images for a mere fraction of a second. Minor jumps or blips are automatically smoothed out by the brain. Since animation frames are shot at very fast rates, most individuals see the movement without stoppages.

1. Traditional animation

Traditional animation (also called cel animation or hand-drawn animation) was the process used for most animated films of the 20th century (Figure 11-5). The individual frames of a traditionally animated film are photographs of drawings, which are first drawn on paper. To create the illusion of movement, each drawing differs slightly from the one before it. The animators' drawings are traced or photocopied onto transparent acetate sheets called cels, which are filled in with paints in assigned colors or tones on the side opposite the line drawings. The completed character cels are photographed one-by-one onto motion picture film against a painted background by a rostrum camera.

The traditional cel animation process became obsolete by the beginning of the 21st century. Today, animators' drawings and the backgrounds are either scanned into or drawn directly into a computer system. Various software programs are used to color the drawings and simulate camera movement and effects. The final animated piece is output to one of several delivery media, including traditional 35 mm film and newer media such as digital video. The "look" of traditional cel animation is still preserved, and the character animators' work has

Figure 11-5 An example of traditional animation, a horse animated by rotoscoping from Eadweard Muybridge's 19th century photos.

remained essentially the same over the past 70 years. Some animation producers have used the term "tradigital" to describe cel animation which makes extensive use of computer technology.

Examples of traditionally animated feature films include Pinocchio (United States, 1940), Animal Farm (United Kingdom, 1954), and Akira (Japan, 1988). Traditional animated films which were produced with the aid of computer technology include The Lion King (US, 1994) Sen to Chihiro no Kamikakushi (Spirited Away) (Japan, 2001), Treasure Planet (USA, 2002) and Les Triplettes de Belleville (2003).

➢ Full animation refers to the process of producing high-quality traditionally animated films, which regularly use detailed drawings and plausible movement. Fully animated films can be done in a variety of styles, from more realistically animated works such as those produced by the Walt Disney studio (Beauty and the Beast, Aladdin, Lion King) to the more "cartoony" styles of those produced by the Warner Bros. animation studio (Iron Giant, Quest for Camelot, Cats Don't Dance). Many of the Disney animated features are examples of full animation, as are non-Disney works such as The Secret of NIMH (US, 1982) and The Iron Giant (US, 1999), Nocturna (Spain, 2007).

➢ Limited animation involves the use of less detailed and/or more stylized drawings and methods of movement. Pioneered by the artists at the American studio United Productions of America, limited animation can be used as a method of stylized artistic expression, as in Gerald McBoing Boing (US, 1951), Yellow Submarine (UK, 1968), and much of the anime produced in Japan. Its primary use, however, has been in producing cost-effective animated content for media such as television (the work of Hanna-Barbera, Filmation, and other TV animation studios) and later the Internet (web cartoons). Some examples are; Spongebob Squarepants (USA, 1999-present), The Fairly OddParents (USA, 2001-present) and Invader Zim (USA, 2001-2006).

➢ Rotoscoping is a technique, patented by Max Fleischer in 1917, where animators trace live-action movement, frame by frame. The source film can be directly copied from actors' outlines into animated drawings, as in The Lord of the Rings (US, 1978), used as a basis and inspiration for character animation, as in most Disney films, or used in a stylized and expressive manner, as in Waking Life (US, 2001) and A Scanner Darkly (US, 2006). Some other examples are: Fire and Ice (USA, 1983) and Heavy Metal (1981).

➢ Live-action/animation is a technique, when combining hand-drawn characters into live action shots. One of the earlier uses of it was Koko the Clown when Koko was drawn over live action footage. Other examples would include Who Framed Roger Rabbit? (USA, 1988), Space Jam (USA, 1996) and Osmosis Jones (USA, 2002).

Stop-motion

Stop-motion animation is used to describe animation created by physically manipulating real-world objects and photographing them one frame of film at a time to create the illusion of movement [2] (Figure 11-6). There are many different types of stop-motion animation, usually named after the type of media used to create the animation. Computer software is widely available to create this type of animation.

Figure 11-6 A Stop-motion Animation of a Moving Coin

➢ Puppet animation typically involves stop-motion puppet figures interacting with each other in a constructed environment, in contrast to the real-world interaction in model animation. The puppets generally have an armature inside of them to keep them still and steady as well as constraining them to move at particular joints. Examples include The Tale of the Fox (France, 1937), Nightmare Before Christmas (US, 1993), Corpse Bride (US, 2005), Coraline (US, 2009), the films of Jiří Trnka and the TV series Robot Chicken (US, 2005-present).

Puppetoon, created using techniques developed by George Pal, are puppet-animated films which typically use a different version of a puppet for different frames, rather than simply manipulating one existing puppet.

➢ Clay animation (Figure 11-7), or Plasticine animation often abbreviated as claymation, uses figures made of clay or a similar malleable material to create stop-motion animation. The figures may have an armature or wire frame inside of them, similar to the related puppet animation, which can be manipulated in order to pose the figures (Figure 11-8). Alternatively, the figures may be made entirely of clay, such as in the films of Bruce Bickford, where clay creatures morph into a variety of different shapes. Examples of clay-animated works include The Gumby Show (US, 1957—1967), Morph shorts (UK, 1977—2000), Wallace and Gromit shorts (UK, as of 1989), Jan Švankmajer's Dimensions of Dialogue (Czechoslovakia, 1982), The Trap Door (UK, 1984). Films include Wallace and Gromit: Curse of the Were-Rabbit, Chicken Run and The Adventures of Mark Twain.

Figure 11-7　Clay Animation

Figure 11-8　A Clay Animation Scene from a Finnish Television Commercial

➢ Cutout animation is a type of stop-motion animation produced by moving 2-dimensional pieces of material such as paper or cloth. Examples include Terry Gilliam's animated sequences from Monty Python's Flying Circus (UK, 1969—1974); Fantastic Planet (France/Czechoslovakia, 1973); Tale of Tales (Russia, 1979), The pilot episode of the TV series (and sometimes in episodes) of South Park (US, 1997).

➢ Silhouette animation is a variant of cutout animation in which the characters are backlit and only visible as silhouettes. Examples include The Adventures of Prince Achmed (Weimar Republic, 1926) and Princes et princesses (France, 2000).

➢ Model animation refers to stop-motion animation created to interact with and exist as a part of a live-action world. Intercutting, matte effects, and split screens are often employed to blend stop-motion characters or objects with live actors and settings. Examples include the work of Ray Harryhausen, as seen in films such Jason and the Argonauts (1961), and the work of Willis O'Brien on films such as King Kong (1933 film).

➢ Go motion is a variant of model animation which uses various techniques to create motion blur between frames of film, which is not present in traditional stop-motion. The technique was invented by Industrial Light & Magic and Phil Tippett to create special effects scenes for the film The Empire Strikes Back (1980). Another example is Vermithrax from Dragonslayer (1981 film).

➢ Object animation refers to the use of regular inanimate objects in stop-motion animation, as opposed to specially created items.

➢ Graphic animation uses non-drawn flat visual graphic material (photographs, newspaper clippings, magazines, etc.) which are sometimes manipulated frame-by-frame to create movement. At other times, the graphics remain stationary, while the stop-motion camera is moved to create on-screen action.

➢ Pixilation involves the use of live humans as stop-motion characters. This allows for a number of surreal effects, including disappearances and reappearances, allowing people to appear to slide across the ground, and other such effects. Examples of pixilation include The

Secret Adventures of Tom Thumb and Angry Kid shorts.

2. Computer animation

Computer animation encompasses a variety of techniques, the unifying factor being that the animation is created digitally on a computer.

(i) 2D animation

2D animation figures are created and/or edited on the computer using 2D bitmap graphics or created and edited using 2D vector graphics (Figure 11-9). This includes automated computerized versions of traditional animation techniques such as of tweening, morphing, onion skinning and interpolated rotoscoping.

Analog computer animation, Flash animation and PowerPoint animation belong to 2D animation

(ii) 3D animation

3D animation figures are digitally modeled and manipulated by an animator. In order to manipulate a mesh, it is given a digital skeletal structure that can be used to control the mesh (Figure 11-10). This process is called rigging. Various other techniques can be applied, such as mathematical functions (ex. gravity, particle simulations), simulated fur or hair, effects such as fire and water and the use of Motion capture to name but a few, these techniques fall under the category of 3D dynamics. Many 3D animations are very believable and are commonly used as Visual effects for recent movies.

Figure 11-9 A Short Gif Animation of Earth

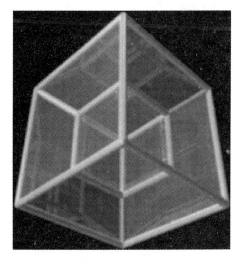

Figure 11-10 A 3D Computer Animation of Hypercube

2D animation techniques tend to focus on image manipulation while 3D techniques usually build virtual worlds in which characters and objects move and interact. 3D animation can create images that seem real to the viewer.

3. Other animation techniques

• Drawn on film animation: a technique where footage is produced by creating the images directly on film stock, for example by Norman McLaren, Len Lye and Stan Brakhage.

• Paint-on-glass animation: a technique for making animated films by manipulating slow drying oil paints on sheets of glass, for example by Aleksandr Petrov.

• Erasure animation: a technique using tradition 2D medium, photographed over time as the artist manipulates the image. For example, William Kentridge is famous for his charcoal erasure films.

• Pinscreen animation: makes use of a screen filled with movable pins, which can be moved in or out by pressing an object onto the screen. The screen is lit from the side so that the pins cast shadows. The technique has been used to create animated films with a range of textural effects difficult to achieve with traditional cel animation.

• Sand animation: sand is moved around on a backlighted or frontlighted piece of glass to create each frame for an animated film. This creates an interesting effect when animated because of the light contrast.

• Flip book: A flip book (sometimes, especially in British English, called a flick book) is a book with a series of pictures that vary gradually from one page to the next, so that when the pages are turned rapidly, the pictures appear to animate by simulating motion or some other change. Flip books are often illustrated books for children, but may also be geared towards adults and employ a series of photographs rather than drawings. Flip books are not always separate books, but may appear as an added feature in ordinary books or magazines, often in the page corners. Software packages and websites are also available that convert digital video files into custom-made flip books.

Part 3　Application of Multimedia[①]

Multimedia finds its application in various areas including, but not limited to, advertisements, art, education, entertainment, engineering, medicine, mathematics, business, scientific research and spatial temporal applications. Several examples are as follows:

Creative Industries

Creative industries use multimedia for a variety of purposes ranging from fine arts, to entertainment, to commercial art, to journalism, to media and software services provided for many of the industries. An individual multimedia designer may cover the spectrum throughout their career. Requests for their skills range from technical, to analytical, to creative.

Commercial

Much of the electronic old and new media used by commercial artists is multimedia. Exciting presentations are used to grab and keep attention in advertising. Business to business (Figure 11-11), and interoffice communications are often developed by creative services firms

---

① http://en.wikipedia.org/wiki/Multimedia

for advanced multimedia presentations beyond simple slide shows to sell ideas or liven-up training. Commercial multimedia developers may be hired to design for governmental services and nonprofit services applications as well.

Figure 11-11 A presentation using Powerpoint. Corporate presentations may combine all forms of media content.

Entertainment and Fine Arts

In addition, multimedia is heavily used in the entertainment industry, especially to develop special effects in movies and animations. Multimedia games are a popular pastime and are software programs available either as CD-ROMs or online. Some video games also use multimedia features. Multimedia applications that allow users to actively participate instead of just sitting by as passive recipients of information are called Interactive Multimedia (Figure 11-12). In the Arts there are multimedia artists, whose minds are able to blend techniques using different media that in some way incorporates interaction with the viewer. One of the most relevant could be Peter Greenaway who is melding Cinema with Opera and all sorts of digital media. Another approach entails the creation of multimedia that can be displayed in a traditional fine arts arena, such as an art gallery. Although multimedia display material may be volatile, the survivability of the content is as strong as any traditional media. Digital recording material may be just as durable and infinitely reproducible with perfect copies every time.

Figure 11-12 Virtual reality uses multimedia content. Applications and delivery platforms of multimedia are virtually limitless.

Education

In Education, multimedia is used to produce computer-based training courses (popularly called CBTs) and reference books like encyclopedia and almanacs. A CBT lets the user go through a series of presentations, text about a particular topic, and associated illustrations in various information formats. Edutainment is an informal term used to describe combining education with entertainment, especially multimedia entertainment.

Learning theory in the past decade has expanded dramatically because of the introduction of multimedia. Several lines of research have evolved (e.g. Cognitive load, Multimedia learning, and the list goes on). The possibilities for learning and instruction are nearly endless.

The idea of media convergence is also becoming a major factor in education, particularly higher education (Figure 11-13). Defined as separate technologies such as voice (and telephony features), data (and productivity applications) and video that now share resources and interact with each other, synergistically creating new efficiencies, media convergence is rapidly changing the curriculum in universities all over the world. Likewise, it is changing the availability, or lack thereof, of jobs requiring this savvy technological skill.

Figure 11-13　VVO Multimedia-Terminal in Dresden WTC (Germany)

Journalism

Newspaper companies all over are also trying to embrace the new phenomenon by implementing its practices in their work. While some have been slow to come around, other major newspapers like The New York Times, USA Today and The Washington Post are setting the precedent for the positioning of the newspaper industry in a globalized world.

News reporting is not limited to traditional media outlets. Freelance journalists can make use of different new media to produce multimedia pieces for their news stories. It engages global audiences and tells stories with technology, which develops new communication techniques for both media producers and consumers. Common Language Project is an example of this type of multimedia journalism production.

Engineering

Software engineers may use multimedia in Computer Simulations for anything from entertainment to training such as military or industrial training. Multimedia for software interfaces are often done as collaboration between creative professionals and software engineers.

Industry

In the Industrial sector, multimedia is used as a way to help present information to shareholders, superiors and coworkers. Multimedia is also helpful for providing employee training, advertising and selling products all over the world via virtually unlimited web-based technology.

Mathematical and Scientific Research

In mathematical and scientific research, multimedia is mainly used for modeling and simulation. For example, a scientist can look at a molecular model of a particular substance and manipulate it to arrive at a new substance. Representative research can be found in journals such as the Journal of Multimedia.

Medicine

In Medicine, doctors can get trained by looking at a virtual surgery or they can simulate how the human body is affected by diseases spread by viruses and bacteria and then develop techniques to prevent it.

Document Imaging

Document imaging is a technique that takes hard copy of an image/document and converts it into a digital format (for example, scanners).

Disabilities

Ability Media allows those with disabilities to gain qualifications in the multimedia field so they can pursue careers that give them access to a wide array of powerful communication forms.

Part 4　Multimedia System[①]

A Multimedia System is a system capable of processing multimedia data and applications (Figure 11-14). A Multimedia System is characterized by the processing, storage, generation, manipulation and rendition of Multimedia information.

---

① http://www.cs.cf.ac.uk/Dave/Multimedia/node1.html

Figure 11-14　One Example of Multimedia System

Characteristics of a Multimedia System

A Multimedia system has four basic characteristics:
- Multimedia systems must be computer controlled.
- Multimedia systems are integrated.
- The information they handle must be represented digitally.
- The interface to the final presentation of media is usually interactive.

Challenges for Multimedia Systems

Supporting multimedia applications over a computer network renders the application distributed. This will involve many special computing techniques—discussed later. Multimedia systems may have to render a variety of media at the same instant—a distinction from normal applications. There is a temporal relationship between many forms of media (*e. g.* Video and Audio. There are forms of problems here:
- Sequencing within the media—playing frames in correct order/time frame in video
- Synchronization—inter-media scheduling (*e. g.* Video and Audio). Lip synchronization is clearly important for humans to watch playback of video and audio and even animation and audio. Ever tried watching an out of (lip) sync film for a long time?

The key issues multimedia systems need to deal with here are:
- How to represent and store temporal information.
- How to strictly maintain the temporal relationships on play back/retrieval
- What process is involved in the above.

Data has to represented digitally so many initial source of data needs to be digitize—translated from analog source to digital representation. The will involve scanning (graphics, still images), sampling (audio/video) although digital cameras now exist for direct scene to digital capture of images and video.

Desirable Features for a Multimedia System

Given the above challenges the following features are desirable (if not a prerequisite) for a Multimedia System:
- Very High Processing Power

— needed to deal with large data processing and real time delivery of media. Special hardware commonplace.
- Multimedia Capable File System

— Needed to deliver real-time media, e.g. Video/Audio Streaming. Special Hardware/Software needed, e.g RAID technology.
- Data Representations/File Formats that support multimedia

— Data representations/file formats should be easy to handle yet allow for compression/decompression in real-time.
- Efficient and High I/O

— input and output to the file subsystem needs to be efficient and fast. Needs to allow for real-time recording as well as playback of data. E.g. Direct to Disk recording systems.
- Special Operating System

— to allow access to file system and process data efficiently and quickly. Needs to support direct transfers to disk, real-time scheduling, fast interrupt processing, I/O streaming etc.
- Storage and Memory

— large storage units (of the order of 50 —100 Gb or more) and large memory (50 — 100 Mb or more). Large Caches also required and frequently of Level 2 and 3 hierarchy for efficient management.
- Network Support

— Client-server systems common as distributed systems common.
- Software Tools

— User friendly tools needed to handle media, design and develop applications, deliver media.

Components of a Multimedia System

Now let us consider the Components (Hardware and Software) required for a multimedia system. A multimedia system should contain the following components:
- Capture devices

— Video Camera, Video Recorder, Audio Microphone, Keyboards, mice, graphics tablets, 3D input devices, tactile sensors, VR devices, Digitising/Sampling Hardware.
- Storage Devices

— Hard disks, CD-ROMs, Jaz/Zip drives, DVD, etc.

- Communication Networks
— Ethernet, Token Ring, FDDI, ATM, Intranets, Internets.
- Computer Systems
— Multimedia Desktop machines, Workstations, MPEG/VIDEO/DSP Hardware.
- Display Devices
— CD-quality speakers, HDTV, SVGA, Hi-Res monitors, Colour printers *etc.*

New Words

synonymous *adj.* 同义词的,同义的,意思相同的
haptic *adj.* 触觉的
artifact *n.* (= artefact) 人工制品(尤指原始工具),假象,石器,后生物
pseudo *adj.* [口]假的,伪的,冒充的
volatile *adj.* 易变的,反复无常的,易激动的,(液体或油)易挥发的
tube *n.* 管,筒,装牙膏或颜料的小软管,管状器官,电子管,地铁
synthetic *adj.* 综合(性)的,合成的,人造的,假想的;虚伪的,不自然的,不诚恳的
acoustic *adj.* 声音的,听觉的
phonic *adj.* (声)音的,语音的,有声的,浊音的
pedantic *adj.* 卖弄学问的,学究式的,迂腐的
acoustic *adj.* 声音的,听觉的
magnetic *adj.* 有磁性的,(可)磁化的,磁的,吸引人心的,有魅力的,催眠的
puppet *n.* 木[玩]偶,傀儡,(行动,思想等)受别人操纵的人[集团]
survivability *n.* 生存能力
reproducible *adj.* 能繁殖的,可再生的,可复写的
synergistical *adj.* 增效的
temporal *adj.* 暂时的,短暂的,非永恒的,世俗的,现世的,时间的
synchronization *n.* 同一时刻;同步

Notes

[1] In this wider sense, images can also be rendered manually, such as by drawing, painting, carving, rendered automatically by printing or computer graphics technology, or developed by a combination of methods, especially in a pseudo-photograph.

译文:在这个更广泛的意义上,图像也可以手工制作,例如素描、绘画、雕刻、印刷,也可以通过打印或计算机图形技术自动生成,或者用各种方法合成,尤其对一个假照片来说更是如此。

[2] Stop-motion animation is used to describe animation created by physically manipulating real-world objects and photographing them one frame of film at a time to create the illusion of movement.

译文：停格动画是用来描述这样一种动画,它是通过物理方式控制现实世界的对象,并一次把他们拍摄下来作为影片中的一帧,从而创造了运动假象的动画。

- created by 通过……而创作,created 是被动语态,属于定于从语句的缩略形式,完整形式应在其前加上 which (that) is.
- at a time 依次,逐一,每次

Selected Translation

Part 1

多媒体介绍

什么是多媒体?

多媒体是使用不同内容形式的组合媒体。这个词可以用作名词(具有多种内容形式的媒体)或作为一个形容一种具有多种内容形式的媒介的形容词。此词是用来与只使用印刷或手工制作的材料的传统形式的媒体对比。多媒体包括文字、音频、静态图像、动画、视频和互动内容形式的组合。

多媒体通常用信息内容处理的设备来记录和播放、展示或存取,如电脑和电子设备,但也可以是一个现场演出的一部分。多媒体(作为一个形容词)也用来描述用于存储和体验多媒体内容的电子媒体设备。多媒体区别于美术品中的混合绘画法,例如与音频混合,它具有更广泛的范围。术语"多元媒体"是互动多媒体的代名词。超媒体可以被视为一个特定的多媒体应用。

现在你可以以你希望的方式通过创建包括文字、图形、视频、多媒体动画、声音等形式的演示文稿来呈现多媒体。你可以设置你的演讲如何与电脑键盘、鼠标、触摸屏等互动,也可以在互联网、独立式的 CD 上发布你的演讲并将其显示出来,或使用等离子大屏幕来呈现广告或信息。

多媒体主要特点

我们可以亲身在在舞台上观看多媒体演示,也可以用媒体播放器在本地播送或播放多媒体演示。一个广播可能是直播或录制的多媒体演示。广播和录音可以是模拟或数字电子媒体技术。数字在线多媒体可以下载或在线播放。流媒体可直播或点播。多媒体游戏可以在一个特定的物理环境中使用,比如有特殊效果,多个用户在一个在线网络上,或有一台离线的本地计算机,有游戏程序等。各种格式的技术多媒体或数字多媒体可能是为了增强用户的体验,例如,在娱乐或艺术上使其更容易、更快速地传递信息或超越日常体验。

由于组合媒体内容的多种形式而使媒体互动性的增强成为可能。随着时间的推移,网上多媒体越来越有面向对象和数据驱动的趋势,用多种内容形式促进合作的终端用户创新和个性化应用。除了视听,触觉技术使人们能感受到虚拟的物体。涉及味觉和嗅觉幻想的新兴技术也可能增强多媒体体验。

Exercises

1. What is multimedia?
2. What are the differences between 2D animation and 3D animation?
3. What aspects can multimedia be applied in?

投稿指南

一、如何选题

科技论文是科学工作者对创造性成果进行理论分析和科学总结,并进行发表或答辩的文字表达形式。科技论文的关键要素是创新性,如何寻找创新性则需要在选题上下工夫。

随着科技的进步与发展,像牛顿、爱因斯坦、爱迪生时代依靠灵感与天才寻找原始火花已经非常困难了。许多人选题喜欢标新立异,然后再从杂志上找题目,似乎这才是创新。显然这样做出的文章难有创新性,几年,甚至十几年的工作一下子就看透了,并且发现了问题所在。如果这时匆匆忙忙写文章,退稿率会很高。

一般而言,研究者应多与导师讨论,听取导师的看法,不要只追求标新立异,在大方向上不要偏离导师的研究方向,这样才能取得导师的指导和帮助。一般的建议是:

- 按导师指导的方向大量阅读,增加自己的知识储备量,了解本学科和本方向的研究历史与现状,明确过去已经进行了哪些研究,有什么成果,哪些问题尚未得到解决。要泛读和精读相结合,合理搭配,节约宝贵时间。
- 研究领域不要涉及太广,要选几个自己感兴趣的领域深挖,逐步从广泛性中找出特殊性,即先广再博。
- 善于总结。注意平常思考的记录,尤其是对突然来临、转瞬即逝的灵感的记录。
- 勤于思考。一旦发现问题,要抛开对权威刊物的迷信,抛开原定的结论,穷追下去,应该充分运用自己的思考力,通过分析、综合、演绎、归纳、分类、组合、加减、反逆、类推等等,对文献资料进行积极的加工,这是一种创造性的想象,缺少它就得不到新的题目。
- 在确定选题之前,要了解选题的创新性和价值性。一般要通过检索来证实这个想法是否具有创新性。此外,还要注意这个选题的现实意义或者长远意义。
- 可行性论证,这包括方法、材料、资金、设备等。

一旦创新性与可行性得到初步保证,则得到了一个不错的选题,从而有可能得到一份很有份量的研究结论。

二、投稿过程与投稿信(COVER LETTER)

1. 投稿过程

写论文的真正意义在于把你的知识与别人分享而获得肯定的那种成就感,尽管大多数人写科技论文的直接目的是为了获得某种荣誉,如晋职、晋级、获得学位等。目的不同,但目标一致,将论文刊出。正确的投稿将有助于科技论文的发表,一般应该注意以下问题:

(1) 正确选择期刊:首先要掂量一下自己文章的分量,想想在哪个杂志上发表最合适。因为期刊种类繁多,即使在同一学科也有许多期刊,且各个期刊的办刊宗旨、专业范围、主题分配、栏目设置及各种类型文章发表的比例均不相同。因此,选择一本恰当的期刊并非易事,然而这是论文得以发表的一个极其重要的环节。选择期刊应考虑的因素:

- 论文主题是否在刊物的征稿范围内。投稿论文可能极为优秀,但如果不适合该刊物,则不可能在该刊物被发表。
- 期刊的学术水平高,其声望就高。当然期刊声望越高,被引用的可能性就越大,影响力就越大。
- 期刊的审稿周期。一般而言,期刊声望越大审稿周期越长。当然,期刊又分为一般期刊、快报(Letters)等(如 IEEE Communication Letters、Physics Review Letters 等),通常快报的效率较高。

(2) 认真阅读投稿须知:确定期刊后,要阅读投稿须知,认真浏览目录,以确定该刊物是否发表你研究领域的文章及发表的比例有多大。一般应该注意:

- 注意栏目设置,确定拟投稿件的栏目。
- 了解稿件的撰写要求。
- 根据刊登文章的投稿日期、接收日期以及见刊日期,估算发表周期,以便出现问题及时与编辑沟通。

(3) 正式投稿:一般来说,投稿程序分以下三步进行:

- 准备投稿信(Cover letter or submission letter)
- 投稿及其包装:目前投稿更多的提倡网络在线投稿,无论是网络投稿还是邮寄投稿,一般要把稿件及其拟投期刊所需的伴随资料一并寄出,一般包括:投稿信、刊物要求的稿件(包括文题页、文摘页、正文、致谢、参考文献、图注、表及图)、版权转让声明、作者地址等。有些还需要提供程序、图片等。
- 稿件追踪:如果投稿两周仍无任何有关稿件收到的信息,也可打电话、发电子邮件或写信给编辑部核实稿件是否收到。

2. 投稿信

对国外期刊投稿时,除了正文文章外,还需要写一封信投稿信。一封好的投稿信可以起到很好的作用,就好比求职时的自荐信一样,如果能吸引编辑的注意,你就成功了一半了。

投稿信的主要目的是希望编辑详细了解文章的主要内容,因而要突出文章的创新性价值,还有你为什么要发表这篇文章,还可以简要指出目前该领域的发展方向。此外,特别要注意用语恰当与格式规范等。

实例1：

Dear Dr：

Enclosed are three copies of a manuscript by XXXXX, XXXXX, and XXXXX titled "XXXXXXXXXXXXXXXXXXXXX". It is submitted to be considered for publications a "Original Article" in your journal. This paper is neither the entire paper nor any part of its content has been published or has been accepted elsewhere. It is not being submitted to any other journal. We believe the paper may be of particular interest to the readers of your journal because XXXXXXXXXXXXXXXXXXXXXXX.

Correspondence and phone calls about the paper should be directed to XXXXXXX at the following address, phone and fax number, and e-mail address：

Department of XXXXXXXXX,

Tsinghua University,

Beijing, 10084,

P. R. China

Tel：XXXXXX

Fax：XXXXX

E-mai：XXXXX

实例2：

Dear Prof. XXX：

I want to submit our manuscript with title "XXXXXXXXX" for publication in "XXXXXXXXX". It is not being submitted to any other journal or is under consideration for publication elsewhere.

The authors claim that none of the material in the paper has been published or is under consideration for publication elsewhere.

I am the corresponding author and further information is as follows：

Address：Department of XXXXX,

Huazhong Normal University,

Wuhan, HuBei, 430079,

P. R. China.

Tel：XXXXXXX

Fax：XXXXXXX

E-mail：qushaocheng@ mail. ccnu. edu. cn

Thanks very much for your attention to our paper.

Sincerely yours,

Shao-cheng Qu

三、审稿过程以及与编辑的沟通

1. 审稿过程

一般不同领域,审稿的过程可能不太一样,大致过程是初选、送审、修改和终审。一般要了解以下基本步骤与内容:

(1) 编辑内部审查:一般包括论文文字、格式的审查与论文题材方面的检查,这种审查通常是编辑部内部的专家进行的。由于一些重要期刊投稿众多,许多好的中文期刊内部审查拒稿率达到 60%;投稿英文期刊时因英文表达不好拒稿率也相当高。如果论文形式不合格,无论你论文内容多么好,都有可能直接被拒绝,因为你的稿件根本没有到真正专家的手中。此外,如果编辑觉得论文题材不适合所投刊物,也会回信退稿。

(2) 正式审稿:编辑会挑选 2—5 名同行对论文的创新性和正确性进行审查。有些期刊采取匿名审稿,有些公开审稿。国内审稿一般有少量审稿费,国外评审是自愿花时间评阅论文,由于评阅人一般是已经在本领域建立了地位,比较忙,因此评审时间较长,投稿者应对此予以理解。审稿期间,作者一般应耐心等待。除按收稿通知建议时间与编辑联系外,一般应给评审 4—6 个月时间。若仍无消息,可以与编辑联系催促一下。

(3) 评审内容:主要包括论文内容的创新性;采用理论、方法和数据的正确性;论文表述方法、写作缺陷等提出批评。

(4) 评审结果一般有以下情况:

- 接收(Accepted or without minor revision):如果接收,作者会收到最终稿的指南,有时需要补充提供数字文件等。
- 修改后可接收(Conditional acceptance upon satisfactory revision):这种情况,应按照评审意见修改论文,将修改部分单独写成报告提供给编辑。一般来说编辑比评审者更具同情心,一般可以最终接受。
- 可以修改后再投:这种情况要分析评审意见,如果编辑希望继续修改提高,不要轻易放弃,修改后被接收的机会还是很大。对于高质量的杂志,多数论文第一次投稿时都会被按这种情况退回来。作者应根据评审意见认真修改。当然也可以提出对某些部分不修改的理由。
- 拒绝:这种情况应根据评审意见修改文稿,然后投往其他刊物。千万不要较劲与编辑过不去,甚至谩骂编辑,这样会对你所在学校甚至国家类似的投稿带来永久的障碍。

(5) 论文发表:收到印刷编辑寄回的校样后,应尽快订正,尽快寄还给印刷编辑。寄校样时,出版商会要求填写版权转让书(Transfer of Copy Right),并告知支付版面费的办法和订购单行本的方法。许多刊物不收版面费,但对特殊印刷(如彩版印刷)收费。有的超过定额免费页数的页面还可能按页面收费。不少收版面费的刊物费用都挺高,不过作者可以写信告知自己的情况,申请免费。

总之,作者对审查意见首先应高度重视,考虑审稿人为什么要提出这些建议。审稿人毕竟是来自一个旁观者的意见,总有一定道理。有的作者觉得审稿人没有读懂自己的文章,拒绝修改,这当然不好。当然,尽管审稿人是同领域的专家,但隔行如隔山,审稿人可能提出一些并不十分中肯的意见也不奇怪。好在评审人一般为三人以上,这至少最小化了由个人偏见而产生的不公正现象。

2. 与编辑的沟通

在投稿期间,为及时了解稿件信息,难免要与编辑进行沟通;对评阅人的审稿意见,作者要认真对待,因而与评阅人进行沟通也是必要的。

与编辑进行沟通,主要是询问稿件状况。下面给出几个例子:

例1:Dear Editor:

I want to know if you have received our manuscript with the title "XXXXXXXX" for submission in "XXXXXXXX". We submit our manuscript from e-mail: XXXXXXXX on Friday, 27, Feb, but we cannot receive the reply. Thank you for your kindly consideration of this request.

Sincerely yours,
XXXXXXXXX

例2:Dear Editor,

I'm not sure if it is the right time to contact you again to inquire about the status of my submitted manuscript(Paper ID: XXXXXXXXX; Title of Paper: XXXXXXXXXXXXX) although nearly one month have passed since I contacted you last time. I would be greatly appreciated if you could spend some of your time check the status for me.

Best regards,
XXXX

例3:Dear Editor:

Thanks for your reply for time and patient. We have sent many dates and figures to you according to reviews. We want to know if you have received it.

Please contact us, if you have any question.

We are looking forward to hearing from your letters.

由于同行评审是匿名的,评审人的批评通常是直率、无情的,甚至是错误的,有些学者认为论文被要求修改或者被拒绝很丢面子,甚至认为这些批评是人身攻击。事实上,事情可能没有那么复杂。作者主要目的是发表论文,因而按照审稿人的意见修改论文显得尤为必要;如果对自己论文很有信心,认为评审人的意见是错误的,这时候一定要讲究策略。一般而言,要对每一个审稿人的意见都要逐个回答,如果可能的话,应该在回复中附上审稿人提出的意见,这样可以简化审稿人的二审工作,也能显示作者的真诚以及对审稿人工作的尊重。

根据审稿人意见完成论文修改之后,作者还应该写一封信对责任编辑表示感谢,同时表明你已经考虑了每一位审稿人的意见。绝对不能对审稿人写了很长的解释,但对论文本身却没有多少修改。一般而言,评阅人对按照他们的建议所付出的努力及其有条有理的修改工作会留下深刻的印象,这样你的工作得到评阅人承认的可能性就越大。

Dear Editor:

　　We have revised the manuscript according to reviews and your comments. Our point-to-point response attached below. At the same time, we would like to thank you and anonymous reviewers for your kindly patience and constructive suggestions, which are very important information to revise this paper.

　　With my king regards,
　　Faithfully yours, XXXX

四、如何修改论文

　　不管在哪里,稿件的评审都不可能是百分之百的公平的。丘吉尔曾说过:同行评审(peer review)是最坏的体系。一般说来,作者拿出的初稿都不是尽善尽美的,有必要进行认真的修改和润色,正如唐朝李沂所说:"能改则瑕可为瑜,瓦砾可为珠玉。"下面介绍几种常用的改稿方法。

　　其一,诵读法。初稿写成后要诵读几遍,一边读,一边思考,并把文气不接、语意不顺的地方随手改过来。叶圣陶先生十分推崇这种"诵读法";鲁迅先生写完文章后,总要先读读,"自己觉得拗口的,就增删几个字,一定要它读得顺口。"可见,诵读法实在是一种简便易行、效果显著的方法。

　　其二,比较法。比较是认识事物的有效方法。把自己的初稿和同类文章中的优秀范文对照、比较,反复揣摩,分析得失,然后加以修改。这是初学者最需要掌握的。

　　其三,旁正法。"三人行,必有我师焉",在修改稿件上,多听取各方面的意见,扬长避短,去粗取精,是大有益处的,作者必须高度重视修改这一环,通过反复推敲、加工,使文稿从内容到形式都达到精粹、完美的高度。

五、如何进行学术报告

　　进行学术报告对一个学者是至关重要的,它不仅展示了你的研究成果,同时也锻炼了你把握事情的能力。通常中国出国留学的学生遇到的最苦闷的事情就是作报告(Presentation),这当然是由中西教育上的差异造成的。目前,许多高校教学中正在积极鼓励作报告。

　　好的论文并不等于好的报告。要做好报告,准备充分是关键。一般应考虑一下因素:
- 好的报告工具,如PPT。
- 清晰的报告结构。
- 适当的字体。
- 得体的姿势与肢体语言,包括手势、语调等。
- 适中的语速。
- 掌握好时间。

　　必须要记住,报告人感兴趣的内容听众不一定感兴趣,报告人的任务是所讲的内容让听众感兴趣,因而必须提倡以听众为中心的报告风格。

　　下面是一段注意力与时间关系图的论述。

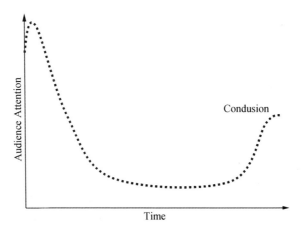

Figure 1　Typical Attention the Audience Pays to an Average Presentation

　　The average attendee of a conference is by all means willing to listen to you, but he is also easily distracted. You should realize that only a minor part of the people have come specifically to listen to your talk. The rest is there for a variety of reasons, to wait for the next speaker, or to get a general impression of the field, or whatever. Figure 1 illustrates how the average audience pays attention during a typical presentation of, let's say, 30 minutes. Almost everyone listens in the beginning, but halfway the attention may well have dropped to around 10-20% of what it was at the start. At the end, many people start to listen again, particularly if you announce your conclusions, because they hope to take something away from the presentation.

　　下面是文章与报告结构安排上的区别。

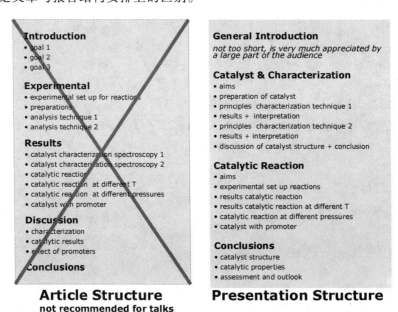

六、科技论文中常见的错误

科技论文是一种专门的文体,由于许多科技论文都由英文写成,加之众多国内学者没有海外求学经历,因而想写出一篇准确规范的英文科技论文还是有相当的难度,正如弗利西亚·布利特曼所言,即使以英语为母语的学生要写出一篇规范的科技论文也需要半年到一年的训练时间。下面是弗利西亚·布利特曼总结的中国学生撰写科技论文时的常见错误。

- The single most common habit is the omission of articles a, an, and the.
- Very long sentences are especially common in Chinese-English writing because the writers often translate directly from Chinese to English. A example as follows:

Too long: The clear height of the case is 6.15 meters; the thickness of the roof is 0.85 meters; the thickness of the bottom is 0.90 meters, the overall width is 26.6 meters, the overall length of the axial cord is 304.5 meters, the length of the jacking section is about 148.8 meters; the weight of the case is about 24127 tons.

Modification:

- Case clearance height 6.15 meters
- Roof thickness 0.85 meters
- Bottom thickness 0.90 meters
- Overall width 26.6 meters
- Overall length of the axial cord 304.5 meters
- Length of the jacking section 148.8 meters (approx.)
- Weight of the case 24127 tons (approx.)
- Prefacing the main idea of a sentence by stating the purpose, location or reason first.

Incorrect: For the application in automobile interiors, this paper studies the nesting optimization problem in leather manufacturing.

Correct: This paper studies the nesting optimization problem in leather manufacturing for application in automobile interiors.

- Tendency of placing phrases which indicate time at the beginning of a sentence

Incorrect: When U is taken as the control parameter, the BDs for $\Delta = 0.0, 0.001, 0.005$ are shown in Figure 8.

Correct: Figure 8 shows the BDs for $\Delta = 0.0, 0.001$, and 0.005 when U is taken as the control parameter.

- Place the most important subject at the beginning of the sentence for emphasis.

Incorrect: Based on the triangulation structure built from unorganized points or a CAD model, the extended STL format is described in this section.

Correct: The extended STL format is described in this section based on the triangulation structure built from unorganized points or a CAD model.

- Avoid redundancy in the following types of phrases frequently used by Chinese English writers

Instead of	Say
Research work	Research or work
Limit condition	Limit or condition
Layout scheme	Layout or scheme
Arrangement plan	Arrangement or plan
Output performance	Output or performance
Simulation results	Simulation or results
Application results	Application or results
Knowledge information	Knowledge or information

- Certain words demand that the noun they modify is plural. These include different, various, and number words.

Don't write	Instead write
Different node	Different nodes
Various method	Various methods
Two advantage	Two advantages
Fifteen thermocouple	Fifteen thermocouples

Chapter 12 Web Design

▲ **Knowledge Objectives**

When you have completed this unit, you will be able to:

• Understand the meaning of web design and know something about how to make an accessible web.

• Know about the technologies involved in the process of designing a web, such as the HTML, XML, XHTML, CSS, JavaScript, VBScript, PHP, ASP and etc.

• Know the functions of some tools in making webs, such as Photoshop, Dreamweaver, Flash, Fireworks, etc.

• Understand and state some of the types of webs and their applications.

▲ **Professional Terms**

ASP	动态服务器页面
CSS	层叠样式表
HTML	超文本链接标示语言
JavaScript	Java 描述语言
PHP	超级文本预处理语言
VBScript	VB 描述语言
XHTML	可扩展超文本链接标示语言
XML	可扩展标示语言

Part 1 Overview of Web Design

Web Design

Web design is the skill of creating presentations of content (usually hypertext or hypermedia) that is delivered to an end-user through the World Wide Web, by way of a Web browser or other Web-enabled software like Internet television clients, microblogging clients and RSS readers [1]. The intent of Web design is to create a website—a collection of electronic documents and applications that reside on a Web server/servers and present content and interactive features/interfaces to the end user in form of Web pages once requested [2]. Such elements as text, bit-mapped images (GIFs, JPEGs) and forms can be placed on the page using HTML/

XHTML/XML tags. Displaying more complex media (vector graphics, animations, videos, sounds) requires plug-ins such as Adobe Flash, QuickTime, Java run-time environment, etc. Plug-ins are also embedded into web page by using HTML/XHTML tags.

Improvements in browsers' compliance with W3C standards prompted a widespread acceptance and usage of XHTML/XML and in conjunction with Cascading Style Sheets (CSS) it is better to position and manipulate web page elements and objects. Typically Web pages are classified as static or dynamic:

• Static pages don't change content and layout with every request unless a human (web master/programmer) manually updates the page. A simple HTML page is an example of static content.

• Dynamic pages adapt their content and/or appearance depending on end-user's input/interaction. Content can be changed on the client side (end-user's computer) by using client-side scripting languages (JavaScript, JScript, Actionscript, etc.) to alter DOM elements (DHTML). Dynamic content is often compiled on the server utilizing server-side scripting languages (Perl, PHP, ASP, JSP, ColdFusion, etc.). Both approaches are usually used in complex applications.

Web design is a kind of graphic design intended for development and styling of objects of the Internet's information environment to provide them with high-end consumer features and aesthetic qualities. The offered definition separates Web design from web programming, emphasizing the functional features of a web site, as well as positioning web design as a kind of graphic design.

The process of designing web pages, web sites, web applications or multimedia for the Web may utilize multiple disciplines, such as animation, graphic design, human-computer interaction, information architecture, interaction design, marketing, photography, search engine optimization and typography. Web pages and websites can be static pages, or can be programmed to be dynamic pages that automatically adapt content or visual appearance depending on a variety of factors, such as input from the end-user, input from the Webmaster or changes in the computing environment (such as the site's associated database having been modified).

Accessible Web Design

To be accessible, Web pages and sites must conform to certain accessibility principles. These accessibility principles are known as the WCAG (Web Content Accessibility Guidelines) when talking about content. These can be grouped into the following main areas.

• Use semantic markup that provides a meaningful structure to the document (i.e. Web page)

• Semantic markup also refers to semantically organizing the web page structure and publishing web services description accordingly so that they can be recognized by other web services on different web pages. Standards for semantic Web are set by IEEE.

- Use a valid markup language that conforms to a published DTD or Schema
- Provide text equivalents for any non-text components (e.g. images, multimedia)
- Use hyperlinks that make sense when read out of context. (e.g. avoid "Click Here")
- Don't use frames
- Use CSS rather than HTML tables for layout
- Author the page so that when the source code is read line-by-line by user agents (such as screen readers) it remains intelligible. (Using tables for design will often result in information that is not.)

However, W3C permits an exception where tables for layout either make sense when linearized or an alternate version (perhaps linearized) is made available. Website accessibility is also changing as it is impacted by Content Management Systems that allow changes to be made to webpages without the need of obtaining programming language knowledge. It is very important that several different components of Web development and interaction can work together in order for the Web to be accessible to people with disabilities. These components include:

- content—the information in a Web page or Web application, including:
  - natural information such as text, images, and sounds
  - code or markup that defines structure, presentation, etc.
- Web browsers, media players, and other "user agents"
- assistive technology, in some cases—screen readers, alternative keyboards, switches, scanning software, etc.
- users' knowledge, experiences, and in some cases, adaptive strategies using the Web
- developers—designers, coders, etc., including developers with disabilities and users who contribute content
- authoring tools—software that creates Web sites
- evaluation tools—Web accessibility evaluation tools, HTML validators, CSS validators, etc.

Website Design

Web design is similar (in some way) to traditional print publishing. Every website is an information display container, just as a book is a container; and every web page is like the page in a book. However, web design uses a framework based on digital code and display technology to construct and maintain an environment to distribute information in multiple formats. Taken to its fullest potential, web design is undoubtedly the most sophisticated and increasingly complex method to support communication in today's world.

For the typical web sites, the basic aspects of design are:
- The *content*: the information on the site should be relevant to the site and should target the area of the public that the website is concerned with.
- The *usability*: the site should be user-friendly, with the interface and navigation simple

and reliable.

• The *appearance*: the graphics and text should include a single style that flows throughout, to show consistency. The style should be professional, appealing and relevant.

• The *visibility*: the site must also be easy to find via most, if not all, major search engines and advertisement media.

A web site typically consists of text and images. The first page of a web site is known as the Home page or Index. Some web sites use what is commonly called a Splash Page. Splash pages might include a welcome message, language or disclaimer. Each web page within a web site is an HTML file which has its own URL. After each web page is created, they are typically linked together using a navigation menu composed of hyperlinks. Faster browsing speeds have led to shorter attention spans and more demanding online visitors and this has resulted in less use of Splash Pages, particularly where commercial web sites are concerned

Once a web site is completed, it must be published or uploaded in order to be viewable to the public over the internet. This may be done using an FTP client. Once published, the web master may use a variety of techniques to increase the traffic, or hits, that the web site receives. This may include submitting the web site to a search engine such as Google, Yahoo, and exchanging links with other web sites, creating affiliations with similar web sites, etc.

Multidisciplinary Requirements

Web site design crosses multiple disciplines of multiple information systems, information technology and communication design. The web site is an information system whose components are sometimes classified as front-end and back-end. The observable content (e.g. page layout, user interface, graphics, text, audio) is known as the front-end. The back-end comprises the organization and efficiency of the source code, invisible scripted functions, and the server-side components that process the output from the front-end. Depending on the size of a Web development project, it may be carried out by a multi-skilled individual (sometimes called a web master), or a project manager may oversee collaborative design between group members with specialized skills.

Issues

By its very nature, web design is conflicted, involving rigid technical conformance and personal creative balance. Rapid technological change complicates acquiring and deploying suitable resources.

Form versus Function

A web developer may pay more attention to how a page looks while neglecting other copywriting and search engine optimization functions such as the readability of text, the ease of navigating the site, or how easily the visitors are going to find the site. As a result, the designers may end up in disputes where some want more decorative graphics at the expense of keyword-rich text and text links. In many cases form follows function. Because some graphics serve communication purposes in addition to aesthetics, how well a site works may depend on the graphic design ideas as well as the professional writing considerations.

When using a lot of graphics, a web page can load slowly, often irritating the user. This has become less of a problem as the internet has evolved with high-speed internet and the use of vector graphics. However there is still an ongoing engineering challenge to increase bandwidth and an artistic challenge to minimize the amount of graphics and their file sizes. This challenge is compounded since increased bandwidth encourages more graphics with larger file sizes.

When faced with a large database and many requirements, a design group may throw far too much information for a server to manage. Alternative technology or additional structure (even another server or site) may be required to fit the demand.

Layout

Layout refers to the dimensioning of content in a device display, and the delivery of media in a content related stream. Web design layouts result in visual content frameworks: these frameworks can be fixed, or they can provide fluid layout with proportional dimensions. Many units of measure exist, but here are some popular dimension formats:

> Pixel measure results in fixed or static content
> Em measure results in proportional content that is relative to font-size
> Percent measure results in fluid content that shrinks and grows to "fit" display windows

Proportional, liquid and hybrid layout are also referred to as dynamic design. Hybrid layout incorporates any combination of fixed, proportional or fluid elements within (or pointing to) a single page. The hybrid web design framework is made possible by digital internet conventions generally prescribed by the W3C. If any layout does not appear, it is very likely that it does not conform to standard design principles, or that those standards conflict with standard layout elements. Current knowledge of standards is essential to effective hybrid design.

Hybrid design maintains most static content control, but is adapted to textual publishing, and for readers, to conventional (printed) display. Hybrid layouts are generally easy on the eye and are found on most sites that distribute traditional images and text to readers. For some sites, hybrid design makes an otherwise cold text column appear warm and balanced.

Device

On the web the designer has no control over several factors, including the size of the browser window, the web browser used, the input devices used (operating system, mouse, touch screen, voice command, text, teletype, cell phone, and etc), and the size, design, and other characteristics of the fonts that users have available (installed) and enabled (preference) on their device. Web designers do well to study and become proficient at removing competitive device and software markup so that web pages display as they are coded to display.

Part 2   Technologies Involved in Web Design

Markup Languages

A markup language is a modern system for annotating a text in a way that is syntactically distinguishable from that text. The idea and terminology evolved from the "marking up" of manuscripts, i. e. the revision instructions by editors, traditionally written with a blue pencil on authors' manuscripts. Examples are typesetting instructions such as those found in troff and LaTeX, and structural markers such as XML tags. Markup is typically omitted from the version of the text which is displayed for end-user consumption. Some markup languages, like HTML have presentation semantics, meaning their specification prescribes how the structured data is to be presented, but other markup languages, like XML, have no predefined semantics.

A well-known example of a markup language in widespread use today is HyperText Markup Language (HTML), one of the document formats of the World Wide Web. HTML is mostly an instance of SGML (though, strictly, it does not comply with all the rules of SGML) and follows many of the markup conventions used in the publishing industry in the communication of printed work between authors, editors, and printers. Let's introduce some markup languages in the following.

1. HTML

HTML, which stands for HyperText Markup Language, is the predominant markup language for web pages. It provides a means to create structured documents by denoting structural semantics for text such as headings, paragraphs, lists, links, quotes and other items. It allows images and objects to be embedded and can be used to create interactive forms. It is written in the form of HTML elements consisting of "tags" surrounded by angle brackets within the web page content (Figure 12-1). It can embed scripts in languages such as JavaScript which affect the behavior of HTML webpages. HTML can also be used to include Cascading Style Sheets (CSS) to define the appearance and layout of text and other material. The W3C, maintainer of both HTML and CSS standards, encourages the use of CSS over explicit presentational markup.

```
<!doctype html>
<html>
  <head>
    <title>Hello HTML</title>
  </head>
  <body>
    <p>Hello World!</p>
  </body>
</html>
```

Figure 12-1   One example of HTML

By 1991, it appeared to many that SGML would be limited to commercial and data-based applications while WYSIWYG tools (which stored documents in proprietary binary formats) would suffice for other document processing applications. The situation changed when Sir Tim Berners-Lee, learning of SGML from co-worker Anders Berglund and others at CERN, used SGML syntax to create HTML. HTML resembles other SGML-based tag languages, although it began as simpler than most and a formal DTD was not developed until later. Steven DeRose argues that HTML's use of descriptive markup (and SGML in particular) was a major factor in the success of the Web, because of the flexibility and extensibility that it enabled (other factors include the notion of URLs and the free distribution of browsers). HTML is quite likely the most used markup language in the world today.

2. Semantic HTML

Semantic HTML is a way of writing HTML that emphasizes the meaning of the encoded information over its presentation (look). HTML has included semantic markup from its inception, but has also included presentational markup such as ⟨font⟩, ⟨i⟩ and ⟨center⟩ tags. There are also the semantically neutral span and div tags. Since the late 1990s when Cascading Style Sheets were beginning to work in most browsers, web authors have been encouraged to avoid the use of presentational HTML markup with a view to the separation of presentation and content.

In a 2001 discussion of the Semantic Web, Tim Berners-Lee and others gave examples of ways in which intelligent software 'agents' may one day automatically trawl the Web and find, filter and correlate previously unrelated, published facts for the benefit of human users. Such agents are not commonplace even now, but some of the ideas of Web 2.0, mashups and price comparison websites may be coming close. The main difference between these web application hybrids and Berners-Lee's semantic agents lies in the fact that the current aggregation and hybridisation of information is usually designed in by web developers, who already know the web locations and the API semantics of the specific data they wish to mash, compare and combine.

Good semantic HTML can improve the accessibility of web documents. For example, when a screen reader or audio browser can correctly ascertain the structure of a document, it will not waste the visually impaired user's time by reading out repeated or irrelevant information when it has been marked up correctly.

3. XML

XML (Extensible Markup Language) (Figure 12-2) is a meta markup language that is now widely used. XML was developed by the World Wide Web Consortium, in a committee created and chaired by Jon Bosak. The main purpose of XML was to simplify SGML by focusing on a particular problem — documents on the Internet. XML remains a meta-language like SGML, allowing users to create any tags needed (hence "extensible") and then describing those tags and their permitted uses.

```
<?xml version="1.0" encoding="UTF-8"?>
<!DOCTYPE recipe PUBLIC "-//Happy-Monkey//DTD RecipeBook//EN"
"http://www.happy-monkey.net/recipebook/recipebook.dtd">

<recipe>
    <title>Peanut-butter On A Spoon</title>

    <ingredientlist>
        <ingredient>Peanut-butter</ingredient>
    </ingredientlist>

    <preparation>
        Stick a spoon in a jar of peanut-butter,
        scoop and pull out a big glob of peanut-butter.
    </preparation>

</recipe>
```

Figure 12-2   A simple markup language based on XML for creating recipes. The markup can be converted to HTML, PDF and Rich Text Format using a programming language or XSL.

XML adoption was helped because every XML document can be written in such a way that it is also an SGML document, and existing SGML users and software could switch to XML fairly easily. However, XML eliminated many of the more complex and human-oriented features of SGML to simplify implementation environments such as documents and publications. However, it appeared to strike a happy medium between simplicity and flexibility, and was rapidly adopted for many other uses. XML is now widely used for communicating data between applications. Like HTML, it can be described as a 'container' language.

4. XHTML

Since January 2000, all W3C Recommendations for HTML have been based on XML rather than SGML, using the abbreviation XHTML (Extensible HyperText Markup Language). The language specification requires that XHTML Web documents must be well-formed XML documents—this allows for more rigorous and robust documents while using tags familiar from HTML.

One of the most noticeable differences between HTML and XHTML is the rule that all tags must be closed: empty HTML tags such as 〈br〉 must either be closed with a regular end tag, or replaced by a special form: 〈br /〉 (the space before the '/' on the end tag is optional, but frequently used because it enables some pre-XML Web browsers, and SGML parsers, to accept the tag). Another is that all attribute values in tags must be quoted. Finally, all tag and attribute names must be lowercase in order to be valid; HTML, on the other hand, was case-insensitive.

5. Other XML-based applications

Many XML-based applications now exist, including Resource Description Framework (RDF), XForms, DocBook, SOAP and the Web Ontology Language (OWL).

Style Sheet Languages

A style sheet language or style language is a computer language used to describe the presentation of structured documents. A structured document which doesn't break the schema it is designed to conform to is "well-formed". A program processing the document must model the schema, and can present it in different formats, fonts, and order, as well as with other effects, by using different sets of style rules contained in different style sheets.

One modern style sheet language with widespread use is Cascading Style Sheets, which is used to style documents written in HTML, XHTML, SVG, XUL, and other markup languages. One of the most attractive features of structured documents is that the content can be reused in many contexts and presented in various ways. Different style sheets can be attached to the logical structure to produce different presentations.

For content in structured documents to be presented, a set of stylistic rules—describing, for example, colors, fonts and layout—must be applied. A collection of stylistic rules is called a style sheet. Style sheets in the form of written documents have a long history of use by editors and typographers to ensure consistency of presentation, spelling and punctuation. In electronic publishing, style sheet languages are mostly used in the context of visual presentation rather than spelling and punctuation.

1. Components of Style Sheet Languages

All style sheet languages offer functionality in these areas:

(i) Syntax

A style sheet language needs a syntax in order to be expressed in a machine-readable manner. For example, here is a simple style sheet written in the CSS syntax (Figure 12-3):

```
h1 { font-size: 1.5em }
```

Figure 12-3　A simple style sheet written in the CSS syntax

(ii) Selectors

Selectors specify which elements are to be influenced by the style rule. As such, selectors are the glue between the structure of the document and the stylistic rules in the style sheets. In the example above, the "h1" selector selects all h1 elements. More complex selectors can select elements based on, e.g., their context, attributes and content.

(iii) Properties

All style sheet languages have some concept of properties that can be given values to change one aspect of rendering an element. The "font-size" property of CSS is used in the above example. Common style sheet languages typically have around 50 properties to describe the presentation of documents

(iv) Values and Units

Properties change the rendering of an element by being assigned a certain value. The value can be a string, a keyword, a number, or a number with a unit identifier. Also, values can be lists or expressions involving several of the aforementioned values. A typical value in a visual style sheet is a length; for example, "1.5em" which consists of a number (1.5) and a unit (em). The "em" value in CSS refers to the font size of the surrounding text. Common style sheet languages have around ten different units.

(v) **Value Propagation Mechanism**

To avoid having to specify explicitly all values for all properties on all elements, style sheet languages have mechanisms to propagate values automatically. The main benefit of value propagation is less-verbose style sheets. In the example above, only the font size is specified; other values will be found through value propagation mechanisms. Inheritance, initial values and cascading are examples of value propagation mechanisms.

(vi) **Formatting Model**

All style sheet languages support some kind of formatting model. Most style sheet languages have a visual formatting model that describes, in some detail, how text and other contents are laid out in the final presentation. For example, the CSS formatting model specifies that block-level elements (of which "h1" is an example) extends to fill the width of the parent element. Some style sheet languages also have an aural formatting model.

2. Cascading Style Sheets

Cascading Style Sheets (CSS) is a style sheet language used to describe the presentation semantics (the look and formatting) of a document written in a markup language. Its most common application is to style web pages written in HTML and XHTML, but the language can also be applied to any kind of XML document, including SVG and XUL.

CSS is designed primarily to enable the separation of document content (written in HTML or a similar markup language) from document presentation, including elements such as the layout, colors, and fonts. This separation can improve content accessibility, provide more flexibility and control in the specification of presentation characteristics, enable multiple pages to share formatting, and reduce complexity and repetition in the structural content (such as by allowing for tableless web design). CSS can also allow the same markup page to be presented in different styles for different rendering methods, such as on-screen, in print, by voice (when read out by a speech-based browser or screen reader) and on Braille-based, tactile devices. While the author of a document typically links that document to a CSS style sheet, readers can use a different style sheet, perhaps one on their own computer, to override the one the author has specified.

CSS specifies a priority scheme to determine which style rules apply if more than one rule matches against a particular element. In this so-called cascade, priorities or weights are calculated and assigned to rules, so that the results are predictable.

Prior to CSS, nearly all of the presentational attributes of HTML documents were contained within the HTML markup; all font colors, background styles, element alignments, borders and sizes had to be explicitly described, often repeatedly, within the HTML. CSS allows authors to move much of that information to a separate style sheet resulting in considerably simpler HTML markup.

Headings (h1 elements), sub-headings (h2), sub-sub-headings (h3), etc., are defined structurally using HTML. In print and on the screen, choice of font, size, color and emphasis for these elements is presentational.

Prior to CSS, document authors who wanted to assign such typographic characteristics to, say, all h2 headings had to use the HTML font and other presentational elements for each occurrence of that heading type. The additional presentational markup in the HTML made documents more complex, and generally more difficult to maintain. In CSS, presentation is separated from structure. In print, CSS can define color, font, text alignment, size, borders, spacing, layout and many other typographic characteristics. It can do so independently for on-screen and printed views. CSS also defines non-visual styles such as the speed and emphasis with which text is read out by aural text readers. The W3C now considers the advantages of CSS for defining all aspects of the presentation of HTML pages to be superior to other methods. It has therefore deprecated the use of all the original presentational HTML markup.

3. Extensible Stylesheet Language

In computing, the term Extensible Stylesheet Language (XSL) is used to refer to a family of languages used to transform and render XML documents.

Historically, the XSL Working Group in W3C produced a draft specification under the name XSL, which eventually split into three parts:

- XSL Transformations (XSLT): an XML language for transforming XML documents
- XSL Formatting Objects (XSL-FO): an XML language for specifying the visual formatting of an XML document
- the XML Path Language (XPath): a non-XML language used by XSLT, and also available for use in non-XSLT contexts, for addressing the parts of an XML document.

As a result, the term XSL is now used with a number of different meanings:

- Sometimes it refers to XSLT: this usage is best avoided. However, "xsl" is used both as the conventional namespace prefix for the XSLT namespace, and as the conventional filename suffix for files containing XSLT stylesheet modules
- Sometimes it refers to XSL-FO: this usage can be justified by the fact that the XSL-FO specification carries the title Extensible Stylesheet Language (XSL); however, the term XSL-FO is less likely to be misunderstood
- Sometimes it refers to both languages considered together, or to the working group that develops both languages
- Sometimes, especially in the Microsoft world, it refers to a now-obsolete variant of

XSLT developed and shipped by Microsoft as part of MSXML before the W3C specification was finalized

4. Client-side Scripting

Client-side scripting generally refers to the class of computer programs on the web that are executed *client-side*, by the user's web browser, instead of *server-side* (on the web server) [3]. This type of computer programming is an important part of the Dynamic HTML (DHTML) concept, enabling web pages to be scripted; that is, to have different and changing content depending on user input, environmental conditions (such as the time of day), or other variables.

Web authors write client-side scripts in languages such as JavaScript (Client-side JavaScript) and VBScript.

5. JavaScript[①]

JavaScript (Figure 12-4) is an implementation of the ECMAScript language standard and is typically used to enable programmatic access to computational objects within a host environment. It can be characterized as a prototype-based object-oriented scripting language that is dynamic, weakly typed and has first-class functions. It is also considered a functional programming language like Scheme and OCaml because it has closures and supports higher-order functions.

```
<html>
  <head><title>LCM Calculator</title></head>
    <body>
      <font face="Courier New" size="3">
      <script type="text/javascript">
/* Finds the lowest common multiple of two numbers */
function LCMCalculator(x, y) { // constructor function
    function checkInt(x) { // inner function
        if (x % 1 != 0)
            throw new TypeError(x + " is not an integer"); // exception throwing
        return x;
    }
    //semicolons are optional (but beware since this may cause consecutive lines to be
    //erroneously treated as a single statement)
    this.a = checkInt(x)
    this.b = checkInt(y)
}
// The prototype of object instances created by a constructor is
// that constructor's "prototype" property.
LCMCalculator.prototype = { // object literal
    gcd : function() { // method that calculates the greatest common divisor
        // Euclidean algorithm:
        var a = Math.abs(this.a), b = Math.abs(this.b), t;
        if (a < b) {
            t = b; b = a; a = t; // swap variables
        }
        while (b !== 0) {
            t = b;
            b = a % b;
            a = t;
        }
        // Only need to calculate gcd once, so "redefine" this method.
        // (Actually not redefinition - it's defined on the instance itself,
```

Figure 12-4 One Example Written in JavaScript

JavaScript is primarily used in the form of client-side JavaScript, implemented as part of a web browser in order to provide enhanced user interfaces and dynamic websites. However, its use in applications outside web pages is also significant.

---

① http://en.wikipedia.org/wiki/JavaScript

JavaScript and the Java programming language both use syntaxes influenced by that of C syntax, and JavaScript copies many Java names and naming conventions; but the two languages are otherwise unrelated and have very different semantics. The key design principles within JavaScript are taken from the Self and Scheme programming languages.

The primary use of JavaScript is to write functions that are embedded in or included from HTML pages and that interact with the Document Object Model (DOM) of the page. Some simple examples of this usage are:

- Opening or popping up a new window with programmatic control over the size, position, and attributes of the new window (e.g. whether the menus, toolbars, etc. are visible).

- Validating input values of a web form to make sure that they are acceptable before being submitted to the server.

- Changing images as the mouse cursor moves over them: This effect is often used to draw the user's attention to important links displayed as graphical elements.

Because JavaScript code can run locally in a user's browser (rather than on a remote server), the browser can respond to user actions quickly, making an application more responsive. Furthermore, JavaScript code can detect user actions which HTML alone cannot, such as individual keystrokes. Applications such as Gmail take advantage of this: much of the user-interface logic is written in JavaScript, and JavaScript dispatches requests for information (such as the content of an e-mail message) to the server. The wider trend of Ajax programming similarly exploits this strength.

A web browser is by far the most common host environment for JavaScript. Web browsers typically use the public API to create "host objects" responsible for reflecting the DOM into JavaScript. The web server is another common application of the engine. A JavaScript webserver would expose host objects representing an HTTP request and response objects, which a JavaScript program could then manipulate to dynamically generate web pages.

Because JavaScript is the only language that the most popular browsers share support for, it has become a target language for many frameworks in other languages, even though JavaScript was never intended to be such a language [4]. Despite the performance limitations inherent to its dynamic nature, the increasing speed of JavaScript engines has made the language a surprisingly feasible compilation target.

6. VBScript

VBScript (Visual Basic Scripting Edition) (Figure 12-5) is an Active Scripting language developed by Microsoft that is modelled on Visual Basic. It is designed as a "lightweight" language with a fast interpreter for use in a wide variety of Microsoft environments. VBScript uses the Component Object Model to access elements of the environment within which it is running; for example, the FileSystemObject (FSO) is used to create, read, update and delete files.

```
<% Option Explicit
%><!DOCTYPE HTML PUBLIC "-//W3C//DTD HTML 4.01 Transitional//EN"
    "http://www.w3.org/TR/html4/loose.dtd">
<html>
    <head>
        <title>VBScript Example</title>
    </head>
    <body>
        <div><%
            ' Grab current time from Now() function.
            Dim timeValue
            timeValue = Now() %>
            The time, in 24-hour format, is
            <%=Hour(timeValue)%>:<%=Minute(timeValue)%>:<%=Second(timeValue)%>.
        </div>
    </body>
</html>
```

Figure 12-5　One Example of VBScript

VBScript has been installed by default in every desktop release of Microsoft Windows since Windows 98; in Windows Server since Windows NT 4.0 Option Pack; and optionally with Windows CE (depending on the device it is installed on).

A VBScript script must be executed within a host environment, of which there are several provided with Microsoft Windows, including: Windows Script Host (WSH), Internet Explorer (IE), and Internet Information Services (IIS). Additionally, the VBScript hosting environment is embeddable in other programs, through technologies such as the Microsoft Script Control (msscript.ocx).

Although VBScript is a general-purpose scripting language, several particular areas of use are noteworthy. First, it is widely used among system administrators in the Microsoft environment. This situation may change with the promotion and increased use of Windows PowerShell. Second, VBScript is the scripting language for Quick Test Professional, a test automation tool. A third area to note is the adoption of VBScript as the internal scripting language for some embedded applications, such as industrial operator interfaces and human machine interfaces.

7. Server-side scripting

Server-side scripting is a web server technology in which a user's request is fulfilled by running a script directly on the web server to generate dynamic web pages. It is usually used to provide interactive web sites that interface to databases or other data stores. This is different from client-side scripting where scripts are run by the viewing web browser, usually in JavaScript. The primary advantage to server-side scripting is the ability to highly customize the response based on the user's requirements, access rights, or queries into data stores.

When the server serves data in a commonly used manner, for example according to the HTTP or FTP protocols, users may have their choice of a number of client programs (most modern web browsers can request and receive data using both of those protocols). In the case of more specialized applications, programmers may write their own server, client, and communications protocol that can only be used with one another.

(i) PHP

Hypertext Preprocessor is a widely used, general-purpose scripting language that was originally designed for web development to produce dynamic web pages. For this purpose, PHP code is embedded into the HTML source document and interpreted by a web server with a PHP processor module, which generates the web page document. As a general-purpose programming language, PHP code is processed by an interpreter application in command-line mode performing desired operating system operations and producing program output on its standard output channel. It may also function as a graphical application. PHP is available as a processor for most modern web servers and as standalone interpreter on most operating systems and computing platforms.

PHP (Figure 12-6) was originally created by Rasmus Lerdorf in 1995 and has been in continuous development ever since. The main implementation of PHP is now produced by the PHP Group and serves as the *de facto* standard for PHP as there is no formal specification. PHP is free software released under the PHP License.

```
<html>
  <head>
    <title>PHP Test</title>
  </head>
  <body>
  <?php
  echo "Hello World";
  /* echo("Hello World"); works as well, although echo isn't a
  function, but a language construct. In some cases, such
  as when multiple parameters are passed to echo, parameters
  cannot be enclosed in parentheses. */
  ?>
  </body>
</html>
```

Figure 12-6 PHP Code Embedded within HTML Code

PHP is a general-purpose scripting language that is especially suited to server-side web development where PHP generally runs on a web server. Any PHP code in a requested file is executed by the PHP runtime, usually to create dynamic web page content. It can also be used for command-line scripting and client-side GUI applications. PHP can be deployed on most web servers, many operating systems and platforms, and can be used with many relational database management systems. It is available free of charge, and the PHP Group provides the complete source code for users to build, customize and extend for their own use.

PHP primarily acts as a filter, taking input from a file or stream containing text and/or PHP instructions and outputs another stream of data; most commonly the output will be HTML. Since PHP 4, the PHP parser compiles input to produce bytecode for processing by the Zend Engine, giving improved performance over its interpreter predecessor.

Originally designed to create dynamic web pages, PHP now focuses mainly on server-side scripting, and it is similar to other server-side scripting languages that provide dynamic content from a web server to a client, such as Microsoft's Active Server Pages, Sun Microsystems' JavaServer Pages, and mod_perl. PHP has also attracted the development of many frameworks that provide building blocks and a design structure to promote rapid application development (RAD). Some of these include CakePHP, Symfony, CodeIgniter, and Zend Framework, offering features similar to other web application frameworks.

The LAMP architecture has become popular in the web industry as a way of deploying web applications. PHP is commonly used as the *P* in this bundle alongside Linux, Apache and MySQL, although the *P* may also refer to Python or Perl or some combination of the three.

(ii) **Active Server Pages (ASP)**

Active Server Pages (ASP), (Figure 12-7) also known as Classic ASP or ASP Classic, was Microsoft's first server-side script-engine for dynamically-generated web pages. Initially released as an add-on to Internet Information Services (IIS) via the Windows NT 4.0 Option Pack (ca 1998), it was subsequently included as a free component of Windows Server (since the initial release of Windows 2000 Server). ASP.NET has superseded ASP.

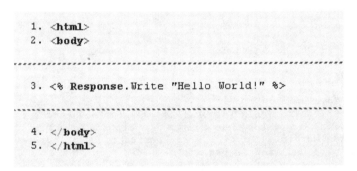

Figure 12-7 The Default Scripting Language (in classic ASP) is VBScript

ASP 2.0 provided six built-in objects: Application, ASPError, Request, Response, Server, and Session. Session, for example, represents a cookie-based session that maintains the state of variables from page to page. The Active Scripting engine's support of the Component Object Model (COM) enables ASP websites to access functionality in compiled libraries such as DLLs.

Web pages with the *.asp* file extension use ASP, although some web sites disguise their choice of scripting language for security purposes (e.g. still using the more common *.htm* or *.html* extension). Pages with the *.aspx* extension use compiled ASP.NET (based on Microsoft's .NET Framework), which makes them faster and more robust than server-side scripting in ASP, which is interpreted at run-time; however, ASP.NET pages may still include some ASP scripting. The introduction of ASP.NET led to use of the term *Classic ASP* for the original technology.

Programmers write most ASP pages using VBScript, but any other Active Scripting engines can be selected instead with the @ Language directive or the ⟨script language = "language" runat = "server"⟩ syntax. JScript (Microsoft's implementation of ECMAScript) is the other language that is usually available. PerlScript (a derivative of Perl) and others are available as third-party installable Active Scripting engines.

Many people regard ASP. NET as the newest release of ASP, but the two products use very different technologies. ASP. NET relies on the. NET Framework and is a compiled language, whereas ASP is strictly an interpreted scripting language.

(ⅲ) **Database technologies**

A database consists of an organized collection of data for one or more uses, typically in digital form. One way of classifying databases involves the type of their contents, for example: bibliographic, document-text, statistical. Digital databases are managed using database management systems, which store database contents, allowing data creation and maintenance, and search and other access [5].

A database management system (DBMS) consists of software that operates databases, providing storage, access, security, backup and other facilities. Database management systems can be categorized according to the database model that they support, such as relational or XML, the type(s) of computer they support, such as a server cluster or a mobile phone, the query language(s) that access the database, such as SQL or XQuery, performance trade-offs, such as maximum scale or maximum speed or others. Some DBMS cover more than one entry in these categories, e. g. , supporting multiple query languages.

MySQL (Figure 12-8) is a relational database management system (RDBMS) that runs as a server providing multi-user access to a number of databases. It is named for original developer Michael Widenius's daughter My.

Figure 12-8 MySQL Workbench in Windows, Displaying the Home Screen Which Streamlines Use of Its Full Capabilities

The MySQL development project has made its source code available under the terms of the

GNU General Public License, as well as under a variety of proprietary agreements. MySQL is owned and sponsored by a single for-profit firm, the Swedish company MySQL AB, now owned by Sun Microsystems, a subsidiary of Oracle Corporation.

Members of the MySQL community have created several forks such as Drizzle, OurDelta, Percona Server, and MariaDB. All of these forks were in progress before the Oracle acquisition (Drizzle was announced 8 months before the Sun acquisition).

Free-software projects that require a full-featured database management system often use MySQL. Such projects include (for example) WordPress, phpBB, Drupal and other software built on the LAMP software stack. MySQL is also used in many high-profile, large-scale World Wide Web products including Wikipedia, Google and Facebook.

The "M" in the acronym of the popular LAMP software stack refers to MySQL. Its popularity for use with web applications is closely tied to the popularity of PHP (the "P" in LAMP). Several high-traffic web sites (including Flickr, Facebook, Wikipedia, Google (though not for searches), Nokia and YouTube) use MySQL for data storage and logging of user data.

(iv) Multimedia

Multimedia is usually recorded and played, displayed or accessed by information content processing devices, such as computerized and electronic devices, but can also be part of a live performance. Multimedia (as an adjective) also describes electronic media devices used to store and experience multimedia content. Multimedia is distinguished from mixed media in fine art; by including audio, for example, it has a broader scope. The term "rich media" is synonymous for interactive multimedia. Hypermedia can be considered one particular multimedia application.

(Please refer to unit 11 for more information about multimedia)

(v) Microsoft Silverlight

Microsoft Silverlight (Figure 12-9) is a web application framework that provides functionalities similar to those in Adobe Flash, integrating multimedia, graphics, animations and interactivity into a single runtime environment. Initially released as a video streaming plugin, later versions brought additional interactivity features and support for CLI languages and development tools. The current version 4 was released to developers on 12 April 2010, and the end-user runtime was released on 15 April 2010.

Chapter 12 Web Design

Figure 12-9 A Silverlight 1.0 application hosted in Internet Explorer. Interactivity is provided by Silverlight, but user input controls are HTML controls overlaid on top of Silverlight content.

It is compatible with multiple web browsers used on Microsoft Windows and Mac OS X operating systems. Mobile devices, starting with Windows Phone 7 and Symbian (Series 60) phones, are likely to become supported in 2010. A free software implementation named Moonlight, developed by Novell in cooperation with Microsoft, is available to bring most Silverlight functionality to Linux, FreeBSD and other open source platforms.

Silverlight (Figure 12-10) provides a retained mode graphics system similar to Windows Presentation Foundation, and integrates multimedia, graphics, animations and interactivity into a single runtime environment. In Silverlight applications, user interfaces are declared in Extensible Application Markup Language (XAML) and programmed using a subset of the .NET Framework. XAML can be used for marking up the vector graphics and animations. Silverlight can also be used to create Windows Sidebar gadgets for Windows Vista.

Silverlight supports Windows Media Video (WMV), Windows Media Audio (WMA) and MPEG Layer III (MP3) media content across all supported browsers without requiring Windows Media Player, the Windows Media Player ActiveX control or Windows Media browser plugins. Because

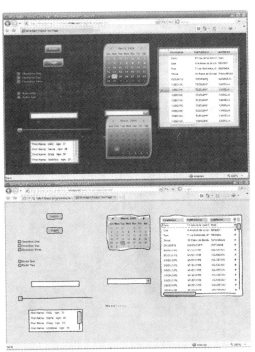

Figure 12-10 A set of Silverlight controls rendered with different skins.

Windows Media Video 9 is an implementation of the Society of Motion Picture and Television Engineers (SMPTE) VC-1 standard, Silverlight also supports VC-1 video, though still only in an Advanced Systems Format (ASF) container format. Furthermore, the Software license agreement says VC-1 is only licensed for the "personal and non-commercial use of a consumer". Silverlight, since version 3, supports the playback of H. 264 video. Silverlight makes it possible to dynamically load Extensible Markup Language (XML) content that can be manipulated through a Document Object Model (DOM) interface, a technique that is consistent with conventional Ajax techniques[6]. Silverlight exposes a Downloader object which can be used to download content, like scripts, media assets or other data, as may be required by the application. With version 2, the programming logic can be written in any .NET language, including some derivatives of common dynamic programming languages like IronRuby and IronPython.

Part 3 Tools for Web Design

Photoshop[①]

Adobe Photoshop is a graphics editing program developed and published by Adobe Systems.

Adobe's 2003 "Creative Suite" rebranding led to Adobe Photoshop 8's renaming to Adobe Photoshop CS. Thus, Adobe Photoshop CS5 is the 12th major release of Adobe Photoshop. The CS rebranding also resulted in Adobe offering numerous software packages containing multiple Adobe programs for a reduced price. There are two versions of Photoshop: Basic and Extended, with Extended having extra features available. Adobe Photoshop Extended is included in all of Adobe's Creative Suite offerings except Design Standard, which has the Basic version.

Features of Photoshop

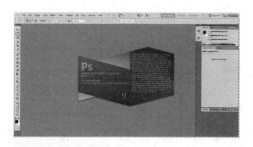

Figure 12-11 Adobe Photoshop CS 5 × 64 Running on Windows 7 ×64

Photoshop (Figure 12-11) has ties with other Adobe software for media editing, animation, and authoring. The .PSD (Photoshop Document), Photoshop's native format, stores an image with support for most imaging options available in Photoshop. These include layers with masks, color spaces, ICC profiles, transparency, text, alpha channels and spot colors, clipping paths, and duotone settings. This is in

---

① http://en.wikipedia.org/wiki/Adobe_Photoshop

contrast to many other file formats (e. g. .EPS or .GIF) that restrict content to provide streamlined, predictable functionality.

Photoshop's popularity means that the .PSD format is widely used, and it is supported to some extent by most competing software. The .PSD file format can be exported to and from Adobe Illustrator, Adobe Premiere Pro, and After Effects, to make professional standard DVDs and provide non-linear editing and special effects services, such as backgrounds, textures, and so on, for television, film, and the Web. Photoshop is a pixel-based image editor, unlike programs such as Macromedia FreeHand (now defunct), Adobe Illustrator, Inkscape or CorelDraw, which are vector-based image editors.

Photoshop uses color models RGB, lab, CMYK, grayscale, binary bitmap, and duotone. Photoshop has the ability to read and write raster and vector image formats such as .EPS, .PNG, .GIF, .JPEG, and Adobe Fireworks.

CS3

Smart Layers display the filter without altering the original image (here on Mac OS X).

New features propagating productivity include streamlined interface, improved Camera Raw, better control over print options, enhanced PDF support, and better management with Adobe Bridge. Editing tools new to CS3 are the Clone Source palette and nondestructive Smart Filters, and other features such as the brightness and contrast adjustment and Vanishing Point module were enhanced. The Black and White adjustment option improves control over manual grayscale conversions with a dialog box similar to that of Channel Mixer. Compositing is assisted with Photoshop's new Quick Selection and Refine Edge tools and improved image stitching technology.

CS3 Extended contains all features of CS3 plus tools for editing and importing some 3D graphics file formats, enhancing video, and comprehensive image analysis tools, utilizing MATLAB integration and DICOM file support.

CS4

Photoshop CS4 features a new 3D engine allowing painting directly on 3D models, wrapping 2D images around 3D shapes, converting gradient maps to 3D objects, adding depth to layers and text, getting print-quality output with the new ray-tracing rendering engine. It supports common 3D formats; the new Adjustment and Mask Panels; Content-aware scaling (seam carving); Fluid Canvas Rotation and File display options. On 30 April, Adobe released Photoshop CS4 Extended, which includes all the same features of Adobe Photoshop CS4 with the addition of capabilities for scientific imaging, 3D, and high end film and video users. The successor to Photoshop CS3, Photoshop CS4 is the first 64-bit Photoshop on consumer computers (only on Windows—the OS X version is still 32-bit only.)

CS5

Photoshop CS5 was launched on April 12, 2010. In a video posted on its official

Facebook page, the development team revealed the new technologies under development, including three dimensional brushes and warping tools.

A version of Adobe Photoshop CS5 Extended was used for a Prerelease Beta. A large group of selected Photoshop users were invited to beta test in Mid-February of 2010.

Adobe Dreamweaver[①]

Adobe Dreamweaver (formerly Macromedia Dreamweaver) is a web development application originally created by Macromedia, and is now developed by Adobe Systems, which acquired Macromedia in 2005.

Dreamweaver is available for both Mac and Windows operating systems. Recent versions have incorporated support for web technologies such as CSS, JavaScript, and various server-side scripting languages and frameworks including ASP, ColdFusion, and PHP.

Features of Adobe Dreamweaver

Dreamweaver allows users to preview websites in locally-installed web browsers. It provides transfer and synchronization features, the ability to find and replace lines of text or code by search terms and regular expressions across the entire site, and a templating feature that allows single-source update of shared code and layout across entire sites without server-side includes or scripting. The behavior panel also enables use of basic JavaScript without any coding knowledge, and integration with Adobe's Spry AJAX framework offers easy access to dynamically-generated content and interfaces.

Dreamweaver can use third-party "Extensions" to extend core functionality of the application, which any web developer can write (largely in HTML and JavaScript). Dreamweaver is supported by a large community of extension developers who make extensions available (both commercial and free) for most web development tasks from simple rollover effects to full-featured shopping carts.

Dreamweaver, like other HTML editors, edits files locally then uploads them to the remote web server using FTP, SFTP, or WebDAV. Dreamweaver CS4 now supports the Subversion (SVN) version control system (Figure 12-12).

---

① http://en.wikipedia.org/wiki/Adobe_Dreamweaver

Figure 12-12　Adobe Dreamweaver CS5 under Windows 7

Syntax highlighting

As of version 6, Dreamweaver supports syntax highlighting for the following languages out of the box:

- ActionScript
- Active Server Pages (ASP).
- ASP. NET (no longer supported as of version CS4-http://kb2. adobe. com/cps/402/kb402489. html)
- C#
- Cascading Style Sheets (CSS)
- ColdFusion
- EDML
- Extensible HyperText Markup Language (XHTML)
- Extensible Markup Language (XML)
- Extensible Stylesheet Language Transformations (XSLT)
- HyperText Markup Language (HTML)
- Java
- JavaScript
- JavaServer Pages (JSP)
- PHP: Hypertext Preprocessor (PHP)
- Visual Basic (VB)
- Visual Basic Script Edition (VBScript)
- Wireless Markup Language (WML)

It is also possible to add your own language syntax highlighting. In addition, code completion is available for many of these languages.

Adobe Fireworks[①]

Adobe Fireworks (formerly Macromedia Fireworks) (Figure 12-13) is a bitmap and vector graphics editor. It was originally developed, using parts of xRes, by Macromedia, which Adobe acquired in 2005, and aimed at web designers (with features such as: slices, the ability to add hotspots etc.) for rapidly creating website prototypes and application interfaces. It is designed to integrate easily with other former Macromedia products, such as Dreamweaver and Flash. It is available as a standalone product or bundled with Adobe Creative Suite. Previous versions were bundled with Macromedia Studio.

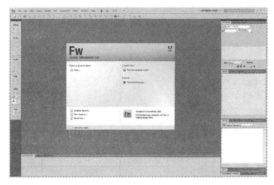

Figure 12-13   The Interface of Fireworks

Features and Functionalities

- Hierarchical Layers

Fireworks supports layering the graphic file. Deep child layers are also possible. All the layers can be accessed from the Layers panel.

- Smart Guides

When Smart Guides are enabled, dashed lines will appear as you use the Selection tool to drag any object around on the canvas. Smart Guides intuitively "line up" with any other element, so that you can visually see when two objects are aligned by their top, sides, bottom or center. Also by dragging out guide lines and pressing the Shift Key, numeric indicators display the distances between guides and the edges of the canvas. This feature was added with the release of CS4.

- 9 Slice scaling

This feature ensures that rounded rectangles maintain their roundness when transformed depending on where the guides are placed. CS4 has this feature exposed as a tool. With this feature introduction in CS3 version, its usage was limited to symbols.

---

① http://en.wikipedia.org/wiki/Adobe_Fireworks
http://www.vtc.com/products/AdobeFireworksCS4/GettingStarted/82412

- Symbols

Reusable elements can be converted into symbols and placed at multiple pages or on the same page. When the master symbol is edited, the changes are propagated to all the instances of that symbol automatically.

- Image Optimization

Fireworks was created specifically for web production and in terms of image compression, it is known to have a better compression rate than Photoshop with JPEG, PNG and GIF images.

- Adobe Creative Suite Integration

Fireworks understands the file formats ai, psd, eps, which designers use in a team allowing for better workflows across multiple Adobe applications.

- Export

A file can be exported as TIFF, flat PNG (8,24,32 bit), JPEG, GIF (both animated and non-animated), PSD, SWF, PICT, BMP, WBMP. The individual pages of a file can also be converted into a single PDF.

- States

Previously known as Frames, these are used for animation purposes. They are also used for defining the behaviors in cases of symbol buttons like Up, Down, Over.

Flash[1]

Adobe Flash (formerly Macromedia Flash) (Figure 12-14) is a multimedia platform used to add animation, video, and interactivity to Web pages. Flash is frequently used for advertisements and games. More recently, it has been positioned as a tool for "Rich Internet Applications" ("RIAs").

Figure 12-14 Adobe Flash CS5 Professional (11.0.0.485) under Windows 7

Flash manipulates vector and raster graphics to provide animation of text, drawings, and still images. It supports bidirectional streaming of audio and video, and it can capture user input via mouse, keyboard, microphone, and camera. Flash contains an Object-oriented

---

[1] http://en.wikipedia.org/wiki/Adobe_Flash

language called ActionScript.

Flash content may be displayed on various computer systems and devices, using Adobe Flash Player, which is available free of charge for common Web browsers, some mobile phones and a few other electronic devices (using Flash Lite).

Flash files are in the SWF format, traditionally called "ShockWave Flash" movies, "Flash movies," or "Flash games", usually have a .swf file extension, and may be used in the form of a Web-page plug-in, strictly "played" in a standalone Flash Player, or incorporated into a self-executing Projector movie (with the .exe extension in Microsoft Windows). Flash Video files[spec 1] have a .flv file extension and are either used from within .swf files or played through a flv-aware player, such as VLC, or QuickTime and Windows Media Player with external codecs added.

The use of vector graphics combined with program code allows Flash files to be smaller — and thus for streams to use less bandwidth — than the corresponding bitmaps or video clips. For content in a single format (such as just text, video, or audio), other alternatives may provide better performance and consume less CPU power than the corresponding Flash movie, for example when using transparency or making large screen updates such as photographic or text fades.

Over the releases of new versions of Flash, Macromedia has made Flash more and more controllable via programming, where they have it positioned as a competitor to HTML to build interactive web sites and applications such as an e-commerce store. Macromedia argues that Flash is the way to go instead of HTML because of the following reasons:

• Flash movies load faster and save on download time because Flash is vector based whereas HTML is not.

• Flash intelligently 'caches' it's movies so they don't have to be reloaded.

• Flash gives the user (the person viewing/using the Flash movie) a more responsive 'rich-client' like experience.

All of these points are true, but they can be true for HTML pages as well (except for the vectors). However, the opposite points are as follows:

Flash pages can be made to load faster, but most of the time, the way they are designed in the real world, they do not. That is not a Flash problem, it is more an issue of the Flash developers going nuts with fancy and heavy Flash movies. While HTML caches pages as well, once images are downloaded they are held in your browser's cache. The cached images are then used instead of downloading them from the server again. What's more, with new technology like ASP .net and Java Server Faces, HTML now can react just like a 'rich-client' application. Even without these new tools, properly designed HTML for most dynamic sites can provide a good user experience.

Part 4 Type and Application of Web[①]

There are many varieties of websites, each specializing in a particular type of content or use, and they may be arbitrarily classified in any number of ways. A few such classifications might include:

• Affiliate: enabled portal that renders not only its custom CMS but also syndicated content from other content providers for an agreed fee. There are usually three relationship tiers. Affiliate Agencies (e.g., Commission Junction), Advertisers (e.g., eBay) and consumer (e.g., Yahoo!).

• Archive site: used to preserve valuable electronic content threatened with extinction. Two examples are: Internet Archive, which since 1996 has preserved billions of old (and new) web pages; and Google Groups, which in early 2005 was archiving over 845,000,000 messages posted to Usenet news/discussion groups.

• Answer Site: Answer site is a site where people can ask questions & answer questions like Yahoo!

• Blog (web log): sites generally used to post online diaries which may include discussion forums (e.g., blogger, Xanga).

• Brand building site: a site with the purpose of creating an experience of a brand online. These sites usually do not sell anything, but focus on building the brand. Brand building sites are most common for low-value, high-volume fast moving consumer goods (FMCG).

• City Site: A site that shows information about a certain city or town and events that takes place in that town. Usually created by the city council or other "movers and shakers". The same as those of geographic entities, such as cities and countries. For example, Richmond.com is the geodomain for Richmond, Virginia.

• Community site: a site where persons with similar interests communicate with each other, usually by chat or message boards, such as MySpace or Facebook.

• Content site: sites whose business is the creation and distribution of original content (e.g., Slate, About.com).

• Corporate website: used to provide background information about a business, organization, or service.

• Electronic commerce (e-commerce) site: a site offering goods and services for online sale and enabling online transactions for such sales.

• Forum: a site where people discuss various topics.

---

① http://en.wikipedia.org/wiki/Website#Types_of_websites

• Gripe site: a site devoted to the critique of a person, place, corporation, government, or institution.

• Humor site: satirizes, parodies or otherwise exists solely to amuse.

• Information site: contains content that is intended to inform visitors, but not necessarily for commercial purposes, such as: RateMyProfessors.com, Free Internet Lexicon and Encyclopedia. Most government, educational and non-profit institutions have an informational site.

• Java applet site: contains software to run over the Web as a Web application.

• Mirror site: A complete reproduction of a website.

• Microblog: a short and simple form of blogging.

• News site: similar to an information site, but dedicated to dispensing news and commentary.

• Personal homepage: run by an individual or a small group (such as a family) that contains information or any content that the individual wishes to include. These are usually uploaded using a web hosting service such as Geocities.

• Phish site: a website created to fraudulently acquire sensitive information, such as passwords and credit card details, by masquerading as a trustworthy person or business (such as Social Security Administration, PayPal) in an electronic communication (see Phishing).

• Political site: A site on which people may voice political views.

• Porn site: A site that shows sexually explicit content for enjoyment and relaxation, most likely in the form of an Internet gallery, dating site, blog, social networking, or video sharing.

• Rating site: A site on which people can praise or disparage what is featured.

• Review site: A site on which people can post reviews for products or services.

• School site: a site on which teachers, students, or administrators can post information about current events at or involving their school. U.S. elementary-high school websites generally use k12 in the URL, such as kearney.k12.mo.us.

• Search engine site: a site that provides general information and is intended as a gateway or lookup for other sites. A pure example is Google, and well-known sites include Yahoo! Search and Bing (search engine).

• Shock site: includes images or other material that is intended to be offensive to most viewers (e.g. rotten.com).

• Social bookmarking site: a site where users share other content from the Internet and rate and comment on the content. StumbleUpon and Digg are examples.

• Social networking site: a site where users could communicate with one another and share media, such as pictures, videos, music, blogs, etc. with other users. These may include games and web applications.

• Video sharing: A site that enables user to upload videos, such as YouTube and Google Video.

- Warez: a site designed to host or link to materials such as music, movies and software for the user to download.
- Web portal: a site that provides a starting point or a gateway to other resources on the Internet or an intranet.
- Wiki site: a site which users collaboratively edit (such as Wikipedia and Wikihow).

Some websites may be included in one or more of these categories. For example, a business website may promote the business's products, but may also host informative documents, such as white papers. There are also numerous sub-categories to the ones listed above.

Websites are constrained by architectural limits (e.g., the computing power dedicated to the website). Very large websites, such as Yahoo!, Microsoft, and Google employ many servers and load balancing equipment such as Cisco Content Services Switches to distribute visitor loads over multiple computers at multiple locations.

New Words

semantic   *adj.* 〈语〉语义的；语义学的
equivalent   *n.* 同等物，等价物，相等物；*adj.* 相等的，相当的，同意义的，等效的
annotate   *vt. & vi.* 注解，注释
syntactical   *adj.* 依照句法的
manuscript   *n.* 手稿，原稿，底稿；*adj.* 手抄的，手写的
hierarchical   *adj.* 分等级的
aggregation   *n.* 集合，集合体，聚合
hybridisation   *n.* 〈主英〉杂交，杂种培植，配种
propagation   *n.* 繁殖，增殖，传导，传播；普及，散发，伸延
tactile   *adj.* 触觉的，触觉感知的
Pseudo   *adj.* 假的；虚伪的

Notes

[1] Web design is the skill of creating presentations of content (usually hypertext or hypermedia) that is delivered to an end-user through the World Wide Web, by way of a Web browser or other Web-enabled software like Internet television clients, microblogging clients and RSS readers.

译文：网页设计是通过万维网利用网页浏览器或其他能够浏览网页的软件如有网络功能的电视客户端软件、微博客户端和RSS阅读器等来呈现要传输给终端用户的内容（通常是超文本或超媒体技术）的一种技能。

- that is delivered to an end-user through the World Wide Web 是定语从句，用来修饰限定 content。
- by way of 通过，利用

[2] The intent of Web design is to create a website—a collection of electronic

documents and applications that reside on a Web server/servers and present content and interactive features/interfaces to the end user in form of Web pages once requested.

译文：网页设计的意图是建立一个网站——将电子文档和应用程序存储在网页服务器或服务器上，并且一旦终端用户发出请求则服务器会以网页的形式呈现内容和互动的专题或界面给用户。

* a collection of electronic documents and applications 是同位语，用来解释说明 a website。
* that reside on a Web server/servers and present content and interactive features/interfaces 是定语从句，用来修饰限定 electronic documents and applications。
* in form of 以……形式

[3] Client-side scripting generally refers to the class of computer programs on the web that are executed client-side, by the user's web browser, instead of server-side (on the web server).

译文：客户端描述语言通常是指网页上的计算机程序类，它们是利用用户的网页浏览器在客户端执行，而不是服务器端（不是在服务器网页上）执行。

* refer to 引用，指代，参考
* that are executed client-side 是定语从句，用来修饰限定 computer programs。
* instead of 代替；而不是；不……而……

[4] Because JavaScript is the only language that the most popular browsers share support for, it has become a target language for many frameworks in other languages, even though JavaScript was never intended to be such a language.

译文：因为 Java 描述语言是最流行的浏览器互相支持的唯一的一种语言，所以即使 Java 描述语言从来没有想要成为这样一种语言，与其他语言相比，它还是成为很多框架指定的语言。

* that the most popular browsers share support for 是定语从句，用来修饰限定 the only language
* even though 尽管，即使，纵然

[5] Digital databases are managed using database management systems, which store database contents, allowing data creation and maintenance, and search and other access.

译文：数字化的数据库是利用数据库管理系统来管理的，数据库管理系统中存储了数据内容，允许数据的创建、维护搜索以及其他方法。

* using database management systems 现在分词做伴随状语。
* which store database contents 是定语从句，用来修饰限定 database management systems。
* allowing data creation and maintenance, and search and other access 是现在分词做伴随状语。

[6] Silverlight makes it possible to dynamically load Extensible Markup Language (XML) content that can be manipulated through a Document Object Model (DOM) interface,

a technique that is consistent with conventional Ajax techniques.

译文：Silverlight 使动态装载可扩展标记语言内容成为可能,动态标记语言能通过与传统的 Ajax 技术一致的技术——文档对象模块界面来控制。

◆ makes it possible 使……成为可能

◆ that can be manipulated through a Document Object Model（DOM）interface 是定语从句,用来修饰限定 Extensible Markup Language（XML）content。

◆ that is consistent with conventional Ajax techniques 是定语从句,用来修饰限定 a technique。

Selected Translation

Part 1

网页设计概述

网页设计

网页设计是通过万维网利用网页浏览器或其他能够浏览网页的软件如有网络功能的电视客户端软件、微博客户端和 RSS 阅读器等来呈现要传输给终端用户的内容（通常是超文本或超媒体技术）的一种技能。网页设计的意图是建立一个网站——将电子文档和应用程序存储在网页服务器或服务器上,并且一旦终端用户发出请求则服务器会以网页的形式呈现内容和互动的专题或界面给用户。像文本、位图图像(GIF 图像、JPEG 文件)和表格等元素可使用 HTML／XHTML／的 XML 标签放置在网页中,而要显示更复杂的媒体(如矢量图形、动画、视频、音频等)需要利用插件(如 Adobe Flash、QuickTime、Java 运行环境等插件)。插件也使用 HTML／XHTML 标签嵌入到网页中。

浏览器的改进与 W3C 的标准促进了 XHTML／XML 的广泛的接受与使用,它与层叠样式表(CSS)的同时使用能更好地定位和操作网页内容和对象。网页通常被归类为静态或动态网页两大类。

• 静态页面不会根据要求来改变内容和布局,除非一个人(网站管理员/程序员)手动更新页面。一个简单的 HTML 网页就是静态网页。

• 动态网页会依据终端用户的输入/交互来调整其内容和(/或)外观。用户可以在客户端(终端用户的计算机)利用客户端脚本语言(JavaScript、JScript、Actionscript 等)来改变 DOM 元素(DHTML),从而网页内容就可以发生变化。动态内容通常是服务器端脚本语言(Perl、PHP、ASP、JSP、ColdFusion,等等)在服务器端进行编译。这两种方法通常在复杂的应用中使用。

网页设计是一种平面设计,它的目的就是为了在互联网信息环境中形成并风格化物体,从而呈现它们高端的消费特征和美学特性。已有的定义将网络编程和网页设计区分开来,强调了网站的功能特征,并将网页设计定位为一类平面设计。

设计网页、网站、网络应用程序或用于 Web 的多媒体的过程可以利用多种形式,例如动画、平面设计、人机交互、信息架构、交互设计、市场营销、摄影、搜索引擎优化和排版等。网页和网站可以是静态页面,我们也可以编程使其成为自动根据各种因素如终端用户的输入、网络管理员或计算环境的变化（如该网站的相关数据库已被修改）等调整内容或外观的动态网页。

可被访问的网页设计

要使网页和网站更易于被访问，它们必须符合一定的访问原则。当谈到网页内容时，这些原则被称为网站内容可访问指导方针，其可以归纳为以下几个主要方面。

- 使用语义标记，它能为文档提供有意义的结构（即网页）；
- 语义标记也指语义地组织网页结构并因此发布 Web 服务的描述，以便它们能够被不同网页上的其他网络服务识别。语义 Web 标准是由 IEEE 规定的；
- 使用一个有效的符合已发布的 DTD 或模式的标记语言；
- 为任何非文字部分的内容（如图片、多媒体）提供文本描述；
- 为避免断章取义使用合理超链接（例如避免"点击这里"）；
- 不要使用框架；
- 使用 CSS 而不是 HTML 表格进行布局。
- 编著页面，这样当由用户代理（如屏幕阅读器）一行一行地读取的源代码时仍然可以理解。（使用表格进行设计往往会造成信息错乱）

然而，W3C 中有一种例外，那就是当是线性的或者候补版本是可访问的时候，使用表格进行布局也是可以的。网站的可访问性也在发生变化，因为它是受内容管理系统影响的，内容管理系统允许在没有获得编程语言知识的情况下来改变网页。非常重要的是，Web 开发和互动的几个不同的组成部分可以共同合作，从而使得身体不方便的人也容易访问网页。这些组成部分包括：

- 内容——Web 页面的信息或 Web 应用程序，包括：
  ➢ 信息，如文本、图像和声音；
  ➢ 定义结构和呈现方式等的代码或标记；
- Web 浏览器、媒体播放器和其他"用户代理"；
- 某些情况下的辅助技术—— 屏幕阅读器、替代键盘、开关、扫描软件等；
- 用户的知识、经验以及某些情况下使用网络自适应策略；
- 开发者——设计师、程序员、制作者等，包括残疾开发者和提供内容的用户；
- 制作工具软件——创建网站的软件；
- 评估工具——网页可获取性评估工具，如网页校验器、CSS 校验器等。

网页设计

网页设计（在某些方面）与传统的印刷出版相似。每一个网站是一个信息陈列容器，就像一本书是一个容器，每个网页就像书中的一页。然而，网页设计采用基于数字编码和显示技术的框架来构建和保持一种环境，从而用多种版式来分布信息。若发挥其最大潜能，网页设计无疑是支持当今世界交流沟通的最先进和日益复杂的方法。

对于特定的网站，设计的基本方面主要有：

- 内容：网站上的信息应是与网站相关的，并应针对该网站所指向的对象所需要的方面。
- 易用性：网站应具有用户友好的界面，并且导航简单和合理。

- 外观:图形和文本应该包括统一的风格,整个网站的图形和文本都一致,以显示网站的一致性。网站类型应该是专业的、有吸引力的和相关的。
- 能见度:网站还必须容易找到,应能通过主要的(并不是所有的)搜索引擎和广告媒体找到。

一个网站通常包括文字和图像。网站的第一页通常称为主页或索引。有些网站还使用了欢迎页面(通俗点说就是鼓吹页面)。欢迎页面可能包括欢迎信息、语言或声明。网站的每一个网页都是一个 HTML 文件,都有自己的网址。每次创建网页后,它们通常利用有超链接的导航菜单连接在一起。更快的浏览速度会导致较短的注意广度和更多的在线访客,这也减少了欢迎页面的使用,也是商业网站非常在意的。

一旦网站建成后,它必须发布或上载,以便公众可以通过互联网进行浏览。这可以通过使用 FTP 客户端来完成。一旦发布后,网站管理员可以使用各种技巧来增加网站获得的浏览数或访问量。增加浏览数或访问量的方法包括将网站与谷歌、雅虎等搜索引擎相链接,与其他网站相互链接,与其他类似的网站相连等。

多学科要求

网页设计跨越多个信息系统、信息技术和通信设计的多个学科。网站是一个信息系统,其有时分类为前台和后台。可视的内容(如页面布局、用户界面、图形、文字、声音)被称为前台。后台包括源代码、无形的脚本功能以及处理前台输出的服务器端的组织和性能。根据一个网页开发项目的规模,网站可能是一个具有多种技能的个人(有时称为网站主人)创建,或在一个项目经理监督下具有专门技能的小组成员协同设计。

问题

由于其本身的性质,网页设计会发生冲突,涉及严格的技术一致性和个人创作的平衡。技术的迅速变化使得获得和调配适当的资源变得更复杂了。

形式与功能

一个网页开发人员可能更加注意网页的外观如何,而忽略诸如复制和搜索引擎优化功能,如文本的可读性、网页导航的排列,或访客怎么才能更容易找到该网站等。因此,设计者之间最终会产生争端,可能一些设计者想要以关键字丰富的文字和文字链接为代价而排列更多的装饰图形符号。在许多案例中形式服从功能。因为某些图形除了有美学的作用还有沟通的目的,一个网站运行得怎么样,取决于图形设计理念以及专业写作的考虑。

当使用很多图形时,网页会加载得很慢,常常会令用户不快。这已经不再成为一个问题,因为互联网已经变成了高速互联网,而且使用了向量图形。但是仍然有一个持续的增加带宽的工程挑战,以及尽量减少图形文件的数量和大小的艺术挑战。这一挑战变得更加复杂,因为带宽的增加又鼓励了更多的较大的图形。

当面对一个大型数据库和许多要求,设计小组可能会抛出一个服务器难以承受的太多的信息让服务器来管理。可能需要替代技术或额外的结构(甚至另一台服务器或网站)以适应其需求。

布局

布局是指在显示设备上内容的尺寸以及与内容相关的媒体数据流的传送。网页设计布局即可视的内容框架:这些框架可以是固定的,或者它们可以用比例尺寸提供动态布局。有许多的测量单位,但这里有一些流行的尺寸样式:

- 像素测量的结果是固定或静态的内容;
- 内容比例电磁测量的结果是与字体有关的比例内容;
- 流体含量百分比测量的结果是缩小或增长到"适合"显示窗口的动态内容。

比例、动态和混合布局也被称为动态设计。混合布局采用单个页面中任何固定的、比例的或动态元素(或指向)的组合。这种混合网页设计框架是由 W3C 规定的数字互联网公约而制定的。如果任何布局没有出现,很可能它不符合标准的设计原则,或者说这些标准与标准布局元素相冲突。目前关于标准的知识对有效的混合设计是必不可少的。

混合设计包括大多数静态内容的控制,但是适合于文字出版、读者浏览以及传统(印刷)显示。混合式布局更容易观看,并且可以在大多数发布传统图片和文字的网站上见到。对于某些网站,混合设计让毫无生机的文字排列变得让人觉得更温暖和更平衡。

设备

在网络上,设计师在某些因素上是没有控制权的,包括浏览器窗口大小、使用的网页浏览器、使用的输入设备(操作系统、鼠标、触摸屏、语音命令、文本、电传、手机,等等),用户在他们设备上可用的(安装的)和喜欢的字体大小、设计和其他的特征。网站设计者努力学习并在消除设备竞争和软件的标记方面非常精通,以便网页显示是按照他们编码的方式来显示的。

Exercises

1. What is web design? And what's the intent of web design?
2. What is the markup language? What markup languages do we usually use in designing the web?
3. According to part 4, what areas can the web be applied in?

应用文写作

一、信函

(一)信函的基本原则和种类

一直以来,信函都是人们交际的一种重要的手段,即使在通信技术高度发达的今天,信函在社会交际和商业事务中仍然扮演着非常重要的作用,这是其他交际形式所无法取代的。信函具有独特的结构、格式和一些惯用的表达方式,掌握这些特点是十分重要的。信函的侧重点在于传递信息、表达情感,它要求内容简明扼要、条理清楚、表意准确、礼貌适度。随着时代的发展,写信的原则(Writing Principles)已从最原始的 3 个"C":Conciseness(简洁)、Clearness(清晰)、Courtesy(礼貌),发展到 5 个"C": Clearness(清晰)、Conciseness(简洁)、Correctness(正确)、Courtesy(礼貌)、Consideration(周到),继而到现在的 7 个"C",它在"5C"的基础上又增加了 Completeness(完整)和 Concreteness(具体)。

具体来说,信函可以分为商业信函或公函(Business Letter or Official Correspondence)和个人信函(Private Letter)两种。商业信函一般谈论或处理重要事物,可以是推荐信、邀请信或者询问、答复某事。个人信函一般比较随意,只需要满足以上的"5C"原则即可,我们在后面也将会以实例进行讲解。而对于商业信函,在此基础上我们还需要加上"完整"和"具体"这两个要求,因为商业信函精确的特点决定了它必须"完整"和"具体",完整而具体的书信更能达到预期的目的;更有助于建立友善的关系;还可以避免不必要的麻烦。

(二)信封的写法

1. 邮票应该贴在信封右上角。
2. 寄信人的姓名、地址应该写在信封的左上角。
3. 收信人的姓名、地址应该写在信封的正中或右下角四分之一处。
4. 也有人喜欢把收件人的名字、地址写在信封正面中央,把寄件人的姓名、地址写在信封的反面。
5. 如果信是由第三者转交给收信人,则要在收信人姓名下面写明转交人的姓名,其前加(C/O = Care Of)。
6. 住址的写法与中文相反;英文住址原则上是由小至大,如必须先写门牌号码、街路名称,再写城市、省(州)和邮政区号,最后一行则写上国家的名称。

(三)信函的组成部分和格式

英语书信通常包括下面几个组成部分:信内地址、称呼、开头语、正文、结束语、签名、附件等。我们逐一来介绍。

1. 信内地址(Inside Address, Introductory Address)

信内地址指收信人的姓名和地址,写在信纸的左上角,从信纸的左边顶格开始写,低于写信人地址和发信日期一两行,也分并列式和斜列式两种,但应与信端(即信头)的书写格式保持一致。其次序是,先写收信人姓名、头衔和单位名称,占一两行,然后写地址,可占二至四行,例如:

(1)并列式

Ms. Zhang

Wuhan University

Hongshan District, 430022

Wuhan

China

(2)斜列式

Ms. Zhang

  Wuhan University

    Hongshan District, 430022

      Wuhan

        China

2. 称呼(Salutation)

称呼是收信人展开信后最先看到的文字,所以称呼很有讲究。对收信人的称呼一般自成一行,写在低于信内地址一两行的地方,从信纸的左边顶格开始写,每个词的开头字母要大写,末尾处的符号,英国人用逗号,但美国和加拿大英语则多用冒号。称呼用语可视写信人与收信人的关系而定。

常用的收信人称呼有:Mr. 先生(男人);Mrs. 夫人(已婚);Miss 小姐(未婚);Ms. 夫人、小姐统称;Mr. and Mrs. 夫妇俩人。

3. 开头语(Initial Sentences)

开头语一般是一些寒暄语,用来引出正文。可以表示对对方的真挚的问候,也可以是表示对对方来信的感谢,还可以是对对方的想念之情。一些常用的开头语有:

- Many thanks for your last kind letter.
- I hope everything goes well.
- I miss you so much that...
- I beg to inform you that...
- I have the pleasure to tell you that...
- I regret to inform you that...
- I feel indebted for the kind note which you sent me on Saturday.
- I am going to answer your letter immediately and with pleasure.
- I am sorry that I have delayed answering your letter of recent date.

4. 信的正文(Body of the Letter)

信的正文每段第一行应往右缩进约四五个字母。在写事务性信件时,正文一般开门见山,内容简单明了,条理清楚,易读,语气要自然诚恳。在写私人信件时,信写好之后若有什么遗漏,可用 P. S. 表示补叙。

5. 结束语(Complimentary Close)

结束语是指写信人的结尾套语。结束语一般低于正文一二行,可写在左边,也可以从信纸的中间或偏右的地方开始写。第一个词的开头字母要大写,末尾用逗号。结束语视写信人与收信人的关系而定,例如写给机关、团体或不相识的人的信,一般用:Yours (very) truly、Yours (very) sincerely、Yours (very) respectfully、Yours appreciatively、Comradely yours,等等。

在欧洲一些国家里,多把 Yours 放在 sincerely 等词的前面。在美国和加拿大等国,则多把 yours 放在 Sincerely 等词之后。Yours 一词有时也可省略。

6. 签名(Signature)

信末的签名一般低于结束语一二行,从信纸中间偏右的地方开始写。若写信人是女性,与收信人又不相识,则一般在署名前用括号注上 Miss、Mrs. 或 Ms.,以便对方回信时知道如何称呼。

7. 附件(Enclosure)

信件若有附件,应在左下角注明 Encls. 或 Enc.。若附件不止一个,则应写出 2(或 3、4、5 等)Encls.,例如:

Enc.: Resume

Encls.: Grade Certificate

（四）范例

1. 祝贺信

在国际交往中，祝贺信使用场合很多。国家之间、团体之间以及个人之间常对一些值得庆祝的大事互致祝贺，这也是增进国家之间的关系、加强个人的友谊的一种方式。这类书信也有正式的和普通的两种。正式的祝贺主要用于政府间、官员间，普通的祝贺则多用于个人交往。前者用词拘谨，经常使用一些套语，后者用词亲切，不拘格式，但也有些常用的词句。

（1）祝贺新年

Your Excellency Mr. Ambassador,

On the occasion of New Year, may my wife and I extend to you and your wife our sincere greetings, wishing you a happy New Year, your career success and your family happiness.

Minister of Foreign Affairs

（2）祝贺信常用套语

- On the occasion of..., I wish to extend to you our warm congratulation on behalf of... and in my own name.

值此……之际，我代表……，并以我个人的名义，向你致以热烈祝贺。

- As..., may I, on behalf of the Chinese people and Government, express to you and through you to the people and Government of your country the heartiest congratulations.

当……之时，我代表中国人民和政府，向你并通过你向你们的人民和政府表示衷心的祝贺。

- May the friendly relations and co-operation between China and Japan develop daily.

祝愿中日两国友好合作关系日益发展。

- May your session be a complete success.

祝大会圆满成功。

2. 感谢信

感谢信在国际交往中是一种很常见的书信形式。按照西方的惯例，当收到邀请、接待、收到祝贺、慰问、接受礼品、帮助等，都应该写信致谢，以示礼貌。感谢信没有固定格式。语言要求诚恳、适当，不宜过长。

（1）感谢招待

Dear Minister,

I am writing this letter to thank you for you warm hospitality accorded to me and my delegation during our recent visit to your beautiful country. I would also like to thank you for your interesting discussion with me which I have found very informative and useful.

During the entire visit, my delegation and I were overwhelmed by the enthusiasm expressed by your business representatives on cooperation with China. I sincerely hope we could have more exchanges like this one when we would be able to continue our interesting discussion on possible ways to expand our bilateral economic and trade relations and bring our business people together.

I am looking forward to your early visit to China when I will be able to pay back some of the hospitality I received during my memorable stay in your beautiful country. With kind personal regards。

Faithfully yours,
Chao Cai
Minister of Economic Cooperation

（2）感谢讲学

Dear Mr. Brown

I am writing on behalf of all members of our department to say how much we all enjoyed your excellent lecture on Tuesday. We have learned a lot about the changes in present-day Information Technology and are very grateful to you for coming to our university and giving us such an interesting and informative talk.

Thank you very much and we look forward to hearing you again.

Yours sincerely,

（3）用于各种场合的感谢语

- I can't sufficiently express my thanks for your thoughtful kindness.

对你给予我们的无微不至的关怀,我难以充分表达我的谢意。

- This is to thank you again for your wonderful hospitality.

再次感谢你的盛情款待。

- We acknowledge with gratitude your message of good wishes.

感谢你的良好的祝愿。

- Many thanks for the fine desk lamp that you send me, and I feel deeply moved by this token of your affection.

非常感谢你送给我的精致的台灯。这一友情的象征,使我深受感动。

3. 投诉信

投诉信一般是用来向被投诉单位的领导或者负责人提出交易过程中出现的失误,可能是服务的质量问题、态度问题,还有可能是所需商品没有及时达到,或者数量上或者质量上存在问题。这个时候,我们可以写一封投诉信,向对方的负责人说明情况。

Dear Sir/Madam：

I am writing to you to complain about your hotel. I had a terrible stay in room 3008 of your hotel from the 4th to the 16th of August 2006, when I came to Guangzhou on business.

Firstly, the air-conditioning in my room could not be turned down or switched off. When I asked the reception staff to do something about it, they laughed and told me it was better than being hot. I asked your front of house manager and she told me she would send someone to my room immediately. No one came. As a result, I was very cold every time I was in the room.

Secondly, I found the bathroom dirty and the hot water was always warm.

Thirdly, the noise at night was extremely loud and I found it difficult to sleep. I asked to change rooms, but was told it was impossible because the hotel was full.

I paid a lot for my stay in your hotel and expect much better service from such a well-known hotel. In future, I will not be staying at your hotel again and will inform my business associates of the terrible service. Wish your service can be improved.

4. 道歉信

在日常生活中难免会出现一些差错,因为失约、损坏了别人的东西等。在这种情况下,应及时写信表示道歉,以消除不必要的误会。写道歉信时应注意态度要诚恳,原委要解释清楚、措辞要委婉。

来看一个因未能及时还书致歉的例子。

Dear Miss Liu:

Excuse me for my long delaying in return to you your *Robinson Crusoe* which I read through with great interest. I had finished reading the book and was about to return it when my cousin came to see me. Never having seen the book, she was so interested in it that I had to retain it longer. However, I hope that in view of the additional delight thus afforded by your book, you will overlook my negligence in not returning it sooner.

Thank you again for the loan.

Sincerely yours,

* * * * * * * *

5. 申请信

申请信的篇幅一般不超过一页,其语气必须诚恳。申请信的正文一般由三至四个段落组成,内容大致如下:

(1) 说明向某单位申请工作的理由,例如见广告应征、熟人介绍、本人专业与该单位业务对口等。

(2) 概括本人经历和特长,表明自己能够胜任此项工作。

(3) 希望聘方积极考虑和尽早答复;按西方惯例,录用前,聘方对申请人进行面试(interview),因此,申请信经常以要求安排面试结尾。

我们来看一个申请任汉语教师的例子。

Dear Dr Smith:

Mr. Liu Yang who has just returned to China from your university informed me that you are considering the possibility of offering a Chinese language course to your students in the next academic year and may have an opening for a teacher of the Chinese language. I'm very much interested in such a position.

I have been teaching Chinese literature and composition at college level since 2000. In the past six years, I have worked in summer programs, teaching the Chinese language and culture to students from English speaking countries. As a result, I have got to know well the common problems of these students and how to adapt teaching to achieve the best results.

With years of intensive English training, I have no difficulty conducting classed in English and feel quite comfortable working with American students.

I will be available after July 2006. Please feel free to contact me if you wish more information. Thank you very much for your consideration and I look forward to hearing from you.

Sincerely yours,
Liu Wei

二、简历

简历是我们打开人生之门的钥匙,现在社会的竞争日益激烈,在求职的过程中,简历的重要性不言而喻。

(一) 英文简历的组成及常见的类型

1. 简历的组成部分和内容

简历是针对自己想应聘的工作把求职意向、经验、个人情况等简要地列举出来,以达到向雇主推销自己的目的,所以在简历中,应该突出自己的强项。一般来说,简历可以由以下几部分组成:

- 姓名、地址、电话(Name, Address, Telephone Number)
- 个人资料(Personal data)
- 求职目标和资格(Objective and Qualifications)
- 经历(Work Experience)
- 学历(Education)
- 著作/专利(Publications or Patents)
- 外语技能(Foreign Languages Skills)
- 特别技能(Special Skills)
- 课外活动/社会活动(Extracurricular Activities or Social Activities)
- 业余爱好/兴趣(Hobbies or Interests)
- 证明材料(References)

以上各项不需要全部列举。一般而言,各项内容根据个人的具体情况或应聘的职位而定。

2. 常见的英文简历类型

个人简历没有固定的格式,应聘者可以根据个人情况,对简历的某些方面有所侧重。例如,对于即将毕业的学生或工作经验很短的人而言,简历可以以学历为主;对于工作经历丰富的人来说,工作经历和工作成绩是简历的亮点。按照简历的不同侧重点,我们把简历分为四类。

(1) 以学历为主的简历

以学历为主的简历的重点是学习经历,适合于即将毕业的学生或有很短工作经历的人。它一般包括以下几项内容:

- 个人资料

- 学历(Education):一般从最高学历写起,写出就读学校的名称、所获学位、所学专业、各阶段学习的起止时间、与应聘职位相关的课程以及成绩、所获得的奖励(如奖学金、优秀学生称号)等。
- 兼职
- 特别技能
- 兴趣爱好

(2)以经历为主的简历

有工作经验的应聘人写简历时可以侧重自己的工作经历,把和应聘工作有关的经历和业绩写出来。此类简历主要包括以下几项内容:

- 个人资料
- 求职目标
- 工作经历(Work Experience):按照时间顺序列出所工作单位的名称、负责的工作、工作业绩等,最好是工作的创新点和收获是可以重点写的内容。
- 特别技能

(3)以技能、业绩或工作性质为中心的简历

此类简历主要是强调应聘人的技能和工作业绩,即以所取得的成绩或具备的技能等来概括工作经历,即把成绩和技能先行列出,不再是将工作经历按照时间顺序一一列出,工作经历在最后可简单地提及。

(4)综合性简历

这是以上第三种和第四种简历的综合,既要突出技能与业绩,也要把工作经历列出。所以简历的书写不能一概而论,可以根据自身的情况做出选择。

(二)英文简历常用词汇与句型

1. 常用词汇

(1)个人情况

Name(姓名),Sex(性别),Male(男),Female(女),Height(身高),Birth(出生),Birth date(出生日期),Born(生于),Province(省),City(市),Street(街),Road(路),District(区),Citizenship(国籍),Address(地址),Postal code(邮政编码),Home phone(住宅电话)。

(2)学历

Education(学历),Curriculum(课程),Major(主修、主课、专业),Minor(选修、辅修),Courses Taken(所学课程),Part-Time Job(业余工作、兼职),Professor(教授),Summer Jobs(暑期工作),Vacation(假期工作),Social Activities(社会活动),Rewards(奖励),Scholarship(奖学金),Semester[学期(美)],Term[学期(英)],President(校长),Vice-president(副校长),Abroad Student(留学生),Master(硕士),Department Chairman(系主任),Guest Professor(客座教授),Teaching Assistant(助教),Doctor(博士),Bachelor(学士)。

(3)经历

Achievements(业绩),Earn(获得、赚取),Cost(成本、费用),Effect(效果、作用),

Direct(指导), Assist(辅助), Guide(指导、操纵), Accomplish[完成(任务等)], Create(创造), Launch[开办(新企业)], Lead(领导), Manage(管理、经营), Analyze(分析), Profit(利润), Manufacture(制造), Reinforce(加强), Spread(传播、扩大), Motivate(促动), Mastered(精通的激发), Negotiate(谈判)。

(4) 其他

Hobbies(业余爱好), Fishing(钓鱼), Boating(划船), Golf(高尔夫球), Oil painting(油画), Skiing(滑雪), Interests(兴趣、爱好), Skating(滑冰), Boxing(拳击), Writing(写作), Jogging(慢跑), Traveling(旅游), Dancing(跳舞), Cooking(烹饪), Collecting Stamps(集邮), Swimming(游泳)。

2．实用句型举例

(1) 求职目标

• A responsible administrative position that will provide challenge where I can use my creativity and initiative.

负责行政事务的、具有挑战性、能发挥创造力与开拓精神的职位

• A position as an editor that will enable me to use my knowledge of editing.

能发挥所学编辑知识的编辑之职

• A position as a Chinese language instructor at college or university level.

大学汉语讲师之职

• Editor of a publishing company.

出版公司的编辑

• To apply my accounting experience in a position offering variety of assignments and challenges with opportunity of advance.

申请能提供各种机遇、挑战、提升机会以及能发挥本人在财会方面经验的职位

• Seeking a teaching position where my expertise in American literature will be employed.

能运用我在美国文学方面专业知识的教师职位

• To offer my training in business administration in a job leading to a position of senior executive.

能运用我在商业管理方面知识的职位,最终目标是高级主管

• To devote my talent in computer science as a computer engineer to a position with growth potential to a computer systems manager.

发挥我在电脑方面才能的电脑工程师之职,并有晋升为电脑系统部经理的机会

• To employ my professional training in the area of electronics engineering.

能运用我在电子方面专业知识的职位

• To begin as a system analyst and eventually become a technical controller.

从系统分析员开始,最终成为技术管理人员

• An administrative secretarial position where communication skills and a pleasant attitude toward people will be assets.

寻求行政秘书之职位,且用得上交际技巧和与人为善的态度为好
(2) 学历及所学课程
- Major courses contributing to management qualifications:

对管理资格有帮助的主要课程:
- Among the pertinent courses I have taken are...

所学的有关课程是……
- Courses taken that will be useful for secretarial work:

所学的对秘书工作有用的课程:
- Academic preparation for electronics engineering:

电子工程方面的专业课程:
- Completed four years of technical training courses at college:

完成大学4年的技术培训课程:
- Specialized courses pertaining to foreign trade:

与外贸有关的专业课程:
- To fulfill the plan for continued study in the field of computer science, I have completed the following courses:

为完成在计算机方面的继续深造的计划,已完成以下课程:
- Following college graduation, I have taken courses in English at Peking University as part of self-improvement program.

大学毕业后,作为进修计划的一部分,已完成北京大学的以下英语课程:
(3) 经历
- Engineering sales specialist, responsible for petroleum sales and technical support to the industrial and commercial industries of the Boston metropolitan area.

工程销售专家,负责推销石油并向波士顿市区内工业及商业性工业提供技术援助。
- Sales manager. In addition to ordinary sales activities and management of department, responsible for recruiting and training of sales staff members.

销售部经理,除正常销售活动和部门管理之外,还负责招聘与训练销售人员。
- Computer Programmer. Operate flow-charts, collect business information for management, update methods of operation.

电脑程序员,管理流程表,收集管理商务信息,掌握最新的操作方法。
- As a senior market researcher, responsible for collection and analysis of business information of interest to foreign business offices stationed in the Building.

高级市场研究员,负责收集和分析住在大厦内的外国商务办事处的商业信息。
(三) 英文简历范例

对于已经有工作经验的人来说,我们可以参考以下的范例:

1. 电子工程师

BACKGROUND:

Over Eight years of extensive electronics experience. Versed in both digital and analog electronics with specific emphasis on computer hardware/software. Special expertise in designing embedded system. Proficient in VHDL and C# programming languages. Excellent in PCB.

WORK EXPERIENCE:

51-singlechip Systems, Shanghai, China, 1997-1999

Sales Engineer, 1999-2000

Responsible for the characterization and evaluation of, and approved vendors list for: Power supplies, oscillators, crystals, and programmable logic used in desktop and laptop computers. Evaluated and recommended quality components that increased product profitability. Interacted with vendors to resolve problems associated with components qualification. Technical advisor for Purchasing.

Design Evaluation Engineer, 2000-2003

Evaluated new computer product designs, solving environmental problems on prototype computers. Conducted systems analysis on new computer products to ensure hardware, software and mechanical design integrity.

Assistant Engineer, 2003-2005

Performed extensive hardware evaluation in prototype computers, tested prototype units for timing violation using the latest state-of-the-art test equipment, digital oscilloscopes and logic analyzers. Performed environmental, ESD and acoustic testing. Designed and built a power-up test used to test prototype computers during cold boot.

EDUCATION:

Bachelor of Science in Electrical Engineering

— Peking University, 1997

Job descriptions:

Work that is related to the analyzing, designing and evaluation of the embedded system.

2. 市场营销员

Chinese Name: Wei Zhang

English Name: Andy

Sex: Male

Born: 7/18/82

University: Tsinghua University

Major: Marketing

Address: 110#, Tsinghua University

Telephone: 1356 * * * *321

Email: * * * *@yahoo.com.cn

Job Objective:

A Position offering challenge and responsibility in the realm of consumer affairs or marketing.

Education:

2002-2006   Tsinghua University, College Of Commerce

Graduating in July with a B.S. degree in Marketing.

Fields of study include: psychology, economics, marketing, business law, statistics, calculus, sociology, product policy, social and managerial concepts in marketing, marketing strategies, consumer behavior, sales force management, marketing research and forecast.

1999-2002   The No.2 Middle School of Beijing.

Social Activities:

2000-2002   Class monitor.

2003-2005   Chairman of the Student Union.

Summer Jobs:

2004 Administrative Assistant in Sales Department of Beijing Samsung Company. Responsible for selling, correspondence, expense reports, record keeping, inventory catalog.

Hobbies:

Swimming, Internet-surfing, music, travel.

English Proficiency:

College English Test-Band Six.

Computer Skills:

Dream weaver, Flash, Adobe Photoshop, AutoCAD, Microsoft office, etc.

References will be furnished upon request.

三、求职信

（一）求职信的内容和技术要求

1. 求职信的特点

求职信（Application letter）属于商业信件，因此文体及格式要正式；语言要简洁、客观、明了；表达要准确；语气要客气。

（1）正式的文体及格式

求职信的文体及格式要正式，这表明求职者的尊重和礼貌，也反映求职人的性格和办事作风。如果求职信写得很随便，会让读信人认为求职者不重视此事或给人马马虎虎的感觉。

（2）简洁、客观、明了的语言

求职人要以客观、实事求是的态度、运用简练的语言把事情表达清楚；要做到主题突出、层次分明、言简意赅。表达要直接，不可绕圈子。此外，不要提与主题不相关的事；在说明个人经历或能力时，要说出具体的业绩，不可笼统概括。

（3）准确的表达

表达不要模棱两可，不可过多使用形容词和副词。要避免生僻的词。对有疑问的词语，要多请教他人或词典。

（4）客气的语气

话语要礼貌，充满自信。既要表现出对对方的尊重，又不要表现得过分热情或恭维。

2. 求职信的内容

一般来说，求职信包括以下四个方面的内容：(1) 你得知这份工作的渠道。(2) 学历及经历的概要。(3) 你的个性以及能力。(4) 联络地点、联络方式，以及最后的感谢语等，可以发挥创意的空间非常大。求职信在于延续履历表的内容，更清楚地表现工作企图心、个性、特质等。

3. 写英文求职信要点

（1）篇幅不易过长，简短为好；态度诚恳，不需华丽词汇；让对方感觉亲切、自信、实在即可。

（2）纸张的选用：建议你用黄褐色或米色纸作最终打印信纸，象牙色也是可以接受的；灰色或任何其他颜色的信纸因缺乏对比度不易看清最好不用。当然还应该注意要配合信封的颜色。

（3）书写：字体要写得整洁可辨，使用打字机把信打出来，显得有专业感。98%的求职信和简历都是用黑墨打印在白纸上的。

（4）附邮票：英语求职信内需附加邮票或回址信封。这会给别人的回信带来方便，而且也会让别人感受到你的真心。

（5）语法：准确无误的语法和拼写使读信人感到舒畅。错误的语法或拼写则十分明显，一目了然。千万不要把收信人的姓名或公司地址拼错。

（6）标点：正确的使用标点符号可以更好地表达自己的意愿。这里也有一些要注意的：

• 标题中除冠词(a、an、the)外每一个字都要大写，4个字母以下的介词(of、in)等不大写，第一个单词始终要大写。

I have read Gone With the Wind.

• 书籍和杂志用斜体或下划线表示：

The business Women

• 所有商标一律大写：

Coca Cola

• 家庭成员的称呼在不用名字时大写：

When I have problems with my homework, I always turn to Brother.

I cried, "Father, help me!"

• 带名字称呼其他亲属时要大写：

My Aunt Kate had promised, but she didn't make it.

（7）数字：数字的使用也有一定的规则，争取正确地使用它们也是非常重要的。

• 从1到10的数字须拼出；11以上都是多音节词，须用阿拉伯数字。如果把120写成 one hundred and twenty，读起来就不方便。

• 数字出现在句子开头时必须拼出：Twenty years is the term contained in the contract.

- 数字组合和数字和词组合在一起使用时须用连字符。

150-ton goods/ 56-miles from the harbor/thirty-two years ago.

- 如果一句中有一个数字在10以下,另一个大于10,按规则都用数字。

I asked for 6 Yuan, but Father gave me 16.

(8) 引号

引号成对使用,一半在引语之前,一半在引号之后。至于在使用引语时逗号和句号位置的确定,只要掌握下面的规则即可:所有的逗号和句号都在引号内(注意逗号和其他标点符号在引语前的用法);而冒号和分号始终在引号之外。

He said in a low voice, "How much time left to us?" and was told," Don't worry! We still have plenty of time".

"We will call you back", this phrase is popular with interviewers.

(9) 问号根据句子的结构可以放在引号之内或引号之外。

Where can we find the "real romance"?

My teacher asked me, "Have you finished your homework?"

(10) 缩写词

省略语是一个词的缩写,为了节约篇幅和便于使用它被用来代替一个完整的词。省略的规则是在被省略的词后面加下圆点。例如:Dr.、A. M.、P. M.等。

有些是我们熟知的省略语已经不再用他们的全称了,而更多的是要使用缩略语,例如:B. A. 而不说 Bachelor of Arts, M. B. A. 而不说 Master of Business Administration。

4. 求职信常用句型

(1) 开头句型

- My interest in the position of Sales Manager has prompted me to forward my resume for your review and consideration.
- The sales Manager position advertised in *China Daily* on July 12 intrigues me. I believe you will find me well-qualified.
- With my thorough educational training in accounting, I wish to apply for an entry-level accounting position.
- Your advertisement for a network support engineer in *China Daily* has interested me very much. I think I can fill the vacancy.
- Attention of Human Resource Manager: Like many other young men, I am looking for a position. I want to get started. At the bottom, perhaps, but started.
- I am very glad that you are recruiting a programmer! I hope to offer my services.
- I am very delighted to know that you have an opening for an English teacher in *Beijing Evening News*.
- I am forwarding my resume in regard to the opening we discussed in your Marketing Department.
- I want a job. Not any job with any company, but a particular job with your company. Here are my reasons: Your organization is more than just a company. It is an institution in the

minds of the Chinese public.

（2）说明经历的句型

• Since my graduation from Beijing Foreign Studies University 6 years ago, I have been employed as an interpreter in a foreign trade company.

• My three years of continuous experience in electrical engineering has taught me how to deal with all the phases of the business I am in right now.

• As the executive manager assistant of LingDa(China) Investment Co., Ltd, I have had a very extensive training in my field.

（3）说明教育程度的句型

• I have a PhD from Peking University of Aeronautics and Astronautics in electronics engineering and was employed by Samsung Computer for 4 years.

• I received my Mater's degree in Chinese literature from Huazhong Normal University in 2000.

• I am a graduate student in the Chemistry Department of Beijing Normal University and will receive my Mater's degree in March this year.

• My studies have given me the foundation of knowledge from which to learn the practical side international trade.

• My outstanding record at school and some experience in business have prepared me for the tasks in the work you are calling for.

• I have a good command of two foreign languages: English and Japanese.

• I am quite proficient in three computer languages: BASIC, C#, .Net

• I can speak and write English very well and have worked as an interpreter for two years.

（4）说明薪金待遇的句型

• I should require that your factory provide me with an apartment.

• With regard to salary, I leave it to you to decide after experience of performance in the job.

• I should require a commencing salary of 5,000 Yuan per month.

• My hope for welfare is to enjoy free medical care.

• The yearly salary I should ask for would be 100,000 Yuan, with a bed in the school's dormitory.

• The monthly salary of 3,800 Yuan will be acceptable if your company houses me.

（5）推荐自己的句型

• I am presently looking for a position where my experience will make a positive contribution to the start-up or continuing profitable operation of a business in which I am so well experienced.

• I am an innovative achiever. I feel that in nowadays society where competition is fierce, there is a need for a representative who can meet and beat the competition. I feel that I have all the necessary ingredients to contribute to the success of Any Corporation. All I need is a starting point.

• Your advertisement in the June 20th issue of *Lawyers Monthly* appeals to me. I feel that I have the qualifications necessary to effectively handle the responsibilities of Administrative Judge.

• My ten years employment at the LIDOO Company provides a wide range of administrative, financial and research support to the Chief Executive Officer. I have a strong aptitude for working with numbers and extensive experience with computer software applications.

• As you will note, I have twelve years of educational and media experience. I am proficient in the operation of a wide variety of photographic, video, and audio equipment. I am regularly responsible for processing, duplicating, and setting up slide presentations, as well as synchronized slide and audio presentations.

（6）结束语句型

• I should appreciate the privilege of an interview. I may be reached by letter at the address given above, or by telephone at 98675213.

• I feel that a personal meeting would give us the opportunity to discuss your shout and long-term objectives and my ability to direct your organization towards successfully achieving those goals.

• I should be glad to have a personal interview, and can present references if desired.

• Thank you for your consideration.

• I have enclosed a resume as well as a brief sample of my writing for your review. I look forward to meeting with you to discuss further how I could contribute to your organization.

• Thank you for your attention to this matter. I look forward to speaking with you.

• The enclosed resume describes my qualifications for the position advertised. I would welcome the opportunity to personally discuss my qualifications with you at your convenience.

• I would welcome the opportunity for a personal interview with you at your convenience.

5. 求职信范例

（1）软件工程师

Reading *Beijing Youth Daily* on the web yesterday, I was very impressed by an article on your company's contribution to the development of China's IT industry. I would like to offer my experience in computer science and am writing to inquire whether your company has any position available.

I will graduate in June from Tsinghua University of Science and Technology with a Bachelor's degree in computer's science. Courses taken include Programming, System Design and Analysis, Operating System, .NET, etc. In addition, I have experience with programming as I have worked as a part-time programmer for almost two years in a software company. I have passed College English Test Band 6 and got a score of 650 in TOFEL.

Working in a company like yours would be a great way to expand my skills and contribute something to the development of computer science. If there is a position available in your company, I do hope that you will consider me. Enclosed is a copy of my resume. I will appreciate if you could give me an opportunity of a personal interview at your convenience. In any event, thank you very much for your time.

Yours sincerely,
Wang Lei

(2) 电脑工程师

Dear Sir or Madam,

In reply to your advertisement in today's Job51, I am respectfully offering my service as an engineer for your company. My college educational background and work experience in the field of IT industry have prepared me for the task in the work you are calling for.

I have worked as a computer programmer in HuaWei Company for three years, during which I become more and more expert in programming. I developed a sales and management software and won a prize for The Administration of Hotel system software. I am a diligent worker and a fast learner and really interested in coping with difficulties in computer science.

However, in order to get a more challenging opportunity, I'd like to fill the opening offered in your company, which I am sure will fully utilize my capability, With regard to salary, I leave it to you to decide after experience of my performance in the job.

I would appreciate it if we could set an appointment so you can get to know me better. Thank you for your kind attention. I hope to hear from you.

Yours sincerely,
Zhang Wei

四、合同书

(一) 合同书的构成和分类

合同是缔约双方通过协商就某一项具体事务划定双方各自的权利和义务，达成的文字契约。随着我国对外开放的不断扩大，各类涉外合同协议日益增多。能够正确理解与撰写涉外合同协议已成为当今国际交往中的一个重要而必不可少的环节。由于合同协议是具有法律效力的契约性文件，条款是否周全、措辞是否严谨、是否能体现平等互利原则，都事关重大。

国际贸易中使用的英文合同书通常由以下内容构成：标题、前言、正文部分和结尾部分。

合同分为贸易合同(Contract of Trade)和聘约合同(Contract of Employment)。

(二) 贸易合同写法与格式

贸易合同是进口出口双方当事人依照法律并通过协商就各自的权利和义务所达成的具有法律约束力的协议。贸易合同不论采用文字条款或表格形式，都必须规定得具体和明确,不得有差错。

一份完整的贸易合同通常包含以下内容:

CONTRACT(合同)

- Date(日期)
- Contract No. (合同号码)
- The Buyers(买方)   The Sellers(卖方)
- This contract is made by and between the Buyers and the Sellers; whereby the Buyers agree to buy and the Sellers agree to sell the under-mentioned goods subject to the terms and conditions as stipulated hereinafter(兹经买卖双方同意按照以下条款由买方购进,卖方售出以下商品)

(1) Article No. (货号)

(2) Description & Specification(品名及规格)

(3) Quantity(数量)

(4) Unit price(单价)

(5) Total Value(总值)

(6) Packing(包装)

(7) Country of Origin and manufacture(生产国别和制造厂家)

(8) Terms of Payment(支付条款)

(9) Time of Shipment(装运期限)

(10) Port of Lading(装运口岸)

(11) Port of Destination(目的口岸)

(12) Insurance: To be effected by buyers for 110% of full invoice value covering _____ up to _____ only. (保险:由卖方按发票全额 110% 投保至_____为止的_____险。)

(13) Payment: By confirmed, irrevocable, transferable and divisible L/C to be available by sight draft to reach the sellers before _____/_____/_____. (付款条件:买方须于_____年____月____日将保兑的,不可撤销的,可转让可分割的即期信用证开到卖方。)

(14) Documents(单据)

(15) Claims: Within 45 days after the arrival of the goods at the destination, should the quality, specifications or quantity be found not in conformity with the stipulations of the contract except those claims for which the insurance company or the owners of the vessel are liable, the Buyers shall, have the right on the strength of the inspection certificate issued by the C.C.I.C and the relative documents to claim for compensation to the Sellers. (索赔:在货到目的口岸 45 天内如发现货物品质、规格和数量与合同不符,除属保险公司或船方责任外,买方有权凭中国商检出具的检验证书或有关文件向卖方索赔换货或赔款。)

(13) Arbitration: All disputes in connection with the execution of this Contract shall be settled friendly through negotiation. In case no settlement can be reached, the case then may be submitted for arbitration to the Arbitration Commission of the China Council for the Promo-

tion of International Trade in accordance with the Provisional Rules of Procedure promulgated by the said Arbitration Commission. The Arbitration committee shall be final and binding upon both parties, and the Arbitration fee shall be borne by the losing parties.（仲裁：凡有关执行合同所发生的一切争议应通过友好协商解决，如协商不能解决，则将分歧提交中国国际贸易促进委员会按有关仲裁程序进行仲裁，仲裁将是终局的，双方均受其约束，仲裁费用由败诉方承担。）

（三）聘约合同

1. 聘约合同的内容

聘约合同多为我国一些高等院校和企事业单位和外国专家本人签订的服务合同，一般规定有聘期、受聘方的工作任务、聘方的要求、受聘方的工资和生活待遇、受聘方应遵守的法律和制度、聘约的生效、终止、解除和延长等。

一般来说，聘约合同里有很多常用的句型，而有一些常用的句型基本上也已经程序化了，成为常用术语，譬如在开头我们通常这样说："This contract is made on the _____ day of _____ 20 ____ between _____ as Seller and _____ as Buyer. Both Parties agree to the sale and purchase of _____ under the following terms and conditions"。

那么下面我们看看聘约合同常用的一些句型即所包含的内容，这些内容又分别用英文怎么表达，在最后，我们再来看一个实例。一般说来，聘约合同的内容组成如下：

• The two Parties, in a spirit of friendly cooperation, agree to sign this contract and pledge to fulfill conscientiously all the obligations stipulated in it.（合同双方在自愿的基础上签订合同。）

• The period of service will be from the _____ day of _____ to the _____ day of _____.（合同的起始和终止时间。）

• The duties of Party B.（受聘方的责任。）

• Party B's monthly salary will be Yuan RMB（About USD）, the pay day is every month _____. If not a full month, the salary will be will be prorated (days times salary/30).（聘用期间报酬的计算。）

• Party A's Obligations：（甲方的义务和职责：）

• Party B's obligations：（乙方的义务和职责：）

• Revision, Cancellation and Termination of the Contract（关于修订、取消和终止合同的一些说明）

• Breach Penalty（违反的处罚）

2. 聘约合同实例

Contact of Employment

The Foreign Language Department of Huazhong Normal University (the engaging party) has engaged Mr. Smith (the engaged party) as a teacher of English. The two parties in the spirit of friendship and cooperation have entered into an agreement to sign and to comply with the present contract.

1. The term of service is two years, that is, from Sept 1, 2006, the first day of the term of office, to Sept 1, 2008, the last day of the term of office.

2. By mutual consultation the work of the engaged party is decided as follows:

(1) Training teachers of English, research students and students taking refresher courses;

(2) Conducting senior English classes and advising students on extra-curricular activities of the language;

(3) Compiling English textbooks and supplementary teaching materials, undertaking tape recording and other work connected with the language;

(4) Having 18 up to 22 teaching periods in a week.

3. The engaged party works five days a week and eight hours a day. The engaged party will have legal holidays as prescribed by the Chinese Government. The vacation is fixed days by the school calendar.

4. The engaging party pays the engaged party a monthly salary of Three Thousand *Yuan* (Chinese Currency) and provides him with various benefits.

5. The engaged party must observe the regulations of the Chinese Government concerning residence, wages and benefits, and travel for foreigners when entering, leaving and passing through the territory of the country, and must follow the working system of the engaging party.

The engaged party welcomes any suggestion put forward by the engaged party and will take them into favorable consideration in so far as circumstances permit. The engaged party will observe the decisions of the engaging party and is to do his work in the spirit of active cooperation to accomplish the tasks assigned.

6. Neither party shall without sufficient cause or reason cancel the contract.

If the engaging party finds it imperative to terminate the contract, then, in addition to bearing the corresponding expenses for wages and benefits, it must pay the engaged party one month's extra salary as compensation allowance, and arrange for him and his family to go back to their own country within a month.

If the engaged party submits his resignation in the course of his service, the engaging party will stop paying him his salary from the day when his resignation is approved by the engaging party, and the engaged party will no longer enjoy the wages and benefits provided. When leaving China, the engaged party and his family will have to pay for everything themselves.

7. The present contract comes into effect on the first day of the term of service herein stipulated and ceases to be effective at its expiration. If either party wished to renew the contract, the other party shall be notified before it expires. Upon agreement by both parties through consultation a new contract may be signed.

8. The engaged party agrees to all the articles in this contract.

9. The present contract is done in Chinese and English, both versions being equally valid.

...（The engaging party）
...（The engaged party）
August 20, 2006
Wuhan, Hubei

五、产品说明书

随着科学和经济的发展,各种现代化的机械、化工、电子产品层出不穷。说明书的主要目的是用来说明产品的性能、特点、用途和使用方法,其语言应当简洁,通俗易懂、准确,注意科学性和逻辑性,使消费者一看便知道所购商品的用途、安装、使用方法和保养方法,以免由于对产品的不了解,造成不必要的差错或损失。

（一）产品说明书的结构

英语产品说明书,根据产品的性能、特点、用途和使用方法的不同,其语言形式也有所不同。一般来讲,产品说明书由标题(包括副标题)和正文两部分组成。有的说明书在最后还附注厂商的名称。

1. 说明书标题

说明书标题,并不如广告的标题那么重要,所以有些英文产品说明书中并没有标题。但从宣传效果上讲,其标题也很重要,在说明中会起到很好的引导作用,如广告标题,说明书标题同样分为直接性标题和间接性标题,有时也附有副标题。

2. 说明书正文

说明书正文的主要目的是用来说明产品的性能、特点、用途和使用方法。其语言应当简洁、通俗易懂、准确,注意科学性和逻辑性,使消费者一看便知道所购买商品的用途、安装、使用方法和保养方法。

各类产品的性质和用途不同,产品说明书的方法及内容也各不相同。正文究竟包括哪几个部分,应根据不同产品的具体情况来确定。

一般来说,各类产品的说明书应包括的内容不尽相同,分类如下:

(1) 饮料类的产品说明书应包括以下几点:
- 食品的主要成分,即组成成分和配料;
- 冲调方法,水的比例,水的温度,即服用方法;
- 要表明生产厂家;
- 保质期;
- 存放方法。

(2) 医药用品的说明书包括:
- 药品的主要成分;
- 药品的主要功效以及适用哪些症状;
- 药品的用法及用量;
- 存放方法;
- 注意事项(包括禁忌,以及药品的副作用);
- 有效期。

（3）电子产品的说明书一般包括：
- 技术参数或产品规格；
- 各部件名称、或称为功能指示；
- 使用方法、控制及操作程序；
- 使用时的注意事项；
- 接地线、天线说明；
- 确保安全要点；
- 节电注意事项；
- 操作方法；
- 机器的维护和保养；
- 常见故障及排除方法；
- 生产厂家、联系地址、电话、邮箱及网站等。

（4）化学产品说明书的内容包括：
- 产品成分；
- 用途；
- 产品的性能特点；
- 产品的适用范围；
- 使用方法；
- 注意事项；
- 保存期。

（二）产品说明书的语言特征

产品说明书的语言不同于广告语言，它的目的不像广告那样在于宣传，而是朴实详细地说明产品的功能和用途等，所以其鼓动性不及广告语言强。一般来说，产品说明书的语言要求简练朴实，切忌夸大其词，以免造成不良的影响和后果。总的来说，产品说明书的语言有以下一些特征：

1. 多用简单句

由于说明书的语言具有简洁、清晰的特点，而且其层次结构明了，所以说明书中常采用简单的句子结构。

- The battery life should be about one year under normal use.
- It is an ideal instrument.
- Purified water for drinking.

2. 多用名词短语

名词性短语使用频繁也是英语产品说明书的一大特色，这些句型大多是祈使句型的动词省略。

- Three times daily. = Take it three times everyday.
- Two tablets each time.
- Cooking time 15 minutes. = The cooking time is 15 minutes.
- Adults and children over 12 years old.

3. 常用祈使句

因为产品说明书通常用来告诉消费者如何正确的使用某种产品,所以祈使句是一种很好的表达方法,它能给人亲切的感觉。

- Do keep out of the reach of children.
- Press the record button when you start to record.
- Adjust the sound Volume with the -/+ buttons.
- Set the Washer Timer to the time you want.
- Store in upright position.

4. 常用复合名词

在英文产品说明书中,复合名词的使用能够简洁而准确的表达产品说明书中所要说明的内容。

- Purified water 纯净水
- Needle-head 针头
- Multi-vitamins 多种维生素
- Push-pull button 推拔式按钮

5. 非谓语结构多

英语中的非谓语动词有动词的不定式、现在分词和过去分词。在产品的英文说明书中,使用非谓语动词,不仅可以提高语言的表达层次,还可以精炼句子的结构。

- Insert batteries with the poles in the right direction as marked.
- Shake well before taken.
- Adjust the echo effect to your taste with the Echo Control while singing.

(三) 产品说明书范例

现代家庭生活已经离不开电子产品,大中小型企业更是如此。电子产品的问世,给生活带来了方便,也给生产带来了活力和效益。但是电子器械如果不按说明书安装或使用,会造成经济的损失甚至是人员的伤亡,因此这类产品说明书应具体、详细,哪怕是一个小螺钉、小线头,都要标明,总体来说,最起码应该写出产品性能、特点、适用范围,即产品简介。我们来看一个说明书的例子。

Precautions in the Use of Microwave Ovens for Heating Food

(1) Inspection for Damage. A microwave oven should only be used if an inspection confirms all the following items.

1. The grill is not damaged or broken.
2. The door fits squarely and securely and opens and closes smoothly.
3. The door hinges are in good condition.
4. The door does not open more than a few millimeters without an audible operation of the safety switches.
5. The metal plates of the metal seal on the door are neither buckled nor deformed.
6. The door seal are neither covered with food nor have large burn marks.

(2) PRECAUTIONS Microwave radiation ovens can cause harmful effects if the following

precautions are not taken:

1. Never tamper with or inactivate the interlocking devices on the door.

2. Never poke an object, particularly a metal object, through the grille or between the door and the oven while the oven is operating.

3. Never place saucepans, unopened cans or other heavy metal objects in the oven.

4. Clean the oven cavity, the door and the seals with water and a mild detergent at regular intervals. Never use any form of abrasive cleaner that may scratch or scour surfaces around the door.

5. Never use the oven without the trays provided by the manufacture.

6. Never operate the oven without a load(an absorbing material such as food or water) in the oven cavity unless specifically allowed in the manufacturer's literature.

7. Never rest heavy objects such as food containers on the door while it is open.

8. Do not place sealed containers in the microwave oven.

使用微波炉烹调应注意的事项

(1) 检查是否有损坏

使用微波炉前应先按下列各项检查:

1. 烤架是否损坏。

2. 炉门是否妥当,开关是否良好。

3. 门栓是否妥当。

4. 除非听到安全开关的操作讯号,炉门不能开启。

5. 炉门上镶着金属绝缘孔网的金属板不可弄曲或变形。

6. 炉门上的绝缘孔网不可沾上食物或积聚油污。

(2) 预防事项:如未采取以下措施,微波炉可能造成危害。

1. 切勿损坏炉门的安全锁。

2. 当微波炉操作时,请勿置入任何物品,特别时金属物体。

3. 不要把平底锅、未开封的罐或其他重金属物体放进炉内。

4. 经常清洁炉内,使用温和洗洁液清理炉门及绝缘孔网,不可使用具有腐蚀性的清洁剂,以免损坏炉门。

5. 使用微波炉时必须应用附属的转盘。

6. 使用微波炉时,炉内应放有可吸收能量的物质(例如:食物,水),除本说明书特别许可的情况外。

7. 炉门开启时,请勿在炉门上放置重物。

8. 切勿使用密封的容器于微波炉内。

General Use

1. In order to maintain high quality, do not operate the oven when empty. The microwave energy will reflect continuously throughout the oven if no food or water is present to absorb energy.

2. If a fire occurs in the oven, touch the STOP/RESET Pad and Leave Door Closed, or

turn TIMER to zero and Leave Door Closed.

3. Do not dry clothes, newspapers or other materials in oven. They may catch fire.

4. Do not use recycled paper products or other materials, as they may contain impurities which may cause sparks and/or fires when used.

5. Do not use newspapers or paper bags for cooking.

6. Do not hit or strike control panel. Damage to control may occur.

7. POT HOLDERS may be needed as heat from food is transferred to the cooking container and from the container to the glass tray. The glass tray can be very hot after removing the cooking container from the oven.

8. Do not store flammable materials next to, on top of, or in the oven. It could be a fire hazard.

9. Do not cook food directly on glass tray unless indicated in recipes.

10. Do not use this oven to heat chemicals or other non-food products. Do not clean this oven with any product that is labeled as containing corrosive chemicals. The heating of corrosive chemicals in this oven may cause microwave radiation leaks.

一般使用

1. 为保持微波炉的质量,切勿让微波炉空操作,因为当没有食物或水分在炉内吸收能量的情况下,微波能量会不停地在炉内反射。

2. 如果炉内着火,请紧闭炉门,并按停止或重置或关掉计时器,然后拔下电源导线,或关闭电路闸刀板或保险丝的开关。

3. 不要在炉内烘干布类、报纸或其他东西。

4. 不可使用再生纸制品类,因其含有容易引起电弧和着火的杂质。

5. 不可将报纸或纸盒用于烘烹。

6. 不可敲击控制板以免导致控制器损坏。

7. 取出烘完的食物时,必须使用锅夹,因为热力会从高温的食物传至烹饪容器,然后再由烘烹容器传至玻璃盛盒,当烘烹容器从炉内取出,玻璃盒会非常热。

8. 不可将易燃物放在烘箱内或烘箱上,以免导致起火。没有放入玻璃盒和轴环时则不可使用烘箱。

9. 如非食谱所指定,不可直接在玻璃盘上烘烹食物。

10. 请勿使用微波炉加热化学剂或其他非食制品。不可用含有腐蚀性化学剂的制品洗涤烘炉。在炉内加热腐蚀性化学剂可能会引起微波外泄。

FOOD

1. Do not use your oven for home canning or the heating of any closed jar. Pressure will build up and the jar may explode. In addition, the microwave oven can't maintain the food at the correct canning temperature. Improperly canned food may spoil and be dangerous to consume.

2. Do not attempt to deep fat fry in your microwave oven.

3. Do not boil eggs in their shell.

4. Potatoes, apples, egg yolks, whole squash and sausages are examples of foods with nonporous skins. This type of food must be pierced before cooking, to prevent bursting.

5. Stir liquids several times during heating to avoid eruption of the liquid from the container, e.g. water, milk or milk based fluids.

6. To check the degree of cooking of roasts and poultry use a Microwave Thermometer. Alternatively, a conventional meat thermometer may be used after the food is removed from the oven. If undercooked, return meat or poultry to the oven and cook for a few minutes at the recommended power level. It is important to ensure that meat and poultry are thoroughly cooked.

7. Cooking Times given in the cookbook are APPROXIMATE. Factors that may affect cooking time are preferred degree of moisture content, starting temperature, altitude, volume, size, shape, of food and utensils used. As you become familiar with the oven, you will be able to adjust for these factors.

8. It is better to Undertake Rather Than Overcook foods. If food is undercooked, it can always be returned to the oven for future cooking. If food is overcooked, nothing can be done. Always start with minimum cooking times recommended.

食物

1. 不可用密封罐将食物或瓶子放入微波炉,当气压增加,瓶子可能会爆炸,而且微波烘箱不可能使食物维持在适当温度,可能会引起罐装食物变质。

2. 不可用微波炉煎炸食物。

3. 不可煮带壳的鸡蛋,因压力会使鸡蛋爆裂。

4. 土豆、苹果、蛋黄、板栗、红肠等带皮的食物在烘烹之前必须用叉或刀穿孔以防止烘焦。

5. 在加热含有气体的液体时,请搅动数次以避免液体溢出容器。

6. 使用微波炉测肉温计检查牛肉或鸡肉的烘烹结果。如果烘烹不足,则再放入微波炉用适当温度多烘几分钟。确保牛肉和鸡肉充分烹制非常重要。

7. 烘烹手册提供了烘烹的大约时间,影响烘烹时间的因素有:所喜欢的烘烹程度、开始温度、海拔高度、分量、大小、食物形状和盛载器皿。如果你熟悉烘箱操作,则可以适当参照以上这些因素加以修正烘烹时间。

8. 烘烹食物时宁可烘烹不足,也不要烘烹过度。如果食物烘烹不足则可以重新再加以烘烹,但如果烘烹过度则无法补救。启动时请用最短时段烘烹。

Important Instructions

Warning—to reduce the risk of burns, electric shock, fire, injury to persons or excessive microwave energy:

1. Read all instructions before using microwave oven.

2. Some products such as whole eggs and sealed containers may explode and should not be heated in microwave oven.

3. Use this microwave oven only for its intended use as described in this manual.

4. As with any appliance, close supervision is necessary when used by children.

5. Do not operate this microwave oven, if it is not working properly, or if it has been damaged or dropped.

6. To reduce the risk of fire in the oven cavity:

a. Do not overlook food. Carefully attend microwave oven if paper plastic, or other combustible materials are placed inside the oven to facilitate cooking.

b. Remove wire twist-ties from bags before placing bag in oven.

c. If materials inside the oven should ignite, keep oven door closed, turn oven off at the wall switch, or shut off power at the fuse or circuit breaker panel.

使用指南

为避免产生烧伤、触电、火灾、人员伤亡或过多的能量外泄：

1. 在使用本设备前，请参阅使用要点。

2. 生鸡蛋及密封盒之类的东西容易引起爆裂，故不能放入烘箱加热烘烹，细节请参照烹调书。

3. 本设备只适用于本指南所指示之用途。

4. 儿童使用本设备时必须注意看管。

5. 当烘箱操作不正常时，或受损坏掉下时，应停止继续使用。

6. 为避免烘箱起火：

a. 不可过度烘烹食物，若在炉内放入纸塑包装或其他易燃物品等材料要特别注意。

b. 放盒子入箱时，请撤去金属包装带。

c. 万一烘箱内的东西着火，请保持烘箱内紧闭，然后拔去电源插头，或关掉屋内电源总联。

Earthing Instructions

This microwave oven must be earthed. In the event of an electrical short circuit, earthing reduces the risk of electric shock by providing an escape wire for the electric current.

This microwave oven is equipped with a cord having an earthing with an earthing plug. The plut must be plugged into an outlet that is properly installed and earthed.

Warning—Improper use of the earthing plug can result in a risk of electric shock.

接地线说明

本设备必须接地线，万一漏电，则接地线可以提供电流回路，以避免触电。本设备配有接地线以及一个接地线插头，此插头必须接插在确实接地的插座上。警告：不当使用接地插头可导致电击风险。

Warning

1. The appliance should be inspected for damage to the door seal and door seal areas. If these areas are damaged the appliance should not be operated but be delivered to the manufacturer to service.

2. It is dangerous for anyone other than a service technician trained by the manufacture to service appliance.

3. If the supply cord of this appliance is damaged, it must be replaced by the special cord available only from the manufacture.

注意事项

1. 需检查这套设备的用具的门边线缝,若有损坏,必须停止使用,并送到制造商处让服务修理员修理。

2. 必须由指定制造商所训练的修理员做调整或修理服务,如让其他人修理,会有危险。

3. 产品的电源若有损坏,必须更换由制造商提供的指定电源线。

Care of Your Microwave Oven

1. Turn the oven off and remove the power plug from the wall socket before cleaning.

2. Keep the inside of the oven clean. When food splatters or spilled liquids adhere to oven walls, wipe with a damp cloth. Mild detergent may be used if the oven gets very dirty. The use of harsh detergent or abrasives is not recommended.

3. The outside oven surfaces should be cleaned with a damp cloth. To prevent damage to the operating parts inside the oven, water should not be allowed to seep into the ventilation openings.

4. Do not allow the Control Panel to become wet. Clean with a soft, damp cloth. Do not use detergents, abrasives or spray on cleaners on the Control Panel. When cleaning the Control Panel, leave the oven door open to prevent the oven from accidentally turning on. After cleaning touch STOP/RESET Pad to clear display window, make sure oven timer is set to off position.

5. If steam accumulates inside or around the outside of the oven door, wipe with a soft cloth. This may occur when the microwave oven is operated under high humidity conditions and in no way indicates malfunction of the unit.

6. It is occasionally necessary to remove the glass tray for cleaning. Wash the tray in warm sudsy water or in a dishwasher.

7. The roller ring and oven cavity floor should be cleaned regularly to avoid excessive noise. Simply wipe the bottom surface of the oven with mild detergent, water or window cleaner and dry. The roller ring may be washed in mild sudsy water or dish washer. Cooking vapours collected during repeated use will in no way affect the bottom surface or roller ring wheels. When removing the roller ring from cavity floor for cleaning, be sure to replace in the proper position.

8. When it becomes necessary to replace the oven light, please consult a dealer to have it replaced.

微波炉的保养

1. 清洗微波炉前,须关闭,并从插座上拔下插头。

2. 保持炉内清洁。如溅出的食物或漏出的液体积在微波炉壁上,则请用湿布擦去。如微波炉十分肮脏,则可以使用中性洗剂。最好不要使用低劣低涤剂或磨损剂。

3．请用微湿布来清洗微波炉表面部分，为防止损伤微波炉内的操作部分，不要让水分由通口渗入。

4．如控制面板湿了，则请用软的干布抹擦，不能用粗糙、磨损性的物体擦控制板。擦控制板时请将炉门打开，以防止不小心启动微波炉。擦完之后按停止/重置以消除显示窗上的显示或确保定时计回到零时的位置。

5．如有水蒸汽积在微波炉内或炉门周围，可用软布擦净。这种情形在微波炉正常运装盒温度高的情况下都可能产生。

6．必须经常清洗玻璃盘，可用温肥皂水清洗或置于洗碗机内清洗。

7．必须经常擦洗轴环盒烘箱壁以避免产生噪音，请用中性洗剂或擦窗剂洗微波炉底面。而轴环则可用热肥皂水清洗。从箱底下取下轴环清洗后必须妥善放回原位。

8．如需要更换炉灯，请向有关厂商查询后更换。

Answers to Exercises of Each Chapter

Chapter 1
略
Chapter 2
略
Chapter 3

1. A raster image is composed of pixels with each pixel having a specific value. A vector image is composed of instructions on how to form shapes with specific values and does not use pixels. Vector is math-based. That is why a vector image can be scaled to any size and will still retain its sharpness, whereas raster image has a set resolution and if it is enlarged it becomes blurry.

2. The formats of digital images mainly contain TIFF—in principle, a very flexible format that can be lossless or lossy; PNG— also a lossless storage format; GIF, which creates a table of up to 256 colors from a pool of 16 million; JPG, which is optimized for photographs and similar continuous tone images that contain many, many colors; RAW—an image output option available on some digital cameras; BMP—an uncompressed proprietary format invented by Microsoft; PSD, PSP, etc.—proprietary formats used by graphics programs.

3. Power your camera—Locate and push the arrow buttons on your digital camera to explore how they function—Explore the playback mode. —Pushing the menu button will give you a variety of choices such as recording, setup and other functions— Push and hold a round button located on top of your digital camera for up to eight seconds to take a digital photo. —Ensure your batteries are charged—Push gently, grasp with thumb and forefinger to remove your memory card. —To use your camera as a video camera, make this selection first on the menu—Add a special touch such as "night" or "scenery" photography by setting the dial to that setting or set it up in the screen menu ahead of time in your digital camera— Understand that the number of pictures you can take varies with your memory card.

4. It mainly contains Drum Scanners, Flatbed Scanners, Film Scanners, Hand Scanners. A flatbed scanner is usually composed of a glass pane (or platen), under which there is a bright light (often xenon or cold cathode fluorescent) which illuminates the pane, and a moving optical array in CCD scanning.

5. Toner-based printers; Liquid inkjet printers; Solid ink printers; Dye-sublimation printers; Inkless printers; Thermal printers; UV printers.

Chapter 4

1. The key difference between analogy and digital technologies is that analog technologies record waveforms as they are, while digital technologies convert analog waveforms into sets of numbers, recording the numbers instead. When played back, the numbers are converted into a voltage stream that approximates the original analog wave.

2. There are three major groups of audio file formats:

Uncompressed formats: WAV, AIFF, AU or raw header-less PCM;

Lossless compression: FLAC, APE, WavPack, Monkey's Audio;

Lossy compression: MP3, ACC, lossy WAV.

3. We can capture digital audios from Electrical Recording, Magnetic Tape Recording, Digital Recording, Libraries of Sound Effects and so on.

4. Cool Edit Pro is an advanced multi track sound editing program for Windows. It has the following (but not limited to) main capabilities:

(1) Sound Filters via DSPE (Digital Signal Processing Effect). (2) Multi track function: Up to 64 simultaneous tracks. (3) Accepts plug-ins to expand its capability. (4) Ability to create batch process files.

5. We can output digital audios throught Audio CD. Audio CD is an umbrella term that refers to many standards of means of playing back audio on a CD. It mainly contains Compact Discs and DVD-audio.

Chapter 5

1. Digital video cameras come in two different image capture formats: interlaced and progressive scan. Interlaced cameras record the image in alternating sets of lines: the odd-numbered lines are scanned, and then the even-numbered lines are scanned, then the odd-numbered lines are scanned again, and so on. One set of odd or even lines is referred to as a "field", and a consecutive pairing of two fields of opposite parity is called a frame.

A progressive scanning digital video camera records each frame as distinct, with both fields being identical. Thus, interlaced video captures twice as many fields per second as progressive video does when both operate at the same number of frames per second.

2. MPG: MPG stands for Moving Picture Experts Group。MPG is very popular in the video world. And there are a number of MPG formats that you should consider-all with different purposes, for example, MPEG-1, MPEG-2 and MPEG-4.

AVI: The acronym AVI comes from Audio Video Interleave. It is often used as a container video format by compression codecs such as Xvid and Divx. AVI is so versatile, that it can be a container for practically any video file.

MOV: The MOV file extension was created by Apple as a means to store and play video files. MOV files are often used to store videos due to its awesome compression ability. Videos created from a number of digital cameras are automatically stored in MOV format. his file can only be played on QuickTime Player.

ASF: ASF (short for Advanced Systems Format) is similar to AVI in that it was created by Microsoft and is a container format which makes use of various codecs as a means of file compression. ASF files can only be played using WMP, which can be a pain for those who use another media player, such as RealPlayer (RP) or iTunes.

WMV: Very similar to ASF, WMV (Windows Media Video) is for all practical purposes an ASF file, only with a specific codec-the WMV codec. hey are arguably the most popular and widely used streaming media format on the Internet (maybe neck and neck presently with FLV).

RM: RealMedia is suitable for use as a streaming media format, which is viewed while it is being sent over the network. Streaming video can be used to watch live television, since it does not require downloading the video in advance.

FLV: Flash videos are composed of complex codecs, but the video quality is very good. FLV files work fairly good streaming over the web, and can be played by pretty much any media player created. Adobe Flash Player is practically universally accepted.

3. VCDs are often bilingual. This is similar to selecting a language track on a DVD, except it's limited to 2 languages, due to there being only two audio channels (left and right). Also the audio track effectively becomes monoaural.

VCDs also cost less than DVDs. The VCD format has no region coding, so discs can be played on any compatible machine worldwide.

VCD's growth has slowed in areas that can afford DVD-Video, which offers most of the same advantages, as well as better picture quality (higher resolution with fewer digital compression artifacts) due to its larger storage capacity.

DVD uses 650 nm wavelength laser diode light as opposed to 780 nm for CD. This permits a smaller pit to be etched on the media surface compared to CDs (0.74 μm for DVD versus 1.6 μm for CD), allowing for a DVD's increased storage capacity.

Chapter 6

1. The literary world, having gingerly learned to manipulate pixeled print ("pixels" are "picture elements", the dots that electronically paint the letters onto the computer screen) through word processing, has found personal computer handy engines to produce printed texts about printed texts. But our thinking has not gone much further than that. Meanwhile, the electronic word has been producing profound changes in the outside world. Some of the billions of dollars American business and government spend to train their employees are being spent in redefining the "textbook"—and, almost in passing, the codex book itself—into an interactive multimedia delivery system. Sooner or later, such electronic "texts" will redefine the writing, reading, and professing of literature as well.

2. Text file: A text file is a kind of computer file that is structured as a sequence of lines. A text file exists within a computer file system. The end of a text file is often denoted by placing one or more special characters, known as an end-of-file marker, after the last line in a

text file.

DOC: In computing, DOC or doc (an abbreviation of 'document') is a file extension for word processing documents; most commonly for Microsoft Word. Historically, the extension was used for documentation in plain-text format, particularly of programs or computer hardware, on a wide range of operating systems.

PDF: Portable Document Format (PDF) is an open standard for document exchange. Formerly a proprietary format, PDF was officially released as an open standard on July 1, 2008, and published by the International Organization for Standardization as ISO/IEC 320001:2008.

Chapter 7

1. Digital layout and design on a computer has truly revolutionized the graphic design profession. In its most basic form, page layout programs bring type, graphics, and photographs together in a single document.

Prior to the traditional and mechanical cut-and-paste techniques, digital layout and design, a new graphic design environment, is a revolution in publishing. Type and text could be brought together and combined in the computer. Text styles, the text font, size, and spacing could all be seen on the screen and problems corrected or changed. The relationship of the type to graphics or photos could be adjusted almost endlessly. Changes in composition or content could be completed without having to send out new specifications to a printer, eliminating the once-typical loss in time and money.

2. The publishing experienced Papyrus scroll, codex wax, tablet and so on. These various forms of early writing publishing may have their own characters, however, are in certain ways similar to today's.

3. At first, you should understand what the support programs of digital layout and design are. They are mainly graphic editing, word processing and vector-based illustration programs. Then you ought to have an idea of you project, design it, finally do on it with the help of the support programs.

4. Have an idea of what you are going to do, design the layout of the stamp, then complete the work with the help of the method mentioned in this chapter according to the requests.

Chapter 8

1. Traditional animation, also referred to as classical animation, cel animation, or hand-drawn animation, is the oldest and historically and the most popular form of animation. In a traditionally-animated cartoon, each frame is drawn by hand. 2D animation had developed from the traditional animation.

2. It mainly contains three formats of 2D animation, they are SWF, GIF, EXE.

The file format SWF is a partially open repository for multimedia and vector graphics. Intended to be small enough for publication on the web, SWF files can contain animations or applets of varying degrees of interactivity and function.

The Graphics Interchange Format (GIF) is a bitmap image format that was introduced by

CompuServe in 1987 and has since come into widespread usage on the World Wide Web due to its wide support and portability.

EXE is the common filename extension denoting an executable file (a program) in the DOS, OpenVMS, Microsoft Windows, Symbian, and OS/2 operating systems. Besides the executable program, many EXE files contain other components called resources, such as bitmaps and icons which the executable program may use for its graphical user interface.

3. The overall capture of creating a 2D animation is divided into three parts: pre-production, production, and post-production.

Pre-production involves establishing the plot of the completed animation.

In the production stage, you can make animation at the aid of relative software.

In the post-production, music and sound effects, as well as visual effects (glows, hazes, etc.) should be added.

4. First of all, you should have a general idea of the work of what you attend to create, then design the script of the animation, finally create the animation according the method referred to in the text. You can make your work with your own characteristic.

Chapter 9

1. (1) CGI is short for computer-generated imagery or computer-generated imaging.

Computer animation is also called CGI animation, is the art of creating moving images with the use of computers. It is a subfield of computer graphics and animation.

(2) It is a phenomenon when the eye and brain work.

From moment to moment, the eye and brain working together actually store whatever one looks at for a fraction of a second, and automatically "smooth out" minor jumps.

The eye and brain will think that they were seeing a smoothly moving object, if the pictures should be drawn at around 12 frames per second or faster (a frame is one complete image).

(3) It is a method to create 3D computer animation by using skeleton models.

In most 3D computer animation systems, an animator creates a simplified representation of a character's anatomy, analogous to a skeleton or stick figure.

In human and animal characters, many parts of the skeletal model correspond to actual bones, but skeletal animation is also used to animate other things, such as facial features.

2. (1) For example, computer games, animation films, architectural composition and advertisement.

You can reference some other documents and detail applications of compute animation at these aspects.

(2) Step 1: Setting up your scene, Step 2: Modeling objects, Step 3: Using materials, Step 4: Placing lights and cameras, Step 5: Animating your scene, Step 6: Rendering your scene.

3. 略

Chapter 10

1. (1) Entertainment medium, business, manufacturing, medicine and psychiatry. You can detail applications of virtual reality at these areas.

(2) Virtual reality can be used at many areas and makes our lives more convenient and enjoyable.

For example, you will enjoy the immersion when play games if you take on the HMD and gloves.

2. (1) 略

Chapter 11

1. Multimedia is media and content that uses a combination of different content forms.

Multimedia includes a combination of text, audio, still images, animation, video, and interactivity content forms.

2. 2D animation figures are created and/or edited on the computer using 2D bitmap graphics or created and edited using 2D vector graphics. 3D animation figures are digitally modeled and manipulated by an animator. 2D animation techniques tend to focus on image manipulation while 3D techniques usually build virtual worlds in which characters and objects move and interact. 3D animation can create images that seem real to the viewer.

3. Multimedia finds its application in various areas including, but not limited to, advertisements, art, education, entertainment, engineering, medicine, mathematics, business, scientific research and spatial temporal applications.

Chapter 12

1. Web design is the skill of creating presentations of content (usually hypertext or hypermedia) that is delivered to an end-user through the World Wide Web, by way of a Web browser or other Web-enabled software like Internet television clients, microblogging clients and RSS readers. The intent of Web design is to create a website—a collection of electronic documents and applications that reside on a Web server/servers and present content and interactive features/interfaces to the end user in form of Web pages once requested.

2. A markup language is a modern system for annotating a text in a way that is syntactically distinguishable from that text. The markup languages we usually use in designing the web are HTML, XML, XHTML. The Resource Description Framework (RDF), XForms, DocBook, SOAP and the Web Ontology Language (OWL), and etc.

3. The web can be applied in the research areas, the entertainment, the learning area and the commercial areas and etc.

北京大学出版社
教育出版中心 精品图书

大学之道丛书
哈佛：谁说了算　　[美]理查德·布瑞德利 著　48元
麻省理工学院如何追求卓越
　　　　　　　　　[美]查尔斯·维斯特 著　35元
大学与市场的悖论　[美]罗杰·盖格 著　48元
现代大学及其图新 [美]谢尔顿·罗斯布莱特 著　60元
美国文理学院的兴衰——凯尼恩学院纪实
　　　　　　　　　[美]P. F. 克鲁格 著　42元
教育的终结：大学何以放弃了对人生意义的追求
　　　　　　　　　[美]安东尼·T.克龙曼 著　35元
大学的逻辑（第三版）　张维迎 著　38元
我的科大十年（续集）　孔宪铎 著　35元
高等教育理念　　　[英]罗纳德·巴尼特 著　45元
美国现代大学的崛起　[美]劳伦斯·维赛 著　66元
美国大学时代的学术自由 [美]沃特·梅兹格 著　39元
美国高等教育通史　[美]亚瑟·科恩 著　59元
哈佛通识教育红皮书　哈佛委员会撰　38元
高等教育何以为"高"——牛津导师制教学反思
　　　　　　　　　[英]大卫·帕尔菲曼 著　39元
印度理工学院的精英们
　　　　　　　　　[印度]桑迪潘·德布 著　39元
知识社会中的大学　[英]杰勒德·德兰迪 著　32元
高等教育的未来：浮言、现实与市场风险
　　　　　　　　　[美]弗兰克·纽曼等 著　39元
后现代大学来临？[英]安东尼·史密斯等 主编　32元
美国大学之魂　　[美]乔治·M.马斯登 著　58元
大学理念重审：与纽曼对话
　　　　　　　　[美]雅罗斯拉夫·帕利坎 著　35元
当代学术界生态揭示
　　　　　　[英]托尼·比彻　保罗·特罗勒尔 著　33元
德国古典大学观及其对中国大学的影响
　　　　　　　　　陈洪捷 著　22元
大学校长遴选：理念与实务　黄俊杰 主编　28元
转变中的大学：传统、议题与前景　郭为藩 著　23元
学术资本主义：政治、政策和创业型大学
　　　　　[美]希拉·斯劳特　拉里·莱斯利 著　36元
什么是世界一流大学　丁学良 著　23元
21世纪的大学　　[美]詹姆斯·杜德斯达 著　38元
公司文化中的大学　[美]埃里克·古尔德 著　23元
美国高等教育史　[美]约翰·塞林 著　69元
哈佛规则：捍卫大学之魂
　　　　　　　　　[美]理查德·布瑞德利 著　48元
美国公立大学的未来
　　[美]詹姆斯·杜德斯达　弗瑞斯·沃马克 著　30元
高等教育公司：营利性大学的崛起
　　　　　　　　　[美]理查德·鲁克 著　24元
东西象牙塔　　　　孔宪铎 著　32元

21世纪引进版精品教材·学术道德与学术规范系列
如何为学术刊物撰稿：写作技能与规范（英文影印版）
　　　　　　　　　[英]罗薇娜·莫 编著　26元
如何撰写和发表科技论文（英文影印版）
　　　　　　　　　[英]罗伯特·戴 等著　28元
给研究生的学术建议 [英]戈登·鲁格 等著　26元
做好社会研究的10个关键
　　　　　　　　　[英]马丁·丹斯考姆 著　20元
阅读、写作和推理：学生指导手册
　　　　　　　　　[英]加文·费尔贝恩 著　25元
如何写好科研项目申请书
　　　　　　[英]安德鲁·弗里德兰德 等著　25元
高等教育研究：进展与方法
　　　　　　　　　[英]马尔科姆·泰特 著　25元

学术规范与研究方法丛书
教育研究方法：实用指南（第六版）
　　　　　　　　　[美]乔伊斯·高尔 等著　98元
社会科学研究的基本规则（第四版）
　　　　　　　　　[英]朱迪斯·贝尔 著　32元
如何撰写与发表社会科学论文：国际刊物指南
　　　　　　　　　蔡今中 著　30元
如何查找文献　　[英]萨莉拉·姆齐 著　35元

21世纪高校教师职业发展读本
如何成为卓越的大学教师（第二版）
　　　　　　　　　肯·贝恩 著　32元
给大学新教员的建议　罗伯特·博伊斯 著　35元
如何提高学生学习质量[英]迈克尔·普洛瑟 等著　35元
学术界的生存智慧　[美]约翰·达利 等主编　35元
给研究生导师的建议（第2版）
　　　　　　　　　[英]萨拉·德拉蒙特 等著　30元

21世纪教师教育系列教材·物理教育系列
中学物理微格教学教程（第二版）
　　　　　　张军朋　詹伟琴　王恬 编著　32元
中学物理科学探究学习评价与案例
　　　　　　　　　张军朋　许桂清 编著　32元

21世纪教育科学系列教材·学科学习心理学系列
数学学习心理学　　孔凡哲　曾峥 编著　29元
语文学习心理学　　李广 主编　29元
化学学习心理学　　王后雄 主编　29元

21世纪教育科学系列教材
现代教育技术——信息技术走进新课堂
　　　　　　　　　冯玲玉 主编　39元
教育学学程——模块化理念的教师行动与体验
　　　　　　　　　闫祯 主编　45元
教师教育技术——从理论到实践　王以宁 主编　36元
教师教育概论　　　李进 主编　75元
基础教育哲学　　　陈建华 著　35元
当代教育行政原理　龚怡祖 编著　37元
教育心理学　　　　李晓东 主编　34元

书名	作者	价格
教育计量学	岳昌君 著	26元
教育经济学	刘志民 著	39元
现代教学论基础	徐继存 赵昌木 主编	35元
现代教育评价教程	吴钢 著	32元
心理与教育测量	顾海根 主编	28元
高等教育的社会经济学	金子元久 著	32元
信息技术在学科教学中的应用	陈勇 等编著	33元
网络调查研究方法概论（第二版）	赵国栋	45元

教师资格认定及师范类毕业生上岗考试辅导教材

书名	作者	价格
教育学	余文森 王晞 主编	26元
教育心理学概论	连榕 罗丽芳 主编	35元

21世纪教师教育系列教材·学科教学论系列

书名	作者	价格
新理念化学教学论	王后雄 主编	38元
新理念科学教学论（第二版）	崔鸿 张海珠 主编	36元
新理念生物教学论	崔鸿 郑晓慧 主编	36元
新理念地理教学论（第二版）	李家清 主编	39元
新理念历史教学论	杜芳 主编	29元
新理念思想政治（品德）教学论（第二版）	胡田庚 主编	36元
新理念信息技术教学论（第二版）	吴军其 主编	32元
新理念数学教学论	冯虹 主编	35元

21教师教育系列教材·学科教学技能训练系列

书名	作者	价格
新理念数学教学技能训练	冯虹	33元
新理念生物教学技能训练（第二版）	崔鸿	33元
新理念思想政治（品德）教学技能训练（第二版）	胡田庚 赵海山	29元
新理念地理教学技能训练	李家清	32元
新理念化学教学技能训练	王后雄	28元

王后雄教师教育系列教材

书名	作者	价格
教育考试的理论与方法	王后雄 主编	35元
化学教育测量与评价	王后雄 主编	45元

西方心理学名著译丛

书名	作者	价格
拓扑心理学原理	[德] 库尔德·勒温	32元
系统心理学：绪论	[美] 爱德华·铁钦纳	30元
社会心理学导论	[美] 威廉·麦独孤	36元
思维与语言	[俄] 列夫·维果茨基	30元
人类的学习	[美] 爱德华·桑代克	30元
基础与应用心理学	[德] 雨果·闵斯特伯格	36元
格式塔心理学原理	[美] 库尔特·考夫卡	75元
动物和人的目的性行为	[美] 爱德华·托尔曼	44元
西方心理学史大纲	唐钺	42元

心理学视野中的文学丛书

书名	作者	价格
围城内外——西方经典爱情小说的进化心理学透视	熊哲宏	32元
我爱故我在——西方文学大师的爱情与爱情心理学	熊哲宏	32元

21世纪教育技术学精品教材（张景中 主编）

书名	作者	价格
教育技术学导论（第二版）	李芒 金林 编著	33元
远程教育原理与技术（第二版）	王继新 张屹 编著	39元
教学系统设计理论与实践（第二版）	杨九民 梁林梅 编著	29元
信息技术教学论（第二版）	雷体南 叶良明 主编	32元
网络教育资源设计与开发	刘清堂 主编	30元
学与教的理论与方式	刘雍潜	32元
信息技术与课程整合（第二版）	赵呈领 杨琳 刘清堂	42元
教育技术研究方法（第二版）	张屹 黄磊	39元
教育技术项目实践	潘克明	32元

21世纪教育技术学精品教材·教育装备系列

书名	作者	价格
教育装备学导论	胡又农	32元
教育装备运筹规划	李慧	26元
教育装备评价简明教程	胡又农	26元

21世纪信息传播实验系列教材（徐福荫 黄慕雄 主编）

书名	价格
多媒体软件设计与开发	32元
电视照明	32元
播音与主持艺术	38元
广告策划与创意	26元
传播学研究方法与实践	26元
摄影基础	32元
数字动画基础与制作	24元
报刊电子编辑	32元
广播电视摄录编	25元
网络新闻实务	32元

21世纪信息传播与新媒体丛书

书名	作者	价格
融合新闻学导论	石长顺	38元
视听评论	何志武	32元